W. S. Merwin:
Essays on the Poetry

GRADUATION: PRINCETON 1947
(To those who are not graduating with our classes, because they are
dead)

X Grim lectures from ~~bad lectures~~, *a chap's delivered*
X A somewhat single school that mouths ~~its~~ years, *our*
   That th~~ieved~~ some of our friends away
   Having forgotten us ~~until~~ this day
   ~~At least, from what remains~~
   We, being young and walking, stay and take |
X ~~A certain standard of our single make.~~

X Step we away from this ~~year's gone~~, *diploma — mistake*
   Advance ~~a light distance~~ toward some sun,
   Pacing ~~an uncertain~~ pave, and leave
   Somewhat together ~~through the~~ push and move,
   Booed by who changed
   Battles for books, blood for beer;
   Their schooling murdered them, "That year!".

   And some of us will leave learning,
   And leave knowing, some, and turning
X ~~The head's impression of this place,~~   *School & acropolis behind the face*
   And all, afterwards, in fear or some God's grace,
   Eventually
   Forget (terror) and tool
   And Time's schooled bauble turning on its spool.

pierced
X With ~~small remembering~~ to do
   In world's ~~pied~~ places, ~~ill-fitted~~ to ... to ...   *sake*
   Be worked, we are supposed to go
   And pour oil in old wounds, and grow
   Most of us
   By common vintage, common hive,
   Being somewhat unified, somewhat alive.

+ Note to Committee: Since you presented me with a subject and asked me
  to write a poem on it, in a sense what you asked me to do was to react
  to the given subject in my own way. At least that is what I have done.
  And if the requisite sentiments and unqualifted optimism are nowhere to
  be found in the poem, that is so merely because I could nowhere find them
  in myself, looking upon the occasion as I do, with little optimism for
  the future. ~~Indeed.~~ But I believe the poem to be poetically reasonably
  sound and reasonably appropriate, and submit it as such.

+ Graduation Committee   WSM

(Time's burden, diploma, measure, and mistake)

With small relief and bandage in our head,
Large the incisions of the nearly dead
We are bungled up to suture, clothe
Set our own heads, their
errors close;

Diploma & officially measurement & mistake

Blow we away from the year's gun
running distance toward some sun,
Roiling an uncertain rut, & leave

A draft of "Graduation," an unpublished poem that Merwin read at the 1947
Princeton graduation ceremonies. He was listed on the program as "senior
poet."

W. S. Merwin: Essays on the Poetry

EDITED BY

Cary Nelson and Ed Folsom

University of Illinois Press

URBANA AND CHICAGO

This book is printed on acid-free paper.

Library of Congress Cataloging-in-Publication Data
Main entry under title:

W. S. Merwin: essays on the poetry.

Bibliography: p.
Includes index.
1. Merwin, W. S. (William Stanley), 1927–
—Criticism and interpretation—Addresses, essays,
lectures. I. Nelson, Cary. II. Folsom, Ed, 1947–
PS3563.E75Z97 1987   811'.54   85-24531
ISBN 0-252-01277-1 (alk. paper)

The editors wish to thank the following for permission to reprint essays which they originally published:
Charles Altieri, "The Struggle with Absence," *Enlarging the Temple* (Lewisburg, Pa.: Bucknell University Press, 1979).
Jarold Ramsey, "The Continuities of W. S. Merwin: 'What Has Escaped Us We Bring with Us,'" *Massachusetts Review,* 14 (Summer, 1973). Reprinted from *The Massachusetts Review,* © 1973 The Massachusetts Review Inc.
Robert Scholes, "Semiotics of the Poetic Text," *Semiotics and Interpretation* (New Haven: Yale University Press, 1982). © 1982 Yale University.

W. S. Merwin's poetry appears by permission of Atheneum Publishers Inc. and Harold Ober Associates: W. S. Merwin, "Separation," "Finally," "Dead Hand," "The Poem," "Daybreak" from *The Moving Target.* Copyright © 1963 W. S. Merwin. "The Animals," "Caesar," "Whenever I Go There," "Wish," "The Asians Dying," "Looking East at Night," "December among the Vanished," "The Cold before the Moonrise," "The Room," "Dusk in Winter," "For the Anniversary of My Death," "Divinities," "When the War Is Over," "Looking for Mushrooms at Sunrise" from *The Lice.* Copyright © 1967 W. S. Merwin. "The Birds on the Morning of Going," "The Well," "The Gardens of Zuñi," "Beginning of the Plains," "The Thread," "Beginning," "The First Darkness," "Elegy," "In the Time of the Blossoms" from *The Carrier of Ladders.* Copyright © 1970 W. S. Merwin. "Early One Summer," "Eyes of Summer," "End of Summer," "The Distances," "Looking Back," "The Old Boast," "The Day," "Words," "Folk Art" from *Writings to an Unfinished Accompaniment.* Copyright © 1973 W. S. Merwin. "Epitaph" from *The First Four Books of Poems.* Copyright © 1975 W. S. Merwin. "Epitaph" from *A Mask for Janus,* copyright © 1952 Yale University Press; copyright renewed 1980 W. S. Merwin. "The Horses," "The Counting Houses," "St. Vincent's," "The Fig Tree" from *The Compass Flower.* Copyright © 1977 W. S. Merwin. "The Oars," "Sunset Water," "Son," "Sun and Rain," "Yesterday," "Tidal Lagoon," "Green Water Tower," "The Middle of Summer," "The Black Jewel," from *Opening the Hand.* Copyright © 1983 W. S. Merwin.

"After Some Years" first appeared in *Harper's,* 214 (June 1957) and is reprinted here by permission of the poet.

"The Complaint of My Family" first appeared in *Evergreen Review,* 9 (Mar. 1965) and is reprinted here by permission of Grove Press.

Contents

Illustrations

Preface

W. S. Merwin: Essays on the Poetry includes new essays by Edward Brunner, Thomas B. Byers, Ed Folsom, Michael Greer, Walter Kalaidjian, Charles Molesworth, Marjorie Perloff, and William H. Rueckert. The essays by Charles Altieri and Cary Nelson are substantially revised and updated since their last appearance. The essays by Jarold Ramsey and Robert Scholes are largely unchanged.

The editors have also compiled a substantial bibliography and written an overview of the archival resources available to those interested in Merwin's work. Since Merwin has not kept records of his early publications and since existing bibliographies and indexes cover small magazines very poorly, we have had to search rather extensively to assemble this list; it should surprise even those who know Merwin's work well. In addition to listing Merwin's own voluminous work, the bibliography cites major criticism about Merwin, and, in paragraph summaries with abbreviated citations, records reviews of his various books. Our work here would have been impossible without the assistance of Victoria Brehm, Lâle Demirtürk, Sharon Lewis, and Donald Scheese at the University of Iowa, Michael Greer and Tom Callanan at the University of Illinois, and Edward Brunner, and without help from a number of libraries—particularly the Rare Book Room at the University of Illinois at Urbana-Champaign, the Inter-Library Loan departments of the University of Iowa and the University of Illinois libraries, the Poetry Collection at the State University of New York at Buffalo, the Special Collections department at the Washington University Library, the Lilly Library at Indiana University, the Humanities Research Center at the University of Texas at Austin, the Pattee Library at the Pennsylvania State

University, the Special Collections department at the University of Delaware Library, and the Ford Foundation Archives. The Theater Collection at Harvard University, the Princeton University Archivist, and Serendipity Books in Berkeley were helpful in answering specific questions. The University of Illinois Campus Research Board provided a personal computer to assist with editing, the School of Humanities provided photocopying, and the English department provided travel funds and funds for photocopying at other libraries. Michael Greer at the University of Illinois transcribed a number of manuscripts and Karen Ford proofread several essays. Harry Ford at Atheneum and Claire Smith at Harold Ober Associates were generous in arranging permissions. The editors are also grateful for support and services provided by University House, University of Iowa.

The acquisition of the W. S. Merwin archive, manuscripts from which are reproduced throughout the book with the poet's permission, was made possible through an endowment from the John Needles Chester Fund of the University of Illinois Foundation, in association with the University of Illinois Library Friends, the University Library, Research Board, College of Liberal Arts and Sciences, School of Humanities, English department, and English departmental library. A number of the manuscripts have been reproduced at approximately their original size. This includes the manuscripts of "St. Vincent's."

An earlier version of Appendix 1 was published as Cary Nelson, *W. S. Merwin's Other Career: The Manuscript Archive of the University Library* by the University of Illinois Library Friends, in the form of an illustrated brochure printed to accompany an exhibit at the University of Illinois Rare Book Room. Publication of the expanded version of the Appendix here and of the reproductions of Merwin manuscripts was made possible by a grant from the University of Illinois Library Friends. The editors wish to express their appreciation for this assistance.

Library Friends at Urbana-Champaign was founded in 1972. It is a nonprofit annual fund membership group designed to benefit the University of Illinois Library. Its goals are to promote private support for the library and to develop public awareness of the library's vast resources. Library Friends supports the library's general goals of strengthening the collections and providing service to the patrons of the library.

Abbreviations

ED FOLSOM AND CARY NELSON

Introduction

It is appropriate that when W. S. Merwin looks back to the tradition of modern American poetry, he generally talks about Ezra Pound. Like Pound, Merwin was a student of romance languages and has made a career of translating poetry from a wide variety of languages (from ancient Sanskrit to contemporary Spanish and French); he has, like Pound, translated drama. In his own poetry he has tried out rhythms and images derived from his translations, seeking as did Pound to "make it new," to make the English language sound like it never sounded before by melding foreign rhythms into it, to value translation "as a means of continually sharpening a writer's awareness of the possibilities of his own language" (STa, viii). Like Pound, too, he has written a great deal of prose: about books, about poetic traditions, about politics and the folly of current human habits in the Western world. Recalling his not altogether happy graduate student days at Princeton when he grew a beard to match Pound's ("I was trying to look like Ezra Pound"), Merwin says, "I was being Ezra Pound. . . . Pound's criticism, which I was avidly ingesting along with the required French literature, did not help my tact or my status as a student there." But his enthusiasm—"I had great admiration for Pound when I was in college. . . . my debt to him began very early" (Folsom and Nelson, "Interview," p. 53)—led to a meeting with Pound at St. Elizabeth's Hospital in the late 1940s, just before Merwin followed the older poet's model of expatriation by going to Europe for seven years. Pound told him to write voraciously: "He said that if you take seriously the wish to be a poet, you should write every day. You should practice it." Merwin followed Pound's advice.

All essays and reviews referred to and quoted from in the Introduction are cited in the Bibliography at the back of this volume.

Pound told him to "read seeds, not twigs," to go back to sources, to translate the Spanish *Romancero*, to stay close to the originals.

If the range of Merwin's work—particularly his translations and his ability to tap into and bring to life a vast array of traditions—reminds us of Pound, his energetic original work across the genres might remind us of William Carlos Williams, the other American modernist that Merwin speaks most fondly of. Like Williams, Merwin has written stories, memoirs, autobiographies, plays, and cultural essays in addition to his poetry. "I really do love Williams," says Merwin, "and I read him over and over when I was about twenty; I still read him. I go back to him, how shall I say it, as an engraver. It's the visual quality of individual moments in Williams" (Folsom and Nelson, "Interview," p. 58). So when Merwin made the major shift in his poetic voice, removing punctuation, shortening his lines, the early Williams—who engraved his poems without punctuation and freed the flow of his syntax, moving his poems from set paths into fields of action—served as a model. (Punctuation, Merwin says, "seemed to staple the poem to the page, but if I took the staples out the poem lifted itself right up off the page. . . . All this gave the poetry new rules, a new way of being" [Folsom and Nelson, "Interview," p. 62].) Merwin's recent verse—attached so intimately to the things of the world, brief moments capturing the perception of sounds and sensations—associates him tonally even more clearly with Williams.

But Merwin has probably been linked by critics more to Wallace Stevens than to Pound and Williams. Cheri Davis's book on Merwin dwells on the comparison. Other critics have invoked Stevens to describe Merwin's early metaphysics and his "mind of winter" during the *Lice* period, beholding the "Nothing that is not there and the nothing that is." Merwin certainly shares Stevens's belief in the vast and unutterable silence of "reality," but he has come to doubt the power of our fictive music to turn that chaotic and alien reality into formed beauty; to Stevens's comforting "After the final no there comes a yes," Merwin offers a bleak "We are the echo of the future / . . . We were not born to survive" (*L*, 33). Merwin has, more than any other American poet, come to doubt the ability of language to be a positive force; at the heart of Merwin's work, there is a severe doubt about language, a fear that to write is to enter into a complicity with a human mind whose hermeneutics is destruction. If Merwin's early poetry indulged in an extravagant Stevensian vocabulary, the later work grew more restrained and stripped, rejecting linguistic complexity for a stark lexical modesty.

Merwin explores the plight and possibility of a poet writing in a world "littered with words" (*MT*, 2), a world where language has spoken its symbols into the depths of oceans, the expanses of deserts, the layered ice at the poles. Our language has granted us an unlucky dominion, and the only things that are safe from us are the things we have not yet named. We name things in order to control them, often to destroy them; thus our history is littered with empty names, names for animals we never saw, never will see. Merwin listens in long silence to the world around him, hoping to hear a few sounds out of the welter of words attach themselves to what is really there. Merwin lets these words call on him, and again and again we experience with him that fragile point, balancing between destruction and regeneration, where we try to live in the world without arrogating it, where we can learn to read what the five poplars are writing on the void. (Nothing, Stevens would say, and Merwin would agree, but would listen longer.)

In his most recent work, Merwin realigns language so that words— a few uncluttered words—brief and tentative, can offer themselves to things, can guide us to a place where the words seem to be appropriated by things, instead of things by words. But this effort does not come easily. Alan Williamson, in a chapter in his *Introspection and Contemporary Poetry* called "Language against Itself," places Merwin among a generation of poets who have "a special and in some ways hostile attitude toward language itself." These poets hold the view, says Williamson, "that language is one of the most powerful agents of our socialization, leading us to internalize our parents', our world's, definitions, and to ignore the portions of our authentic experience—the experience of the body and of the unconscious—that do not express themselves directly in verbal terms." Consequently, the "truly important educative experiences" become "experiences of unlearning." Merwin, of course, is the extreme case of this distrust of language: "Merwin in his later poetry rejects language more radically than his contemporaries do, reducing it to the mere gesture of beginning, or an inarticulate cry. And concurrently what is gestured at seems less and less a distinct though pre-verbal creaturely state and more and more an uncreated, mystical or nihilistic Void. One wonders how far this line of development in Merwin can be attributed to his initial etherealness; how far, on the contrary, to a fear that there is more literariness to be purged in his own beginnings than in his contemporaries." As Williamson suggests, Merwin's "initial etherealness" and "literariness" are qualities of his poetic language that would worry many early commentators on his work; the diminishment, disappearance, and occasional reoccurrence of qualities like these in Merwin's poetry have given rise to a good deal of critical comment.

Given Merwin's notions of language and his dramatic shifts from an elegant, allusive, and formal verse to a sparse and fragmented poetry and more recently to a familiar and at times conversational language, it is no surprise that his poetic reputation has in large part developed as a reaction to his changing ideas of poetic language. The changes in Merwin's use of language have been so remarkable, in fact, that many early comments about his work by other poets and by critics now sound surprisingly inappropriate, as if they are referring to another poet. W. H. Auden introduced Merwin in the foreword to *A Mask for Janus* by placing him firmly into an orthodox formal tradition: "With his concern for the traditional conception of Western culture as expressed in its myths, Mr. Merwin combines an admirable respect for its tradition of poetic craftsmanship" (*MJ*, vii). Robert Bly, on the other hand, writing about Merwin just before *The Moving Target* appeared, categorized him as a prosy and prolix poet: "Much of his work is certainly on a lower level of intensity than true poetry." Bly went on: "If we consider the flat sound, the pale rhythm, the absence of the senses, we realize this is simply prose, appearing as if by forgetfulness in a poem. . . . Mr. Merwin is trying to write poetry with a language never intended for poetry at all. The language he uses was conceived for strictly descriptive—that is, prose—purposes." Bly found "the most striking characteristic" of Merwin's verse to be "wastage of words": "the words follow each other like ants in one of their vast battles in Africa, as lemmings in their migrations into the sea, or as minor characters in some huge and sprawling novel of the 19th century. When we look closely at his poems, in fact, we see a use of language which we associate with a novel: instead of diving to the core of the emotion, as in poetry, the language moves horizontally." Bly saw the autobiographical poems "about the coal mining section of Pennsylvania where Mr. Merwin was born" (appearing in *The Drunk in the Furnace*) as the most "poetic" things Merwin had written: "The superiority of these poems to those on Jason's Voyage is nearly infinite. The new poems exist in

a real landscape and the people are real, not shadows out of a book."
In recent years, of course, other critics have complained about this
autobiographical element in Merwin's work, finding that *it* made his
poems prosy and prolix. But Bly would remain consistent; nearly
twenty years after these comments he would still complain about
"the insistent generality" in Merwin's work: "Somehow objects and
emotions float in space. That means the task of detaching them
from their context has been done . . . but I feel the task of reattach-
ing them to a new context, born out of the vision, has not been done
by Merwin."

Writing in 1961 about *The Drunk in the Furnace*, James Dickey
shared Bly's concerns and complained too about what he felt to be a
calculating, distanced voice in Merwin: "What he has lacked up to
now, and still lacks, is intensity, some vital ingress into the *event* of
the poem which would cause him to lose his way among the intricacies of what is so easy for him to say concerning almost anything on
earth and suffer a little at the hands of his subjects: in a word, *earn*
them emotionally. Control of one's material is one thing, and dicta-
torship over it is another." Another poet, Thom Gunn, writing at the
same time, echoed Dickey: "Merwin lacks that *absorption* in his
subject matter which paradoxically ends by making a poem look
outward, to the rest of the world. As it is, his poetry tells us something about a thing or an event with great accuracy, but is curiously
barren of individual emotions or ideas." Gunn found a "beautiful
self-sufficiency" in each poem, but a "sameness" in the language,
"an evenness of texture, and a lack of any real contrast." Dickey,
however, sensed something quite different from a sameness or mo-
notony in the language; while he felt that there was "still far too
much gilded stuffing rounding out the contours of Mr. Merwin's
poems" and that he was still too hidden behind "his various masks,"
nonetheless he found that "a new, strange kind of simplicity is now
becoming available to Merwin, and the fact that it is slowly emerging from the techniques of one of the master prosodists of our time
makes its advent doubly worth watching."

The autobiographical impulse that Bly celebrated, the relaxing of
the tense distancing and the emerging simplicity that Dickey antici-
pated, all would come, but not until the late 1970s. First Merwin's
language would enter a period when it would become more distanced, more difficult, more detached from contexts. No one antici-
pated *The Moving Target* and the three books that would follow it;

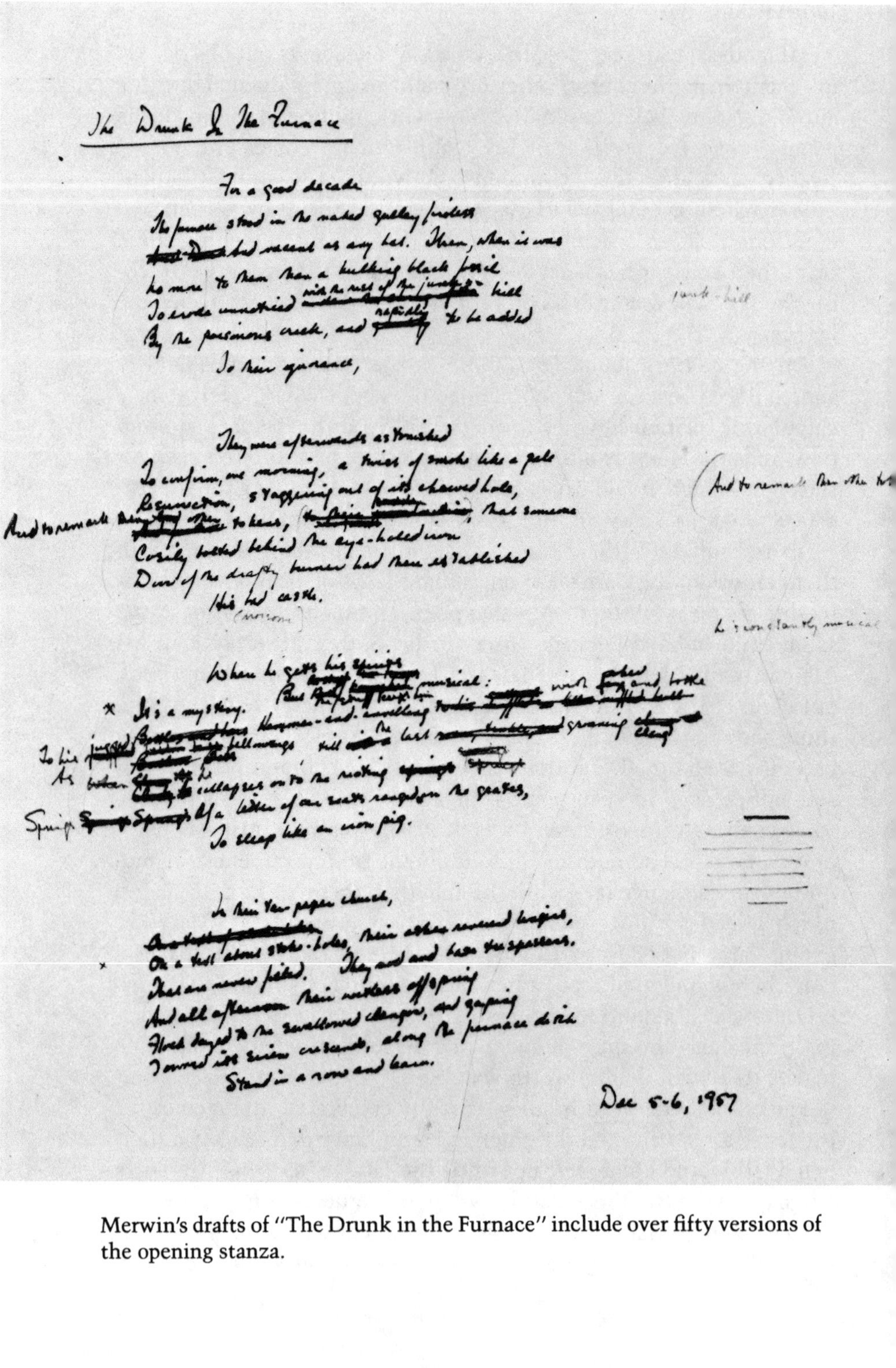

The Drunk In The Furnace

For a good decade
The furnace stood in the naked gully, fireless
And vacant as any hat. Then, when it was
No more to them than a hulking black fossil
To erode unnoticed with the rest of the junk-hill
By the poisonous creek, and rapidly to be added
To their ignorance,

They were afterwards astonished
To confirm, one morning, a twist of smoke like a pale
Resurrection, staggering out of its chewed hole,
And to remark then other tokens that someone
Cozily bolted behind the eye-holed iron
Door of the drafty burner had there established
His bad castle.
([illegible])

When he gets his spirits
It's a mystery. [illegible]
[illegible]
collapses onto the rusting springs
of a ladder of raw seats ranged on the grates,
To sleep like an iron pig.

In their tar-paper church,
On a text about stoke-holes, their other reverend begins,
That are never filled. They sit and hear the spoilers.
And all afternoon their nettles offspring
Flock dazed to the swallowed clangour, and gaping
Towered its siren crescents, along the furnace ditch
Stand in a row and learn.

junk-hill

(And to remark then other to

Is constantly musical

Dec 5-6, 1957

Merwin's drafts of "The Drunk in the Furnace" include over fifty versions of the opening stanza.

When for a good decade

~~The~~

It had stood friesless and vacant as any had,
And was no more to them than a naked fossil
~~Fossil in the Harsh gulley~~ ~~~~

—
—
—

When for a good decade
It had stood in the stripped gulley, friesless,
Dark And vacant as any had, and was
No more to them than a naked fossil
~~In the stripped gulley~~ ~~~~   To be ignored among

When for a good decade
It had stood ~~in the stripped~~ friesless and vacant as any
Had

When for a good decade
It had stood ~~first~~ ~~friesless and vacant as any had,~~

When for a good decade

~~It~~
~~had stood~~
It had stood in the stripped gulley, friesless
And vacant as any had, ~~whose bricks 'as~~ black
Was As unregenerate as ever, it was

When for a good decade

~~Friesless and vacant as~~
It had stood, in the stripped gulley, friesless
And vacant as any had,

For a good decade
Fireless and vacant as any had, the furnace

When for a good decade
The furnace had stood in the stripped gulley, fireless
And vacant as any had

For a good decade
The furnace stood in the stripped gulley, fireless
And vacant as any had.

Then when it was

No more to them than a naked fossil
To erode unnoticed,

For a good decade
The furnace stood in the stripped gulley, fireless
And vacant as any had.

Then when it was
No more to them than a naked fossil
To be ignored, in the shrug of the hill

To crumble ignored,

For a good decade
The furnace stood in the stripped naked gulley, fireless
Dark vacant as any had. Then when it was
No more to them than a hulking black fossil
To erode unnoticed, under the shrug of the hill
By the poisoned creek, and quickly to be added
To their ignorance,

They were afterwards astonished

Dickey's descriptive phrase—"a new, strange kind of simplicity"—
might fit these poems, but we would need to put an unnatural emphasis on *new* and *strange*.

When *The Moving Target* appeared, there was a great deal of con-
sternation about how to describe and talk about these poems.
Edward Dorn, admitting that "Merwin is as good a poet as any other
I know of," found himself puzzled: "Why does the verse need to be so
metaphorical? For all the use of the concrete, to my eye what remains is a suggestion, in context surprisingly abstract." Falling back
on Bly's unease with generality, vagueness, and elegance in Merwin's work, Dorn found Merwin's language "elegant at times, fine at
others, and most times boldly enigmatic." For the next fifteen years,
"enigma" became a common part of the vocabulary in Merwin criticism. Paul Carroll spoke of how one poem in *The Moving Target*,
after he studied it for five years, remained "an enigma . . . simple yet
obscure and even disturbing."

Along with the enigmatic simplicity, readers began to sense an
apocalyptic tone in Merwin's poetry. Merwin had been expressing
his concerns about nuclear and ecological disaster since the mid-
1950s; his 1958 review of two books about birds, for example, began
with the comment that "as I perused these two books the question
of survival kept up a dull *continuo* in my head, intruding itself on
my pleasure at intervals like the sound of a faucet left running somewhere. . . . I go on the assumption . . . that there is some link between a society's threat to destroy itself with its own inventions, and
the same society's possibly ungovernable commitment to industrial
expansion and population increase, which in our own country remove a million acres from the world every year, and which threaten
more and more of the wild life of the globe." And in 1962 Merwin
published *A New Right Arm*, a Swiftian satire about the advantages
of conscripting into the armed forces mutants generated by the
atomic age. Dorn found that essay more moving and more effective
than the poetry that was expressing the same stark anger, but more
and more readers were finding themselves haunted by the sparse, unpunctuated language of the new poems, stark prophecies calmly an-
nouncing the extinction of the human species. Writing of *The Lice*
in 1968, Denis Donoghue found that Merwin's new style was the
perfect vehicle for his new tone: "The apocalyptic note is not new; it
was clearly audible in the second half of *The Moving Target. . . .* But

in *The Lice* the note is much more powerful, more dramatically sustained by the impression of man as a stranger on this cooling planet. This is a world without syntax, inhabited by a man who thought he had read the signs correctly and now, revising his texts, concludes that he was wrong."

Part of what readers were responding to was Merwin's growing distrust of language, his desire not to have his poems enter into complicity with the arrogating tendencies of human symbol-making activities. Donoghue saw the *Lice* poems as Merwin's search "for a natural syntax in which relations between one thing and another are given: to be discovered, not imposed by will or whim." Some readers, like William Dickey, found Merwin's new language not so much stark and silent as "empty," but even Dickey saw the dramatic change that was occurring: "*The Lice* moves with disquieting force into failures, vacancies, into a true reversal of Merwin's earlier assumption that poetic language is in fact able to determine experience." What beliefs Merwin may once have shared with Stevens about the efficacy of supreme fictions now seemed shattered, and commentators increasingly focused on Merwin's radical departures from his early formal work with its luxuriance of words. Vern Rutsala found that in reading *The Lice* and thinking of Merwin's career to that point, "it becomes apparent that Merwin has shed a great deal in order to get at a naked kind of statement." And Kenneth Rexroth noted how "each of Merwin's books has been a step from that academic fashion of imitation baroque, which he handled with great skill, toward evergreater modesty and immediacy of utterance."

But Merwin's immediacy of utterance, like his "strange simplicity," was not so easily grasped; it was an immediacy with distancing, a simplicity with complexity. Laurence Lieberman noted the "peculiar distancing" of the voice in *The Lice*:

It is as though the voice filters up to the reader like echoes from a very deep well, and yet it strikes his ear with a raw energy—a sustained inner urgency—that is rare even in poetry of the direct and explicit type. It is as though the artist's spirit, in fighting free of his human personality, layer by layer, has won through to the frontier of great impersonal being, and, in poem after poem, his spirit stands before us and speaks in utter simplicity and nakedness with no loss of personal immediacy. And yet, the voice has a strangely disembodied quality: it seems to speak across a very great barren distance. The poems must be read very slowly, since most of their uncanny power is hidden in overtones that must be listened for in silences between lines, and still stranger silences within lines.

To read this new poetry, suggested Lieberman, we had to become translators:

> To learn to read any major poet correctly, we must train the ear to listen for nuances of language and line movement that may be as unfamiliar and inaccessible, at first reading, as those of a foreign language. These difficulties, and the rewards that may be earned by surmounting them, are larger in Merwin's new poetry than in the work of most other contemporaries. As we hunt the pauses we missed on first reading, we are forced to hesitate, and Merwin's mastery is nowhere more evident than in his consistent power to turn these inevitable hesitations to advantage. Nearly always, the reader finds that there are images with hidden meanings and statements with a potential doubling effect; ambiguities that were hidden on first reading somehow become perfectly available during repeated readings, since the rhythmical pauses left by elided punctuation are exquisitely timed in relation to moments of revelation waiting to be grasped in line and image.

Richard Howard, reviewing *The Carrier of Ladders*, poems that were "intimate . . . but not in the least personal," found that in reading Merwin's work one had to follow the *via negativa:* "That is the real goal of these poems: . . . a quality of life which used to be called visionary, and which must be characterized by its negatives, by what it is not, for what it is cannot be spoken." Sandra McPherson agreed, positing that Merwin "builds his style on his use of denials," and is "researching the erasures of the universe" with his "negative aesthetic."

Harold Bloom probed for the cultural source of this negative aesthetic, this oddly bare and barren elegance. Looking for the Emersonian "visionary strain" in Merwin, Bloom found him to be uncomfortable in the role of "an American visionary poet"—he wrote "a dark postscript to the Emersonian insistence that poets are as liberating gods." Merwin's "predicament," for Bloom, was "that he has no

Transcendental vision, and yet feels impelled to prophesy." As a result, what we got in his poetry was "the constant attempt at self-reliance in the conviction that only thus will the poet *see*," but Merwin's "lust for discontinuity," for self-begetting, played against his traditional elegance of style and his ingrained respect for his precursors. Bloom sensed that Merwin at heart is more the "honorable, civilized, representative poet" (like Longfellow) than the "American Orphic bard," but Merwin, in the 1960s, assumed the bardic stance out of a historical and aesthetic necessity: "Only the *situation* of the Emersonian Transcendentalist or Orphic Poet survives in Merwin; it is as though for him the native strain were pure strain, to be endured because endurance is value enough, or even because the eloquence of endurance is enough." So, for Bloom, Merwin's cryptic new language was the result of his Emersonian posturing in a non-Transcendentalist world: "Merwin seems condemned to write a poetry that is as bare of true content as it is so elegantly bare in diction and design."

Merwin's language continued to strike more and more readers as emptied of conventional connotation, speaking its meaning only through its dark tonalities. Denis Donoghue's reading of *Carrier* went so far as to suggest that the "words are emptied of all allegiance except what remains in their cadence: that is, Mr. Merwin does by cadence what other poets do by image and figure." Donoghue continued: "The words do not call attention to themselves as words, they have hardly more than the modest aim of connectives, establishing rhythmic sequences on which later efforts depend. . . . Merwin's new poems issue from severence. They are not messages, swiftly delivered from poet to reader, but tokens of fracture; the only hope is to begin again with a rediscovered ABC of feeling."

James Dickey's 1961 call for emotional "intensity" in Merwin's work was dismissed by Donoghue: "I now think it is vulgar to demand 'passion' from such a poet as Mr. Merwin, if we mean something hieratic or Yeatsian. . . . Passion in the new book, if the word is to be used, is the energy of the book as a whole, the entire record of loss, fear, and hope." Merwin's style was being accepted, probed on its own terms, recognized as the work of a master at the height of his powers. Readers stretched further and further for images to try to capture the odd phenomenon of spoken silences that they found in the poetry. Lieberman, reviewing *Writings to an Unfinished Accompaniment*, talked of Merwin's fantastic linguistic shorthand, in which the few irreducible lines and images chosen (or has he mastered, rather, the power of perfect submission, passivity, in allowing the inevitable lines and images to choose *him*, the translator's genius?) guide the reader's ear by unerringly exact bridges across the very hinges— invisible overlaps and interlockings—between the words to the silences behind, or surrounding, the spoken utterances. This wizardry is accomplished by chains of sound and echoes, the echoes of echoes, the tones and overtones—all matings that tie or bind sound to silence, tongue to its dumbness, voice to its muteness.

Lieberman's would not be the first or the last critical vocabulary to collapse under the strain of describing what is going on in these books of the 1960s and early 1970s. But what Lieberman did make clear is that Merwin seemed to have achieved a poetry of "submission" or "passivity" where things, events, words choose him instead of him forcing his patterns on events, things, words. Stephen Spender defined this quality as "animism"—"seeing things reversed, the person who acts and looks as acted upon and looked at." Spender worried that this technique might be a "trick" and found its use in *Writings* "a bit monotonous"; still, he felt a remarkable power in the writing:

> these poems communicate a sense of someone watching and waiting, surrounding himself with silence, so that he can see minute particles, listen to infinitesimal sounds, with a passivity of attention, a refusal to disturb with his own observing consciousness the object observed. It is as though things write their own poems through Merwin. At their best they are poems of total attention and as such they protest against our world of total distraction. He gives the reader the feeling that the things we see in nature can be withdrawn from our eyes and returned to their integral separateness.

Hayden Carruth heard the same tone in Merwin's poetry, but reacted quite differently; reading *The Compass Flower*, he found the poetry moving "toward expressive but still vague silence," and he believed Merwin's practice is to give us a "written poem that is a guide to an unwritten one." He objected to Merwin's "distrust of the medium," and was appalled that, just when we needed it most, "we should be abandoning one of the few good and beautiful things that

prior civilizations have striven to create—language." Merwin, of
course, never abandoned language, though there was a time, after
The Lice, when he was not sure he could write any more, when
he seemed at the end of words—"there was really no point in it"
(Folsom and Nelson, "Interview," p. 46). But he has always been
aware that, as he said in the mid-1960s, "absolute despair has no art,
and I imagine the writing of a poem, in whatever mode, still betrays
the existence of hope, which is why poetry is more and more chary
of the conscious mind, in our age. And what the poem manages to
find hope for may be part of what it keeps trying to say" ("Notes,"
272). Merwin's poems have persevered, and what they have been trying to say in recent years has seemed more accessible for most
readers.

Probably no other contemporary poet has been as universally recognized as a major talent and simultaneously so criticized, prodded,
reprimanded, and challenged at every stage of his career as Merwin
has been. In 1970, Helen Vendler chastized Merwin for "maintaining
his starved and mute stance so long" that she felt an "urge to ask
him to eat something, anything, to cure his anemia," to give body to
his "voice singing out of empty cisterns and exhausted wells with
the toneless cry of *The Waste Land*." She felt his poetry was manufactured and insincere, "written not so much from sentiments requiring expression as from obsessive counters demanding manipulation." (Ironically, this is precisely the quality that makes Merwin
"uneasy" about Whitman's poetry—"you decide on a stance and
then you bring in material to flesh out that stance, to give details to
your position. . . . The stance is basically *there;* and much of the
poetry simply adds detail to it" [Folsom and Nelson, "Interview,"
p. 32].) Vendler identified a "Merwin dictionary" of word-talismans
that he "endlessly pushes around." (Robert Peters would expand on
this idea and catalogue at length Merwin's "Can't-Fail Concoction"
of images, landscapes, myths, totems—"Merwin's recipes for whip-
ping up prizewinning delectables for the great American poetry bake-
off.") But Vendler finds, over Merwin's "elusive pallors," a "faint cast
of sentimentality . . . that persuades the reader that he could, by
taking thought, add a cubit to his stature and raise sturdier offspring."

Many readers would find the poems of *The Compass Flower, Finding the Islands,* and *Opening the Hand* to be those sturdier off-

spring, more accessible, more voiced, more grounded in recognizable places and events. New forms have accompanied the new voice: a brief, three-line aphoristic stanza, and a more absorptive "broken-back" line with a spaced pause in the middle, creating a meditative and suggestive double line-break in each line. But with the new forms, the new attentiveness, come new criticisms, new complaints, as well as new recognitions of mastery. The process goes on, as it must for any major talent whose career keeps upsetting critics' predictions, whose work continually keeps his readers off balance, sure only that they can expect what they haven't yet expected. The essays in this volume pick up on and expand the issues and concerns raised by the poets and critics discussed here—poets and critics who in many ways set the terms for the ongoing discussion of Merwin's poetry.

As this narrative makes clear, the reviews of Merwin's books have, viewed collectively, been the site of much disputation. Yet most of the full-length essays on his work have been positive. No doubt this partly reflects most critics' tendency to write extensively only about poets they admire, a tendency reinforced by the New Critical tradition of close readings of individual poems. (Highly detailed but negative readings are difficult to sustain without seeming pointless; moreover, negative close readings are often at odds with the hidden phenomenological ground of many technical analyses.) As a result, collections of the sort we offer here are often limited to positive essays. Consequently, they have a tendency to detach themselves from the context of contemporary debate, appealing instead, perhaps prematurely, to the idealizations of the canon.

We have aimed here for a different effect: for a combination of positive and negative essays, making a collection that thereby gives extended treatment to the issues shaping contemporary debate on Merwin's work. To do this, we had to assure our contributors repeatedly that we would indeed accept good essays that took issue with all or part of Merwin's output. (Despite this, contributors who emphasized negative judgments all felt it necessary to assure us they would understand if we rejected their essays. One wonders about the politics of other collections on contemporary poets.) The result is a volume that, though weighted toward the positive, also includes distinct differences of opinion, sometimes even with opposing readings of individual poems. Readers interested in tracking this debate can compare, for example, Marjorie Perloff's negative reading of "The Asians Dying" with Cary Nelson's positive one, countering both of these with William Rueckert's suggestion that the poem is so strong and clear it does not need *any* reading. Or they can compare Charles Altieri's doubts about Merwin's most recent work with the very specific strengths both Edward Brunner and Thomas Byers find there, Altieri after writing approvingly of *The Lice* and *The Carrier of Ladders*, Brunner in the context of a positive essay on *Opening the Hand*, Byers as part of an essay that faults some of Merwin's recent impulses but applauds others. Similarly, Charles Molesworth's gentle dissent about most of Merwin's poetry since *The Lice* contrasts with readings in many of the other essays here. Yet even when these authors approve or disapprove of Merwin's work they use rather different strategies. Perloff attacks quite directly the very poems in *The Lice* that Rueckert, Altieri, Robert Scholes, and Jarold Ramsey, among others, would consider Merwin's greatest accomplishments. Molesworth, on the other hand, takes poems that Nelson, among others, might consider among Merwin's weaker ones and treats them as representative and decisive. Thus it would be possible to agree with Molesworth's assessments of particular poems but reject his overall reading of Merwin's career.

In addition to foregrounding questions of evaluation, the essays here give a good basis for thinking about the relation between methodology or critical discourse and the language of literary texts themselves. Readers will note, for example, that the theoretical allegiances of these essays vary considerably: from Robert Scholes's use of a naturalized semiotics to Marjorie Perloff's value judgments grounded in an interested version of literary history, from Edward Brunner's psychological interpretation of technique to Walter Kalaidjian's relentless poststructuralism, from Charles Altieri's and Cary Nelson's phenomenological close readings to Ed Folsom's model of an individuated cultural history; from Thomas Byers's partly psychoanalytic conclusions to William Rueckert's journal record of the struggle between his autobiographical and New Critical responses to *The Lice*. Yet there is one thing all the essays have in common—the persistence of Merwin's voice as a component of the essays themselves. Whether Merwin is quoted, imitated, or caricatured here, whether his style is echoed or forcefully distanced, all the essays must deal with the tendency of his writing to permeate whatever one writes about it. Thus in one very significant sense the methodological differences among these essays are swept aside by their common struggle (with Merwin himself) for priority of voice.

This tension is, of course, heightened by the question of evaluation, a question long deflected in contemporary criticism in general by its concentration on the established canon, but a question that is at issue again in literary studies, in part because of increased self-reflection in critical practice, in part because issues of racial, sexual, and national difference have thrown the canon into uncertainty. But the politics, the rhetoric, the stresses, the ambitions, and the delusions built into literary evaluation are particularly evident in evaluating our contemporaries, where judgments are strikingly theatrical and unstable. In regarding the canon, we tend to think of earlier periods as regrettably but instructively burdened with their own historicity in exercising evaluative judgment. Conversely, we tend to see ourselves as existing at the ideal moment (so far) to make universal and timeless judgments.

In the debates over a contemporary poet, however, such confidence is often comical, since rival claims that are mutually exclusive exist simultaneously. At its best, that is the risk and perhaps the excitement of judging contemporary poetry—the risk that our readings are subject at every moment to complete deflation. At its worst, evaluation then seems little more than a local effect of the dynamics of power. But that does not make it ungenerous, demonic, or trivial. For it is part of the culture's effort to define who we are and who we may become. Those questions are no more decidable than the question of whether Merwin's "The Asians Dying" is or is not a good poem, but those larger cultural questions are involved in the evaluation of that poem and in the evaluation of his work as a whole. In that process, all these essays work to convince the reader and make claims on the reader's sympathies and cultural identity. Nelson, for example, aims to increase the historical burden the poem places on the reader; Perloff aims to limit the poem's power. These readings are not liberally available alternatives but devastating commentaries on each other's judgments and on our place in history. We dedicate this book to that vertiginous sense of necessity. And on the issue of evalua-

tion, we give Merwin the last word, in the form of the last two
stanzas from his poem "Berryman":

> I had hardly begun to read
> I asked how can you ever be sure
> That what you write is really
> any good at all and he said you can't
>
> you can't you can never be sure
> you die without knowing
> whether anything you wrote was any good
> if you have to be sure don't write

JAROLD RAMSEY

The Continuities of W. S. Merwin: "What Has Escaped Us We Bring with Us"

I wrote this essay in 1970, and it was published not long after *The Carrier of Ladders* appeared and (with a certainty of deservedness rare for our literary awards) won the Pulitzer Prize. It is tempting now, looking back over a dozen unpredictable years, to follow Merwin's continuities on through his writing since those days of Kent State, Cambodia, and Spiro T. Agnew. One would want to notice, for example, how, beginning with *Carrier*, the poet has tended to pursue his haunted intuitions of selfhood in the light of a fuller awareness of other people, whose value to the speaker is often grasped and uttered in times of absence and separation. From *Carrier* on, an *elegiac* note has attended the poetry, not to be found in the emotional austerity of *The Lice.*

> I am the son of farewells and one of me will not come back but
> one of me never forgets.
> ("Psalm: Our Fathers," *CL*, 95)

Indeed, since *The Lice* the general emotional range of Merwin's poetry has widened considerably, reminding us that the peculiar icy poise of that collection could not be—ought not to be—sustained. Still, I feel now as I did in 1970 that I could say what I most wanted to say about Merwin's poetry by focusing on a book as absolute, as pure and formally achieved as *The Lice.* In its time it is fully the peer, I believe, of *Life Studies, Seventy-Seven Dream Songs*, and *The Far Field;* and if we now incline to respond to its apocalyptic insistence, "Well, now, we have survived after all," poems like "When the

War Is Over" seem timeless in their power to check such witless
complacency about the world and our present purchase on it:

> The dead will think the living are worth it we will know
> Who we are
> And we will all enlist again
>
> (L, 64)

I

Too much has been made, probably, of the New Departures in W. S.
Merwin's poetry since he began his career in 1952 with *A Mask for
Janus*. Remarkable differences there are, to be sure, between those
ripely elegant, sometimes precious early poems of high mythic density, and the downright, Lowellesque family mythologizings in *The
Drunk in the Furnace*; or between these pieces and the austere
poems in *The Lice* and *The Carrier of Ladders*. Yet—such is Merwin's achievement in all phases of his career—it is finally the continuity more than the variety that is worth pursuing. Men perish, in
Alcmaeon's dictum, because they cannot join the end to the beginning: and one of the measures of a poet's achievement, I think, is the
vitality with which his beginnings in the art are subsumed and kept
alive in the end of it—or, in Merwin's case, happily, in the ongoing
forms of it.

Thus, in every one of Merwin's books there is his peculiar grammar of emblems, the signatures of his imagination: the bells, mirrors, gloves, stones, doorways; the birds, the whales; and behind
them all, inexhaustible in its numinousness, the sea. Whether the
style runs toward elegant copiousness or discursiveness or a riddling
austerity, there is from first to last his gift for the indelibly expressive image:

> I am the ash that walk.
> ("Blind William's Song," *MJ*, 23)

> her hands lost in her bright hair . . .
>   ("The Wakening," *GB*, 27)

> While the children they both had begotten
> With old faces now, but themselves shrunken
> To child-size again, stood ranged at her side,
> Beating their little Bibles till he died.
> ("Grandfather in the Old Men's Home," *DF*, 41)

> For speaking either truth or comfort
> I have no more tongue than a wound.
>
>   I go . . .
> Through the standing harvest of my lost arrows . . .
>   ("The Nails" and "In the Night Fields," *MT*, 18, 30)
>
> a people blind as hammers . . .
>   ("Unfinished Book of Kings," *L*, 14)
>
> my mind infinitely divided and hopeless
> like a stockyard seen from above . . .
>   ("Plane," *CL*, 3)

There is always the sympathy with animal modes of consciousness, tending lately toward an explicit totemism. And always the extraordinary sensitivity to the *genii* of seasons and places; and the reliance on the two great verbs of human life: *to set out* and *to dream*. And the lines of development in which one tangent of his career eventually intersects other tangents—the translating of primitive and French modernist poetry bearing fruit in the style and vision of the most recent poetry, for example, and the fabulistic verse-narratives in *Green with Beasts* ("The Mountain," "The Station," "The Master") opening the way to the "fictions" in *The Miner's Pale Children*.

If there were a Collected or Selected Poems (and after so many books there ought to be), the condition of latency in style and matter that unites the phases of Merwin's career would, I think, be obvious. But for now two token illustrations of what I mean must suffice. On the one hand, near the imaginative heart of *The Carrier of Ladders* stands a wonderful poem titled "The Judgment of Paris"—and it is written with all the rhetorical elegance and loving attention of the details of myth that characterize *A Mask for Janus*. And on the other hand, in that first volume, across the page from a rather overblown myth piece, "Suspicor Speculum: To Sisyphus," one encounters this bleak, echoing little poem that would be at home in *The Lice*.

EPITAPH

> Death is not information.
> Stone that I am,
> He came into my quiet
> And I shall be still for him.
>   (*MJ*, 39)

Instead of sharp breaks, then, there is a kind of latency of talent and craft; a continuity of possibilities looking backward and forward for which Janus would be the appropriate sign.

Now there is nothing on the face of it very special about a poet's work being ultimately a piece and yet in its stages strikingly varied: the careers of Lowell and Roethke come immediately to mind. But the terms of continuity in Merwin's work have not been fairly recognized—and in what follows, I want to examine the poet's sixth book, *The Lice*, in an attempt to place it in his career, and to show how its form as a collection and its individual poems testify to his deep concern with the continuities of his life as a poet and of human life in general.

II

As all the reviewers of *The Lice* have declared, its first premise is an intuition of apocalypse. The poet's long-standing concern with inklings of his own mortality now flows inexorably into the apprehension, little short of certainty, that we are all living out the end of something. Men, having arrogated to themselves the power of annihilating all earthly life, including their own race, must now pay the cost of such unforgivable knowledge—enduring the death of the civilization that has for so long shaped their human selves, their purposes, their words. What makes *The Lice* special in a decade of writing that will be remembered for its apocalyptic obsessions, is an eerie sense of bearing witness to a world already in mid-apocalypse. These are not portentous poems so much as notations on the experience that it is all but over and done with, that we are merely "the echo of the future," and "tomorrow belongs to no one." In his preface to *A Mask for Janus*, W. H. Auden noted how Merwin caught "the feeling which most of us share of being witnesses to the collapse of a civilization, a collapse which transcends all political differences and for which we are all collectively responsible, and in addition feeling that this collapse is not final but that, on the other side of disaster, there will be some kind of rebirth, though we cannot imagine its nature" (*MJ*, viii).

But this intuition of rebirth beyond catastrophe is, with some notable exceptions, lacking in *The Lice*. The Last Days are surely at hand for the secular imagination when the future becomes literally

EPITAPH

Stone that I am,
He came into my quiet,
And I speak for him.
He was not my friend
But walked in hand with summer
But was claimed to this place.
There was no cure, no cure.
And now He can make no message
That was not known before.
Now None beg at his door;
He was not rich nor poor;
He owns nothing any more.
And he tells me nothing;
He has forgotten
How it was, and when,
That Death drew upon him;
After whatever words,
What will whispers.
And What which in other places,
Here Now his lips are stilled
With firmer thing than fingers;
His tongue is most secret;
His eye is folded
From whatever was seen;
He was not foolish nor wise,
But listened, and now lies
Now In a long hush, not waiting:
Death is not without information.
He wore many colors
But was cold in winter,
But was cold in season.
Name and body have gone
From what they have been;
So little I knew him,
I can give but slight character:
He was warm, uneasy restless, walked in the weather,
And now is at home always;
He was changeable,
But he has learned patience;
He lived out his fashion
And keeps one mode forever.

A draft of "Epitaph," a poem that Merwin condensed to four lines before publishing it. See Jarold Ramsey's comments on the version published in *A Mask for Janus.*

unimaginable—as it appears to be in this late, bitter invocation of
Janus, in which (as so often) the poet's sense of his own mortality
underlies the general apocalyptic burden:

> When you look back there is always the past
> Even when it has vanished
> But when you look forward
> With your dirty knuckles and the wingless
> Bird on your shoulder
> What can you write
>
>   ("It Is March," *L,* 17)

What can you write: in the face of such intuitions, what redemp-
tions of imagination, of art? At the far edge of history, what continues? What remains to be seen? In his one extended prose commentary to date on the age, a coldly ferocious indictment titled
"Notes for a Preface" (p. 272), Merwin acknowledges that "absolute
despair has no art," and in *The Lice* the poems voice their way
through that silent condition, I think, in a quest for the continuities
by which the imagination may be redeemed from its deathly grip on
the End.

As it is, the poems in *The Lice,* even more than those in *The Moving Target,* convey the hush and chill of hostages of silence; more
than any other American poetry, in their forms, they seem really to
follow the mind's first unpurposive gathering of images and words
before it is forced to move toward concepts, conclusions, public utterance. In their logical thrust they are *preconceptual,* eschewing (as
Merwin always has) even the circumstantialities by means of which
most modern American poetry is logically anchored in a kind of
emotional cause-and-effect: "I was *here,* (and so) I came to feel. . . ."
If absolute despair has no art, then there must be degrees; partial despair over an often unthinkable and unspeakable age must find its
poetic voice in regions of the mind somewhere below the orderly
circles of discursive thought. As Merwin has put it in the "Notes"
just cited, "I imagine the writing of a poem, in whatever mode, still
betrays the existence of hope, which is why poetry is more and more
chary of the conscious mind in our age" (p. 272). What it more and
more turns to, in Merwin's writing preeminently, is the preconceptual and intuitive mind.

Here, of course, we touch on not just Merwin's practice, but more
generally on one of the distinguishing features of postwar poetry—

one of the strategies by which many of our best writers have attempted to come to terms with the age. Prufrock pointed the way for what might be labeled a "neuropoetics" with his wish for a manner of expression so direct and unmediated it would be "as if a magic lantern threw the nerves in patterns on a screen";[1] and latterly, writers like Theodore Roethke, James Dickey, Robert Bly, and Charles Olson have striven (often with elaborate explanations) to create a poetic style which, in Roethke's formula, is able "to catch the very movement of the mind itself."[2] That is, the mind's habitual private motions, elusive, fishlike, "deep": perhaps, on the very threshold of cognition, beneath the constraining forms of logic, syntax, and punctuation, poetry can establish a foothold on the realities of a disordered, unaccountable time.

In Merwin's case, the *syntax* of his verse is straightforward enough, and such a rationale operates most obviously in *The Lice* in the total abandonment of punctuation. The reader is thereby forced to attend to the semantic movements of the verse very closely and openmindedly; without the formal syntactical signals of commas, periods, question marks to simplify things for him, he generally has several possible meanings opening before him at once. He thus cannot extrapolate to likely conclusions about the gist of a sequence of lines (as we all do to some extent in reading conventional poetry); indeed, often Merwin's lineation is mischievous, deliberately setting cognitive traps for the reader, as in the following lines from "Fly." A tame pigeon having died following his efforts to get it to fly again, the speaker says

> So that is what I am
>
> Pondering his eye that could not
> Conceive that I was a creature to run from
>
> I who have always believed too much in words
> (L, 73)

As a sense unit complete in itself, the first line is a brutally direct and exclusive identification of the speaker as the killer of a trusting animal: he is *that*; but when this sense is drawn into the succeeding lines, the initial recognition, without being denied or minimized, is tellingly developed in terms of the human paradox of being a "creature" and yet having the power to "ponder" and believe in words.

More generally, if Merwin is among those poets who pursue the

truth to be gotten in catching "the very movement of the mind,"
then in *The Lice* he often seems to be after a particular preconceptual mode—that of the riddle. As Aristotle points out in the *Rhetoric*, riddles and metaphors have much in common. And, as with a
metaphor, in attending to a posed riddle we are not interested so
much in "solving" it as in fully imagining the unfamiliar, maybe impossible union of details, which, we take it on faith, will be revealed
to us as something familiar, now to be seen in a new light. "What
small children die of old age and their parents are still young people?"
The meaning and certainly the pleasure of the riddle don't lie, I submit, in getting the answer itself, "leaves of a tree," but rather in the
"willing suspension of disbelief" which the riddle licenses, the
opening of the imagination to the possibility of such illogical circumstances, and the skewed perception of familiar objects which
follows. The riddling imagination in Merwin is rarely so playful or
direct; but in his persistent abrupt personification of natural objects
and forces, in his omission of logical connections and transitions (as
well as punctuation), in the way his titles so often seem to stand to
their poems as answers to riddles, and overall in the way the poems
metaphorically occupy, tease, short-circuit the workaday mind and
liberate the preconceptual faculties, he really does seem to be prac-
ticing, in the line of Verlaine and Dickinson, a poetry of riddle.[3]

III

As a book, an ordering of poems, of course, *The Lice* is anything but
preconceptual. It is remarkable in Merwin's career or anybody's for
the rightness and beauty of its articulate shape: whether by fidelity
to the order of composition or by editorial architecture, it is a triumph of imaginative *ordonnance*. The aimlessness and confusion of
a search for ways of joining the past and the present to a hardly imag-
inable future are given, as poem follows poem, an eloquent continuity. The individual poems, which would be impressive in their consistency and purity of tone in any ordering, are made to add up to a
totality of meaning that is much more than their sum as mere parts.
     Let us begin: on a fundamental level of organization, *The Lice*
proceeds according to a strict *seasonal* sequence—as if Merwin,
in whom the language of the seasons has always registered deeply,
were offering himself the certainty of at least one long continuum,

everything else having failed or promised failure. It is winter when the book opens, apparently. Later, in a series of broadly political poems that are undated but wintry in their bleakness, comes "It Is March." Another undated interval, then "April," then "The River of Bees," with its memories of a hopeful summer. In the following poem, "The Widow," autumn has come, and the poet wonders at the blessed subsequence of the natural order, so chastening to our human discontinuities:

> How easily the ripe grain
> Leaves the husk
> At the simple turning of the planet
> (*L*, 34)

Three poems later and the planet has swung on to November, in "A Debt," and then follows a memorable sequence of eleven short poems meditating on the passage of autumn into winter—"In Autumn," "Crows on the North Slope," "New Moon in November," "December Night," "After the Solstice," "December among the Vanished," "Glimpses of the Ice," "The Cold before the Moonrise," "Early January," "The Room," and "Dusk in Winter." But lest there be any expectation that in the book's seasonal progression these reflections on the bleakness within and without will give way to a joyful Shelleyan spring-that-is-never-far-behind, the succeeding poem, "A Scale in May," though it continues the turning of the year, is a Swiftian excoriation of human presumptuousness: "Of all the beasts to man alone death brings justice" (p. 50). In such incongruities—the seasons rolling on indifferently without toil while amid them men act out their pride and debasement—one inevitably hears bitter echoes of Ecclesiastes and, more to the point of Merwin's title, of Heraclitus.

From this poem of cheerless spring, the book advances into its second summer, in a progression of short poems like "How We Are Spared," with its haunting opposition, underscored by the title, of catastrophe and song—an opposition characteristic of Merwin.

> At midsummer before dawn an orange light returns to the
>   mountains
> Like a great weight and the small birds cry out
> And bear it up
> (*L*, 53)

Summer gives way to early autumn, and in the season of ripening
and harvest, the poet contemplates his own barrenness against the
coming on of winter:

> The flocks are beginning to form
> I will take with me the emptiness of my hands
> ("Provision," *L*, 55)

Soon enough it is winter again—in "In the Winter of My Thirtieth
Year," the poet, waking in fog and rain, now finds his mood sorting
rather than jarring with the season—

> Of course there is nothing the matter with the stars
> It is my emptiness among them
> While they drift farther away in the invisible morning
> (*L*, 61)

It is needless to trace the seasonal continuum of *The Lice* further
in detail. The book's second winter drifts on by implication, not direct mention, in a series of especially bleak and unsparing poems of
political animus, until, in "Avoiding News by the River," as the poet
wrestles with his anger and shame over "the news," he realizes that
another solstice has come round: "In an hour it will be summer."
And in this third summer, the book ends with "Looking for Mushrooms at Sunrise." With a measure of hope, it seems: now the season
is a time for "looking" rather than "avoiding," and where in other
summers the poet wearily assayed his emptiness against the fullness
of the season, now he seems to embrace its fulfillment of the promise of renewal. He has found, for the moment, a season and place
"without grief," with enormous personal implications, as will be
seen later on.

On another level of organization, the poems in *The Lice* are ar-
rayed in what amounts to a withering denunciation of modern man,
for his persistence in ways and purposes that will inevitably result in
the end of all continuities, his own included. Beyond most contemporary excursions in apocalypse, Merwin's "protest poems" (and how
feeble that label is!) have an authentically misanthropic dimension.
Perhaps this is why they seem to cut so much deeper than, say, the
outcries of Robert Bly or Denise Levertov—in which there is generally a residue of party-righteousness, "we few" versus "them." At
any rate, Merwin's misanthropy is a version of Swift's—the capabil-
ity of loving individual men while despising the abstract Man and
his Works. Merwin has often cited with approval one of Swift's

"Thoughts on Various Subjects": "I never wonder to see men wicked, but I often wonder to see them not ashamed."[4] And in *The Lice*, it is the shameproof, rationalizing arrogance of men that drives him to such raptures of bitterness.

In particular, from the beginning of his career, and in addition to his ban-the-bomb activities, Merwin has been deeply concerned with our good humanistic exploitation of the natural world, through which whole families of fellow creatures are harried to extinction, and the world becomes more and more hideously "human," and we grow correspondingly less and less humane. By the 1960s, the lively sympathy for our brother animals which occasions so many poems in *Green with Beasts* and *The Dancing Bears* has been joined by its misanthropic complement, a bitter indignation over man's despoliation of the world he shares with them. In the "Notes for a Preface" already cited, Merwin declares that "among my peculiar failings is an inability to believe that the experience of being human, that gave rise to the arts in the first place, can continue to be nourished in a world contrived and populated by nothing but humans" ("Notes," 271). And no American poet since Robinson Jeffers (the comparison is otherwise strange) has so relentlessly unparagoned man amongst the animals.

In *The Lice*, the animus behind Merwin's excoriation of what he has called "the activities of an emergent and epidemic species which scorns all life except its own withering existence" ("Notes," 272) most often expresses itself in ferocious comparisons between rampant man and the doomed, silently reproachful creatures of the earth:

> Men think they are better than grass . . .
> ("The River of Bees," *L*, 32)

> The extinct animals are still looking for home
> Their eyes full of cotton
> ("In Autumn," *L*, 41)

Thus, the first poem in the book, "The Animals," introduces the poet as Adam, the would-be Namer of Animals, but frustrated by the disappearance of his subjects—

> I with no voice

> Remembering names to invent for them
> Will any come back will one
> (*L*, 3)

And near the beginning of the main "political" sequence (which runs on from "Some Last Questions" to "The Gods," more than a third of the whole collection) stands one of Merwin's most widely admired poems, "The Last One"—his myth of man's uncreation of the natural world, inspired in form and spirit, it would seem, by his translation of a South American Indian myth, "The Creation of the Moon" (STa, 28–30).

In this sardonic ecological version of apocalypse, men have "made up their minds to be everywhere because why not / Everywhere was theirs because they thought so" (L, 10). So for no apparent reason except to gratify their "own withering existence" they prepare to cut down "the last one." But in long parallel lines in which the mounting terror is ironically deepened by the casual, "primitive" style, the natural order at last rises up, turns on its human destroyers, and, reversing the days of creation, engulfs them in an omnivorous annihilating "shadow." Only a few are spared—"The lucky ones with their shadows"—meaning, perhaps, the animal mortality they shared all along with all of created life, but now are "lucky" enough to be forced to acknowledge.

Though they spring, I think, from this vision of man's impending death, as it were, from ultimate "natural causes," most of the poems in the sequence take a more narrowly political view of the end, focusing on such final evidence as the perversion of democratic institutions, the Vietnam War, and so on. The titles alone are eschatologically resonant: "Some Last Questions," "An End in Spring," "Unfinished Book of Kings," "Bread at Midnight." In the first of these, Merwin dismembers the corrupt Body Politic with characteristic surreal savagery; the poem's form is that of an inverted riddle:

> What is the tongue
>   A. The black coat that fell off the wall
>   With sleeves trying to say something
> What are the hands
>   A. Paid
>
>   (L, 6)

It is concluded that the "compatriots" of today are those who "make the stars of bone." In "An End in Spring," the "it" that has reached an end seems to be our epoch in history, our civilization, more specifically our nation—"Ceasing to exist it becomes a deity"; meanwhile

> The compatriots stupid as their tables
> Go on eating their packages
> Selling gloves to the clocks
> Doing alright
>
> (L, 7)

As throughout the collection, these poems interpret and reinforce each other by close juxtaposition; the skewing of *compatriot* is a good example.

In such a context, "I Live Up Here" strikes me as a prophetic excoriation of the institutionalized Old Liberalism of Detached Good Intentions—such as would not be heard in this country for several years after the poem was written. The speaker condemns himself with his complacent political apologia—"I live up here / And a little bit to the left / And I go down only / For the accidents"—still, when "silence comes with the plate," he gives "what I can / Feeling *it's worth it*"—because he is so confident the democratic system is working, for him at least—

> I see
> What my votes the mice are accomplishing
> And I know I'm free
>
> (L, 8)

In "Unfinished Book of Kings," which follows "The Last One," Merwin dramatizes the final collapse of that system and the nullity of American political life generally, by referring what sounds like an American campaign to the dreary biblical account of the decline and fall of the Jewish state after Solomon. This very ambitious poem is, I think, too arbitrary in its personifications of doom, too dense in its surreal details to be ultimately successful: but its burden emerges eloquently enough—the votes have indeed become mice, the people, "blind as hammers," prepare for a hollow inaugural "of Their Own the last of the absences"—the last, it seems in a long line of rulers "whose blessing was as the folding and unfolding of papers."

Merwin continues to ask "What can continue" in such circumstances, in "Bread at Midnight" ("Well now that it is over / I remember my homeland the mountains of chaff") (L, 18); "Caesar," with its unforgettable image of a "compatriot" wheeling a hopelessly invalided ruler "past the feet of empty stairs / Hoping he's dead" (L, 19); and "The Moths," where "an audience of rubber tombstones is

watching / The skulls of / The leaders / Strung on the same worm"
(*L*, 23). The sequence seems to grow more explicit—the "There" in
"Whenever I Go There" is, apparently, a less and less credible United
States in which, he recognizes, "the beginning is broken"; in the
Spenglerian pieces "Wish" and "The Wave," it is the terrible necessity of the collapse of his own country and its traditions that
he must confront—"I inherited the wake of a long wave" (*L*, 26).
(Again, Robinson Jeffers comes to mind.) Most explicit of all, "News
of the Assassin" is surely one of the most eloquent poems occasioned by the killing of President Kennedy and its shabby political
legacies—

> An empty window has overtaken me

> After the bees comes the smell of cigars
> In the lobby of darkness
> > > > (*L*, 28)

This political sequence concludes with a poem titled "The Gods,"
the mood and imagery of which may be properly called postapocalyptic. It begins by establishing a condition of despair quite beyond protest and denunciation—"If I have complained I hope I have done
with it," and it goes on to meditate on the bankruptcy of a history
that has led to Vietnam and, indeed, to the guilty speaker himself:
"I / Am all that became of them / Clearly all is lost." Asking, as
throughout the sequence, "What is man that he should be infinite,"
the speaker ultimately looks *beyond* man to a natural world as desolate as T. S. Eliot's visions of the end. It is another version of the
posthuman world of "The Last One":

> clearly this is

> The other world
> These strewn rocks belong to the wind
> If it could use them
> > > > (*L*, 30–31)

At this point in the overall movement of the book, Merwin's political and eschatological preoccupations are subsumed in more broadly
personal subjects—but the burden of "men think they are better
than grass" is never far beneath the surface ("There is no season /
That requires us" ["The Widow," *L*, 30]), and it finally breaks out
again, seeming to interrupt a series of introspective pieces, in the

only straightforward Vietnam poems in the book, "The Asians Dying" and the wonderfully sardonic new stanza for Mrs. Howe's "Battle
Hymn," "When the War Is Over." But the unspeakable war is treated
as only one especially outrageous symptom of the end: in "The Dry
Stone Mason" and "Peasant: His Prayer to the Powers of the World,"
the poet turns his unsparing eye on the collapse, in the name of modern progress, of life-giving traditions among the rural poor. It is the
fate of the dry-stone mason, an artist in his trade who joined stones
as honestly as a poet might hope to join words, to survive into "the
age of mortar." And in his long ironic prayer to the industrial powers
that be, the Peasant describes in wonder the synthetic, wasteful, *un-
real* life that has come to usurp and rule his own simplicity, even his
language—

> What could I do I thought things were real
> Cruel and wise
> And came and went in their names
>
> (*L*, 65)

At first reading, those powers of the modern world appear to speak
themselves in the following poem, "For a Coming Extinction," the
latest in Merwin's pod of whale poems, all owing something to Jonah
and Job, and having to do with the terrible human implications of
animal extinctions. But the tone of the poem is not so simple: as
in other poems of its kind in the book, Merwin's spokesman em-
ploys a complex kind of sarcasm rather than the consistently self-
incriminating irony of a conventional persona. The speaker's monu-
mentally arrogant statement on behalf of the heedless despoilers of
life shifts intermittently to direct evocation of the pity, outrage, and
guilt that the prospect of the whale's extinction demands, and in this
mood he defines the terrible burden under which the poetic imagination must labor in *The Lice:*

> I write as though you could understand
> And I could say it
> One must always pretend something
> Among the dying
>
> (*L*, 68)

In the last poem of portent in the collection, "My Brothers the Silent," this unstably sarcastic voice is replaced by what seems to be
the anguished voice of an Everyman who fitfully, uncomprehendingly

recognizes that his race is busily humanizing the earth and thus de-humanizing itself. He feels complicity without understanding:

> I do not know what my hands are for
> I do not know what my wars are deciding . . .
>
> Look how I am attached to the ends of things . . .

Thus attached, the speaker quails before the human image he sees reflected in the eyes of sheep, which

> When I meet them on the roads raise toward me
> Their clear eyes unknowable as days
> And if they see me do not recognize me do not
> Believe in me
>
> (L, 78)

Something of the moral and perceptual continuity in Merwin's work can be measured by comparing these lines with the last lines of a characteristic poem in *Green with Beasts,* "Dog Dreaming," with its unsettling but undismaying evocation of a dog's awareness of the human—

> So little that is tamed, yet so much
> That you would find deeply familiar there.
> You are there often, your very eyes . . .
> Strange only to yourself, and loved, and only
> A sleeping beast knows who you are.
>
> (GB, 55)

IV

One striking feature of Merwin's austere rhetoric in *The Lice* is his reliance on an unusual form of personification. Again and again, in a landscape notable for its bleakness and human emptiness, the sur-viving natural objects and forces appear in a ghostly human form—

> Evening again the old hat without a head . . .
> ("Evening," L, 51)

> the winter that lipless man . . .
> ("December among the Vanished," L, 51)

> The sun sets in the cold without friends . . .
> It goes down believing in nothing . . .
> ("Dusk in Winter," L, 49)

> Tomorrow a colorless woman standing
> With her reproach and her bony children
> ("Watchers," *L*, 77)

It is as if the poet, in Richard Howard's phrase, "holed up" somewhere with his indignation and generic shame over man's destructiveness and, banishing the race at large from the properties of his
lonely imagination, is haunted nonetheless by specters of the community of man—displacements of what he has rejected.[5] Often (like
the woman in "Watchers") the personifications are characterized as
unforgiving witnesses of human life, and subtly carry on the chastening comparison between the human order and the natural order
that is, as suggested earlier, one of the organizing principles of the
whole book.

Ultimately, it is the speaker of the poems himself who appears as
chief among the ghosts. Caught between the unconsoling reality of
the season's flow and his meditations on the present unreality of human continuities, haunted by intuitions of a stable self within the
dominant experience of the self's fragmentation, he appears throughout *The Lice* to grope without much success for the threads of his
own identity. The speaker of a poem in the first book asserts that
"We survived the selves we remembered" ("Anabasis II," *MJ*, 5), and
in *Green with Beasts*, "The Wilderness" celebrates the clarification
of existence occasioned by an escape to the wild—"merely surviving
all that is not here" (*GB*, 26)—but in the poems at hand, though the
escape has in a fashion been made, the speaker, as in the end of "The
River of Bees," is obsessed with those remembered selves, and knows
that "we were not born to survive / Only to live" (*L*, 33)—that is,
with the vivid sense of the implications past and future of the moment that is the basis of identity.

Here, I think, lies the central line of imaginative continuity in *The
Lice*—and indeed, in Merwin's career as a whole. A more and more
ironic continuity, of course—a sort of incomplete *cogito:* to question-
beggingly assert "I am" by asking again and again, "Who am I?"
Space forbids a full tracing of the theme of self-confrontation and the
quest for the terms of personal continuity through Merwin's books,
but the following would be, I think, chief titles in that inquiry: in *A
Mask for Janus*, "Anabasis" I and II and "Meng Tzu's Song"; in *The
Dancing Bears*, "Colloquy at Peniel," with its treatment of Jacob's
wrestling match with the angel of selfhood, and the lovely "Cansos,"

with their burden of self-discovery in the love of another being;
"The Prodigal Son" and "Learning a Dead Language" in *Green with
Beasts;* all the family pieces in *The Drunk in the Furnace,* with their
implicit question, Is this what I come from? Is this what I must
come to?—a line of imagination that carries on into the first two
poems of *The Moving Target,* "Home for Thanksgiving" and "A
Letter from Gussie," and comes to real fruition in that book in
the self-directed meditations on his grandfather and his dead elder
brother, "Sire" and "For My Brother Hanson," and in "Finally,"
whose note of urgency anticipates *The Lice:*

> My dread, my ignorance, my
> Self, it is time. Your imminence
> Prowls the palms of my hands like sweat.
>
> · · ·
>
>   Bring
> Integrity as a gift. . . .
>
>   (*MT,* 22)

As odd as it may seem to bracket this most unromantic poet with
Wordsworth, there is in all of Merwin's books, most eloquently in
the last three, a bedeviled impulse to discover how the Child is Father to the Man, how one's days are bound each to each by some form
of natural piety. And the note of personal strangeness, of *déjà vu,*
that pervades *The Lice* is very much like a permanent condition of
Wordsworth's adolescent intuition of being not for that hour nor that
place.[6]

Modern counterparts might be found in Lowell's and Roethke's ag-
onized quests for a viable selfhood—but whereas their quests are revealed in great detail to be conditioned by psychological factors,
Merwin's seems, at least in comparison, chastely unpsychological
in its sources. His unstinting suppression of the personal circumstances of the poems (the family portraits of the 50s and early 60s,
many of them uncollected, being about the nearest he has come to
the hectic "confessionalism" of *Life Studies*) evokes, in the useful
distinction of Richard Howard in *Alone with America,* a sense of intimacy but not of the personal or private.[7] So far "out of it," as the
saying goes, the haunted speaker of *The Lice* declines to enumerate
confessionally his earlier existences so as to find out what, or rather
whom, he is "out of." Thus the task of self-orientation is made that
much more difficult, one would think, but its successful completion

in poetry that much more capable of universality of meaning by *not* being composed of personalized details. In the prophetic words of "Canso" in *The Dancing Bears*, we enter in Merwin's late poetry, especially in *The Lice*, "a domain of déjà vus, / The final most outlandish fastness of / Familiarity without memory" (*DB*, 54).

In that primer of modern apocalyptics, *The Sense of an Ending*, Frank Kermode observes how the experience of déjà vu seems naturally to attend meditations on the End—an observation pertinent to Merwin's vision.[8] The imagination, baffled in its impulse to conceive images of a postapocalyptic future, becomes suffused with an uncanny sense that what is happening has all happened before—a "familiarity without memory," exactly, in which the element of familiarity may or may not hint at possibilities of survival, of continuity of the self.

Here, perhaps, the full propriety of *The Lice*'s title and the riddling Heraclitean epigraph that provides it can be understood: "All men are deceived by the appearances of things, even Homer himself, who was the wisest man in Greece; for he was deceived by boys catching lice: they said to him, 'What we have caught and what we have killed we have left behind, but what has escaped us we bring with us'" (*L*, title page). For his purpose, Merwin has chosen one of the oldest and most widespread riddles known in the West (someone scrawled it on a wall in Pompeii, and versions have been recorded in Hungary, modern Greece, and Iceland)[9]—and the poet's use of a version attributed to Heraclitus is especially revealing. The riddle's significance for the book (and it is absolutely central) can be read roughly as follows. Caught in the brute Heraclitean flow but threatened with its mortal and indeed its apocalyptic stoppage, and unable to grasp the real continuity of his own self within it, the poet, one of Homer's kin, feels possessed by the ghostly presence of what has escaped him because of his human trouble with appearances. The "lice" he paradoxically brings along with him toward the end are the unresolved alternatives, the frustrated purposes, the guilt, missed chances, and unwritten poems of his discontinuous lives. The Heraclitean dictum of "For Now" in *The Moving Target*—"Tell me what you see vanishing and I / Will tell you who you are" (*MT*, 93)—is now recast as ironic first-person wisdom. Contemplating his earlier years and "the things I think I would do differently," the poet concludes, "they are what I am" ("In the Winter of My Thirty-Eighth Year" [*L*, 61]); in "Provision," foreseeing his mortal future, he declares, "What you do not have you find everywhere" (L, 55). It is a profoundly pessimistic version of Roethke's hopeful twisting of Heraclitus—"What slides away / provides."[10] It must, somehow—but how can it? What we catch of personal significance out of the flux we "kill" with imperfect understanding and finite memory, and leave behind; what eludes us about our selves follows to vex but not to nurture us. Is there, within the great indifferent Heraclitean strife and flow among things (itself threatened apocalyptically in our age) the possibility of a human order, a stable scheme of things caught and kept alive in the flux, not "lice" but the real and abiding terms of one's identity?

To return to the opening poem, "The Animals": in terms of the poet's quest for identity, for an integrity of being, those unseen, unreturning animals he is "remembering to invent names for"—are they not analogous to the "lice" of which his self seems chiefly to be composed? In "Is That What You Are," the title's question, ostensibly directed to a "New ghost . . . / Standing on the stairs of water," recoils upon the speaker himself, as he wonders, the baffled quick confronting the enigmatic dead, "What failure still keeps you / Among us the unfinished" (L, 4). The confrontation continues in that weirdly fine monologue, "The Hydra." Of all the poems in The Lice, it seems most truly to follow the first prediscursive stirrings of the mind, as if the poet were beginning to brood upon some ultimate riddle. Once sturdily possessed of the distinction between the living and the dead, the speaker admits that he now forgets "where the difference falls"; yet against the hydra song of Death, which "calls me Everybody," he tries to assert that "I know my name and do not answer." Against his half-envious view of the dead with their finalized identities and their freedom from "hesitations," having just confessed that he has forgotten the difference between them and himself, he characteristically contradicts himself and distinguishes life in the Heraclitean flow in these strange deathly terms:

> One thing about the living sometimes a piece of us
> Can stop dying for a moment
>
> (L, 5)

Are those transcendent moments what we are? Or are we rather the "lice" we bring with us?

Later in this book, in "The Plaster," Merwin describes how for

him the house of an untimely dead writer is haunted by the poems
he or she did not live to write. In the context I am trying to define,
the meditation turns back upon its author, as in "Is That What You
Are"; the last lines seem to return him to the identity half-hidden in
his own incomplete career, with its burden of "lice"; "What is like
you now / Who were haunted all your life by the best of you / Hiding
in your death" (L, 40).

Glossing "The Lost Son," Theodore Roethke wrote that in that
poem and throughout the middle of his career he proceeded from a
belief that "to go forward as a spiritual man it is necessary first to go
back," that is, through his own life.[11] But Merwin, in searching for
the self's lost integrity, will not follow this program of progress-by-
reversion. In one of the most personal poems in *The Lice*, "The River
of Bees," the speaker in a dream recalls a Homeric blind old man
seen fifteen years before who stood in the courtyard of a house beside
a river and sang "of what was older." Rather like "Hydra," the poem
evolves in terms of a vacillation between such affirmative and hopeful private memories of "what is older" and the general unreality and
purposelessness of the present. It would be simpler, the poet might
at least consolidate his despair, if he could forget the old singer, who,
after all, must now be dead, obliterated—and anyway, in Heraclitean
logic, is it not futile to return to the rivers of the past? But, in sequences like the following, something compels him to return in pain
to a once open and *possible* life; having declared with a kind of bitter
exultation against all humanistic aspiration, "Men think they are
better than grass," in the next line he comes back wistfully to a time
when the distinction seemed unimportant—

> I return to his voice rising like a forkful of hay

but then the nullity of the present obscures that voice—

> He was old he is not real nothing is real
> Nor the noise of death drawing water

Harried by this fearful intuition, driven to wonder if "We are the echo
of the future," he goes on asking, How shall I live? and as an artist,
What shall I say? And in the crucible of this great poem, the poet
achieves a brilliant fusion, at once plaintive and authoritative, of his
private lostness and the lostness of an entire age, with its Civil Defense guides to postnuclear survival that no one really believes in—

> On the door it says what to do to survive
> But we were not born to survive
> Only to live
>
>   (L, 32–33)

"How shall we live" in an age that is only the echo of its awful future? How can the song of the old blind goatherd teach us now? It is in such poems as this one (and "The Widow," which follows it), achieving a terrible consonance of personal and public necessity, that Merwin has truly seized, in Laurence Lieberman's praise, "the peculiar spiritual agony of our time, and the agony of a generation which knows itself to be the last, and has transformed that agony into great art."[12]

In addition to his preoccupation with the coming and going of the seasons, Merwin has always been fascinated by the anniversaries and personal celebrations by which we try to affirm the continuity-within-flux of our lives. Thus, in "The Child," occupied with the kind of introspection of parts generally occasioned by birthdays, he finds it "inconceivable that I should be the age I am." How, through the accumulation of what "lice," did he get to this year of what must somehow be one life? Rather like the disoriented, amnesiac characters in Beckett's plays, he tries to remember the stories about himself, but concludes that "something / Else must connect them besides just this me." Then, in the midst of his complex disorientation, the speaker wonders if a simple childlike spirit of affirmation might not restore to him his identity, made whole and continuous again—might not reveal to him how the child is father to the man, bringing at last "The child that will lead you" (L, 37–38). But the biblical and Wordsworthian echoes in this wish give it, I think, a certain rueful and skeptical tone—and in a companion piece, "In the Winter of My Thirty-Eighth Year," finding himself "As far from myself as ever," the poet acknowledges with a harder wisdom that whatever the "natural piety" might be that would unite the pieces of his life, the selves he half-remembers, it is futile to dream of new beginnings in childhood or youth or any age but the present. "There is nothing wrong with my age now probably / It is how I have come to it / Like a thing I kept putting off as I did my youth." In this unsparing mood, even the dim consolations of the pathetic fallacy are rejected: "Of course there is nothing the matter with the stars / It is my emptiness among them . . ." (L, 61).

V

> But is there any comfort to be found?
> Man is in love and loves what vanishes . . .[13]

What are the consolations of the disoriented, fragmented self; toward what, yearning to join beginning and end, can it turn? *The Lice* is a harrowing book, but it is not an emotional or artistic cul-de-sac. What seem like sources of affirmation can be felt if not understood in it, I think, and that is perhaps all we should expect in poems that cut so deeply into the nerves.[14] I have suggested that the style of *The Lice* derives from a radical preconceptualism, the imagination refusing to defer to the discursive faculties, choosing instead to encounter the world as if absorbing a riddle. And what comes through as affirmation is fundamentally an intuition of the ineluctable strangeness and richness of the moment—that finite dimension of the infinite flow of things which, as the poet confesses he did with his whole youth, we keep "putting off." When reduced in these poems to the moments that compose it, life registers as unfamiliar, strange, riddling—but not as inevitably hopeless or terrifying. In these terms, one of the crucial poems in *The Lice*, and fittingly one of the most beautiful, is another one of Merwin's "anniversary" pieces, "For the Anniversary of My Death," and I quote it entire—

> Every year without knowing it I have passed the day
> When the last fires will wave to me
> And the silence will set out
> Tireless traveller
> Like the beam of a lightless star
>
> Then I will no longer
> Find myself in life as in a strange garment
> Surprised at the earth
> And the love of one woman
> And the shamelessness of men
> As today writing after three days of rain
> Hearing the wren sing and the falling cease
> And bowing not knowing to what
>
> (L, 58)

It begins, mordantly enough, even morbidly, with life conceived of as having attained purpose and a measure of identity only when it reaches the end. In a characteristically compressed, mind-boggling figure, the poet imagines the onset of his nonbeing in terms of the terminal flow of light from a burnt-out star, a continuing signal, as it were, for which there is no longer a living source. But in the second section, the poet is drawn back from interstellar space to the forms he knows of that strangeness, sensing in them the sources of life itself and of its renewal—the earth's surprise, the love of one woman precariously balanced, but balanced still, against the shamelessness of men—until he finds he has repossessed "today," no longer significant to him as the hypothetical anniversary of his death, but instead as one day, full of the strangeness of ceased rain, wren song, the renewed flow of his own imagination. In the words of an earlier poem, "The Dragonfly," *It is all here,* somehow—now, not lost, though in his bow he can only gesture his restored reverence for what he cannot understand.

Not that Merwin returns often to love and to poetry for consolation, but what they stand for in this poem, the recognition of the inexhaustible richness of the present, he does seize upon, significantly, in the last poem of the collection, "Looking for Mushrooms at Sunrise"—as at the conclusion of other books, with "Daybreak" in *Moving Target* and "In the Time of the Blossoms" in *The Carrier of Ladders,* he has chosen to end on a note of emotional openness, of renewal. Now it is simply the opulent revivals of the earth and the surprise of finding himself on it at the break of another day, that Merwin celebrates. The day begins; the Heraclitean flux continues; the "lice" of other days haunt him with a powerful sense of déjà vu; the quest for the integrity of the lost and discontinuous Self leads him on—

> Where else am I walking even now
> Looking for me
>
> (*L,* 80)

but now that racking quest has brought him to a "place without grief," a place and season, and ultimately a *poem,* of natural growth and daily renewal where his selves, all full of the richness of one moment—"even now"—might begin to recognize one another at last, and pass from surviving to living.

NOTES

1. T. S. Eliot, "The Love Song of J. Alfred Prufrock," in *T. S. Eliot: The Complete Poems and Plays* (New York: Harcourt Brace, 1952), p. 6.

2. Theodore Roethke, *On the Poet and His Craft: Selected Prose of Theodore Roethke*, ed. Ralph Mills, Jr. (Seattle: University of Washington Press, 1965), p. 10.

3. Given Merwin's persistent interest, both as translator and as poet, in folklore and the oral traditions of tribal societies, it is to be hoped that his critics will soon be following him into this territory, which he knows as well as any of our major poets, including Ted Hughes and Gary Snyder. (For such a reconnaissance on behalf of Hughes, see my "Crow: Or the Trickster Transformed," *Massachusetts Review*, 19 (Spring 1978), 111–27.) By the same token, Merwin's intensive study of traditional Eastern meditative practices has an important bearing on his writing, especially since *The Carrier of Ladders*, but that bearing likewise remains to be explored.

4. Jonathan Swift, "Thoughts on Various Subjects," in *The Prose Works of Jonathan Swift*, vol. 4, ed. Herbert Davis (Oxford: Shakespeare Head Press, 1957), p. 251.

5. Richard Howard, *Alone with America: Essays on the Art of Poetry in the United States since 1950* (New York: Atheneum, 1969), p. 378.

6. Since *The Lice* appeared in 1967, Merwin's poetry has received some first-rate critical attention from critics willing and able to puzzle out, without prejudice, the poet's evolving "program" as a writer. But almost without exception these commentators have ignored his continuing concern with selfhood—perhaps "have shied away from" is a more accurate phrase, given the postmodernist critical attitude toward the old questions of self and identity. Nathalie Sarraute has remarked somewhere that, upon hearing the word *psychology*, a contemporary novelist should look away and blush. She seems to speak for most of Merwin's critics—but not at all for the poetry itself, with its persistent vein of self-encounter.

7. Howard, *Alone with America*, p. 376.

8. Frank Kermode, *The Sense of an Ending* (New York: Oxford, 1968), pp. 44ff.

9. See Archer Taylor, *English Riddles from Oral Tradition* (Berkeley: University of California Press, 1951), pp. 159–60.

10. Theodore Roethke, "Give Way Ye Gates," *The Collected Poems of Theodore Roethke* (Garden City: Doubleday, 1967), p. 80.

11. Roethke, *On the Poet and His Craft*, p. 39.

12. Laurence Lieberman, "Recent Poetry in Review," *Yale Review*, 57 (Summer 1968), 597.

13. W. B. Yeats, *The Collected Poems of W. B. Yeats* (New York: Macmillan, 1960), p. 205.

14. The question of "affirmation" in Merwin's poetry has occupied most of his recent critics, particularly in regard to the tonality of the last poems in his books. Altieri and Nelson, for example, deny such a note, whereas Kyle proclaims it. No use trying to make Merwin out as a poet committed to "creating confidence in life," but at or near the other extreme, it seems to me that some of his most sympathetic and penetrating critics, Altieri and Nelson, for example, come very close to offering a view of the poet's imagi-

native program as nihilistic. Certainly they tend to ignore or undervalue the evidence, in Merwin's poetry since *The Lice*, of a widening of his affective range, so intent are they on construing Merwin's capable negativity, in terms of literary and political assumptions about what our bad age calls for in its writers. If this widened range does not include out-and-out affirmation, it does include elements of the elegiac, the poignant, the tender, the erotic, the nostalgic, the pawkily comic—not to be felt in the rigorous exclusions of *The Lice*.

WILLIAM H. RUECKERT

Rereading *The Lice:*
A Journal

9/29/81

I've been reading and teaching this book of poems since it first came out in 1967. I've been reading Merwin's poems since I was in college. He and I were born a year apart (1926, 1927), and I have always considered him a kind of chronological brother who became the poet I always wanted to be and never was to become. I once thought about writing a book about a group of poets born during or near my birth year—Ginsberg, Bly, O'Hara (a classmate at Michigan, dead in his prime), Ashbery, Snyder, Merwin, Kinnell, Rich, Merrill, Snodgrass—because it would be interesting to see how we lived through the same events (and how we now remember them): the Depression, World War II, McCarthy, the Eisenhower years, Korea, Kennedy and the excitement of the New Frontier, Vietnam, the environmental movement, the Black revolution, feminism, Watergate and the horrors of the Nixon administration, the sexual revolution. I would also follow the development of each poet's poetry from the late forties, when most of them began to publish, to the present, in relation to my own life and work.

But Merwin (along with Snyder and Kinnell) has always meant the most to me, and probably no book of poetry by one of my contemporaries will ever mean to me what *The Lice* has. It has been a sacred text, just as all of Merwin's readings have been holy moments for me, and my meetings with Merwin, before or after his readings, usually with my friend Jerry Ramsey, have meant more to me than any of the other meetings I have had with poets—again with the possible exception of Snyder. Kinnell was sick when I met him; Lowell was drunk and lecherous; Dickey was arrogant and role-playing; Creeley was too remote to make much of; I never really knew O'Hara well; Berryman was so hung over and strung out he was barely human; Hecht never let anyone too near him; Duncan was overwhelming, completely dominating every conversation so one could only circle around the edges of the dazzling talk; Dorn, acerbic as usual, sent small, barbed words at you all the time.

But Merwin and Snyder talked to you the minute they perceived you had actually read their poetry seriously and were trying to engage it and them. Merwin was the best because I met him more often, mostly during the Vietnam years; and because he was not only one of the most beautiful men I have ever seen, but one of the sweetest, and in his person a kind of living contradiction to the deconstructive wisdom of the poems in *The Lice*. Real affinities existed between the two of us. During the readings I heard things I thought no one else had experienced or thought, much less verbalized. Meeting him so often was important because it allowed me to separate, but never divorce, the poetry from the man. It gave me a much purer conception of what it meant to be a poet in our time and of how poetry was relevant to its own time. Talking with Snyder or reading his interviews, you could predict many of his poems; talking with Merwin you could not have predicted the poems of *Lice* or *Carrier of Ladders*. The poems gave one access to a deep, inner imaginative life, to a whole other dimension of reality (as Faulkner's great novels did) not available by any other means. Merwin could not have talked the poems of *The Lice*.

9/30/81

At 8:30, Jordan driven to school, Barbara off to work, the dogs walked, I am ready to begin again. Pure pleasure, writing about Merwin and *The Lice*, though three hours of it drain me for the rest of the day.

How to unravel the book. That was always the question. The months of the year and the seasons, in their repeating orders, give the book a certain deceptive continuity: "An End in Spring," "It Is March," "April," "In Autumn," "New Moon in November," "December Night," "After the Solstice," "December among the Vanished," "Early January," "Dusk in Winter," "A Scale in May," "In the Winter of My Thirty-Eighth Year." There are also many internal references to the months, the seasons, the diurnal rhythms—the realities of natural time and nature itself. They remind us that the poet is in the world, almost without exception a rural, often seemingly pastoral world. But this book is not any version of pastoral. I have to disagree with Jerry Ramsey that the book derives its unity from these sequential references to nature, both as scene and temporal movement. The poems rooted in nature are among the most obscure and troubling. What is one to make of "An End in Spring," a title that contradicts itself, or effects a reversal, and begins, as so many of the poems do, with an antecedentless "It is carried beyond itself a little way / And covered with a sky of old bedding," and continues leaving the "it" without attributes:

> Ceasing to exist it becomes a deity
>
> It is with the others that are not there
> The centuries are named for them the names
> Do not come down to us
>
> $\qquad\qquad\qquad\qquad$ (*L*, 7)

10/1/81

Reread "An End in Spring" many times after yesterday; the whole last part must be quoted, so that the force of the nonreferentials—"it" and "them"—can be felt and the characteristic irresolution of the poem can be understood:

> Ceasing to exist it becomes a deity
>
> It is with the others that are not there
> The centuries are named for them the names
> Do not come down to us
>
> On the way to them the words
> Die

Maybe it does not matter who or what has come to an end in spring, only that something has. There is no internal evidence to use in identifying "it" or "them." They are blanks which cannot be filled; they are simply anything that has come to an end in spring when so much else is beginning again. It has ceased to be; it cannot be named because it has gone into a realm that is beyond words, beyond experi-

ence and knowledge. The only thing we can know is the ending in
spring itself. This is not a poem of mourning, but a poem which
states a fact of our existence. We always want to know what has died
so we can sentimentalize it, memorialize it. Not here. "Ceasing to
exist it becomes a deity" is one of those brutally true and ironic lines
one finds all through the book. The deities come from that other
realm about which we know nothing. That is why the words die on
the way to them, because the words know nothing about this realm
and so cannot name what is in it. This realm, about which so many
words have been written, and from which so many truths have been
derived, is devastated as a source of human value and support. One is
reminded of Yeats's comic and ironic poem on this same subject,
"News for the Delphic Oracle," in which the poet sends news to the
Delphic Oracle about what it is really like over there in the other
realm. Yeats, at least, *imagines* a life in that other realm, but not
Merwin. One of the oldest traditional poetic subjects is simply canceled here.

Take another spring poem, "It Is March," one of the book's bleakest:

> When you look back there is always the past
> Even when it has vanished
> But when you look forward
> With your dirty knuckles and the wingless
> Bird on your shoulder
> What can you write
>
> (L, 17)

And the last line of the poem: "Whatever I have to do has not yet
begun." What you can write if you are a poet are precisely the kinds
of poems Merwin wrote for *The Lice* and parts of *The Carrier of Ladders* and *Writings to an Unfinished Accompaniment*. Many of the
poems in *The Lice* are written from a vantage point Merwin has
achieved by an imaginative projection into an unthinkable future:
"The Animals," "Some Last Questions," "The Last One," "A Scale
in May," "For a Coming Extinction," "The Gods," "The River of
Bees," "The Asians Dying"—and others. But Merwin will not myth-
ologize the future, for the words die on the way to that realm; he is
not going to be another Yeats, nor will he follow Eliot's or Pound's
way. He is going to eat some of Ginsberg's "reality sandwiches," to
look right into the center of the nightmares, as Kinnell did in *The*

Book of Nightmares. He is going to write what he can and try to discover a new beginning. Thus, though it deals in finalities, *The Lice* is not a terminal but a mediating book. It is the book in which Merwin, like William Carlos Williams, makes his descent, to be followed by an ascent. It is his wasteland book in which he also identifies and buries his dead. But Merwin and Eliot are responding to different historical circumstances. In fact, Merwin's dead are the very last things which gave Eliot life toward the end of *The Waste Land* and in "Ash Wednesday." The Western Culture that saved Eliot has died for Merwin, and that is the source of much of the agony in these poems. The last line of "It Is March" refers to the need to find a new ground; no viable future can be projected from the past of Western culture. When Merwin says, at the beginning of "A Scale in May," that "all my teachers are dead except silence" he is not just referring to the death or failure of the culture of the word; he is also referring to Western (white) culture with its anthropocentric view of the world.

So much is dead in this book, and on such a large scale. Putting Merwin and Whitman together is very instructive. There is so much that is alive in Whitman, and the future is always full of promises, as in "Children of Adam" or "Song of the Open Road." Robert Duncan, when we were both reading papers on Whitman at a conference, said this opposition between Whitman and Merwin was false and unfair to Merwin. I've thought a lot about what he said and still think it is correct to polarize the two, especially for *The Lice*, though Merwin abandoned Whitman's America long before *The Lice*. Here, much more than America is being abandoned, so perhaps Duncan is right—it is distracting to bring Whitman into it.

10/2/81

> All those years behind windows
> With blind crosses sweeping the tables
>
> And myself tracking over empty ground
> Animals I never saw
>
> I with no voice
>
> Remembering names to invent for them
>   (*L*, 3)

Beginning the book, one wants badly to make sense of this poem. But making rational sense is one of the first things abandoned here. So many phrases and lines are cut loose from our grammatical, syntactical, and cognitive expectations. Who, what has been all those years behind windows? What windows? The dead, extinct animals? Windows of museums, pet shops? What are blind crosses? Is this literal—a broom in the shape of a cross, blind because brooms don't have eyes? How does the conjunctive "and" function; what does it join and who is "myself" and why is he tracking the animals? Is he Adam, the namer of animals; the poet as Adam the namer of the things of this world? He is certainly not Whitman's New Adam. Is the empty ground an image of devastation or is it just empty of animals? Are they what was all those years behind bars? If he never saw any animals, where was he? Where are they? Extinct? And he has no voice. A Poet and Namer with no voice; mute, wordless. Note the piling on of negatives at the outset. *Blind* crosses. *Empty* ground, animals I *never* saw. I with *no* voice. Then one of the most perfect of Merwin's paradoxical, self-canceling actions: remembering names to invent for them, not reinvent (itself impossible) but invent. You can't reinvent the names, be Adam again, and name them for the first time. It is no new Eden here. So he remembers the names, but has neither voice to speak them, nor things to name.

Emerson said that words and things were still together. Burke said that the word is not the thing it names. Bateson said that the map is not the territory it charts. But we have gone beyond all that here. The voiceless poet remembers the names of the animals, but there are no animals to name. The end of the poem now turns to questions and affirmations which seem to deny themselves—given the negatives at the beginning. "Will any come back will one": note the diminishing movement, another form of negation: from any (indeterminate) to one, as if one would be enough, but of course it wouldn't. Then to the affirmations that are really negations: will one of the animals come back saying "yes," saying "look carefully" (so you can recognize that I am an animal and remember a name to invent for me), saying yes, "we will meet again" (in some future). If the animals are dead it is because we have killed them or destroyed their habitats. And here is one man looking for the lost animals, trying to recover some unity and completeness. But he won't. The final question is rhetorical, a beginning that cancels beginnings.

The Lice offers a particular way of viewing and living in the world by way of language. The poems dance a variety of attitudes—in Burke's metaphor—in stark, beautiful, and disorienting images and a syntax of vision (or perception) that require great patience and effort from the reader. Almost nothing is easy in this book, and one is put into the peculiar position—so characteristic of contemporary literature—of trying to understand how pain can be pleasurable, why one subjects one's mind to repeated painful encounters with these poems.

Consider "Some Last Questions." Last questions are eschatological (Burke might say entelechial) questions about the ends of things. All the questions, until the last two, are about man and are posed anatomically: What is the head? What are the eyes, the feet, the tongue, the hands? What is silence? Who are the compatriots? The questions are answered ironically, in terms of what each part of the body ultimately becomes. Each answer diminishes and deconstructs the arrogant view of man so characteristic of Western culture. It is as if Merwin were setting out to undercut the "What a piece of work is a man" speech in *Hamlet*. Every vital human organ has its essential function canceled by an ironic view of man as matter. The head (the mind, the imagination, the neurological center) becomes ash; the eyes become the sockets in the skull;—but now I'm making a mistake. I am translating the second answer into conventional iconography, and Merwin never does that. In fact, he usually works against just such a procedure, so that the answers are skewed to the questions but the negating principle of the answer is clear—even when the images are impenetrable. The clearest answer to all the questions is the first: head is ash. As the poem progresses the answers become more difficult, and some of the answers are wrong but right at the same time, so that the question/answer technique is brought into question to suggest the folly of received answers to ultimate questions.

> What are the eyes
>   A. The wells have fallen in and have
>   Inhabitants
>
> > (*L*, 6)

The answer is given to us in a metaphor that—but wait, is it a metaphor or simply an image that answers the question in parallel terms:

the wells have fallen in and so no longer can provide water; furthermore, they are now occupied by other (nonspecified) inhabitants,
which simply indicates that they are not what they used to be. One's
previous training in analysis and hermeneutics inclines one toward a
metaphorical reading of the answer based on what happens to flesh,
to those parts of the body most readily subject to decomposition.
The wells become the eyes in the sockets, the inhabitants perhaps
become worms. Yet even if we cannot decide whether we are dealing with a metaphor or an image we understand the import of the
answer.

But when we come to the next answer, all is not as clear:

> What are the feet
> A. Thumbs left after the auction

This is a riddle, an enigma, a wrong answer that is right in some way,
even as it is canceled in the next line: "No what are the feet." Every
question here is about some part of man, but every answer tells us
about the whole and functions as a synecdoche. If the head is ash,
then no enduring spirit dignifies it; no apocalypse will resurrect it
into its former bodily form. The head will be recycled to form other
living matter. Only an anthropocentric view exempts us from this
universal fate and sees us as superior to the biosphere itself.

What are "thumbs left after the auction"? Well, they are something that has become completely useless, because either the rest of
the hand, or the rest of the body, has been auctioned off. This answer
is relevant for all the questions, then, though the other answers are
different in kind because each is specific to the part of the body being
questioned.

It is usually a mistake to work out a complete reading of any of the
major poems in *The Lice*. A complete reading presupposes a kind of
coherence (whether rational, metaphoric, or symbolic) which many
of these poems do not have, or which we have not yet come to understand. I think Merwin deliberately created poems which lack the
kinds of coherence we expect. Indeed, there is no law that says everything in a poem has to make sense. That is a deception perpetrated
by the logical centers of the mind, but the mind has other centers,
and reason cannot encompass the world. In fact, many of the poems
in this book are about the failures of reason and remind us of
Bachelard's beautiful distinction between reason and imagination.
This is a boundary-breaking book of poems. Unlike Duncan, who

often writes Whitmanesque poems that try to unify everything, Merwin makes us suffer through alienation, disjunction, riddles, enigmas, failed visions, irony, as a principle of human evolution: despair without relief, ends with no beginnings; reduction, irresolution, diminishment, loss as the principle of life.

But let us return to the feet:

> Who are the compatriots
> A. They make the stars of bone

A beautiful image which goes from macro (stars) to micro (bones) and creates a Bachelardian intimate immensity. This expansive image, in which the stars are made out of elements from the decayed bones of mankind (the end as beginning again), finally merges man back into what all living matter on earth came from—the cosmos itself. Whitman would have understood this question and its answer perfectly, and without irony. The imagination that conceived these lines was able to project a long way into the future, beyond life on earth, beyond irony of all kinds, including cosmic irony.

10/8/81

Let's go to extremes here and take one of the simplest and shortest poems in the book—"Wish"—and examine it in relation to one of the most obscure poems—"The Wave." They follow each other on pages 25–27.

> WISH
> The star in my
> Hand is falling
>
> All the uniforms know what's no use
>
> May I bow to Necessity not
> To her hirelings

This is clearly an antiwar poem and belongs with the other poems that are overtly political (such as "Caesar") and antiwar (such as "The Asians Dying"). We can read this poem literally or symbolically and get the same results—a phenomenon which is true of many of the poems in the book. The star in line 1 can be the insignia an officer has taken off and is dropping, signifying an end to his commitment to everything the armed forces stand for; or it could be a star falling, something coming to an end. The uniforms of line 3 are what is left after the bodies inside them die. They know that killing is no use because, in terms of this image, they are left empty and useless. Uniforms also identify the enemy. The hierarchical image in line 4 describes a relationship of lower to higher power, a recognition by the individual I that there are greater forces in history. Dying for one's country (*Dulce et decorum est pro patria mori*) has always been presented as a duty and a necessity. In fact, the Modern State has the power to execute you for treason if you refuse to risk your life for it (as in Faulkner's *Fable*). Line 4 identifies this idea as a political lie, not a necessity, and certainly originates from Merwin's revulsion against the Vietnam War. Bowing to this false necessity is a form of mindless servility. True Necessity (Merwin seldom capitalizes internal words) is what many of his poems try to identify. Merwin does not say what it is here, but we can assume it is death. War is merely one of death's "hirelings," one of the many inferior illusions we die for.

This poem is very satisfying because it can be worked out so readily. "The Wave" is another matter. I will make no attempt at a sustained analysis. It is a frustrating, recalcitrant, even maddening poem, absolutely resisting the kind of code-breaking analyses most of us love to do. The only thing one can say with certainty about this poem is that it is about alienation and extreme homelessness and ontological confusion. Bachelard might draw out the opening line because in a sense it was written for him: "I inhabited the wake of a long wave." He might have responded to the other inhabiting/space images: "Envelopes came each enfolding a little chalk / I inhabited the place where they opened them"; "I inhabited the sound of hope walking on water"; "I inhabit the sound of their pens on boxes / Writing to the dead in / Languages"; "I inhabit their wrappings sending back darkness." Space criticism (Bachelard, Blanchot), ontological criticism, and various modes of Burkean analysis might enable us to decode this poem, but I'm not sure decoding would be appropriate. I have only quoted pieces of the poem, but the poem is all of a piece in the power of its negative images—images of loss, homelessness, interminable wandering, searching for a harbor that retreats before you and disappears, images of the futility of writing and language, and finally images of indirection (the futureless future, the absence of any sense of how or where to begin again).

"The Wave" is a poem one hurls one's mind against repeatedly in attempts to overpower it, break it down into its component sense-making parts. But that struggle to master a verbal structure is a mistake here. *The Lice* reminds one again and again of the first line from Heraclitus opposite the title page—"All men are deceived by the appearance of things." After working to read the poem carefully, one should learn when to let go, when to acquiesce to indeterminacy, when to admit that a complete hermeneutic action is impossible. The poem loses none of its power because of this. We are aware from the first line that this poem is going to be a cry of anguish. One might read this poem in conjunction with Whitman's "Out of the Cradle Endlessly Rocking"—a poem also about waves and the sea, but one in which the poet finds instead of laments the loss of direction.

11/9/81

Let's play "A Scale in May."

There are eight notes in a conventional scale, and eight three-line stanzas in the poem. Indeed, it is one of the book's most mathematically regular poems. The poem is also about justice, and it suggests, as many of the poems do, an iconographic imagination—as with death drawing water. A female, nude from the waist up, blindfolded, holding a scale, is the traditional Western symbol for justice. Justice, of course, is blindfolded so that absolute justice may be done, without interference from the senses.

11/10/81

The relationship between the two ways in which "scale" can be understood is neither clear nor obvious. Furthermore, why May? Perhaps because Merwin wrote the poem in May. Merwin has poems dated in almost every month of the year; it seems—empirically— best to recognize the fact that the poems in the book were written serially over a number of years and that Merwin has, without symbolism, simply incorporated the time of writing into many of them. The opening lines of the poem are among the book's finest:

> Now all my teachers are dead except silence
> I am trying to read what the five poplars are writing
> On the void
>
> (*L*, 50)

One of the recurrent themes of *The Lice* is the failure of the accumulated culture of the written word to provide reliable guidance. Worse, perhaps, it provides answers that lead us to destroy both the natural and the man-made world. For a lifelong poet this failure of the written word is a disaster. Many of the poems in *The Lice* and *The Carrier of Ladders* seek a new language for a new kind of poetry. Much of the difficulty with *The Lice* derives from the fact that it rejects so much without being able to provide alternatives (yet) and hence is a sustained act of creative negation. So many dead teachers. So many obituaries. So much pain at being human, at what humans have done to each other and to the nonhuman world. So much unexpiatable guilt. So much injustice. So Merwin turns to his first and last teacher: silence, the preverbal, the nonverbal, the postverbal, and tries to "read what the five poplars are writing / On the void." The five poplars affirm their own being, their sheer presence silhouetted against the sky. They do not tell us what to do to survive; if anything, they tell us we were only born to live.

The first four sections or notes of the poem deal with man; the last four, with the exception of line 17, deal primarily with nature. The dichotomy in the poem is between the human and the nonhuman, between the verbal and the nonverbal. An elegant interpretation of this poem might insist that if one is to play any chords on this scale they must always consist of some combination of notes from 1–4 and 5–8. Better simply to argue that man has been weighed in the scale of justice, found guilty and wanting. "Of all the beasts to man alone death brings justice." The poet would like to free himself from this fate, "To kneel in a doorway empty except for the song." This, of course, is impossible, and much of the agony of the book reflects this ambivalence. The next two sections of the poem consist of some of Merwin's most sardonic aphorisms and riddles. The six lines are organized in terms of obsessive human motives and drives: mechanical or human time, politics, human governance, nationalism and artificial boundaries (frontiers and kingdoms), various criteria for success, and forms of pride, religious and ideological systems. These are some of the dead teachers.

The last four sections of the poem are organized by images of the natural world: the day, stars, an owl, the sun, the evening shadows, flowers, stone, water—or the natural events of the diurnal cycle. What is stressed here is the absence of destructive motives. The poet is trying to learn from this nonhuman source, to read what nature is writing. The yearning here is for a way to be human and avoid the truth of line 4: "Of all the beasts to man alone death brings justice." The wish—it runs through this book and *Carrier of Ladders* and is partially realized in *Compass Flower*—is to be pure song, played from a nondestructive scale in May. But half this scale is destructive; the chords play notes from both halves. Yet the walls of light speak to him; the shadows teach him something about the house beyond death; and the waterfall, the one audible image in the last four sections, teaches him about laughter. All teach him about the world beyond (before) the human world, but none could teach him anything if he did not begin by realizing that his human and verbal teachers are inadequate and ultimately destructive.

After several hours, the head is numb with the effort of working with this marvelous poem; but poetry does not have to be easy. We have earned "A Scale in May" now and it is ours to play over and over, beginning with the dead teachers and ending with the waterfall.

Few events in my critical life have meant as much as earning this book of poems: earning some other poets, perhaps, like Yeats and Hopkins, Dylan Thomas and Robert Duncan, Whitman and Adrienne Rich; working my way into Faulkner's imagination; struggling toward an understanding of Kenneth Burke. But this book remains special, and I write here in part to discover why.

11/11/81

"The Widow" (*L*, 34) is one of Merwin's deepest poems about the relationship of the differences between humans and nature:

> How easily the ripe grain
> Leaves the husk
> At the simple turning of the planet
>
> . . .
>
> You grieve
> Not that heaven does not exist but
> That it exists without us

It is easier to say what the poem is about in a general way than it is to determine who or what the Widow is. (One wonders why a poet would write and publish such a recalcitrant poem, a poem which

THE LICE

(THE GLASS TOWERS)

by

W. S. Merwin

for George Kirstein

Lacan de Loubressac
Lot, France

All men are deceived by the appearances of
things, even Homer himself, who was the wisest
man in Greece; for he was deceived by boys catching
lice: they said to him, "That which we have
caught and that which we have killed we have
left behind, but that which has escaped we
bring with us."
— HERACLITUS

what /
what /

The title page to the first full manuscript of *The Lice*. Note that Merwin's first title was *The Glass Towers*.

seems to cancel its very communicative purpose and hence seems somewhat suicidal.) A widow is a woman who has lost her husband by death and not remarried. There are two specific references: "The Widow rises under our fingernails / In this sky we were born we are born" (ll. 12–13) and "The Widow does not / Hear you and your cry is numberless" (ll. 26–27). The poem's title is not obviously self-defining from internal evidence. Lines 12–13 are very puzzling; lines 26–27 will remain unclear until one can decide who or what the Widow is. Capitalizing Widow suggests, again, a certain icono-graphic, even allegorical, tendency. Like "The Waves," the poem is elliptical and cryptographic. There are key passages that lack ante-cedent pronoun references. Moreover, the pronouns used (us, we, you) vary in their application so that now the speaker of the poem is included and then he seems to exclude himself and refer only to other you's, and sometimes he seems to refer to himself in the second person. The *us* and *we* are always inclusive; the *you* varies, but there is no place where it could, helpfully, refer to the Widow. This poem presents all the problems one has in reading *The Lice*, in an acute form. The deceptions created by the absence of punctuation and in-ternal spacing make it easy to read through syntactical and sense units and run them together incomprehensibly. For example, the line "not seeing the irony in the air" could complete what precedes it; or it could be in a juxtapositional relationship to the harrowing line that follows—"Everything that does not need you is real."

The poem begins with a lovely description of how nature operates according to its own laws, without any help from us. That the corn is planted by us does not vitiate the image, for the lines could as readily apply to trees dropping their leaves or birds migrating. The next two lines make a distinction between humans and nature in one of those reversed, negating images that are so prevalent in *The Lice:* "There is no season / That requires us." We do not normally think of the seasons as requiring anything; we think of them simply coming, year after year. To state matters as Merwin has here separates us from nature in a radical way. Once both the child and husband of na-ture, we have died to that relationship and left nature a Widow, and the Widow no longer requires or needs us in any way.

The next six lines have no antecedent pronoun, but one assumes they refer to all of us. It is we who are "masters of forgetting," who

use ciphers, moralize, construct norms, and "contrive cities." These
actions run counter to nature, as Merwin renders it in the image of
"Threading the eyeless rocks with / A narrow light." The next two
lines bring us back to our grounding in nature (no matter what we
think or do, no matter how many great cities we contrive—and we
must remember that the city is our most complete denial of nature).
We may think we have transcended nature, but this is a function of
our failure to see "the irony in the air"—to realize how completely
dependent we are. We may think we have widowed her, but it is we
who are the losers when "Men think they are better than grass."

The next two stanzas explore the same persistent human drive
Merwin so consistently subjects to ironic treatment: the desire to
have everything fixed and subject to control. The "you" here is
clearly human beings in general; it weeps because it does not know
yet what it can or should be; it keeps yearning to be what it was told
it should be. It wishes it were something as definite as "numbers," so
it multiplies as numbers do. It "grieves" because it cannot be part of
the absolute belief that heaven exists. These recognitions culminate
in "Not seeing the irony in the air." One does not see the air and so
cannot represent it in images and be sure that it is real; but it is the
invisible reality upon which all human life depends; the irony is that
it is more real and necessary than any eye-centered image or visual
representation.

The last three lines tell us what we now have left, which is really
very little, and again leave us at the zero point we must arrive at in
order to be able to begin again:

> This is the waking landscape
> Dream after dream after dream walking away through it
> Invisible invisible invisible
>
> (L, 35)

This may be as certain as we can ever be at the end of this poem. I
have argued that nature is the Widow and that the poem is about
how we have always been deceived by our conception of nature as
mother-wife-helper-succor-female; in reality nature is a Widow, a
woman whose mate has died and who has not remarried, by choice.
She does not need us; she does not hear our cry; yet she rises under
our fingernails and it is we who need her, for we were born out of
her, and can have no life without her. But I would not push this read-

ing further. For if we try to force the poem we will mistreat it as we have mistreated nature and never discover what Merwin is about.

11/16/81

Many of the poems in *The Lice* are not just about, but are actually addressed to nonhuman subjects, subjects that cannot understand human language. "For a Coming Extinction" is one of the best examples. "In a Clearing," "My Brothers the Silent," "The Herds," the cluster of short poems following "In Autumn," "Death of a Favorite Bird," and "Looking for Mushrooms at Sunrise" are others. "In a Clearing," a poem about the way in which animals die and the way in which species immortality replaces our delusion about individual immortality, should be read in conjunction with "The Finding of Reasons." It is one of Merwin's attempts to understand the other, nonhuman world—not to find reasons to explain it away, but to understand it and himself in relation to it. The true brotherhood is the community of all living things. One of the reasons *The Lice* has been so important to me is that it has taken me beyond my local community to the largest community I can comprehend: the eco- or biosphere and my place in it. Yet this is not an offer of escape. *The Lice* never allows you to escape anything; it is all confrontation.

11/17/81

"My Brothers the Silent" is one of the last poems in the book, written with an irony that comes from Merwin's recognition of a condition of simultaneous knowledge and ignorance. This double perspective frees the book from a temptation to either arrogance or sentimentality.

The brothers are part of an "uncharitable" family to which the speaker belongs that has left him his inheritance. The speaker's inheritance is the earth, nature itself, and the speaker is an infant in terms of eonic time. Whoever the brothers are, they suggest our origins. What they are afraid of, and what the speaker, with his double knowledge, is vaguely aware of, is that he—humans—will destroy the earth. The speaker says he does not really know what he wants, he does not know what his hands are for, he does not know why he fights so many wars. These are terrible admissions on the part of

someone who has inherited the earth. He says that he has "the pitiless blood and remote gaze of our lineage" and that he is "attached to
the ends of things." The speaker is also possessed by exclusive possession itself, since he "will leave nothing to strangers." In ecological terms, he is hardly the person you would want as a planet stew-
ard. The last five lines deal with his relationship with the sheep his
brothers used to tend. He clearly has nothing to do with the sheep
any longer, though he regards them as his own. It is a sustained image of alienation, of separation, of a broken relationship between the
inheritor and his inheritance. (Think, here, for the sake of violent
contrast, of Whitman's "There Was a Child Went Forth" and the kind
of ontological interchanges which are enumerated in that poem.)

We have passed well beyond destructive words here and have come
to the most fundamental fear in *The Lice*—which is that man is in
fact a world-eater who does not know what to ask for, what his hands
are for, how to make up his mind about his desires, and, worse, has
intrinsic to him four fatally incapacitating traits: the pitiless blood;
the remote gaze; an extreme self-interest and possessiveness (the refusal to leave anything of his to strangers; the denial of whatever is
not himself or like him); and his attachment to the unvarying ends
or teleology of things. If, as Merwin says in another poem, this is
what brothers have come to, then surely all is lost.

11/18/81

Anyone who has heard Merwin read and talked with him knows that
he has both an acute political and an ecological consciousness. In
fact, the two are not really separable and in some ways all of the ecological poems in *The Lice* are also political. They certainly express a
particular kind of individual response to the political realities of our
time, a feeling of helplessness, despair, and shame. "Unfinished
Book of Kings" is about a massive failure of the kind of vision which
would make a new political leadership possible. The prophets are
all dead and at the end of the poem we have the king of absences
crowned. Perhaps this "Book of Kings" is unfinished because there
are no more kings to write about, there is no one who will lead us
out of bondage and there are no more prophets who can provide the
vision necessary to guide us—the nation—toward a better life.

Three political poems in a row occur on pages 63–68 of *The Lice:* "The Asians Dying," "When the War Is Over," and "Peasant." "When the War Is Over" is one of the most straightforward poems in the book. It is obviously political and ironic and needs no analysis. It belongs to a small group of poems in the book which do not require critical mediation. "The Asians Dying" is Merwin's most explicit anti-Vietnam War poem. Though the poem is neither overtly political nor anti-American, no American reader who lived through that time would need to have the poem's powerful self-accusing political thrust explained. Though the poem mostly concentrates on effects rather than causes, those responsible are everywhere present and indicted in the poem as the "possessors." The "possessors" will be followed and haunted forever by the ghosts of their victims; "nothing they will come to" will be "real" again; the "possessors" have "Death" as "their star"; they become what they do: they have no past and only fire, or destruction, for their future.

"Peasant" is the most complex of these three poems. The subtitle indicates that the poem is the peasant's "Prayer to the Powers of This World," which makes it a kind of dramatic monologue addressed to the rulers and oppressors from the ruled and oppressed, to those with power from one who is powerless and helpless. A strong social consciousness is at work in the poem and makes us think of "Pieces for Other Lives" and, by association, poems such as "For a Coming Extinction," where a comparably strong ecological consciousness is at work. A strong ontological consciousness, of course, is everywhere present in the book.

The poem as prayer. A prayer is an approach to deity in word or thought; an earnest request; a form of entreating, imploring, supplicating; an address with adoration, confession, supplication, or thanksgiving (Webster). Kenneth Burke has said—in *The Philosophy of Literary Form*—that all poetry can be divided into the categories of dream, prayer, and chart. *The Lice* is full of dream poems. By "chart," Burke says he means poems that realistically size up situations, even if they do not always tell us what to do about them. But the poem as prayer. How many other prayers are there in *The Lice:* who or what is there to pray to? The Widow does not hear you and "your cries are numberless." "Peasant" is all irony, or prayer-canceling; it is an indictment of the powers of this world in the form of an ironic prayer to them. It is more chart than prayer when one is done with it and sizes up both the situation of the oppressed and the nature and character of the oppressors. The one authentic prayer in this book is Necessity (Nature?). It is not till *The Carrier of Ladders* that Merwin is able to write prayers, since prayers do have to be addressed to someone or something. *The Lice* is a book of dreams and charts.

ROBERT SCHOLES

Reading Merwin Semiotically

In recent years European and American literary critics, influenced by the structuralist movement, have developed a "semiotic" approach to the reading of literary texts. In this development semiotics can be seen as a sort of new rhetoric: an attempt to codify certain features of literary analysis, to make literary study more systematic, by seeing the literary work as an object produced for communicative purposes. The main features of the semiotic approach to poetic texts are these. The poetic text is seen as "intertextual," based on other texts. The reader's role is held to be a creative, productive one, in which the reader helps to *make* the poem. And the poem is seen as achieving poetic status by violating certain kinds of expectation, achieving the unexpectedness that gives it a high information quotient. These are not radical departures from tradition, but they all tend to stretch the interpretive boundaries set by the New Criticism: looking beyond the work toward the reader, the norms of reading, and the textual background of the poem itself. The most important semiotic critics in this tradition are Roman Jakobson, Umberto Eco, Gérard Genette, Yuri Lotman, and Michael Riffaterre. I will be following them, but not slavishly, in the pages that follow, in which my purpose is simply to illustrate the semiotic method by applying it to some short texts by a poet I admire: W. S. Merwin.

Let us begin with one of the shortest poetic texts in the English language, "Elegy."

ELEGY
Who would I show it to
(*CL*, 137)

One line, one sentence, unpunctuated, but proclaimed an interrogative by its grammar and syntax—what makes it a poem? Certainly, without its title it would not be a poem; but neither would the title alone constitute a poetic text. Nor do the two together simply make a poem by themselves. Given the title and the text, the reader is encouraged to make a poem. He is not forced to do so, but there is not much else he can do with this material, and certainly nothing else so rewarding. (I will use the masculine pronoun here to refer to the reader, not because all readers are male but because I am, and my hypothetical reader is not a pure construct but an idealized version of myself.)

How do we make a poem out of this text? There are only two things to work on, the title and the question posed by the single, colloquial line. The line is not simply colloquial, it is prosaic; with no words of more than one syllable, concluded by a preposition, it is within the utterance range of every speaker of English. It is, in a sense, completely intelligible. But in another sense it is opaque, mysterious. Its three pronouns—who, I, it—pose problems of reference. Its conditional verb phrase—would . . . show . . . to—poses a problem of situation. The context that would supply the information required to make that simple sentence meaningful as well as intelligible is not there. It must be supplied by the reader.

To make a poem of this text the reader must not only know English, he must know a poetic code as well: the code of the funeral elegy, as practiced in English from the Renaissance to the present time. The "words on the page" do not constitute a poetic "work," complete and self-sufficient, but a "text," a sketch or outline that must be completed by the active participation of a reader equipped with the right sort of information. In this case part of that information consists of an acquaintance with the elegiac tradition: its procedures, assumptions, devices, and values. One needs to know works like Milton's "Lycidas," Shelley's "Adonais," Tennyson's "In Memoriam," Whitman's "When Lilacs Last in the Dooryard Bloomed," Dylan Thomas's "Refusal to Mourn the Death by Fire of a Child in London," and so on and on in order to "read" this simple poem properly. In fact, it could be argued that the more elegies one can bring to bear on a reading of this one, the better, richer poem this one becomes. Personally, I would go even further, suggesting that a knowledge of the critical tradition—of Dr. Johnson's objections to "Lycidas," for instance, or Wordsworth's critique of poetic diction—

will also enhance one's reading of this poem. For the poem is, of course, an anti-elegy, a refusal, not simply to mourn, but to write a sonorous, eloquent, mournful but finally acquiescent, accepting—in a word, "elegiac"—poem at all.

Reading the poem involves, then, a special knowledge of its tradition. It also involves a special interpretive skill. The forms of the short, written poem as they have developed in English over the past few centuries can be usefully seen as compressed, truncated, or fragmented imitations of other verbal forms, especially the play, story, public oration, and personal essay. The reasons for this are too complicated for consideration here, but the fact will be apparent to all who reflect upon the matter. Our short poems are almost always elliptical versions of what can easily be conceived of as dramatic, narrative, oratorical, or meditative texts. Often, they are combinations of these and other modes of address. To take an obvious example, the dramatic monologue in the hands of Robert Browning is like a speech from a play (though usually more elongated than most such speeches). But to "read" such a monologue we must imagine the setting, the situation, the context, and so on. The dramatic monologue is "like" a play but gives us less information of certain sorts than a play would, requiring us to provide that information by decoding the clues in the monologue itself in the light of our understanding of the generic model or "architext." Most short poems work this way. They require both special knowledge and special skills to be "read."

To understand "Elegy" we must construct a situation out of the clues provided. The "it" in "Who would I show it to" is of course the elegy itself. The "I" is the potential writer of the elegy. The "Who" is the audience for the poem. But the verb phrase "would . . . show . . . to" indicates a condition contrary to fact. Who would I show it to *if* I were to write it? This implies in turn that for the potential elegiac poet there is one person whose appreciation means more than that of all the rest of the potential audience for the poem he might write, and it further implies that the death of this particular person is the one imagined in the poem. If this person were dead, the poet suggests, so would his inspiration be dead. With no one to write for, no poem would be forthcoming. This poem is not merely a "refusal to mourn," like that of Dylan Thomas, it is a refusal to elegize. The whole elegiac tradition, like its cousin the funeral oration, turns finally away from mourning toward acceptance, revival, renewal, a return to the concerns of life, symbolized by the very writing of the poem. Life goes on; there *is* an audience; and the mourned person will live through accomplishments, influence, descendants, and also (not least) in the elegiac poem itself. Merwin rejects all that. *If* I wrote an elegy for X, the person for whom I have always written, X would not be alive to read it; therefore, there is no reason to write an elegy for the one person in my life who most deserves one; therefore, there is no reason to write any elegy, anymore, ever. Finally, and of course, this poem called "Elegy" is not an elegy.

Am I pushing my interpretation too far? If you go in the right direction, there is no such thing as too far. All the elegies ever written will enrich our understanding of this poem. And all the ramifications of situation that can be developed from the hints in this one line are also relevant. On any line of interpretation one will reach a point of diminishing returns, but the zero point is infinitely far away. Considered semiotically, the important aspects of this little interpretive exercise are these: (1) To read the poem we must know its generic tradition (what Gérard Genette has called "the architext")[1] and a certain number of the texts in that tradition; and (2) we must have some skill at supplying the elements (narrative, dramatic, oratorical, personal) that are lacking because of the elliptical nature of poetic utterance. Combined, these indicate the major premise of any semiotic study of poetry: that a poem is a text connected to other texts, requiring the active participation of a skilled reader for its interpretation.

The other texts need not be parts of a tradition sanctioned by "high" culture; they may just as easily be taken from popular tradition, as another little poem by Merwin will show. It is called "When the War Is Over":

> When the war is over
> We will be proud of course the air will be
> Good for breathing at last
> The water will have been improved the salmon
> And the silence of heaven will migrate more perfectly
> The dead will think the living are worth it we will know
> Who we are
> And we will all enlist again
>
> (*L*, 64)

This is a poem of the 1960s, and one could gloss it by reference to the Vietnam War, but that is hardly a necessary feature of its interpretation. Much more important in the way of information is a folk ditty sung in many wars by soldiers and sailors (I have sung it myself in ports from Newport, R.I., to Yokosuka, Japan, during the Korean "police action") in anticipation of their release from military duties. It is sung to the stirring tune of "The Battle Hymn of the Republic," its words beginning with "When the war is over we will all enlist again" repeated several times, and concluding with a variety of expletivious lines, ranging from "We will, like hell we will" to "In a pig's ass hole we will." The folk song is based on a simple ironic reversal—we *will* enlist again is maintained until the last line, where that sentiment is firmly rejected.

Merwin has made his poem by re-reversing the sentiment of the folk song, saying, in effect, we think we won't enlist again, but, fatally, we will, we will. Formally, he has done this by taking the first line of the folk song—"When the war is over we will all enlist again"—and spreading it out. "When the war is over" becomes the first line of his poem and "we will all enlist again" becomes the last. In the middle is the material that makes this text a poem, for the reader who has the equipment to read it. For our purpose this material can also serve to illustrate some of the principles of poetic discourse formulated by Michael Riffaterre in his *Semiotics of Poetry*.[2] The way this poem grows out of the folk song by its negation or inversion is one of the typical features of poetic discourse. Texts emerge from other "intertexts" or from matrices provided by a discursive tradition. Merwin's development of his material is also quintessentially poetic by Riffaterre's criteria, which, to a considerable extent, I accept. What Merwin does with the central material of the poem is to move gradually from the prosaic to the poetic, before falling back to the prosaic for the last line, which is now transfigured by the preceding material. Let us look more carefully at how this works. "When the war is over / We will be proud of course. . . ." This is a perfectly prosaic sentence; that is, it poses no problems in grammar, syntax, or semantics for the reader—except that the reader himself must close the sentence by mentally inserting the period in the right place. The reader's sense of grammar is not allowed to operate passively but must take an active hand in constructing the poem from the text. Still, the grammatical clues are so straightforward that this gesture of sentence-closure is not difficult to make.

There is only one tiny problem. The sentence could be closed after

Merwin's holograph manuscript of one page (of several) of an unfinished, unpublished poem of the 1960s. "Three Public Songs. To the Tune of 'Vietnam Must Be Made Safe For Democracy.'"

To the Tune of: Vietnam Must Be Made Safe For Democracy

I

Chant of the Great Democracy

We never heard of them in
In Our lives who do they think they are
Trying to keep us from defending them
 keep
When we have experts what
What what kind of nutty
God is that they have puts them up to it and
And who's in back of him

You can't trust them
When you think how we've
Tried to help them sacrificed what did
They ever do/to be worthy of it you
You'd think there was anything in it
For us   To be Worthy of it
When All we want is after all is they should
Vote
Like us

They don't know
Anything all we want after all is
Someday Eventually
They should have civilization themselves schools
Cars   just
Come to And Army / like us having learned about
Our God   / just

You can't trust —— You can't trust
You can't trust them when you think how we've
then you think how we've
Tried to help them sacrificed when you think
Think what we're — Saving them from
What did they ever do to be
To be Worthy of it
You'd think there was anything in it
For us
When all we want after all is they should
Vote After all is they should vote
Like us.

Typed transcription (by C. N.) of "Chant of the Great Democracy."

"proud." The prepositional phrase "of course" can either end the first sentence or begin the second. This is not important, but it is a warning of more significant "ungrammaticalities" to come. There are other traps or invitations to stretch the limits of grammatical and semantic coding as we proceed. Since the text lacks all conventional marks of prosaic punctuation, the conventions of poetic punctuation loom larger. The lines begin with capital letters and end with space. Each line is a discrete unit, something like a sentence. Thus, though we can find a prosaic place for a period in the middle of some lines, we are led toward a different mode of reading as well, with the elements of each line functioning as a grammatical unit. If we take "We will be proud of course the air will be" as a strong syntactical unit, a complete sentence, the parallelism of "we will be" and "the air will be" draws both these auxiliary phrases toward the yoke (or zeugma, in rhetorical parlance) of the main verb phrase, "will be proud." The air will be proud? Impossible! Surely, the poet wouldn't want us to think that. I wouldn't be too sure. Roman Jakobson has cogently argued that parallelism of various sorts is the major feature of poetic grammar. That potential zeugma, with its semantic absurdity, haunts the second line of the poem without insisting that we attend to it. Further on, there will be anomalies too palpable to be ignored.

At this point, however, the text allows us to make a second sentence easily, coming to a full stop comfortably at the end of line 3: "the air will be / Good for breathing at last." The only problem here is the slight semantic strain involved in finding a causal reason for the connection between the improvement in the air and the end of the war. This amounts to a threat against what Riffaterre calls mimesis—that is, our ability to assign referential status to the things apparently designated by the text. If we understand that the air will be "literally," as we say, improved, then we are reading the word "air" mimetically. If, on the other hand, we take the word, as we say, figuratively, then we have been driven from a mimetic reading to what Riffaterre calls a "semiotic" one. This frustration of mimesis by semantic impossibility is a regular feature of poetic texts. In the present case, such familiar figures as "to breathe easier" inhabit the same semantic space as "the air will be good for breathing," but the poet has unpacked the domesticated version and allowed the strangeness of the image to become perceptible again. Still, interpretation continues to be easy; the strangeness is perceived as a kind of noise, not as a message in another code.

With the fourth line the strangeness of poetic speech is fully upon us: "The water will have been improved the salmon." The move from air to water is natural. They are essential substances, frequently associated in poetic discourse. But the causal relationship between the end of the war and the improvement in air can hardly be stretched to water. One may say, O well, after the war even the water will taste better. Perhaps, but there are salmon in this water and they will not go away.

A part of every reader of poetry must be a reader of prose. The effort of making a poem from a poetic text requires the increase of energy caused by frustration of prosaic interpretation. If the reader doesn't strain after prose sense, poetic readings will hardly be attained. The skill required for poetic interpretation involves a strong concern for prosaic meaning combined with a readiness to push beyond the prosaic to generate new meanings. In semiotic terms this often means that the established codes of interpretation, whether grammatical or lexical, may have to be reconstructed. This is work, productive labor. Its immediate reward is the satisfaction of interpretation itself, making a poem from the text, but there are other and perhaps greater rewards for the individual interpreter, in the form of gains in flexibility and verbal skill, along with possession of enriched semantic and syntactic codes.

Returning to the poem, the interpreter must deal with the salmon. They have appeared "naturally" in the water by a familiar process of association: metonymy. But grammatically and logically (causally) they are not easy to fit into the picture. If the line is to be read as a whole and complete sentence, the salmon will have to be read as "improved" along with the water. This is not merely difficult mimetically but virtually impossible. The sensitive interpreter begins at this point to wonder whether impossibility itself may not be presiding over the poem. Improved air is close enough to already coded metaphors that have died and become clichés, so that we breathe easily enough in our interpretation of that metaphor. But improved salmon must give us considerable pause. Perhaps we can solve our problem by inserting a period before the salmon, so that they may leap into the next sentence, where they will indeed go naturally with the verb "migrate," making an old familiar combination. Salmon and migration go together like sardines and crowdedness. We take comfort from these regular associations.

But poetic texts are designed to discomfort us first of all. Any

comfort we get from them must be earned. "The salmon and the silence of heaven will migrate more perfectly"—there is our new next
sentence, and it works fine syntactically. What Riffaterre would call
its "ungrammaticality" comes at the level of semantics and mimesis,
not at the level of grammar as such. Yes, the salmon will migrate
after the war, as they have doubtless migrated all through it, since
they must; they are genetically programmed to do so. But their migration is a part of the order of things on this earth and can scarcely
be improved. And the "silence of heaven" is by any definition beyond
such timebound, earthbound things as migration and improvement.
No, it has not improved, nor will it migrate. Following the poet along
his metonymic trail we have come up against a wall of negation, a
cosmic irony. The disruption of mimesis is absolute, leading us to
read some level of ironic denial into all the poem's assertions. The
textual utterance about the migration of the heavenly silence is the
poetic counterpart of the folk song's utterance about the pig's ass
hole. They are, in their different ways, contradictions sufficiently
powerful to direct all interpreters toward the ironic mode of reading.
    In "The dead will think the living are worth it" and "we will know
/ Who we are" the text offers us two statements that are simple
grammatically but complex semantically and fraught with ironies.
Then comes the "And," the innocent copula, which alerts us to the
poem's impending closure, and joins this statement to all the others.
But where the others are qualified or negated by irony, this one is
perfectly straightforward, though dripping, now, with the sarcasm
that flows from the preceding ironies. We *will* all enlist again, as
surely as the salmon migrate—and *that* is who we are. We need not
literally enlist; the whole poem is an extended metaphor, an allegory
of an aspect of human nature that is despicable: that we enlist again
and again in destructive enterprises, caring not enough about the air,
the water, the living creatures, the dead, the earth, the heavens. And
here is where I part company with Michael Riffaterre. Where he is
content to point out how poetic texts cut themselves off from direct
mimetic or referential connection to reality, I would insist that in
many, perhaps most cases, they circle back allegorically to reference
once again. That is, we, the readers, the interpreters, bring them
back by going through them, to their ends.
    Though Michael Riffaterre has argued that poetry *is* essentially
antimimetic and nonreferential, Yuri Lotman, the most interesting

of the current generation of Soviet semioticians, argues what seems to be the opposite side of the case. Lotman's view of poetry, as articulated in *Analysis of the Poetic Text*,[3] is clear, powerful, and worth considering in some detail. Lotman, in fact, sets poetic discourse against three kinds of "automism," and he means by automism something very like I. A. Richards's notion of "stock response." These are (1) the automism of language, (2) the automism of "common sense," and (3) the automism of our "spatio-visual" picture of the world. Against the inertia of these three systems—habitual modes of perception, of thought, and of speech—the poet and the poem go to work. Let me illustrate with a simple poem by Merwin:

SEPARATION

Your absence has gone through me
Like thread through a needle.
Everything I do is stitched with its color.

(*MT, 9*)

This simple poem is complex in Lotman's sense because it violates expectations in all three of Lotman's frameworks, and poetic information, like any other kind of information, is inversely proportional to its expectedness. In Merwin's little poem the first line seems to start us along the syntactic road of a familiar cliché: "gone through me like a knife," or a needle or some other sharp instrument. The poem then violates our expectation by grasping the unexpected end of the needle. Our common sense tells us that separation is painful. We expect an image to be presented that will concentrate on pain—something that a needle could easily accomplish. But instead the image presented focuses our attention on the ubiquity of the feeling of separation rather than its acuteness. In this reversal of the cliché, separation, taking apart, becomes a kind of sewing together. Finally, our spatial-visual sense tells us that a person cannot be visualized as a kind of needle going around stitching things with a thread the color of absence. We cannot, on this level, even say what color the thread is. It *won't* visualize. But this unvisualizable "image" carries its meaning with the kind of vigor that only poetry can command. To comprehend the image we must move to a higher level of abstraction, where its significance emerges as a concept—pervasiveness, ubiquity, or inevitability—but a concept energized by our movement from the image to the theme it signifies. We might add that the apparent "ordinariness" of the language of the poem may itself be seen as a violation of "poetic" expectations. As Lotman points out, "not only the retreat from the natural norms of language but also their approximation can be a source of artistic effect" (p. 133).

It should be clear that Lotman's view of poetry is in many respects similar to Riffaterre's. They both stress the deviance or ungrammaticality of the poetic text and the need for the reader to actively make meaning, recoding his language and cultural framework as it is necessary to do so. But they appear to differ profoundly on the question of reference. Let me bring this difference to a sharper focus. Riffaterre says, everywhere and often, what we can find him saying of a Victor Hugo poem in *Text Production:* "the comparison of a poem to reality is a critical approach of doubtful value."[4] Lotman says, in no uncertain terms, something that appears completely contradictory: "The aim of poetry, of course, is not 'devices' but a knowledge of the world and the relationship among people, self-knowledge, and the development of the human personality in the process of learning and social communication. In the final summing up, the goal of poetry coincides with the goal of culture as a whole. But poetry realizes this goal specifically, and an understanding of its specific character is impossible if one ignores its mechanism, its internal structure. This mechanism actually is more readily revealed when it enters into conflict with the automism of language" (pp. 132–33).

Behind Riffaterre, Mallarmé; behind Lotman, Victor Shklovsky's insistence that "art exists to help us recover the sensation of life; it exists to make us feel things, to make the stone *stony.*" Both Lotman and Riffaterre are semioticians, but one writes out of a French tradition, the other out of a Slavic one. Even so, I wish to argue that they are not so far apart as they seem. They *both* note that poetic texts challenge our accepted modes of speech, perception, and belief. But where Lotman believes that such challenges bring us dialectically to a greater understanding of the world, Riffaterre is silent, skeptical. Let us say, then, that within semiotic studies the question is open, unsettled. Personally, I am closer to Lotman on this matter, but the question of where the critic stands is far less important than the matter of what the poet is doing. Merwin has been accused of being bloodless, a mere manipulator of words. Being a poet he must weave his garment of words, of course, but in doing so he works for all of us, because like Beckett's Watt, we all desire words to be "applied to our situations." Merwin's words apply. When he says "my words are the garment of what I shall never be / Like the tucked sleeve of a one-armed boy" (L, 62) the words apply to himself first of all, and to all other poets, and finally to all those who work with words. Nobody's words bleed. All poems are bloodless. The gap between the word and the flesh is in fact what is expressed so perfectly in the lines just quoted. The sleeve is not the arm, but there is a relationship between the tucked sleeve and the missing arm, a relationship of form, of resemblance in difference, and the sleeve/arm relationship bears a further resemblance in difference to the word/flesh relationship. Once I had read those lines of Merwin, every such tucked sleeve became for me a "garment of what I shall never be." A good poet does not simply copy the world's meanings. He makes the world meaningful and thereby bearable. As Beckett says of Watt, "He had turned, little by little, a disturbance into words, he had made a pillow of old words, for a head."

NOTES

1. See Gérard Genette, *L'introduction à l'architexte* (Paris: Seuil, 1979).

2. Michael Riffaterre, *Semiotics of Poetry* (Bloomington: Indiana University Press, 1978).

3. Yuri Lotman, *Analysis of the Poetic Text* (Ann Arbor: Ardis, 1976).

4. Michael Riffaterre, *Text Production*, trans. Terese Lyons (New York: Columbia University Press, 1983), p. 182.

CARY NELSON

The Resources of Failure:
W. S. Merwin's
Deconstructive Career

Certain words now in our knowledge we will not use again, and
we will never forget them. We need them. Like the back of the
picture. Like our marrow, and the color in our veins. We shine
the lantern of our sleep on them, to make sure, and there they
are, trembling already for the day of witness. They will be buried
with us, and rise with the rest. [*HT*, 58]

Perhaps, as Merwin suggests in this little hieratic meditation, the
very words most central to our selfhood must remain unspoken. Yet
any reader of Merwin's recent poetry—with its insistent, recurring
vocabulary—will suspect that this poet thinks he knows what those
words are. At the least, Merwin clearly feels that certain words and
images give witness to what cannot be said. These words have gradually become the core of his poetic language; there, they infiltrate the
rest of the language, reducing the whole of discourse to a single ineffable and refracted meaning. Not so long ago—no longer in any case
than 1939 and *Finnegans Wake*—a work demonstrating the interconnectedness of language could be a source of continuing pleasure.
In American poetry, as I argue in *Our Last First Poets: Vision and
History in Contemporary American Poetry*, this verbal interconnectedness imitates a democratic ideal. That cultural pressure keeps
a democratically inclusive aesthetic alive somewhat longer in America, but through the 1960s it becomes increasingly ironic and impossible. With Theodore Roethke's late poetry, like "North American

Sequence," in which he opens his work to broad American landscapes and to a related sense of American history, a democratically
inclusive project is uncertain and unstable, though still possible as
a verbal gesture that is politically gratuitous but emotionally grati-
fying. For this generation, Robert Duncan may be among the last unqualified believers in this central part of Whitman's poetic, but the
historical events of the 1960s undermine even Duncan's faith in verbal community. With Galway Kinnell, the aesthetic of verbal connections becomes frenetic and compulsive; Roethke's graceful rehearsals
of verbal ecstasy now require elaborate connections whose powers of
democratic transformation are fatally damaged by American history.
This development culminates, among others, in Adrienne Rich and
Merwin, in whose poetry history finally triumphs. Yet both Rich
and Merwin regularly opt for radically deconstructed forms that
manage to capture history's powers of dissolution. Rich, however, re-
serves one possibility for a restorative verbal democracy—a female
interconnectedness that can at least counterpoint America's less
successful history. But with Merwin's poetry that joy in tracing the
endless relationships among words seems irrecoverable. One feature
of Merwin's aesthetic is that our delight in watching words echo one
another is relentlessly undercut.

The use of such words, then, involves specific risks that are apparent the first time they are spoken. The selfhood they reveal is intimate but impersonal. The knowledge they bring thus deflates the
subject, but it is an evacuation without much attendant drama. To
speak these words is to experience an uneasiness that cannot be resolved; yet the poet who speaks them may appear, paradoxically, as
Jacques Derrida has come to be viewed in contemporary criticism,
the master of irresolution. The challenge Merwin sets himself in his
best work is to occupy exactly that position—to become the anonymous American figure who announces the harmonizing dissolution
of the language. Merwin thus offers us one final, dark incarnation
of a poetic of democratic openness. In doing so, of course, he has
claimed that signal voice as his own. The contradiction provides him
with a sardonic version of Whitman's prophetic stance, and it gives
his poetry its own grim humor. To be successful, both the inverted
prophecy and the humor must remain muted, for they tend toward
the sententious. At the same time they must be compromised at
every opportunity.

As anyone even casually familiar with his career knows, Merwin has not always written poetry that radically undermines each assertion. In effect, his work from *The Moving Target* through *Writings to an Unfinished Accompaniment* offers us what remained after he rigorously pruned the excesses of his first books and then turned what was left back on itself. In the process Merwin returned to the dark mood of his earliest extant poems, the unpublished poems of the 1946–48 manuscripts (included in the W. S. Merwin Archive at the University of Illinois). The result has been a poetry of extraordinary force, a poetry that inherits the fatalistic despair of the second half of the century but gives it a prophetic new form, a form that ruthlessly deconstructs its own accomplishments. Though the 1946–48 manuscripts establish Merwin's characteristically bleak perspective, dethroning any originary claim we might grant his first books, there would still have been no way of predicting the intense condensation of the poetry of the 1960s and 1970s. But the foundation for Merwin's development is present in his language from the beginning. "Silence," "emptiness," "distance," "death," "darkness"—there are others, but this diction that Merwin shares with Kinnell includes some of his most recurrent words, and they are central in his first extant work.

"No one could make the dark be still," Merwin writes in "In Time of Destruction," an unpublished poem dedicated to "the young men of my generation who have died by violence." Similarly, he dedicates "Graduation: Princeton 1947" to "those who are not graduating with our classes, because they are dead" and appends a remarkable note (somewhat softened in a second draft) to the graduation committee who requested the poem: "if the requisite sentiments and unqualified optimism are nowhere to be found in the poem, that is so merely because I could nowhere find them in myself, looking upon the occasion as I do with little optimism for the future." In these first unpublished poems, then, this diction reinforces a rather specific sense of historical futility, one prompted by the slaughter of World War II. Poems in the 1946–48 manuscripts include, for example, "For a Flier Killed in the Recent Destruction," a flier now buried in "the sharp earth where darkness roots." Similarly, in "The Glove and the Floor (A Commentary on the Streets of Warsaw)," "the sky shudders silent" over a landscape of carrion where "Pluto's three-headed mastiff shakes his shades / And sidles drooling through the Warsaw streets / Defiling death with darkness."

Then in Merwin's first books, a body of work that we can now describe as mounting the first major shift in his career, this vocabulary invokes an ahistorical mythic vantage point, serving to lend mystery to Merwin's new romanticism, a romanticism in which Keats's melancholy is mediated through Yeats's antinomies.[1] To read his first four books in the light of what he has published since 1960 is to discover these key terms, potent and isolated in the later poems, present with their thematic resonance surprisingly spelled out but rendered harmless.[2] Yet the first books almost provide a semantic glossary to the imagery of the later work. In a way, this development duplicates two early modernist concerns: the reaction to Romanticism and the interest in formal condensation. Merwin, however, has now moved toward a typically contemporary irony about the possibility of any kind of formal perfection.

Merwin's first two books offer pleasant and engaging reading. His metrical skills, as Auden notes in his introduction to *A Mask for Janus* (1952), are considerable; his mastery of a wide variety of traditional forms is impressive. Yet the poetry is so ornately complacent that a line like "We survived the selves that we remembered" (*MJ*, 5) is almost cause for self-congratulation; in either the 1946–48 manuscripts or the later poetry it would be more claustrophobic than ironic, free from choice or potential for change and free as well from much conviction about either survival or memory. Yet the line does anticipate his recent work; it is among those passages in his first books that read almost like recipes for his later poetic: "We turned from silence and fearfully made / Our small language in the place of the night" (*MJ*, 8). In isolation, the content of these lines suggests the precarious quality of Merwin's recent language, and it also reflects a verbal helplessness before history that is present, in less definitive form, in many other contemporary poets. But a few lines later Merwin indulges in a dream of "the last oceans where the drowned pursue / The daze and fall of fabulous voyages," and "the place of night" becomes a Romantic conceit. We can permit ourselves to contemplate "drownings / In mirrors," and to "dream of distances," because these transformations occur in a secure rhetorical territory.

Merwin's longest poem, "East of the Sun and West of the Moon" (1954), retells the Norwegian folktale known by the same title; the plot structure is similar to Apuleius's *Cupid and Psyche*. Unlike the more tightly organized poems in these books, this poem is not managed with Merwin's formal grace. The lack of control, however, allows more of his main concerns to surface. His key terms occur more frequently, but they are almost inundated by elegant description. "I sing," he writes, "to drown the silence of far flowers"; "white-tongued flowers shout / Impossible silence on the impossible air" (*DB*, 57, 46). Any threat in such images of silence, or in the several descriptions of the empty distance over which the girl must pursue her lover, is deflected by the elaborate language. Poetic tradition and Merwin's own effusive rhetoric combine to protect her journey "beyond the hueless sighing of drowned days / Into the dark where no shades sigh" (*DB*, 53). It is as if Merwin has rhetorically displaced the sense of catastrophic deluge dominating many of the early unpublished poems: "The fish were drowned under slaughter," he writes in "In Time of Destruction" from the 1946–48 manuscripts, "Darkness was unable to hold the darkness together."

With Merwin's third and fourth books, however, a note of desperation marks another stage in his work. Many of the poems in *Green with Beasts* (1956) and *The Drunk in the Furnace* (1960) are overwritten, repetitive, almost garrulous. But they are not clumsily written, nor do they lack craft. Poems like "Leviathan" (*GB*, 11–12) seem designed instead to exhaust their subject matter through continual variation and reiteration of the same terms and images. Where silence in the unpublished poems evoked a historicized alienation, and in the first published books involved a kind of rhetorical swooning, it now acquires obsessive resonance. The subject matter is generally more explicit; he stops calling so many poems "Song," "Carol," or "Fable," and gives them precise titles. He seems to be confronting brute reality more directly. Yet the apparent attempt to exhaust the topic really signals the poet's need to exhaust his own perceptions, a motive that may also be present in Kinnell's "The Avenue Bearing the Initial of Christ into the New World." Merwin wants to render the mechanism of his verbal apprehension finally knowable and given; if he cannot do that, he will be satisfied to extinguish it.

The poetry presses toward a silence achieved through self-depletion. Thus the descriptive lines piled on one another, as well as the recurring topic of the sea, tend in their massiveness to suggest their obverse—emptiness and evacuation. This traditional connection between everything and nothing, between whales or oceans and nothingness, later develops into the intimate loneliness of Merwin's vast landscapes—landscapes whose empty American immensity suggests the loss of historical possibility—landscapes where distance penetrates everything in sight. Formally, these poems seem wholly unlike the thin, spare poems for which he has become famous. The relationship between the two groups of poems is one of radical difference, and the second change in his writing, beginning with *The Moving Target* (1963), the first major change in his public career, is again one of reversal and rejection. At their core, therefore, they have an essential resemblance—the verbose poems so full of themselves and the meticulously honed poems retaining only the last vestige of speech—each is supremely "a vessel at anchor in its own reflection" (*DF*, 4). Internally, the language in each type of poem is highly consistent. As artifacts, however, the early poems are overblown, whereas the recent poems are contemporary objects that almost eliminate themselves. There is one other crucial comparison: within each group the poems resemble one another to an extraordinary degree. Yet "there must be," Merwin writes toward the end of his second book, "in a kingdom of mirrors a king among / Mirrors" (*DB*, 77); within the two sets of poems, each individual poem would be that king. The earlier poems compete for that honor, but the later poems try to win by losing most thoroughly. For to be a king among mirrors is to proclaim a sovereignty of absolution, to be the perfect image of all otherness. Seen in the light of what he has done since 1960, the excesses of Merwin's overwrought poems reveal a need to create poetry so empty it could contain the world. That covert desire is eventually fulfilled by a poetry that becomes empty in the very act of opening itself to the world. After the unpublished poems of 1946–48, not until the 1960s does a substantial public historical world again exist as an overt subject or background in Merwin's poetry. Once it does, Merwin's tone undergoes another definitive change.

Judged according to its influence on Merwin's subsequent development, *Green with Beasts* (1956) is the most important of the first four volumes. In this book his prolix descriptiveness is most closely tied to the thematic investigation of a self-reflexive emptiness. The book begins with a sequence of five animal poems. We anticipate a bestiary of creatures uniquely individuated through poetry, but the continual reiteration of the same themes and images soon eliminates that expectation. Nor is he quite attempting to pinpoint the otherness common to all animal life. He uses animals to control the redeeming otherness inhering in the whole external world. "When I speak," he wrote earlier, "it is the world / That I must mention" (*DB*, 61), but the world, it seems, has no need to speak of us. Despite his continuing interest in animal poems, then, they do not constitute a separate strain in his poetry. These animal poems actually represent the first fruition of his insight into our dependence on physical objects in general. One of his main purposes is to undermine our security by disclosing the way objects dominate the entire spatiotemporal environment.

A rooster, in this sequence of poems, has a cry that "frames all the silence" (*GB*, 13); he hovers motionless, "his wings as though beating the air of elsewhere," though everything, as Merwin tells us, becomes elsewhere in that moment. His one eye glares "like the sun's self (for there is no other)," and the center of our self is suddenly displaced. Similarly, a dog summons in his unfixed gaze the "shimmering vista of emptiness," the whole summer afternoon around him, "the shining distance that weighs and waves / Like water" (*GB*, 17). He guards "the empty / Distance, the insufferable light losing itself / In its own glare." The dog is used to focus the world's indifferent gaze on us, to render the subject seen in the blind eye of sheer material substance. Perhaps the dog is simply unaware of our presence. No,

> Look again: it is through you
> That he looks, and the danger of his eyes
> Is that in them you are not there.
>   (*GB*, 18)

The terms of the paradox are clear, but Merwin seems compelled to restate them again and again: "behind his eyes / You will be seen not to be there, in the glaring / Uncharactered reaches of oblivion." Pray, he tells us, that we "be delivered / From the vain distance he is the power of," but the real imperative is apparent in the confident irony of his diction: he casually sketches everything we depend on as "the dust you stand in / And your other darlings." Throughout his career, Merwin suggests that naming makes us a possession of the thing named. The real wish is to be consumed.

In the next poem, "White Goat, White Ram," the self-reflective quality in description becomes too conscious. We are not interested in the animals themselves, he writes, but in "conjuring by their shapes / The shape of our desire, which without them would remain / Without a form and nameless" (*GB*, 20). The whiteness of the goat and ram is a symbol, "as we should say those are white who remember nothing"; their whiteness is a mechanism for transforming "the dying riot of random generation," our own "mad menagerie, / The body behind bone" (*DB*, 70, 34) into "a circle of silence, a drying vista of ruin" (*MJ*, 45). But the impulse is too obvious to communicate with any sense of necessity. The poetry becomes slack. He tries unsuccessfully to draw an organizing symbolism from Christ's story by adapting it ironically to fit our situation, "so that our gracelessness may have the back of a goat / To ride away upon." Kinnell makes similar efforts to secularize religious imagery with equally uneasy results. Duncan perhaps succeeds at this for a time, because of his belief in mythic universality, though the dark history of the 1960s troubles Duncan's religious imagery as well. Merwin is not temperamentally suited to unironic religious imagery except as a way to invoke inexplicable ritual violence. However romantic Merwin once may have been, he was not as well (unless much earlier) an unqualified believer. It rings false when he says we would "give speech to the mute tongues / Of angels."[3] If the goats "browse beyond words," then they only recede further beyond this poem.

In the second section of the book, Merwin attempts to derive some structural benefit from his compulsion for repetition. Particularly in "The Prodigal Son" and "The Annunciation," he aims for a musical sense of thematic variation and recurrence. Yet he repeats his key words more overtly than before without the camouflage of different adjectives. In "The Prodigal Son" (*GB*, 28–32) the echoes are so numerous that the whole poem would have to be quoted to account for all of them. "Distance" occurs sixteen times in the poem's five pages, "emptiness" seventeen times, and there are continual references to silence, vacancy, nothingness, hollowness, illusions, and mirages. The poem, like the familiar hot afternoon in which it takes place, should presumably begin to shimmer in our mind's eye "as in its own / Mirage." The metaphysics of this enterprise probably has its roots in Wallace Stevens, but Merwin has rejected Stevens's verbal intricacy for a heavy metronome that approaches self-mimicry.

The poem's story serves primarily to delay and, less successfully, to occasion the resolution we expect from the outset. The images of dissolving forms will collapse into a single harmonious field—the prodigal son will return home. In a setting of motionless summer heat, the father of the absent son sits brooding on empty distance with vacant eyes. His house itself is "an image merely / By which he may know the face of emptiness"; like the poem, it is "a name with which to say emptiness." He is obsessed with his son's absence, though the departure only brought about the inevitable, for "emptiness had lodged with him before." Meanwhile the son, too, contemplates emptiness, having left home in search of "something / Vague because distant," something

> Which, unknowing, he was leaving behind, yet
> Which he had to leave to be able to find. And wasted
> His substance in wild experiment and found
> Emptiness only, found nothing in distance,
> Sits finally in a sty and broods
> Upon emptiness, upon distance.

Abundance and desolation are now more openly connected by the tedium associated with sexual abandon. "My sex," Merwin later writes, "grew into the only tree, a joyless evergreen" (*MT*, 2). The son indulges in women and silks, only to find "his mind turns among / Those vacancies as a mirror hung by a string / In a ruin." Seemingly separated by space and extended in time, the son's gloom and the father's gloom are actually copresent to one another. Out of the same field of mirrored heat and shadow, out of the same silence in which "distance is dead," the son and the father move together. The story comes full circle; in the ghostlike substance of the poem ("unto this / Has been likened the kingdom of heaven") the trinity is restored. Past and future are indeed folded together in the present of this poem, but the reader is left the bemused spectator of a bucolic round.

    If Merwin were to issue a selection of poems, this text should surely be included, not because it is a good poem—it isn't—but because it is dissatisfied with its own inadequacy. The poem's restlessness prepares us for the second great shift in his technique. As the epigraph for *The Dancing Bears*, Merwin chose Flaubert's observation (here in Richard Howard's translation) that "human speech is like a cracked kettle on which we pound out tunes fit to make bears dance when what we want is to win over the stars." As Howard points out, this is "the ironical sign . . . under which Merwin inscribes his elegance and his eloquence."[4] As an epigraph for this book, the quotation is mostly a gratuitous afterthought, the kind of precious disavowal that both distances and protects; he is not yet troubled by the self-conscious element in verbal artifice. The epigraph is really a bridge to the next two collections and their genuine anguish at the limitations of his language. "The stars," he will write, "that came with us this far have gone back" (MT, 32). And more poignantly, "the stars do not believe each other" (CL, 136); when their light reaches us, they are already dead.

There is a lesson here for those reviewers who are unhappy that Merwin's poems reflect some self-imitation. Stylistic consistency often edges toward self-imitation—a fact that many contemporary authors have consciously exploited. Yet Merwin has managed to use this sometimes fruitless reflexiveness to force substantial changes in his style. Each of his stylistic metamorphoses has followed from a self-conscious craft that turned into self-parody and even revulsion, a process perhaps more complex, though no more anguished, than Rich's deliberate rejection of formal perfection in the 1960s. I would sing, he wrote in one of the elaborate love poems at the end of *The Dancing Bears*, "till you have become / The poem in whose arbor we may kiss," but the air of impossibility has already invaded the quest: "in the fraying / Edges of patience the teased harpies / Hone the incredible silence against their tongues" (DB, 82, 83). Not so surprisingly, we open the next volume to the unpretentious futility of the dedicatory poem: "In this world how little can be communicated" (GB, 5). He proceeds, in the next poem, "past bone-wreck of vessels, / Tide-ruin, wash of lost bodies bobbing" (GB, 11), and the resources of the sea bring the book full circle and carry him into the opening poems of *The Drunk in the Furnace*. But there the florid rhetoric, with its echoes of Dylan Thomas, is at war with its empty subject: "Virtues / That had borne us thus far turned on us, peopling / The lashed plains of our minds with hollow voices" (DF, 6).

The most significant features of *The Drunk in the Furnace* are its melancholy, more discursive and less at ease with itself than in his first book, and its self-deprecatory and liberating comedy. The melancholy lacks the force it will have when it finds its true, eroded form. We learn of the fated circularity of Odysseus's journey, of the foghorn that calls "to something men had forgotten, / That stirs under fog" (DF, 3), and of a ship that has passed by the poem's speaker only a few hours before going down in a storm (the old notion of being brushed unknowingly by disaster). The poems are competent, but too self-consciously thoughtful. The wildly ironic poems in the book are closer to the roots of the change at work in Merwin's career. In "Fable" a man clinging to the top branch of a tree accepts the advice of a passerby who says he must save himself by jumping, because the tree is falling. He is killed in the fall and the passerby kindly remarks to the corpse that he really let himself drop because he wanted to die. The macabre is also evident in the story of the one-eyed man, king in the country of the blind, who so tires of describing the visible world to his subjects that at the end he does not even mention "the black thumb as big as a valley" descending on them out of the sky (DF, 35).

Two poems are especially relevant to Merwin's next book. In "Sailor Ashore" a drunk's vision reveals ironically "what unsteady ways the solid earth has / After all" (DF, 7). There follows, masked with buffoonery, the kind of unnerving perception so frequent in Merwin's work since The Moving Target: "the sea is everywhere. / But worst here where it is secret and pretends / To keep its mountains in one place." The drunk's classic perception of the animacy of inanimate objects and forces anticipates what will become one of Merwin's characteristic syntactic and semantic devices.

The final poem in the book, which is also the title poem, is an irrevocable perspective on his work to that point. An empty iron furnace rusts in a trash-ridden gully by a poisonous creek, until a derelict decides to make it his "bad castle." He brings his bottle, bolts the door behind him, and carouses in drunken solitude until he passes out. Written in careful septets, the poem's formal concern for a frivolous occasion mocks all the sonorities of Merwin's previous books. The poem ends with a description of the local adults listening to warnings from their preacher, while their children crowd to the irresistible furnace:

> Their witless offspring flock like piped rats to its siren
> Crescendo, and agape on the crumbling ridge
> Stand in a row and learn.
>
> (DF, 54)

With this burlesque of all his own overwrought rhetoric, Merwin can never return to his earlier style. It is a deliberate aggression.

This rebirth of willful failure is a singularly American trait. It is common to many of our foremost poets, and crucial to many ruined or limited careers whose poetry nevertheless holds us. Of the several hundred poems Merwin has published since 1960, many do not succeed; some, like the run-on Beckettian sentence of "Fear" (CL, 83–86), are simply not appropriate to his new form. A few, like "Line" (CF, 26), which describes the ritual interactions in a supermarket line, deal with prosaic topics that resist Merwin's powers of transformation and thus become comic, a tendency he finally masters in "Questions to Tourists Stopped by a Pineapple Field" (OH, 43–45). Some, like many of his short prose pieces, seem glibly designed to indulge a lazy audience's pleasure in effortless and unspecific mystery. Others demand too much of themselves and of their readers, as when Merwin—like Rich in "Not Somewhere Else, But Here" in The Dream of a Common Language and Duncan in "The Fire" in Bending The Bow—tries to render a series of unconnected images into a condition of heightened apprehension: "an end a wise man fire / other stars the left hand" (WA, 101). Many, such as the haiku-like fragments in "Signs" (CL, 116–18), pale before the overwhelming power of his best work. Yet the production, like Whitman's work, is a single enterprise; the volumes beginning with The Moving Target are all one book, even to the ultimate undermining of the project in the optimistic poems in The Compass Flower and Finding the Islands. The poems reflect one another endlessly, repeat the same messages tirelessly, clarify one another and simultaneously complicate one another until no image can ever be resolved.

It is not merely that we must judge the body of poems entire. It is rather, as with Rich, that the finest poems are always in dialogue with the worst. Though new subjects are frequently introduced, many of the major poems use a vocabulary (silence, emptiness, distance, darkness, whiteness, death) and create images with nouns (gloves, hands, eyes, feet, shoes, water, birds, mirrors, sky, trees, nests, wings) whose familiarity surpasses a verbal signature and becomes almost a form of self-betrayal. What we experience in the best poems is a cohesion *despite* this omnipresent diction. The best wrest themselves from their rhetorical ground and make themselves simultaneously unique and typical. Merwin exploits the most impossible fact of language—that words and images are riddled with received meaning and historical context. Like Kenneth Burke, Merwin believes that language is not merely a web of connotations but also a structured source of motivation. Unlike Burke and Duncan, however, Merwin does not feel that play amidst these verbal connections will be liberating. Language is already a democratic resource, but it is suffocating. Our words speak through us to override any fresh use we may have for them. "On the way to them," he writes, "the words / Die" (L, 7); they are used, given, and they will not live for us. "I can put my words into the mouths / of spirits," he tells us, "but they will not say them" (CL, 17).

Merwin is not the first to have wrestled in this way with poetic tradition; indeed, his first books are damaged by influences never made truly his own. Merwin is, however, unique in so daringly disclosing the echolalic qualities of his own language. Beckett and Burroughs, along with many younger novelists, have taken that risk in prose, but our preconceptions about the formal integrity of poems make the choice more difficult there. Because of those expectations, the ironic formal repetition and verbal self-subversion so common in experimental fiction have yet to be attempted with much success in contemporary poetry.[5] The most radical other example is James Merrill, with the plural, unstable texture he achieves by juxtaposing original metaphors, conversational clichés, and frequent allusion and quotation. It is not surprising that neither Merwin's nor Merrill's very different kinds of self-deflating irony have been successfully imitated, since most open-form contemporary American poetry retains some Whitmanesque hope of projecting an ideally open and democratic society. Merwin's open forms, indeed, have succeeded in mirroring the loss of any real historical possibility. Unlike those poems of the 1960s that are grounded in a reaction against historical actuality, or even those poems that seem to be victimized by history, Merwin's poems manage to give our history its most frightening voice. The revolution in Merwin's style must, then, be understood as an exacting and necessary discipline, one which is highly responsive to the general political environment. (A specific example is his decision, two-thirds of the way through The Moving Target and again early in The Lice, to abandon all punctuation.)[6] This discipline is undertaken, somewhat like Beckett's decision to write in French, in the face of considerable self-doubt and a sensitivity to the supremely self-conscious state of language in this historical moment. He recognizes that poetry exhibits some of the most terrible and most transcendent dreams identified with American culture. "Is it with speech," he asks, that "you combed out your voice till the ends bled" (*L*, 39). "In / our language deaths are to be heard / at any moment through the talk" (*CL*, 56). To give voice to those deaths, as Eliot did in *The Waste Land* and as Merwin has succeeded in doing, is to become for a moment the single voice of an age.

Merwin's failures are parings essential to the carving of that central voice. A device which works in one volume (such as the use of twice-repeated words which comes to fruition as a technique in *The Lice*) is exorcised by repeated use in the next. In *Opening the Hand* a new device—the internal caesura—is mastered and trivialized in the same book. Obviously latent possibilities, which we expect to find but which we know will not convince us, appear in the poetry, as if they must ritually be undone:

> there is no memory
> except the smoke writing writing *wait*
> *wai*
> *w*
>
> (*CL*, 101)

We can excuse this as an amusing visual game, but it will nonetheless persist in our memories as a reduction of Merwin's whole enterprise, a reduction which is therefore implicit throughout his work. Even that value judgment, however, cannot be maintained complacently, for in the same poem he revises an older image and raises it to a new level of discovery:

> the white
> invisible stars they also
> writing
>
> and unable to read

Merwin often generates one splendid line in an otherwise ordinary poem that leaves us indifferent to the quality of the rest. And some poems introduce images weakly, only to have them fulfilled some pages later. Such conflicting levels of quality within a single poem are not in themselves problematic or unusual. But neither individual lines nor individual poems are very easy to isolate from the surrounding intertext of Merwin's output. His best poems are still those that cohere, though they achieve their formal integrity by dominating a score of comparable metaphors which work from other poems to undo the internal relations. That achievement, perhaps we should say counterachievement, reverses what we ordinarily expect to experience through poetic form. It has the effect of an aggression against the core assumptions of New Criticism. It also serves as an attempt to displace the modernist revolution and relocate it in the present moment. The disruptions and discontinuities of *The Waste Land* reappear in Merwin's poetry without recourse to any mythic synthesis and with little implied priority for the poetic text itself.[7]

These accomplishments might seem of small consequence, if they were not so closely tied to a sense of a surrounding culture. With each of Merwin's formal self-subversions, we sense our mutual destiny at work in his poetry. If the hesitance, the repetitiveness, and the runic suggestiveness of his poetry border on preciosity, the fault seems to be ours as well as his. We cannot, in effect, fault him with inadequacies he seems to have drawn out of the language we share. Thus his failed poems are important precisely because they

> Appear
> not as what they are
> but as what prevents them
> (*CL*, 118)

"It has taken me this long," he writes, "to know what I cannot say" (*CL*, 28); this is a universal silence—visionary, figural, and full of its own throttled speech. Only Merwin could dare to give us "and when" as an entire last stanza (*WA*, 109); it is intolerable, of course, but we knew such a provisional gesture was imminent in our language, so we are relieved to have it taken from us, to see it written. "My words," he writes, "are the garment of what I shall never be / Like the tucked sleeve of a one-armed boy" (*L*, 62). This takes to its conclusion a common impulse to achieve in poetry a vision of selfhood not yet possible in actual life. Merwin, however, gives the goal its true historical futility, for the vision now "shall never be." The words of this vision, never consummated in speech, remain at the edge of each unsatisfied utterance. They are not merely his words, he insists; they are not centered in some unique selfhood verbally achieved. They are our words, and he is merely their agent. This role is common to the prophetic impulse in American poetry since Whitman, but it finds in Merwin its most anonymous and universal incarnation.[8] "It would be enough," Merwin says, "for me to know / who is writing this" (CL, 35). In most other poets this Borgesian comment would simply be mystical. We only tolerate Yeats's claim and its attendant system because of the poetry it produced. Yet Merwin's poetry is so close to the destiny of the language he uses—to the pressure the words themselves exercise toward their day of witness—that we must entertain the notion of a collective will: "Again this procession of the speechless / Bringing me their words" (MT, 97).

"Looking for Mushrooms at Sunrise" (L, 80) offers a fine image of poetry as a response to necessities inhering in language itself. As in many of the most effective poems in The Lice, he retains the sense of a specific topic, while simultaneously making the poem reflect the mood and vocabulary of the rest of his work. Before dawn he walks "on centuries of dead chestnut leaves": the surface of the earth is a matrix of every depleted past. It is "a place without grief," seemingly with no human consciousness present to it:

In the dark while the rain fell
The gold chanterelles pushed through a sleep that was not mine
Waking me
So that I came up the mountain to find them

No sleep, he suggests, is entirely our own; we dream collectively. Our speech then flows from the reservoir of things said. The soft, almost shapeless thrust of new mushrooms rising through darkness is a perfect image of the half-awakened consciousness. But the stanza goes further, hinting that our sleep is not exclusively human, that our sleep is the earth's sleep. So the search for mushrooms is also part of a waning hope that mute, essential substances will continue speaking to us in the light. The day seems familiar, as though the landscape were a tapestry woven of past anticipations: "I recognize their haunts as though remembering / Another life." The poem ends in a spirit of unsettled possibility. It resonates in the mind until we choose to break with it. The conclusion is full of pathos controlled both by verbal economy and by hope indistinguishable from anxiety. "Where else am I walking even now," he writes—and the metrical pause before the next line seems endless—"Looking for me."

These poems have a tone of quiet prophecy, as though the final whimper Eliot foretold continues to dwindle forever. In "The Room" (L, 48), he writes of a frail survivor whose apparently approaching

death is really the imprint of inexhaustible renewal. Of course one
version of poetic renewal is reading. Thus "The Room" is also about
our reading the poem. "I," therefore, is not only a poet speaking; the
pronoun belongs equally to the reader, so "all this" is the text we
contemplate:

> I think all this is somewhere in myself
> The cold room unlit before dawn
> Containing a stillness such as attends death
> And from a corner the sounds of a small bird trying
> From time to time to fly a few beats in the dark
> You would say it was dying it is immortal

Finality, for Merwin, is endlessly repeatable. If we are, as Olson
writes, the "last 'first' people," we may continue in that role forever.
That conviction begins in Merwin's earliest unpublished poems
with his sense of postapocalyptic hopelessness after World War II; it
continues in the first published poems with his narratives pursuing
silence and emptiness, then matures in his later work to where it no
longer needs narrative support. Distance and vacuity are eventually
inescapable conditions of all presence: "The horizon I was making
for runs through my eyes. / It has woven its simple nest among my
bones" (*MT*, 10). This is an image of consciousness alienated from
its own substance. We have "been made," Merwin writes in lines
that echo with increased fatalism Olson's sense of the constitutive
role of space in American culture, "Of distances that would not
again be ours" (*L*, 74). Eventually, this image of selfhood as embody-
ing communal absence brings him to attempt poems of considerable
presence which have no apparent subject at all. In *The Moving Target*
and *The Lice*, however, he first explores the tonality of the void, at
the same time linking it to a sense of history as an untraceable but
pervasive disease.

"December among the Vanished" (*L*, 45) is one of the major poems
addressed to the texture of absence:

> The old snow gets up and moves taking its
> Birds with it
>
> The beasts hide in the knitted walls
> From the winter that lipless man
> Hinges echo but nothing opens

> A silence before this one
> Has left its broken huts facing the pastures
> Through their stone roofs the snow
> And the darkness walk down
>
> In one of them I sit with a dead shepherd
> And watch his lambs

The atmosphere of this poem offers snow, but no reviving moisture. Change is only loss; the snow "gets up"—it drifts or evaporates with the insistence of inanimate force, the winter birds (or their tracks) following its course. The beasts hiding in knitted walls anticipate the unprotected sheep of the last stanza, since we may take "knitted walls" as an image of sheep's coats, but the phrase also suggests predators in a forest, or even an animal furtiveness inhering in all matter, as when he wrote of "the night green with beasts as April with grass" (*GB*, 15). In any case, the sense of threat and tension is clear. The winter is a "lipless man," sere and skeletal. The next line, "Hinges echo but nothing opens," is intended to be a complete sentence; the rattling door frames, or even the hinge of potential seasonal change, are the empty vestiges of possibilities now extinct. Yet Merwin's unpunctuated poems often create syntactical ambiguities, so we may also read that "lipless man Hinges" echo the winter. But this human presence, perhaps the hinged jaws of a skull, can neither speak nor alter the landscape. The second stanza begins with an image of broken huts, belonging by virtue of their common origin to a silence receding into the past. We cannot remember if this silence once followed Armageddon; we suspect that it has a historical cause, but we can no longer isolate one. The lines also imply, more metaphorically, that even silence is now unhoused, even nothingness is exposed and unprotected. The pastures are no vista of openness but an encroaching distance. There are no barriers against fortune; with insensible willfulness, the snow and darkness "walk" down through shattered roofs. Everything is penetrated by loss.

The poem to this point is directed toward the last lines, where the tension becomes intolerable. They are among the most anguished lines in contemporary poetry, and their pain has no outlet. In one of those vacant huts, he writes, "I sit with a dead shepherd / And watch his lambs." The ceremony of shepherding, whether that of gods or of men, is gone out of the world; the lambs are born too late to understand their danger. The poem's tone makes the speaker seem a powerless witness, brought forward to watch in paralysis. Yet the resonances of the final verb are very complicated. "Watch" suggests not only mere observation but also protective vigilance, as in "watch over." We are not, however, convinced that the speaker could intervene if the lambs were threatened. The verb also implies the watch kept over the dead, an association which makes the lambs appear even more helpless. What is definitely missing here, what will never return, is the particular, secure relationship between the shepherd and his flock, a relationship Christianity ordinarily renews each December. The act of writing the poem is perhaps an act of witness, though the poet cannot quite become the new shepherd. Inevitably, too, our own loyalties are torn. We yearn to reach out and care for the lambs, but we are also part of that flock whose shepherd is dead.

In a larger sense, the poem itself is very nearly paralyzed. As the poem proceeds, its imagery is filled out, its emotional resonance intensified and newly dramatized, but the poem is also nothing more than another fragment of the world *The Lice* has evoked for forty pages. From that perspective, its broad tonal consistency suggests stasis rather than creative variation. Like so many of Merwin's recent poems, or like Rich's "Shooting Script," it is a sequence of equivalences impinging on one another; if there is a definitive key to their similarities, the poem both desires and evades it. Even the title, "December among the Vanished," straddles redundancy and contradiction—suggesting at once a double extinction and the inconceivable winter of those no longer present.

Many of Merwin's poems do not develop through logical or syntactical progression. They proceed by accretion. Syntax sometimes connects lines and occasionally stanzas, but even syntactical progression is often deliberately subverted by line breaks at awkward points within clauses. With *Opening the Hand* this tendency undergoes a further development, since the caesura sometimes interrupts and thwarts normal speech patterns within the line. The impulse to speak is thus always threatened by closure; the poem at any moment may abort itself into silence. Indeed, many of Merwin's poems seem to end more than once. Often, when the poem reaches the bottom of a page, the internal evidence combines with the physical layout to suggest the poem has concluded. Yet we can only be certain after turning the page. New Criticism has trained us to take the published text as final. Yet with this poet we must admit that even his more tightly organized poems could easily be expanded with lines or stanzas from other poems. His manuscripts reinforce this conclusion, since for many years he has carried small notebooks with him and used them to jot down hundreds of individual lines; the individual line is thus clearly often a self-contained element of his writing practice. Similarly, many poems could be cut or rearranged without necessarily altering their effect. This verbal equalization, the ultimate opening and democratization of form, is entirely appropriate to Merwin's vision. All the poems from *The Moving Target* to *Writings to an Unfinished Accompaniment* may be read as though they were written simultaneously—in the winter of an eternal present.

All seasons, for Merwin, have winter at their core. There is no longer any cruelest month: "April April / Sinks through the sand of names" (*L*, 29). Seasonal change and historical occurrence extend desolation to each new moment. Of spring he writes: "The dead bowmen buried these many years / Are setting out again" (*MT*, 96); they are in motion, but we cannot assume they are alive. When the walnuts fall to the road and split in the autumn, he observes: "here is the small brain of our extinct summer. / Already it remembers nothing" (*MT*, 32). "Extinction," he writes, is "my ancestor" (*MT*, 74); with each arrival, "once more I remember that the beginning / Is broken" (*L*, 24). Time in Merwin has been entirely spatialized. We have finally been given that spatial absolution, that identification of time with the history of the continent, that haunts so much of American literature since the nineteenth century; our history has been given over to a geography of omnipresent distance. "Seeing how it goes," he writes, "I see how it will be" (*MT*, 49); "the past" is "like a day / that would burn unmoved forever" (*WA*, 20). The present is neither a point of departure nor even an origin true to itself; it is merely that eventfulness in which both past and future recur. "We are the echo of the future" (*L*, 33). "The present" is "a wax bell in a wax belfry" (*MT*, 81); in it, "the future woke me with its silence" (*MT*, 97). When he says, "I am the son of the future but my own father" (*CL*, 92), he points to no romantic rebellion against a paternally imposed destiny, but rather to the self-conscious irony with which he recreates the inevitable. "I am the son of ruins already among us" (*CL*, 96), he writes, and the line refers self-reflexively to its own linguistic paternity.

Appropriately, then, Merwin's poetry is always called postapocalyptic. The term is frequently applied to contemporary literature, but it requires some elaboration before it will exactly fit Merwin's vision. Like the silence in "December among the Vanished," the holocaust that leveled our sense of possibility cannot be named or dated in such a way as to distance us from it. Moreover, even the most tangible of present events lack a positivity that can be contained and mastered. Those of Merwin's poems that retain specific historical references, such as "Sheridan" (*OH*, 53–55) or "The Asians Dying" (*L*, 63), demonstrate how history ceases to be an external process or eventfulness that can be known and limited, how it constitutes the present moment by infiltrating everything. History is not something we record; it is what we are.

Merwin's "The Asians Dying" is his most famous poem overtly about the Vietnam War; it merits an analysis by infiltration, a criticism surrounded and deadened by the poem's political echoes. I quote the poem's lines, in order, interspersed with my commentary. "When the forests have been destroyed," he writes, "their darkness remains," their heaviness and their thick foliage weigh on us like our guilt. No defoliation, no consuming fire, is decisive. The landscape, leveled in the outside world, rises again in us. The shadows amongst the trees are now a brooding absence and an inner darkness. In our eyes are traces of each obliteration; our will is choked by compulsion, our sight layered with erasures:

> The ash the great walker follows the possessors
> Forever
> Nothing they will come to is real
> Nor for long

As readers, we too are possessors, but the poem's images *decay* through association. The enlightenment the poem offers is experienced, paradoxically, as suffocation. We are possessed by a past which invades each anticipation; ruinous memories seep into every future. "Over the watercourses / Like ducks in the time of the ducks"—the only remaining migration is our residual unrest—"the ghosts of the villages trail in the sky / Making a new twilight." The only constant is our discontent, the only change the rhythm of returning night-mare. Twilight is the moment when consciousness—itself a confusion of misdeeds—submits to new violence.

The poem is a tapestry of recognition and forgetfulness; its lines comment on one another endlessly. Each image (unique in its context) is immediately enfolded by a torpor of historical sameness; in an age whose destiny is past, each name names everything. The poem is a claustrophobia verbally enhanced by false relief; each new line rediscovers old ground.

But Merwin's fine musical sense always provides for surprises in tempo. These verbal shocks (like their unpunctuated lines) bleed off into silence, but that only increases their hold on us:

> Rain falls into the open eyes of the dead
> Again again with its pointless sound
> When the moon finds them they are the color of everything

These lines are set by themselves on the page. If we could, we might join them to another stanza to deaden their horror. The lines relate a simple fact, one we secretly knew but had not consciously thought of, but the image lends the war an unbearable solitude. It is as though a single and essential benediction were lacking at the core of everything we are. It is too late; death cannot be contained. We cannot bury the dead of Vietnam; raindrops hammer at their delicate eyes, we cannot reach out to close them. Already they are the color of everything, for everything has taken on their color: their violated sight is taken up into the limpidity of the air.

Thus "the nights disappear like bruises but nothing is healed / The dead go away like bruises." Dawn is merely burning darkness. There are no more beginnings. We are not truly healed (nor can the poem heal us); we are uniformly, though not terminally, wounded. The body politic absorbs its crimes; they are its substance: "The blood vanishes into the poisoned farmlands." The war is the absolute limit of knowledge: "Pain the horizon / Remains." Above us, trembling but unfulfilled, "the seasons rock," now unnatural signs that no longer signify; "they are paper bells / Calling to nothing living." For a world that will not be reborn, seasonal change is mockery. And the poem, too, is a paper bell; it tolls no prophecy, for its message was apparent long ago—embedded equally in every historical act and in every line.

Merwin's first draft of "The Asians Dying."

For the Asian Dead

        The ash walks everywhere
                footsteps

        (The smoke turns)

        over the lake - like ducks--ghosts of the villages
                        forests
        Even when the ~~jungles~~ have been burned (destroyed)
                Their darkness remains

The poisoned fields
                In the time when there were
                Ducks over the water courses

Follow the ash like footsteps   As in the time when the ducks
But it leads everywhere

Come with the ash great walker

Ash the great walker follows the possessors
~~Follow~~
~~Everywhere~~

Even the dead disappear   like bruises
                go away

The dead - like bruises

                The world is moving water

The possessors walk into-- ~~like~~ everywhere
Like ~~little~~ flames with no light
~~dust~~
        - of smoke
                fires

(The poisoned fields ruled by absence

                They with
                ~~have~~ no past and a fire
                ~~is~~ Their only future

The possessors move everywhere under
                    under Death their star

The possessors move everywhere under Death their star
Like columns of smoke they ~~move~~ walk into the shadows
Like little flames with no light
They with no past and fire
~~And fire~~ Their ~~only~~ future
                only

                When the moon finds them they are the color of
                                everything

Even when the forests have been burned
Their darkness remains
And through it ash the great walker follows
The possessors

When the forests have been destroyed their darkness remains
The ash the great walker follows the possessors
Forever
Nothing they will come to is real
Nor for long
And Over the water courses as in the time of the ducks
The ghosts of the villages trail in the sky
Making a great twilight
Rain falls into the open eyes of the dead
~~Again again~~ Repeating

The nights disappear like bruises but nothing is healed
The dead go away like bruises
~~Over the poisoned fields the seasons~~
~~Arrive and~~ The blood vanishes into the poisoned farmlands
    The seasons rock over head ~~like paper bells~~
            Paper bells

    Summoning nothing living

A typed transcription (by C. N.) of Merwin's first draft of "The Asians Dying."

"The possessors move everywhere under Death their star," Merwin concludes, but he is naming all of us, not accusing anyone, for the poem too possesses a history it loathes. "Like columns of smoke they advance into the shadows / Like thin flames with no light." What we are has corrupted the elements we are made of; all that we cannot see is unspeakably known to us. "They with no past," he writes, "And fire their only future"; the pronoun reveals not the clarity of distance but a special kind of self-knowledge—forgetfulness and revulsion in contest. The possessors have no past because what they do cannot be distinguished from what they have been. The final line is merely a rebuke, a false seal on the poem's form; fire is the future already with us.[9]

"The Asians Dying" is surrounded by poems virtually identical in tone and import that have no traceable historical referents. Thus the quality of particular historical events is dissipated and generalized as soon as we read any quantity of Merwin's poetry. Finally, though Merwin's desolate landscapes are unquestionably postapocalyptic, they are also pervaded with a sense of uneasy expectation. The apocalypse in our past survives only as a kind of vague dread, as if it were only about to occur. If "it is / the broken windows that look to the future" (CL, 87), then the air of impending doom is undercut when we realize the windows are already broken. "It had been many years," he writes, "since the final prophet had felt the hand of the future how it had no weight" (L, 13). Both our dreams of transcendence and our dreams of disaster are false sympathies, maudlin and self-serving dramas. "I am sure now," he writes in "Glimpse of the Ice" (L, 46), death is "a light under the skin coming nearer." Yet the death will never occur; even if it has already happened we are unable to move beyond it. Postapocalyptic, surely, but obsessed with "The End / That great god . . . Leaving behind it the future / Dead" (L, 68). Moreover, the sense of a faded apocalypse in Merwin is distinctly American. It transcends the conventional references to the Nazi holocaust and to nuclear war to refer more broadly to a sense in America that our origin and continuing presence as a people is apocalyptic. We live in the midst of a resolution we cannot possess, we "sit in the dark praying as one silence / for the resurrection" (CL, 37). Again and again, we rush forward to come into the emptiness of ourselves; we reach out to embrace our special destination. "We run / down onto the wharf named / for us" but "the harbor is empty" (WA, 38):

> . . . our gravestones are blowing
> like clouds backward
> through time to find us
> they sail over us through us
> back to lives that waited
> for us
>
> and we never knew
>
> (*WA*, 38)

This is the end of a poem, and its rhythm is part of the poem's communication. The onrushing tempo builds, hesitates, and then expends itself in indecision. Many of Merwin's last lines are like that, intentionally undercutting the mounting energy, delivered almost flatly. In other cases, the final touch is heavier, and the content tends to be anticipatory, creating a new beginning rather than a conclusion. Such incomplete beginnings leave us hanging with nowhere to go, for the poem is at an end. The two characteristic methods move us from different directions toward the same stasis. Occasionally, he manages both effects at once. "Come back" (*L*, 76) ends with a line without period or question mark: "Is it the same way there"—a line that is thus both query and statement. Our absolution is everywhere around us, but it is like water which "flows through its / Own fingers without end" (*L*, 43). So Merwin can dedicate a poem to "The Anniversary of My Death," an uncertain day he can celebrate every morning. That day will arrive like the constant beam of a star already extinguished. Another poem of dedication is titled "For the Grave of Posterity" (*MT*, 71). The poem celebrates a "stone that is / not here and bears no writing"; the stone "commemorates / the emptiness at the end of / history." The conclusion, properly without final punctuation, is one of vague erasure in the guise of finality: "Whatever it could have said of you is already forgotten."

Each of the dead, Merwin writes, offers us his message: "*I know nothing / learn of me*" (*CL*, 51). It is also the message of each of his poems. In a little prose statement titled "On Open Form," Merwin speculates rather paradoxically about a poetry whose forms are each uniquely anonymous; each form is to have "an unduplicatable resonance, something that would be like an echo except that it is repeating no sound."[10] In "To Where We Are" (*MT*, 61), he concludes with a description of "our neighbors" that is also an invocation to his readers:

> Natives of now, creatures of
> One song,
> Their first, their last,
>
> Listen.

The poetry he has written, since that moment of self-reflexive laughter in *The Drunk in the Furnace*, has been poetry of this univocal, demoniacally democratic song. Its forms are wholly unhinged; they are a species of "Nothing / On which doors were opening" (*L*, 20).

One of the foremost of these poems is "Beginning" (*CL*, 123):

> Long before spring
> king of the black cranes
> rises one day
> from the black
> needle's eye
> on the white plain
> under the white sky
>
> the crown turns
> and the eye
> drilled clear through his head
> turns
> it is north everywhere
> come out he says
>
> come out then
> the light is not yet
> divided
> it is a long way
> to the first
> anything
> come even so
> we will start
> bring your nights with you

One early source for this poem is Merwin's "The Frozen Sea" (*DF*, 6), a poem about antarctic exploration and about the human experience of that landscape. The ice and snow are "the very flesh / No different only colder, as was / The sea itself"; they reflect a "whiteness that we could not bear. It / Turned bloody in our carnal eyes." The wind there shrieks of a violent purification; it would "freeze out / The mortal flaw in us." Its "screaming silence" fills the explorers' minds with hollow animal voices that boast "their / Guts would feed on God." The absolute whiteness and sheer antagonism of the setting invoke comparable human extremes—transcendence and violence. The men are at the center of a vortex; they are so small, these figures "around whom the howling / World turned." Only "a soulless needle" can tell them where they are, though even the magnetic compass is useless near the poles, where the dipping needle stands vertical. They have come to a point of origin that inversely suggests closure. Merwin describes this journey to whiteness in lines he will later directly echo in "Beginning": we have come, he writes, "to the pure south, and whichever way we turned / Was north, the sides of the north everywhere." The choices of direction are infinite, but they are all the same. With the sides of the north surrounding them, they are not liberated but confined. Time seems to have stopped; it awaits only the imprint of the law. In a poem called "The Present" (*MT*, 51), he writes: "The walls join hands and / It is tomorrow."

"Beginning" realizes the figural potential of the earlier poem. The ambiguous title, without the restricting definite article, is at once noun, verb, and adjective; it makes this creation-poem coextensive with all time. It is an eschatology of origins; it binds the course of history to a single core of emptiness. The landscape is again pure whiteness—a white plain under a white sky, possibly separated by the thin seam of the horizon, but perhaps not distinguishable at all. Yet this whiteness is not of substance but of essence; like the sun, it "hangs / in a cage of light" (*CL*, 96). The poem begins "long before spring," which sets it not only before the first spring or the first birth, but also as a seed or source within every renewal. The poem's distance is one of inaccessible proximity; within us and outside time, its beginning is a true origin—an end.

Within these hemispheres of light, like the germ of the poem's movement, is a black needle's eye. The image of the needle's eye combines a sense of the compass, its needle now ascending directly out of its center, with an allusion to Christ's words, "It is easier for a camel to go through the eye of a needle, than for a rich man to enter the kingdom of God." The biblical reference occurs in three earlier poems about Merwin's grandparents (*DF*, 41–44), as in his grandmother's belief that you could get "through . . . the needle's eye if / you made up your mind straight and narrow." The needle's eye is a nexus for these past connections and also an image of vision as a rite of passage. As he writes later in "The Way Ahead" (*WA*, 63):

> An eye is to come
> to what was never seen
> the beginning opening
> and beholding the end
> falling into it

Out of this eye, whose pupil is a doorway into the nothingness of all things, out of this eye which is his nest, rises the king of the black cranes. Metaphorically, kingship here suggests he is the foremost of his kind, selected to bear a destiny of dark flight. Merwin may be aware of the legend alluded to in Christian art that there is indeed a king of the cranes whom the other cranes, each standing on one foot to stay awake, encircle and guard as he sleeps at night. If the legend is relevant here, it can add another dimension to the nest image: the king of the cranes rises out of preexistent watchfulness. In both Western and Eastern art the crane is frequently a positive symbol of justice, vigilance, loyalty, and good works. In Egyptian iconography the crane is associated with the ibis-headed god Thoth, spokesman and arbiter for the gods, patron of wisdom and the arts, and inventor of writing.[11] Yet the crane is also known in a wide range of myths as a sly and wily bird, whose enticements to humans are offered in duplicity. So the crane, dark lord over the bleached plain at the beginning and the end of time, here, at least, is an ambivalent figure.

His crown turns, and his indifferent gaze falls on us. His gaze is empty; it is only a hollow cylinder through which the white landscape is focused. The eye is "drilled clear through his head"; it is an image familiar to us from modern sculpture, a more ruthless version also of the drilled eyes in ancient Greek sculpture. The image is startlingly mechanical, like a periscope or a gun turret. As the eye turns, it progressively renders the crane's whole head empty. The image of the crane's eye is a verbal successor to the black needle's eye in the first stanza. This vacant stare, the eye through which white light fills his black head, makes the opposite colors equivalent. It heralds the collapse of all alternatives, although it is proffered to us as a first moment when distinction is only a perceiving eye moving through uniform white light. "Come out," the crane encourages, "it is north everywhere." In Merwin's work, such enticements are double-edged. "Well they'd made up their minds to be everywhere because why not," he writes in "The Last One" (L, 10); the line presages an empty possessiveness that will cover the earth. Come out, he reasons, and we are tempted, as with his power of flight, by an image of the end disguised as a new beginning. If the light is not yet divided, then we need not fear our own darkness; it will be transparent. If it is north everywhere, then every failure will be an ascent, every cruelty a transfiguration. Come out, the crane demands, we shall now make everything in our image; we no longer need know ourselves at all. Dream, the crane suggests, that no things are yet to be seen; thus everything can be undone. "Everything that does not need you," Merwin wrote earlier, "is real" (L, 35). But these things can be undone. It is a long way before anything will happen, and the crane's offhand "come even so" is the sardonic justification for the death we would want anyway. When "the first / anything" appears it will occur under the sign of everything. "Bring your nights with you," he commands, as though we had any intention of doing otherwise, as though we had any choice. These "nights" are composed of the darkness we have inside us even in the brightest light. From the black needle's eye, our shadow rises to fall over the earth. "Beginning" extends the American myth of a second chance to a dream of a decisive chance—an opportunity to eliminate all uncertainty. Moreover, we may feel uneasily that we have already made the choice, for the crane's invitation, past the midpoint of "Beginning," also reads like a belated invitation to encounter the poem, one we accepted in venturing forth to read.

The poem seems inexorable, yet its form is almost dismantled. Its achievement is to pursue its own deconstruction with sufficient discipline to triumph over it. Full of long pauses, particularly in the last stanza, it has been pushed to the point of faltering. Although a narrative line is maintained throughout, it is reduced virtually to a series of isolated images. Whiteness, blackness, emptiness—the poem pivots about a hollow center which is nonetheless human. It comes almost as close as a poem can to containing nothing; yet it is broadly prophetic, cohering through a coldly democratic generosity that summons all subjects. It attempts to be, and largely succeeds as, an allegory of all situations.

Into its resolving emptiness "Beginning" draws all the political and social poems from *The Moving Target* to *The Carrier of Ladders.* There are no overt references to American history here, but the anguished mixture of loss and hope at the core of poems like "The Trail into Kansas," "Western Country," "Other Travellers to the River," and "The Gardens of Zuñi," the last two addressed respectively to William Bartram and John Wesley Powell, culminates in this poem of ultimate beginnings and endings. In effect, "the black heart of Andrew Jackson" (*CL*, 50) is traced here to its abstract origin outside any ordinary sequence of events. But the poem is also radically anticipatory, bringing America's first and last dreams together. Thus "Beginning" also generalizes Merwin's merciless vision of American history as the representative eschatology of our times. Through the tunnel of the crane's eye pass our celebrations, our songs, our pronouncements of victory and glory, and our incessant violence. A few years earlier, Merwin had written two bitterly sardonic lines indicting and connecting everything that is best and worst in us: "The beating on the bars of the cages / Is caught and parcelled out to the bells" (*MT*, 87). By the time we get to "Beginning," however, the reciprocal halves of this social contract have coalesced into a single wave of sound. Our complicity with our leaders, or our enthusiasm for them (and there are no other choices), is a convulsive "applause like the heels of the hanged" (*CL*, 57). In a poem like "Beginning" the cultural accusation is implicit in the metaphors of sight and light and darkness, worked into that vocabulary in such a way that it cannot be extricated. Thus we hear echoes of his earlier political judgments ("You born with the faces of presidents on your eyelids," he wrote, "and your lies elected" [*MT*, 93, 94]) even in this language, which is reduced to its bare essentials.

This harsh analysis of all of us began, in Merwin's early poetry, with a heavy irony directed toward his own verbal excesses. It has left him even now with a sense of guilt about formal accomplishment. He is one of the very few good poets to consider aesthetic satisfaction not the highest of all emotions, but almost a herd instinct born of fear. There is, of course, no scarcity of poets who reject the notion that the individual poem has to prove itself. The result is most often poetry of little verbal interest; even those more talented poets who take that position, like Duncan and Rich, regularly produce weak poetry as a result. Merwin, however, has realized the necessity of taking meticulous care in deconstructing his poems. Moreover, he has understood the place of a fascination with failed visions in America's controlling myths. So in all his poems we hear the collective movement of our culture's language toward its ends. "How many things," he muses, "come to one name / hoping to be fed" (*CL*, 131); his poetry continually names, but the relief we feel in naming and being named is either pathetic or despicable. "By the time you read this," he writes, and he is willfully playing with his reader, "it is dark on the next page" (*CL*, 131). He has a tendency to give us less and less in his poetry, to demand ever more of us as readers. There is no poet of comparable talent whose work is so exhausting to read; each thing given becomes meaningful only when taken away.

Merwin's poems become a mirror for all of us, one we thought we wanted, but the glass gives no comfort; in it we see the "cold lakes / from which our eyes were made" (*WA*, 42). Yet even that relief, for the vision of our own evil is tantalizing in its finality, is denied us. In some of his work the mirror invites hysteria. In "Glass" (*WA*, 107), a mirror opens and "where the eyes were" is a gray road with a little figure running away. It is Alice's story with a shrill edge to it, for there is no secure return. The figures suddenly multiply, as though the anonymous men who hang like suspended rain in Magritte's famous painting "Golconde" (1953)[12] began to flail in uncontrolled descent: "with their backs to you and their arms in the air / and no shadow." All the visible world flees with them, the stones, the birds, the dust—symbols also in Merwin's art—and it seems "all your terrors" are "running away from you." But it is, he writes almost amusedly, "too late." So "you fall on your knees and try to call to them / far in the empty face."

In poems like this, in *Writings to an Unfinished Accompaniment* and *The Compass Flower*, at times a loss of control threatens. Some of the images seem uncommunicatively runic, and the irony is almost manic. In some of the poems in *The Compass Flower*, Merwin's favorite nouns are used so casually that they are almost trivialized. Unlike Kinnell, whose vocabulary for emptiness and revelation often fails in short poems, Merwin's repeated vocabulary does not require long and elaborate contextualization. Merwin's vocabulary rather needs concise but continually new and unexpected realization. Only then can he use a familiar vocabulary "to make language itself almost something you cannot catch hold of."[13] Nonetheless, Merwin's weaker poems are necessary to his career. For the poems that do cohere, the weaker poems provide a background of unhinged emotion in which suffering loses its hold on prophecy. In the midst of poems whose echoing of past work suffocates, in the midst of fragmentary poems exhibiting the imprint of a form that now has an insistent life of its own, we discover poems of remarkable strength. In only three lines, "The Old Boast" (WA, 13) demonstrates Merwin's new power:

> Listen natives of a dry place
> from the harpist's fingers
> rain

An impossible disjunction exists here between the title and the text. The title is voiced with a deliberately antagonistic irony. It pushes the poem toward alluding to the false sustenance in aesthetic pleasure. But the text is inescapably felicitous. It displays a visionary synesthesia in which sound is water and the harpist's moving fingers appear as falling rain. The harp traditionally implies an unresolved tension between transcendence and sensuality. The poem maintains those forces in ambivalent poise.

"Tidal Lagoon" from Merwin's most recent book (OH, 36) has some of the same strength through compression:

> From the edge of the bare reef   in the afternoon
> children who can't swim   fling themselves forward calling
> and disappear for a moment   in the long mirror
> that contains the reflections   of the mountains

This is a poem that structurally cancels its own temptations toward a narrative unpacking. The visual pattern created by the zigzag caesura oddly duplicates the mountains' reflection in the water, just as the two halves of each line almost serve as semantic reflections of each other. The rapturous, risk-taking leap into the water is in no way resolvable by extracting a story from the text. For the mere reflection of the children is itself, should they only stand there, a flinging of their image into the watery mountains. A gaze directed toward the water is a calling forth, a naming, of the substances (light, water, air, earth) echoing in the gaze. There is a certain pathos in the "children who can't swim" but it is canceled by the poem's cool presentation of a fact of nature. In a strange way I find the poem seems to begin again as soon as it ends, though at the same time it is fixed in its imagist concision in such a way as to appear utterly static.

Another almost ineffably vatic poem is "Folk Art" (*WA*, 67). The title signifies, with flat irony, Merwin's fondness for inadvertent revelation:

> Sunday the fighting-cock
> loses an eye
> a red hand-print is plastered to its face
> with a hole in it
> and it sees what the palms see from the cross
> one palm

In the same volume, Merwin writes that "we were severed / from the animals / with a wound that never heals" (p. 22). In this poem, the wound is not healed, but it does speak. The imagery is reminiscent, not necessarily intentionally, of Lawrence's "The Man Who Died," and it is also relevant to Lawrence's fascination with primitive, violent ritual in Mexico.[14] With a gesture almost too swift for sight, the fighting-cock's eye is pecked out. The image is hardly pleasant. But the shape of the wound suggests a mock benediction, the laying on of bloody hands. It is our own violence, visible, rude, and tangible across a mysterious biological distance. We flinch and are given the second sight we secretly wanted, made possible as it always is by a rite of blood. There is a hole in this red hand, and it is permitted to see what we cannot. We fear, Merwin wrote earlier, that our lives do not go all the way, so we will send this messenger there. We gather again to "call crucify / crucify him" (*CL*, 87). This is no ordinary vision, for the eye is blind. Its sight is a form of mutilated touch: it reaches out to envision a mortality for all substance. It "sees what the palms see from the cross," death, for a moment both fleshly and eternal. That single palm is bared in every open hand.

These three poems include characteristics shared by many of the most successful poems in *The Compass Flower* and *Opening the Hand*. There (and most problematically in *Finding the Islands*) Merwin sometimes attempts to write positively about love and nature, but regularly fails. Straightforward affirmation is a mode Merwin may never be able to recover, a mode as well that public life may have made difficult for other American poets. Merwin needs to write about nature in such a way as to raise essential doubts about our epistemology. His best nature poems display a shocked wonder at the consubstantiality of natural things, displayed, almost inaccessibly,

in language. Thus Merwin can write that the sun mysteriously
shows "all the colors of autumn without the leaves," but he cannot
convincingly say that "marjoram joy of the mountain flowers again"
without making that personification more troubling (CF, 49, 48). Nature for Merwin offers us neither consolation nor salvation. "Past the
bleared pane fields drown," he writes in "Breakfast Piece: Feb. 1948"
from his unpublished manuscripts, and continues a few lines later
by observing that the "wind's language cannot say / Why I should
not let my hands / Hang straight down like the clock's hands." If anything, nature is a model for inaction; indeed, in "The Horse" (CF,
14), Merwin achieves a radical beauty that obliterates even the necessity for human witness:

> In a dead tree
> there is the ghost of a horse
> no horse
> was ever seen near the tree
> but the tree was born
> of a mare
> it rolled with long legs
> in rustling meadows
> it pricked its ears
> it reared and tossed its head
> and suddenly stood still
> beginning to remember
> as its leaves fell

Because there is a dark ecstasy in "The Old Boast," "Tidal Lagoon," "Folk Art," and "The Horse," readers will mitigate their ner-
vousness by convincing themselves that their energy is optimistic. It
would be more accurate to say that these three poems present images
of epistemological transformation radically indifferent to our need
for affirmation. In most of Merwin's work, however, his vision is
more coldly antagonistic. There is an ordinary human reluctance to
face a vision so uncompromisingly negative. Merwin himself faces
it in the moment of writing, but it would be foolish to expect him to
underline his honesty in some less ambiguous confession. Of course
this vision does not prevent him from writing; it is not a nihilism
that blocks discourse. Indeed his vision is a form of verbal productiv-
ity—a highly successful one, judging from the number of poems he
has published since 1960. Yet the fact of continuing production is
not in itself a form of affirmation. Nor does it seem accurate to say

that Merwin provides us with a phenomenology of inhabited absence. If he did, he could argue that, like all phenomenologies, even negative ones, it shows an affectionate, affirmative empathy for its subject matter. Yet the obsessive, almost mechanistic repetition of Merwin's central vocabulary runs counter to the responsiveness we expect from a phenomenological method.

Criticism often capitulates, in its final pages, by finding affirmation in the most bleak of modern works; it is part of the impulse to socialize the experience of reading literature. In criticism of American literature these affirmative conclusions also show that the critic wishes to push the culture's myths toward a positive fulfillment. Yet the easy optimism of American poems in open forms is essentially dead. A criticism that glibly seeks visions of democratic communality in poems devoted to moments of self-extinction or visions of collective dread is a criticism perhaps unwilling to cope with its own relation to history. In Merwin's case the impulse toward affirmation should be resisted. "This way the dust, that way the dust," he writes, sounding for a moment like Roethke, "I listen to both sides" (*MT*, 50), but Roethke's nervous playfulness in Merwin becomes a weighing of dark alternatives. On balance there is little comfort in this stasis. He ends that poem with lines that will be quoted many times as evidence that his vision is finally positive:

> This must be what I wanted to be doing,
> Walking at night between the two deserts,
> Singing.
>
> (*MT*, 50)

Merwin himself has commented that "absolute despair has no art," but a poetry which reveals "the existence of hope" need not be hopeful.[15] There is a trace of pride in the passage above, a pride in speech giving witness to pain. Yet the desert does not bloom. The pain cannot be mastered or transformed. And the first line implies that he has no real choice. Even in his earlier work he knew his poetic terrain to be

> No landscape but a demeanor of distance
> Where interchangeably the poles are death
> And death, as in an opposition of mirrors
> Where no beginning is, no end. . . .
>
> (*DB*, 77)

This is also the landscape of "Nightpiece" from the 1946–48 manuscripts, where "unwelcome birds at dusk convoke for feast," where "shadows, a mountainous disease, infest" the moon. And it is the landscape of "The Pilgrims," from the same group of poems:

> . . . I could find no place
> Out of sight of their palms,
> None past the empty eyes
> That gather me like alms.

He concludes *Writings to an Unfinished Accompaniment* with a poem, "Gift," that will also be enthusiastically misunderstood. The title applies not only to poetic inspiration, to the words he is given to utter, but also to the gift we receive in reading. He has to trust this gift, or he can trust nothing. He will be led by it, as streams are, as are the "braiding flights of birds / the gropings of veins." The first image is unashamedly beautiful. He often gives us, as in the final poem of *The Carrier of Ladders*, a poem whose language seems superficially beautiful without complication. Yet in the earlier poem his final plea, "Sing to me," is addressed to the music of a tree that will not bloom in the time of blossoms. Here, too, the final tone is insidious through its compromised rapture. The braiding flight of birds, for all its pleasure, is a rope endlessly woven and unwoven. It tantalizes, like the uncomprehending "gropings of veins," with a vision of unity always imminent and never forthcoming. The next lines, despite their dry economy, are more openly sardonic. He is led by this gift as are "the thankful days / breath by breath." From this inexorable movement of a destiny indifferent to human difference, the last stanza, a passage of extraordinary force, separates itself. No more decisive plea exists anywhere in Merwin's poetry: I shall be named by this gift, I shall choose willfully to be emptied and undone in this irreversible giving. It is a call, voiced for all of us, not simply to be freed, but to be possessed:

> I call to it Nameless One O Invisible
> Untouchable Free
> I am nameless I am divided
> I am invisible I am untouchable
> and empty
> nomad live with me
> be my eyes
> my tongue and my hands

> my sleep and my rising
> out of chaos
> come and be given

This plea to be taken over by a destiny finally free of uncertain hopefulness seems universal. Yet we diminish its singular appeal and terror if we deny the passage its historical ground. We have to understand "Gift" as a last, dark invocation of Whitman's solitary role as the representative American speaker. In it we should hear an answer, an alternative conclusion, to Merwin's earlier depiction of America's unresolvable communal yearnings:

> Each no doubt knows a western country
> half discovered
> which he thinks is there because
> he thinks he left it
> and its names are still written in the sun
> in his age and he knows them
> but he will never tread their ground
>
> $\qquad\qquad\qquad\qquad$ (*CL*, 48)

This passage is from "Western Country," one of the series of poems in *The Carrier of Ladders* that uses figures from American history as avatars of our national psyche. The poem that follows it, "The Gardens of Zuñi," is about John Wesley Powell (1832–1902), an American geologist and ethnologist who lost his right arm at the battle of Shiloh. Powell later led a number of expeditions into the American West, worked on a scheme to classify Indian languages, and argued for careful agriculture in the dry high plains and irrigation programs in arid portions of the West. At the core of Powell's mixture of pessimism and ambition Merwin sees an exemplary American fatefulness:

> The one-armed explorer
> Could touch only half of the country
> In the virgin half
> the house fires give no more heat
> than the stars
> it has been so these many years
> and there is no bleeding
>
> He is long dead with his five fingers
> and the sum of their touching
> and the memory

of the other hand
his scout

that sent back no message
from where it had reached
with no lines in its palm
while he balanced
balanced
and groped on
for the virgin land

and found where it had been

Acting for all of us, Powell pursues a vision that compels us despite
its temporal and spatial distance. Only his right hand, severed in the
nation's fratricidal war, can still reach for the invisible virgin land we
cannot forget. Our own body, lost to us and insensible, touches in an
irretrievable past the virgin country that cannot be possessed. Only
fifty years ago, Williams could still imagine that a sacrificial marriage between the explorer and the virgin land might provide us with
a model of a restorative American identity. In one of the chapters of
In the American Grain, de Soto dies and his body is literally consumed by the continent. Yet a few chapters later a new kind of
American is born, symbolically, of this grisly union. Even if the continent is no longer virginal, poets can, Williams would believe, continue to explore its image in us. In the first poem of "North American Sequence," just before the 1960s, Roethke can declare himself,
unlike Eliot, still willing to see the poet as an explorer in American
landscapes:

Old men should be explorers?
I'll be an Indian
Ogalala?
Iroquois.[16]

Now, with Merwin, we are no longer free to decide whether to
choose an American identity. That "blindness a hollow a cold source"
is guaranteed for each of us, citizens whose forefathers moved out
"over the prairie" (*CL*, 47). A poetry of open forms imitating a democratic geography is no longer difficult to achieve. Yet the current harvest of Olson's and Williams's composition by field is not always appealing. Seeking America in verse, Merwin "found where it had
been" and what it had become.

NOTES

1. Harvey Gross, "The Writing on the Void: The Poetry of W. S. Merwin," *Iowa Review*, 1 (Summer 1970), 92–106, compares Merwin's stylistic elegance to that of Keats. There are numerous parallels with Yeats: "as though a man could make / A Mirror out of his own divinity, / Wherein he might believe himself, and be" (*DB*, 72);

> What is a man
> That a man may recognize, unless the inhuman
> Sun and moon wearing the masks of a man,
> Weave before him such a tale as he
> —Finding his own face in the strange story—
> Mistakes by metaphor and calls his own
> Smiling, as on a familiar mystery? (*DB*, 41)

2. Jarold Ramsey, "The Continuities of W. S. Merwin," argues that "in every one of Merwin's books there is his peculiar grammar of emblems, the signatures of his imagination: the bells, mirrors, gloves, stones, doorways; the birds, the whales; and behind them all, inexhaustible in its numinousness, the sea" (p. 20). I agree that this vocabulary runs through all of Merwin's books, but I also feel it functions quite differently at each stage of his career.

3. At times Merwin's attitude toward religion is almost sardonic, as when he describes a rocky landscape: "nowhere else / Pillows like these stones for dreaming of angels" (*DF*, 23). Or, with more bitterness: "Unable to endure my world and calling the failure God, I will / destroy yours" (*MT*, 13). Yet he is also both attracted to and irritated by religious mystery. Given that his father was a Presbyterian minister, this ambivalence is hardly surprising.

4. Richard Howard, *Alone with America: Essays on the Art of Poetry in the Unites States since 1950* (New York: Atheneum, 1969), p. 361.

5. For an analysis of the relationship between Merwin's poetry and contemporary fiction, see Evan Watkins's *The Critical Act: Criticism and Community* (New Haven: Yale University Press, 1978).

6. Eliminating punctuation allows for some special effects that might be more self-conscious in a conventionally punctuated poem. Occasionally he will let the last line of a stanza bleed off into empty space: "but when she opened it" (*CL*, 126). Alternatively, he can limit that uncertainty with the following line, in this case the first line of the next stanza: "Someone has just / but no sound reaches the gate" (*CL*, 36). He will frequently embed a quotation within a line, without distinguishing punctuation, so that what would ordinarily be isolated seems instead to emerge inexorably from the preceding words: "I hear the cry go up for him Caesar Caesar" (*L*, 19); "I have prayed O wounds come back from death / and be healed" (*CL*, 96). See also Merwin's own comments on eliminating punctuation in his *Iowa Review* interview.

7. Eliot's influence on Merwin could be the subject of a separate essay, but I should at least note that the relationship goes beyond the ambience of *The Waste Land*. It extends to similarities in diction and rhythm, to the point

where Merwin seems to have deconstructed the early Eliot. Thus Eliot's "the bone's prayer to Death its God" seems almost to belong more properly to Merwin, whereas Merwin's "in this country of stone and dark dew" seems as though it should be returned to Eliot. On the other hand, Eliot's "rats' feet over broken glass" and Merwin's "Large brotherhood of broken stones" could be inserted into poems by either of them. Consider this sequence of lines: "I can hear the blood crawling over the plains" (Merwin); "Over endless plains, stumbling in cracked earth" (Eliot); "its horizon beyond which nothing is known" (Merwin); "Ringed by the flat horizon only" (Eliot); "the horizon I was making for runs through my eyes" (Merwin).

8. Merwin generally eliminates personal references from his poetry even when he knows a poem to have part of its impetus in a particular event in his life. At a reading (University of Illinois, Feb. 4, 1974) Merwin commented that "My Friends" (*MT*, 80–81) was based on a demonstration at the San Francisco Post Office in support of the people who had attempted to sail into a nuclear test site. "My friends without shields walk on the target" becomes a quite specific reference in that context, gaining a particular poignancy and some political force but losing some of its broad power to threaten us with a universal image of a meticulously targeted vulnerability. Similarly, at another reading (Beloit College, Apr. 3, 1981) Merwin introduced "Before That" (*MT*, 69–70) by talking about the kind of urban renewal that wantonly destroys our architectural heritage. He glossed the "City unhealthy pale with pictures of / cemeteries sifting on its windows" by telling the audience that white crosses are painted on buildings about to be demolished. For an audience familiar with Merwin's poetry the effect of seeming to restore this kind of referentiality is partly deflationary and reductive. Moreover, the suggestion that his poetry is grounded in a narrow kind of referentiality is misleading to the extent that it directs our attention away from the poetry as a writing practice. Yet the poetry itself resists a reductive reading, in effect asserting its own plural, aggressive, ironic relation to referentiality. Merwin's impulse in introducing his poetry in this way is apparently equally ambivalent, as his comments on this issue in the *Iowa Review* interview suggest. The impulse is partly a friendly effort to make the poems accessible and to provide relief from a reading's intensity. Yet the poem itself will then force an open, apocalyptic reading of its referent. Thus the introductory comment at once betrays the poem and proves that it cannot be betrayed. This double quality can be most easily demonstrated by citing Merwin's rather different introduction of "The Last One" (*L*, 10–12): "I wish it would become so untopical that no one would understand it at all."

9. In her essay in this book, "Apocalypse Then: Merwin and the Sorrows of Literary History," Marjorie Perloff argues that the publication of "The Asians Dying" in the *New Yorker*—with its visual context of slick ads for expensive consumer goods—demonstrates that the poem has no real political power and represents no threat to the magazine's readers. This claim seems to me to be in error on two grounds. First, the juxtaposition of contradictory messages has long been a feature of magazines that depend on adver-

tizing money. With television and postmodern culture in general, such juxtapositions have become both omnipresent and increasingly jarring. Thus the problem, while meriting discussion, is not unique to the *New Yorker.* Second, the *New Yorker* has a long history of publishing serious political writing, ranging from John Hersey's *Hiroshima* to the "Talk of the Town" series on Vietnam and Central America. That is not to say that the *New Yorker* has always been politically courageous. Merwin's essay "Act of Conscience" was actually scheduled to appear there, but the editor backed down when the Cuban missile crisis intervened, feeling it was not the time to publish something critical of the government. Merwin then called *The Nation,* and they published the essay immediately.

10. W. S. Merwin, "On Open Form," in *Naked Poetry,* ed. Stephen Berg and Robert Mezey (Indianapolis: Bobbs-Merrill Co., 1969), pp. 270–72.

11. Carol Kyle, "A Riddle for the New Year: Affirmation in W. S. Merwin," *Modern Poetry Studies,* 4 (Winter 1973), 288–303, mentions the possible reference to Thoth. Her reading of "Beginning" argues that the poem is essentially affirmative. Kyle also finds Merwin's series of cultural avatars— figures like Columbus or John Wesley Powell—to be entirely affirmative. Since Merwin uses these men as figures for American initiatives that have failed or turned demonic, I find her reading inexplicable.

12. The comparison with Magritte can be extended. When Merwin's surrealism is most visual, in lines like "the glass knights lie by their gloves of blood" (*L,* 8), or "you can see / Eyes lined up to ripen on all the sills" (*MT,* 26), or "at the windows in the knives / You are watching" (*L,* 4), I am reminded of those of Magritte's paintings whose surrealism depends on the improbable juxtaposition or displacement of distinctly bounded objects. One of Merwin's recurring images, that of the human hand, is frequently cast in this mode: "I have seen streets where the hands of the beggars / Are left out at night like shoes in a hotel corridor" (*MT,* 27); "flocks of single hands are all flying / southward" (*WA,* 18). "Dead Hand," a two-line poem, reads: "Temptations still nest in it like basilisks. / Hang it up till the rings fall" (*MT,* 14).

13. W. S. Merwin, "An Interview with W. S. Merwin," *Road Apple Review,* 1 (Spring 1969), 36.

14. The imagery also resembles the description of the "Blue Cockerel": "the spread red hand / Of his comb thrown back and the one eye / Glaring like the sun's self" (*GB,* 13).

15. Merwin, "Notes for a Preface," in *The Distinctive Voice,* ed. William F. Martz (Glenview, Ill.: Scott, Foresman and Company, 1966), pp. 268–72.

16. Roethke, *Collected Poems* (New York: Doubleday, 1966), p. 189.

MARJORIE PERLOFF

Apocalypse Then:
Merwin and the Sorrows
of Literary History

Merwin's sixth book of poems, *The Lice*, appeared in 1967 at the
height of the war in Vietnam. Reviewing the book for the *Yale Review*, Laurence Lieberman declared:

> If there is any book today that has perfectly captured the pecu-
> liar spiritual agony of our time, the agony of a generation which
> knows itself to be the last, and has transformed that agony into
> great art, it is W. S. Merwin's *The Lice*. To read these poems is an
> act of self-purification. Every poem in the book pronounces a
> judgment against modern man—the gravest sentence the poetic
> imagination can conceive for man's withered and wasted con-
> science: our sweep of history adds up to one thing only, a moral
> vacuity that is absolute and irrevocable. This book is a testa-
> ment of betrayals; we have betrayed all beings that had power to
> save us: the forests, the animals, the gods, the dead, the spirit in
> us, the words. Now, in our last moments alive, they return to
> haunt us.[1]

Extreme claims, these, especially now that a younger generation is
proclaiming that *it* is the last, even as its poets are writing in a
"cool" mode, very different from Merwin's.[2] The apocalyptic consciousness of the sixties had no use for the lessons of history: to
write, as Merwin presumably did, about what Altieri calls "the
other side of despair," to "make loss itself the ground for numinous
awareness that might suffice for the attentive imagination"[3]—this, it
was assumed, was to write "the New Poetry" or "Poetry in Open
Forms" or "Postmodern Poetry"—a radical poetry that questions the

assumptions of modernism. Thus Merwin holds a place of honor in Stephen Berg and Robert Mezey's 1969 anthology, *Naked Poetry*, an anthology that grew out of "the firm conviction that the strongest and most alive poetry in America had abandoned or at least broken the grip of traditional meters and had set out, once again, into 'the wilderness of unopened life.'"[4] In his own statement "On Open Form" for *Naked Poetry*, Merwin himself insisted: "I am a formalist, in the most strict and orthodox sense," but that statement could be—and was—safely ignored, for on the same page the poet remarked: "In an age when time and technique encroach hourly . . . on the source itself of poetry, it seems as though what is needed for any particular nebulous unwritten hope that may become a poem is not a manipulable, more or less predictably recurring pattern, but an unduplicatable resonance, something that would be like an echo except that it is repeating no sound" (p. 271).

I find the logic of this statement puzzling: why is ours, more than any other period in history, "an age when time and technique encroach hourly on the source itself of poetry"? And in what sense can any good poem in the late twentieth century have an "unduplicatable resonance"? Never mind: Merwin's "echo . . . repeating no sound" became, for "the generation which knows itself to be the last," a kind of *nouveau frisson*. Reviewing *The Carrier of Ladders* (1970), Richard Howard, whose *Alone with America* devotes more space to Merwin than to any of its other forty poets, declared that "the real goal of these poems . . . [is] a quality of life which used to be called visionary, and which must be characterized by its negatives, by what it is not, for what it is cannot be spoken."[5] And in what is a very different study, Paul Carroll's *Poem in Its Skin* (1968), a book that submits to close reading ten new poems by "the generation of 1962," a generation to which Carroll refers as "Barbarians inside the City Gates," and which includes Allen Ginsberg, Frank O'Hara, Robert Creeley, and John Ashbery, Merwin was called "the prince of the new poets": "In many of his most recent lyrics, one feels as if taken into a country where all is poetry—pristine, totally natural, miracles everywhere. Listen to this brief poem called 'Dead Hand': Temptations still nest in it like basilisks. / Hang it up till the rings fall."[6]

Merwin as New Visionary—this view was codified by Karl Malkoff in his *Crowell's Handbook of Contemporary American Poetry* (1973). Again, Merwin gets more space than any other poet of his generation (the only two poets who receive more than Merwin are Lowell and Roethke) and is called "the representative poet of his time, having gone through a process that is not only common to many of his contemporaries, but a microcosm of the history of modern verse as well."[7] That history, as Malkoff sees it, is the movement "from the formal to the free, from the traditional to the innovative." The poems of *A Mask for Janus* (1952) are "monuments to orderly vision," but by the time he wrote the final section of *The Drunk in the Furnace* (1960), with its more realistic family poems, somewhat in the vein of Lowell, Merwin had emerged "as a practitioner of open form": "the syntax is frequently fragmented, the language is less precious, less archaic, and much tougher" (p. 213). The "new spareness" of the sixties poems, a "language . . . simple but capable of bearing much weight" (p. 215), paradoxically brings Merwin back to the beginnings of his career: "It is as if he had not developed his style by metamorphosis, but rather by a stripping down, so that what we have now in the later poems are the bare elements of his earliest verse reduced to their essential forms" (p. 216). A similar case was made by Cary Nelson in a challenging essay called "The Resources of Failure: W. S. Merwin's Deconstructive Career" (1977): "[Merwin's] recent work offers us what remained after he rigorously pruned the excesses of his first poems and then turned what was left back on itself. The result has been a poetry of extraordinary force, a poetry that inherits the despair of the century but gives it a prophetic new form, a form that ruthlessly deconstructs its own accomplishments."[8]

But even as Merwin's "prophetic new form" was being hailed by the critics, dissenting voices were beginning to question it: Nelson himself, for that matter, remarks that "Merwin's desolate landscapes are pervaded with a sense of uneasy expectation. The apocalypse in our past survives only as a kind of vague dread, as if it were only about to occur" (p. 104). The same point was made more emphatically by Harold Bloom in a 1973 essay called "The New Transcendentalism: The Visionary Strain in Merwin, Ashbery, and Ammons." Like Malkoff, Carroll, and Howard, Bloom calls Merwin "the indubitably representative poet of my generation," but although he admires Merwin's attempt to make himself into "an American visionary poet," he concludes that "Merwin's predicament . . . is that he has no Transcendental vision, and yet feels impelled to prophesy":

> The poignance of his current phase is the constant attempt at self-reliance, in the conviction that only thus will the poet *see*.

Merwin's true precursors are three honorable, civilized representative poets: Longfellow and MacLeish and Wilbur, none of
whom attempted to speak a Word that was his own Word only. In
another time, Merwin would have gone on with the cultivation
of a more continuous idiom, as he did in his early volumes, and
as Longfellow did even in the Age of Emerson. The pressures of
the quasi-apocalyptic nineteen-sixties have made of Merwin an
American Orphic bard despite the sorrow that his poetic tem-
perament is not at home in suffering the Native Strain. No poet
legitimately speaks a Word whose burden is that his generation
will be the very last. Merwin's litanies of denudation will read
very oddly when a fresh generation proclaims nearly the same
dilemma, and then yet another generation trumpets finality.[9]

One may want to quarrel with Bloom's list of legitimate precursors, but his prediction that the poet's "litanies of denudation" will
read oddly to the next generation has already come true: indeed,
the very same year that Bloom published his essay, two young poet-
critics, both political activists, submitted the premises of poems like
"The Asians Dying" to severe questioning. In an essay called "Language against Itself: The Middle Generation of Contemporary Poets,"
Alan Williamson argued that poets like Merwin, Galway Kinnell,
James Wright, and Gary Snyder had turned the search for poetic vision into a kind of "ecological survival technique."[10] As "the first
generation to confront concentration camps and the atomic bomb,
the fully revealed destructiveness of civilized man, while still in the
process of growing up," this generation of poets, so Williamson argues, turned inward, concentrating on "the lessons to be learned
from animals, Indians, primitive or peasant cultures, the wilderness
as well as simple Wordsworthian solitary works; and thus a whole
new repertory of characteristic subjects is created" (pp. 56–57). Merwin and Kinnell, Bly and Wright have a "shared penchant for putting
the 'I' in the simplest of possible sentence structures, pronoun/active
or linking verb, with no modifiers before or between. The 'I' becomes
numb, neutral, universal: a transparency through which we look directly to the state of being or feeling" (p. 58). Indeed, Merwin, by
Williamson's account, denies his natural sensibility which is ethe-
real rather than "concrete or earthly," forcing his poetry to "develop
toward the same tactics as his contemporaries' (the simple, quasi-
narrative sentence, the isolated word, the numb 'I'), toward the same
loyalties, political and symbolic, and above all, toward the same stress

on the inadequacy of language" (p. 65). And Williamson quotes three
lines from "The Gods" (L, 30):

> My blind neighbor has required of me
> A description of darkness
> And I begin I begin but. . . .

James Atlas's essay, published in the same collection, is called "Diminishing Returns: The Writings of W. S. Merwin." Like Williamson, Atlas objects to the poet's "disembodied voice, addressing some unknown Other," to his excessive use of animism (e.g., "the horizon / Climbs down from its tree") which imbues the poems with "Surrealist confusion" (p. 76). What Lieberman calls "a testament of betrayals" is considered by Atlas to be a curious withdrawal from the meaning of political experience. For although Merwin may follow writers like Barthes in believing that only a language of disruption can measure our current history, he "still resists the real significance of what he practices; the disruption of language is no more than a device in *The Lice* (1967) and *The Carrier of Ladders* (1970). Monotonous, interminable, self-imitative, each poem exudes unbearable exhaustion; none supports a close analysis" (p. 78). And Atlas submits "The Night of the Shirts" to some basic questions ("Where is 'here'?" "What is 'it'?" "What is 'the same story'?"), concluding that "excessive transmutation of our 'modern dilemmas' has caused us to misinterpret them; what there should be more of at this time are critiques, poems that situate us in the world, or elaborate on real conditions" (p. 79).

Ironically, then, the very qualities in the poetry that were singled out for praise during what Bloom calls the "quasi-apocalyptic" sixties, have been cited by certain articulate poet-critics, who came of age in just this period, as its defects. For Howard, Merwin's poetry embodies a quality "which used to be called visionary, and which must be characterized by its negatives, by what it is not, for what it is cannot be spoken." To which the student of Wittgenstein might retort: "Whereof one cannot speak, thereof one must be silent." A compelling case against Merwin's rhetoric—or, more accurately, against the rhetoric of "mysterious, bardic hush" as it appears in the poetry of Bly and Wright as well as that of Merwin, has been made by Robert Pinsky in *The Situation of Poetry* (1977). Here is Pinsky on "Whenever I Go There" from *The Lice:*

Whenever I go there everything is changed

The stamps on the bandages the titles
Of the professors of water

The portrait of Glare the reasons for
The white mourning

In new rocks new insects are sitting

With the lights off
And once more I remember that the beginning

Is broken

No wonder the addresses are torn

To which I make my way eating the silence of animals
Offering snow to the darkness

Today belongs to few and tomorrow to no one.

(*L*, 24)

It is possible to think the way this poem proceeds—elliptical, allusive, dark, introspective, abrupt, intimate—as a "contemporary" mode distinct from . . . more traditional method[s]. . . . For that reason, some explicit exposition . . . may be helpful. "There" seems to be an internal place and a region of the mind which the poet chooses repeatedly to visit; knowledge of that place seems necessary to his imaginative life. But "habit" or expectation is useless in this place which never repeats itself. If "there" is the starting place for one's poems, or most valued perceptions, it is an absolute starting place: remembered categories and labels, if not quite discarded, must be subjected to new learning. . . . To put it more simply, each time the poet meditates upon—say—the fact that in some cultures mourners wear white, his sense of the reasons must be new.

The life there is hidden in a nearly impenetrable darkness, and the effort even to describe it is awkward, somewhat farcical, cruelly exposed.[11]

The voice that here, and in related poems, refuses the limitations of the conscious mind is characterized by Laurence Lieberman as one that "filters up to the reader like echoes from a very deep well, and yet . . . strikes his ear with a raw energy—a sustained inner urgency" (p. 260). Richard Howard similarly observes that "All the poems [in

The Lice] appear to be written from one and the same place where the poet has holed up, observant but withdrawn, compassionate but hopeless, isolated yet the more concerned . . . by the events of a public world" (pp. 441–42). Pinsky is more skeptical: "Whenever I Go There," he suggests, may well be *about* difficulty, about the need to renounce habits and expectations, but Merwin's "elliptically 'beautiful' phrases fall with a stylistic ease which we do not question even while we are questioning whether those phrases mean anything":

> . . . in a sense this poem embodies an extreme Romanticism: a pursuit of darkness, of silence, of the soul moving in ways so unlike abstract thought that it burrows into or 'eats' its immobile paradise. On the other hand, the Romanticism is qualified by the form of the last line
>
> Today belongs to few and tomorrow to no one
>
> which, despite the absence of end punctuation, is a summarizing abstract formula. You could nearly call it a moral. . . . in fact the action of this poem, as with most of [Merwin's] best poems, is to create a generic experience. (pp. 93–94)

Which is to say that the poem "moves in a resolutely elliptical way from image to atomistic image, finally reaching a kind of generalization-against-generalizing" (p. 164).

Cautiously stated as this is, Pinsky's charge is serious: he is saying that Merwin's rhetoric of vision is contradicted by a curiously nonvisionary penchant for summarizing moral statement, for the formulated abstract truth. Such questioning of the Merwinian mode is not an isolated case. A decade after Paul Carroll referred to Merwin as the "prince of poets," the British poet Andrew Waterman, reviewing *The Compass Flower* (1977) for the *Times Literary Supplement*, wrote, "Merwin . . . whose poetry has been admired in America for twenty-five years, offers a depressing case of extreme regression. . . . Merwin's is simply banal and devitalized writing . . . [its] enervation of language, sicklily ingenuous tone, and sentimentality are all self-consciously perpetrated."[12] If this dismissal sounds unduly harsh— and of course it is—we should remember that a critic as different in outlook from Pinsky and Waterman as Harold Bloom, who has declared himself to be "not unsympathetic to [Merwin's] work" (p. 128), concludes his discussion of the poetry with the statement, "Merwin seems condemned to write a poetry that is as bare of true content as it is so elegantly bare in diction and design" (p. 129).

It seems, then, that what was regarded a short decade ago as the epitome of "Naked Poetry," as "an Eliotic process of negative mysticism as the way to achieve a 'Poverty' beyond even love,"[13] now looks, to many readers, suspiciously like the Poetic Diction that the "naked poets" were supposedly repudiating. How this process came about, how one generation's "prince of poets" could become, in the words of Turner Cassity, "a very talented practitioner in a very tired tradition,"[14] is my subject.

II

Throughout the sixties and well into the early seventies, the debate between modernism and postmodernism in poetry (or "closed" versus "open" poetry, or poetry as "product" versus poetry as "process") revolved around two questions: the question of verse form ("fixed" versus "free") and the question of "transcendence" versus "immanence" or "presence." Thus, when in the last section of *The Drunk in the Furnace* (1960) Merwin turned from the traditional meters and stanzas of his first three books to the flexible blank verse of the final, more personal section, James Dickey hailed the change with the announcement that "With tools like these ["an odd kind of roughed-up, clunking diction and meter"] and with the discoveries about himself that this book shows him intent on making, Merwin should soar like a phoenix out of the neat ashes of his early work."[15] And soar like a phoenix Merwin did: by the time he published *The Moving Target* (1963), whose poems are written in short, abrupt free-verse units, critics like Richard Howard could speak of "an entirely different mastery of style." "On the page," said Howard, "the generally unpunctuated poems look as though they had been exploded, not written down, the images arranged so that the lines never enclose but instead *expose* them" (p. 436). And in their introduction to *Naked Poetry*, Stephen Berg and Robert Mezey take it as a given that to break "the grip of traditional meters" is to "set out . . . into 'the wilderness of unopened life'" (p. xi). By such an account, Merwin, who had renounced the villanelle and sestina, the rondel and ballad stanza of his first books for the hushed and impassioned free verse of *The Moving Target*, could be nothing less than a creator of the New.

Two things were safely ignored at the time. First, Merwin's free verse, which may have seemed enormously innovative when read against the background of the formalism of the fifties—the mode,

say, of Richard Wilbur or Allen Tate or Howard Nemerov—was nowhere as explosive as the free verse Pound and Williams were writing
by 1916, a free-verse model carried on by Zukofsky and Oppen in the
thirties, and by Olson into the late forties and early fifties. Second, it
should have struck the critics as slightly odd that a poetry so seemingly explosive—the poetry of "the wilderness of unopened life"—
was routinely published in the *New Yorker, Poetry,* the *Hudson Review,* and *Harper's*—hardly the organs of the avant-garde. *The Moving Target* has gone through eight printings between 1963 and 1979;
The Lice, eleven printings between 1967 and 1981. Eleven of the
sixty-three poems in *The Lice* first appeared in the *New Yorker* and
eighteen in *Poetry*. In the case of Merwin's subsequent volumes, this
ratio has increased: in *The Compass Flower* (1977), eighteen out of
sixty-one poems—almost one-third—were published in the *New
Yorker*. How is it that readers of the *New Yorker,* coming across
a poem like "The Asians Dying" on a glossy page between those
gorgeous ads for fur coats and diamonds and resorts in St. Croix,
were not put off by the newness of lines like

> When the forests have been destroyed their darkness remains
> The ash the great walker follows the possessors
> Forever,
>
> (*L*, 63)

by their evident strangeness?

This is a question to which I shall return, but for the moment let
me consider the more difficult question of Merwin's poetics of immanence. It has been argued, most notably by Charles Altieri in his
important book *Enlarging the Temple,* that whereas the great mod-
ernists—Yeats, Eliot, Stevens—adopt the Coleridgean "commitment to the creative, form-giving imagination and its power to affect
society, or at least personal needs for meaning, by constructing coherent, fully human forms out of the flux of experience," postmodern poets follow Wordsworth in developing "an essentially *immanentist* vision of the role of poetry": "Here poetic creation is
conceived more as the discovery and the disclosure of numinous relationships within nature than as the creation of containing and
structuring forms. Hence its basic commitment is to recovering familiar realities in such a way that they appear dynamically present
and invigorate the mind with a sense of powers and objective values

available to it" (p. 17). And again, "In the symbolist aesthetic, especially in the enervated forms of it practiced in the 1950s, the central focus is on the mind's powers to balance opposites and to take up a perspective from which the mind can judge and interpret what it presents. In the aesthetics of presence, on the other hand, poems do not present direct experience but the direct aesthetic illusion of direct experience that depends on style and form as means of seeing the word freshly" (p. 24). And Altieri quotes Robert Duncan's essay, "Towards an Open Universe": "Central to and defining the poetics I am trying to suggest here is the conviction that the order man may contrive or impose upon the things about him or upon his own language is trivial beside the divine order or natural order he may discover in them."[16]

Where does Merwin fit into this scheme? If a postmodern poet like Duncan can discover "natural order" in the "things about him," Merwin, so Altieri argues, is one of his "fallen counterparts" in that "at the very moment of intense awareness of presence there is produced a terrifying self-consciousness of all that cannot be made present or numinously 'here'" (p. 19). This very sense of emptiness or "absence" now becomes "the source of more complex and satisfying modes of inhabiting the other side of despair, however bleak that territory might be. . . . Merwin makes loss itself the ground for numinous awareness that might suffice for the attentive imagination."

It is this sense of loss that accounts for Merwin's penchant for abstract language and surreal image. Altieri says, "The illusory present is more insubstantial than the darkness or painful sense of absence it replaces. Moreover, the language one uses to fix those particulars, or even to comfort oneself by lamenting their passing, eventually mocks one with its inadequacies and its absences" (p. 194). Or, as Cary Nelson puts it, "The challenge Merwin sets himself in his best work . . . is to become the anonymous figure who announces the harmonizing dissolution of the language" (p. 79). Such recurrent words as "silence," "emptiness," and "distance," already present in Merwin's earliest poems, are undercut in the later work, in which language is turned back on itself so as to measure "the loss of any real historical possibility" (p. 90). Indeed, Merwin's "formal self-subversions" mirror our own; they draw out the "inadequacies . . . of the language we share" (p. 92).

My difficulty with these readings is that the sense of loss, of absence, of "the harmonizing dissolution of the language," so interestingly discussed by Altieri and Nelson, seems to me to be asserted rather than explored. Unlike Beckett, to whom he has frequently been compared,[17] Merwin rarely invents a fictional situation in which emptiness, darkness, the failure of the language to mirror "reality" are actually *experienced* by someone. It is time to look at a concrete example.

FOR THE ANNIVERSARY OF MY DEATH

Every year without knowing it I have passed the day
When the last fires will wave to me
And the silence will set out
Tireless traveller
Like the beam of a lightless star

Then I will no longer
Find myself in life as in a strange garment
Surprised at the earth
And the love of one woman
And the shamelessness of men
As today writing after three days of rain
Hearing the wren sing and the falling cease
And bowing not knowing to what

(L, 58)

Karl Malkoff, who calls this "one of the most striking poems in the collection [*The Lice*]," provides an analysis which is worth pondering:

The central idea of the poem is simple: each year contains the date on which the poet will finally die, each year he unknowingly passes the anniversary of his death. But the implications of this premise are complex. They involve nothing less than the total breakdown of conventional modes of apprehending time. Viewing time *sub specie aeternitatis* . . . Merwin labels the linear sense of time—that is, time as inexorable, unfolding, continual movement—as illusory. The "beam of a lightless star" is in one sense a metaphor of Merwin's own language of silence, the silence of death, the silence of meaninglessness. A beam emanating from a lightless star also suggests that from a sufficiently detached perspective, a dead star can appear still alive. . . . This is a fine symbol of the poet's eternal longings. And it is a fine symbol of time as relative in a world of absolute being.

Merwin perceives that his death has already taken place in precisely the sense that the present exists eternally. The temporal distinction is false. In the second stanza, however, he sets up new distinctions to replace the old. He will no longer "Find myself in life as in a strange garment." He will lose his divisive perceptions that isolate him from the rest of being. Merwin's response is characteristically ambivalent. He will no longer be "surprised at the earth / And the love of one woman." The uncomfortable world of time and change is also the realm of specifically human satisfactions. It is finally to this human universe that Merwin must return. (pp. 214–15)

I have cited this reading at such length because it strikes me as wholly typical of what we might call a sixties reading of sixties poetry. What Malkoff goes on to call "the hallmark of Merwin's 'new style'" is that his images consist "not of detailed description, but rather of actions and essential types." Indeed, the types become "almost allegorical. . . . But like all modern allegory, it is not supported by an ordered universe; it is grounded in nothingness" (p. 215). Here Malkoff unwittingly contradicts his own reading of the text, for what he has just shown, painstakingly and convincingly, is that Merwin's allegory, far from being "grounded in nothingness," is grounded in the familiar paradox that time is at once linear and eternal. "Viewing time *sub specie aeternitatis*," the linear view is illusory, as the symbolic "beam" of the lightless star, shining millions of miles from its dead source, suggests. On the other hand, to lose one's linear sense of time is, as the poet says in the second stanza, to lose one's humanity, one's ability to be "surprised at the earth / And the love of one woman." A paradox as neat as any Cleanth Brooks discovered in Wordsworth's "It Is a Beauteous Evening" or Yeats's "Among School Children." Yeats, for that matter, had pondered a similar time/eternity paradox as early as "The Stolen Child."

How, then, is the poem different from the late modernist lyric of the fifties, including Merwin's own early work? For one thing, the "I" is not a persona but quite simply the poet himself—here is a point of departure that seemed much more striking to readers of the sixties than it does to us today. For another, the imagery does not have the texture of W. K. Wimsatt's "concrete universal," of the metaphysical conceit dear to the New Critics. Merwin's language is "simple," if by simple we mean familiar: everyone knows what "day" means, or "fire" or "silence" or "traveller" or "three days of rain." It is also curiously abstract: most of the generic nouns are preceded by an article but not by an adjectival modifier: "the day," "the silence," "the earth," "the beam," "the love," "the shamelessness." In the rare cases when the noun does have a modifier, the adjective works to increase the sense of abstraction—"the tireless traveller," "strange garment," "last fires," "lightless star." Accordingly, the landscape of the poem seems to be mysterious; it has repeatedly been called "dreamlike" or "surreal," even though both these terms are probably misnomers: in a dream, one doesn't think in terms of "Every year" or "Then I will no longer / Find myself" or "today writing after three days of rain"; and "surreal" refers, not to something vaguely mysterious and blurred, but to a landscape, whether in the verbal or the visual arts, in which objects, people, actions, or situations that cannot conceivably coexist in the "real world" are brought together, as in Magritte's painting *Collective Invention* (in which a fish with the lower torso and legs of a woman—a sort of reverse mermaid—is seen lying on a naturalistically painted beach beside the ocean).

But whatever term we use to describe Merwin's images, it is true that they are unlike, say, John Crowe Ransom's metaphors in "The Equilibrists." If "Lemuel's Blessing" is, as Paul Carroll argues, again a poem built around a single paradox ("one who is an archetype of civilized tribal values petitions in a traditionally communal form of prayer that he be allowed to exist outside of civilized communal values . . . and come to share as deeply as possible the nature and characteristics of the wolf" pp. 146–47), that paradox is nevertheless framed differently from Ransom's, an allegorical mode having replaced the symbolist mode of the moderns. This difference aside, Merwin's poetry carried on the tradition of the well-made poem of the fifties. For what distinguishes a poem like "For the Anniversary of My Death" from the "undecidable" texts of a Beckett on the one hand, as from its modernist predecessors on the other, is the marked authorial control that runs counter to the lipservice paid to "bowing not knowing to what." Far from being a poem of *dis-covery*, a text whose "echo repeats no sound," "For the Anniversary of My Death" is characterized by a strong sense of closure.

Consider, for example, the stanzaic division. The first stanza (five lines) describes what happens "Every year"; the second (eight lines) refers to "Then" (when I will be dead). The first concentrates on the silence of eternity, beyond "the last fires," the eternity symbolized by the beam of the lightless star. The second recalls, even as does the final stanza of Yeats's "The Stolen Child," what will be lost when death ends the inexorable forward movement of time, when the "strange garment" of life is shed: namely, the love of one woman, the shamelessness of men, the singing of the wren, the falling of rain, and, yes, the "bowing not knowing to what," which is to say, "bowing" to the premonition of death one has in moments of transition, as when a three-day rain comes to an end.

Does the language "mock the poet with its absences"? Not really, or at least its mockery seems to take place only on the surface. The first line quickly gives the game away: since there is obviously no way to know on what day of the year one will die, the phrase "without knowing it" strikes a rather self-important note. This is the language, not of dream or of mysterious Otherness, but of calculation: the setting up of a hypothetical situation that brings the time/eternity paradox into sharp relief. Again, the reference to "death" as the moment when "the last fires will wave to me" seems to me the very opposite of "spare" (a word regularly applied to Merwin's poetry by his admirers); it is a gestural, a decorative metaphor reminiscent of Dylan Thomas rather than René Char.[18] Indeed, lines 2–5, with their heavy alliteration and assonance, their repetition and slow, stately movement, have the authentic Thomas ring:

> When the last fires will wave to me
> And the silence will set out
> Tireless traveller
> Like the beam of a lightless star

The language of the second stanza is increasingly abstract, conceptual, formulaic, recalling, as Bloom points out, the conservative rhetoric of poets like Longfellow or MacLeish. To call life "a strange garment," to define one's humanity in terms of "the love of one woman" and the need to wrestle with "the shamelessness of men"— such locutions have the accent of the Sunday sermon rather than the surrealist lyric. Given this context, the "bowing not knowing to what" in the unpunctuated last line is a predictable closural device: it points us back to the title with its recognition that one of the days now lived through will, one year, be the day of the poet's death.

The poem's closure is reflected in its formal verse structure. Merwin's heavily end-stopped lines, each followed by a brief rest or hush, are lightly stressed, anapests predominating as in

Like the beám of a líghtless stár

or

And bówing not knówing to whát

but in many lines the pattern is complicated by an initial trochee:

Évery yeár without knówing it
Tíreless tráveller
Heáring the wrén síng.

Syntactic parallelism—"And the silence will set out," "And the love of one woman," "And the shamelessness of men"—provides a further ordering principle. And although the stress count ranges between two and five (and syllable count between five and thirteen), the lines are organized tightly by qualitative sound repetition: Merwin's patterning is extremely intricate, as in the alliteration of t's, r's, and l's in "Tireless traveller," the assonance and consonance in "Find myself in life," and the internal eye rhyme in "And bowing not knowing to what."

"For the Anniversary of My Death" is thus a very elegant, well-made poem; it has a finish that would be the envy of any number of poets, and its theme is certainly universal—just mysterious enough to arrest the reader's attention, yet just natural enough (this is the way we all feel about death sometimes) to have broad appeal. It is, I think, this blend of strangeness and a clear-sighted literalness that makes a poem like "The Asians Dying" memorable. Consider the lines

Rain falls into the open eyes of the dead
Again again with its pointless sound
When the moon finds them they are the color of everything
                                                                    (L, 63)

We don't usually think of rain falling precisely into open eyes, let alone "the open eyes of the dead." The image is an odd one and yet the third line has a kind of photographic accuracy: in the moonlight, the dead bodies, clothed in khaki, would indeed blend with the colors of the forest ground, and so theirs is "the color of everything." Add to this the irony—a rather heavy-handed irony, I think—of Merwin's implication that, in our world, the color of death has become "everything," and you have an intricate enough layering of meanings, which is not to say that Merwin's construction is in any way radical or subversive. Indeed, I submit that nothing in "The Asians Dying" has the startling modernity of

> I was neither at the hot gates
> Nor fought in the warm rain
> Nor knee deep in the salt marsh, heaving a cutlass,
> Bitten by flies, fought.

Cary Nelson has rightly noted Merwin's debt to Eliot (p. 119), but it is a good question whether "Gerontion" doesn't capture what Lieberman calls "the peculiar spiritual agony of our time" at least as well as do poems like "The Asians Dying."

In Merwin's poems of the early seventies, fragmentation of syntax, abstraction, and ellipsis become, as the critics have noted, more marked; these are "difficult" poems in that their nouns are generic and that their spatial and temporal adverbs usually have ambiguous referents. Of *The Carrier of Ladders*, Richard Howard writes: "They are intimate poems, but not in the least personal—there are no persons here, nor even personifications. There are presences, and they support processes which afford the speaking voice an access to prophecy, by which I mean the capacity not to predict the future but rather to release the present: *'key / unlocking the presence / of the unlighted river / under the mountains.'* For Merwin, for the poet who is the one voice raised in Merwin's book, anyone or anything can be the 'key'—another person, his own body, an event, a landscape—the key to darkness, to unconditional life" (p. 444). Let us see how this "unconditional life" is released in "Beginning of the Plains":

> On city bridges steep as hills I change countries
> and this according to the promise
> is the way home
>
> where the cold has come from
> with its secret baggage
>
> in the white sky the light flickering
> like the flight of a wing
>
> nothing to be bought in the last
> dim shops

before the plain begins
few shelves kept only by children
and relatives there for the holiday
who know nothing

wind without flags
marching into the city
to the rear

I recognize the first hunger
as the plains start
under my feet
                          (CL, 80)

"Beginning of the Plains" is the sort of Merwin poem often called Kafkaesque:[19] in a nightmare vision, the poet must climb city bridges "as steep as hills," must "change countries" in a journey that will paradoxically bring him "home," a home dreaded with the premonition that "the cold has come from [it] / with its secret baggage." As he sets out on his journey, the poet passes "dim shops / before the plain begins," but there is "nothing to be bought" in these, only a "few shelves kept only by children / and relatives there for the holiday / who know nothing." The nature of the holiday is not specified but it doesn't matter, for the holiday is, in any case, not destined for him. Rather, he must proceed on his lonely pilgrimage, driven "to the rear" by a "wind without flags," that is to say an empty air mass, one in which nothing flutters, nothing has life. As the poet is swept along by this wind, his exile begins: "I recognize the first hunger / as the plains start / under my feet."

It would be an interesting exercise to study how a poem like "Beginning of the Plains" "deconstructs," to use Cary Nelson's word, earlier journey poems like "Anabasis I," the opening poem of *A Mask for Janus*, which has passages like the following:

Silence about our silence grew;
Beached by the convenient stream

Night is familiar when it comes.
On dim gestures does the mind
Exorcise abandoned limbs,
Disbodied, of that other hand

Estranged almost beyond response.
                          (MJ, 3)

In the later poem, Merwin has abandoned the complex modification and inversion of his first experiments with poetic syntax; he has also purged his language of recondite words like "Disbodied." But the journey into "silence" and "night" has not appreciably changed; it is the journey of life, the eternal Pilgrim's Progress, even if the 1970 poem presents that journey in more abstract, more seemingly mysterious terms, the "I" now being overheard as if speaking in a trance: "I see x, I do y, then I must do z. . . ."

The Kafkaesque rhetoric of "Beginning of the Plains" does not, for all the stress on absence, go very deep. In a Kafka journey, as in a Beckett one, there are very concrete, specific signposts, signposts that yield particular meanings, even as those meanings are undercut by other contradictory signs. But what is indeterminacy in Kafka is mere vagueness here: we don't know *where* the poet must journey or why or in what "city" he now finds himself, but the nature of the journey is nevertheless easily understood. The traveler is afraid, for the projected journey is fraught with danger, pain, and hunger. Moreover, this is not a journey for which one can prepare: "nothing to be bought in the last / dim shops / before the plain begins." One must simply go up those "bridges steep as hills"; there is no choice. It is the familiar allegory of pilgrimage—*nel mezzo del cammin di nostra vita.*

But the working out of this allegory involves Merwin in a certain contradiction between form and meaning. What Howard calls the "key" to the "unconditional life" is found, formally speaking, all too easily. We are told that the journey is difficult, that the beginning of the plains marks a frightening threshold, but the poem unfolds without struggle in what is a continuous narrative made up of simple declarative sentences ("I change countries"; "I recognize the first hunger") and noun phrases ("few shelves kept only by children"; "wind without flags"). Again, the sound structure is reassuring: the nicely measured end-stopped lines with their lightly stressed anapests ("and rélatives thére for the hóliday") foreground intricate patterns of sound repetition:

> in the white sky the light is flickering
> like the flight of a wing

Here we have not only end-rhyme, but internal rhyme ("white"/ "light"/"flight"), assonance of both short and long *i*'s, and alliteration of *f*'s, *l*'s, and *w*'s; the chiming recalls, say, Poe rather than Beckett. Interestingly, when Beckett does, in some of the late prose, use such sound patterns, it is for parodic effect, an effect quite unlike Merwin's solemn, low-key, evenly pitched speech. Indeed, "Beginning of the Plains" presents a progress to a goal:

> I recognize the first hunger
> as the plains start
> under my feet

The "first hunger" marks the turn: the journey, we know, has begun. Punctuated or not, Merwin's last two lines, four syllables each, seem to close the box with the click of a spring on the off-rhyme "start"/"feet."

"Beginning of the Plains" thus makes a series of statements about experience that are curiously at odds with what Howard calls "an access to prophecy" and Bloom, "the Native Strain, the American Orphic vision." Unlike Char or Beckett or Kafka, but like the three poets Bloom cites—Longfellow, MacLeish, and Wilbur (and I would add E. A. Robinson)—Merwin sets up his poems so that they press toward generalization even if the generalization to be made is only that we must recognize the nothing that is. Indeed, John Bayley, in a review of *Writings to an Unfinished Accompaniment* (1973), puts his finger on the problem when he says, referring to the book blurb which reprints the previously cited statement by Richard Howard as well as an even more extravagant one by Adrienne Rich:

> W. S. Merwin seems to me a poet of civility and civilisation, and as such a beautifully sensitive and accomplished one. What can Adrienne Rich mean by saying that he "has been working more privately, profoundly and daringly than any other American poet of my generation? . . . It was not *daring* of Gray to write "The curfew tolls the knell of parting day," though if he had written "The curfew strikes the hour of parting day," he would have failed to produce a line of good poetry. . . . Merwin's poetry, I would have thought, is of a kind not at all common today and decidedly interesting: it is the poetry of a kind of inner cultivation, requiring an audience with something of the same degree of experience and refinement, with expectations and preknowledge of what is going on.[20]

Precisely. That audience is the audience of the *New Yorker* and *Poetry*, of the *Hudson Review* and the *Yale Review*; it is this audience that has kept Merwin's poems in print, unlike almost anyone else's poems one can cite today, going through countless editions in their elegant Atheneum jackets. It is an audience that recognizes that, like Gray, Merwin almost never writes a bad line of poetry: "wind without flags," for example, conveys precisely and economically the sense of emptiness Merwin wants to depict.

Merwin's poetry, Bayley suggests, "is both extremely solitary and extremely fastidious, and yet it seems to need and call for the presence of a roomful of invisible understanders in something of the same way . . . early Augustan poetry needed the presence of that receptive coffeehouse society . . . who were alert to their manifestation of intellectual fine breeding, and concerned to be pleased with it" (p. 117). I think this is a very telling point. From the time that he won the Yale Younger Poets Award for *A Mask for Janus* in 1952 through the mid-seventies—that is to say, for a twenty-five-year span—Merwin could count on that "roomful of invisible understanders" who shared his fastidiousness, his good breeding, his elegant ways of distancing and yet bringing to mind the pain and emptiness of living in a bad time. It was an audience to whom the poet could say, as he does in "Avoiding News by the River," "Milky light flows through the branches / Fills with blood / Men will be waking," and count on their instant response to his circumspect reference to the bloodshed in Vietnam.

But viewed more dispassionately, Merwin, as Bayley puts it, "is not strong meat" (p. 117), and it was inevitable that before long the younger generation, who had been in college and hence more or less on the barricades when the Vietnam War was coming to its climax, would be less well-bred, less receptive to the measured abstractions, the careful distancing in Merwin's poetry about war and suffering and loss. Two things happened. On the one hand, for poets like Robert Pinsky and Alan Williamson, Merwin's elegance came to represent a thinly disguised evasiveness, a turning of one's back on the real world. As Turner Cassity puts it, "I know of no poems from which the apparatuses of industrial revolution have been more rigidly excluded" (p. 295). On the other hand, more experimental writers like the L-A-N-G-U-A-G-E poets of New York and San Francisco or the performance poets associated with Jerome Rothenberg's *New Wilderness Letter* are creating a decentered and playfully deconstructed universe—an undecidability—that exists on the other side of Merwin's "unduplicatable resonance."

In his recent work, Merwin seems to be trying to meet this avant-garde on its own ground: he has, for instance, written a group of poems in long, prosaic lines, whose spacing is meant to mark the pauses in natural speech in what looks superficially like David Antin's "talk poems":

Something continues and   I don't know what to call it
though the language is full of suggestions
in the way of language
                                but they are all anonymous
and it's almost your birthday   music next to my bones

Surely this is writing against the grain, the flippant tone ("though the language is full of suggestions / in the way of language") not according with the more familiar Merwin locutions of lines 8–9:

the leaks in the roof go on dripping   after the rain has passed
smell of ginger flowers   slips through the dark house

locutions that would seem more at home in his usual free-verse stanzas:

                    the leaks in the roof go on dripping
                    after the rain has passed
                    smell of ginger flowers
                    slips through the dark house.

Merwin's poetry has, in many ways, suffered at the hands of his admirers, who have championed it as a "testament of betrayals," a key prophetically unlocking the door of the present. But apocalypse has never been the métier of this fastidious poet, whose gift is perhaps less for revelation than for delicate resonance. Here is a short poem called "Dusk in Winter":

                    The sun sets in the cold without friends
                    Without reproaches after all it has done for us
                    It goes down believing in nothing
                    When it has gone I hear the stream running after it
                    It has brought its flute it is a long way
                                                        (L, 49)

Here, in the compass of five lines, Merwin deftly debunks the pathetic fallacy, the human belief that the sun either does or does not have "friends," that it might "reproach" us for "all it has done for us." All one can do, Merwin implies, is to define how it feels to watch the sun go down—its look and its sound—for the sun has no importance beyond itself or, to quote Wallace Stevens, "beyond ourselves." "When it has gone I hear the stream running after it"—here Merwin defines a commonly experienced aural illusion, an intuition that in nature all things are related. That intuition is confirmed by the last line which stands out both visually and aurally: a run-on sentence made up of ten monosyllables with a delicate echo structure of short *i*'s and *t*'s, the second clause trailing off at the line end— "long way"—thus crossing the basic iambic pentameter rhythm with anapest and spondee:

it has brought its flute it is a long way

The flute metaphor, precisely conveying the dying fall of stream and sun, reinforces this special sound effect. The poem thus ends on the carefully planned downbeat that we have come to recognize as the authentic Merwin signature. It is a signature ill at ease with phrases like "prophecy" or "negative mysticism" or "naked poetry" or "the opening of the field." As for being one of the "Barbarians inside the City Gates," surely Merwin himself knows better. As he puts it in "The Cold before the Moonrise":

> If there is a place where this is the language may
> It be my country
>
> (*L*, 46)

NOTES

1. Reprinted in Laurence Lieberman, *Unassigned Frequencies* (Urbana: University of Illinois Press, 1977), p. 257.

2. For a good overview of the difference between sixties and seventies poetry, see Stanley Plumly's two-part article, "Chapter and Verse," in *American Poetry Review*; Part 1: "Rhetoric and Emotion," 7 (Jan./Feb. 1978), 21–42; Part 2: "Image and Emblem," 7 (May/June 1978), 21–32.

3. Charles Altieri, *Enlarging the Temple* (Lewisburg, [Pa.]: Bucknell University Press, 1979), p. 19. The section on Merwin is revised in this collection as "Situating Merwin's Poetry since 1970."

4. Stephen Berg and Robert Mezey, eds., *Naked Poetry* (Indianapolis: Bobbs-Merrill Co., 1969), p. xi.

5. Richard Howard, *Alone with America: Essays on the Art of Poetry in the United States since 1950* (New York: Atheneum, 1969; enlarged ed. New York: Atheneum, 1980), p. 444. All references are to the second edition unless specified. In the first edition, Merwin gets thirty-two pages, closely followed by John Hollander (thirty-one) and James Dickey (twenty-three). Some other figures to measure against these: John Ashbery (nineteen),

Robert Creeley (nine), Allen Ginsberg (seven), Denise Levertov (thirteen), Frank O'Hara (sixteen).

6. Paul Carroll, *The Poem in Its Skin* (Chicago: Big Table, 1968), pp. 219–20.

7. Karl Malkoff, *Crowell's Handbook of Contemporary American Poetry* (New York: Thomas Y. Crowell, Co., 1973), p. 208.

8. Cary Nelson, "The Resources of Failure: W. S. Merwin's Deconstructive Career," p. 80 (revised from *Our Last First Poets* [Urbana: University of Illinois Press, 1981]).

9. Harold Bloom, *Figures of Capable Imagination* (New York: Seabury Press, 1976), pp. 124, 127.

10. Alan Williamson, "Language against Itself: The Middle Generation of Contemporary Poets," in *American Poetry since 1960: Some Critical Perspectives*, ed. Robert Shaw (Cheadle Hulme: Carcanet Press, 1973), p. 56.

11. Robert Pinsky, *The Situation of Poetry: Contemporary Poetry and Its Traditions* (Princeton: Princeton University Press, 1977), pp. 92–93.

12. Andrew Waterman, "The Illusions of Immediacy," *Times Literary Supplement*, July 29, 1977, p. 836.

13. Altieri, "Situating Merwin's Poetry," p. 172.

14. Turner Cassity, "Dresden Milkmaids: The Pitfalls of Tradition," *Parnassus*, 5 (Fall/Winter 1976), 300.

15. James Dickey, *Babel to Byzantium* (New York: Farrar, Straus and Giroux, Inc., 1968), p. 143.

16. Altieri, *Enlarging the Temple*, pp. 38–39; quoting Robert Duncan, "Towards an Open Universe," in *Poets on Poetry*, ed. Howard Nemerov (New York: Basic Books, 1966), p. 139.

17. See Nelson, "Resources of Failure," p. 90; Robert Peters, *The Great American Poetry Bake-Off* (Metuchen, N.J.: Scarecrow Press, 1979), pp. 259, 267.

18. For the Char connection, see Howard, *Alone with America*, p. 435, and cf. Altieri, *Enlarging the Temple*, p. 196: "Merwin is so disturbing in large measure because his roots are European—in poets like Rilke and Follain who have developed numerous variations on the *via negativa* as the way of enduring presence." It should be noted that Altieri's discussion of Merwin, although not published before *Enlarging the Temple* (1979), was framed, as are the other chapters in the book, prior to 1970.

19. See, for example, Harvey Gross, "The Writing on the Void: The Poetry of W. S. Merwin," *Iowa Review*, 1 (Summer 1970), 105.

20. John Bayley, "How to Be Intimate without Being Personal," *Parnassus*, 2 (Fall/Winter 1973), 116–17.

CHARLES MOLESWORTH

W. S. Merwin:
Style, Vision, Influence

Of the work Merwin has published since 1960, I would rate *The Lice* (1969) as his best poetry and *Unframed Originals* (1982) as his best prose.[1] *Unframed Originals,* one of the finest memoirs of any of the poets of his generation, may in fact be Merwin's single best book. The prose is richly evocative, mythically resonant, and yet histori-cally and sociologically precise. Merwin tells a story of family scenes and identities recast by memory and by the structures of quest-romance. Everything Merwin knows about world literature serves him as he renders justice to the dense particularity of a family his-tory poised between the ordinary world of middle-class aspirations and repossessions, and the twilight world of initiation, concealment, and destiny—perhaps the three great mythic subjects.

I would like to contrast this successful prose with a representative group of poems—the first five poems from *Writings to an Un-finished Accompaniment*—that also attempt a kind of mythic gen-eralization but without the observed detail that grounds *Unframed Originals.* The poems, I would argue, do not succeed, and they point to difficulties I have with much of Merwin's work.

The opening paragraph of *Unframed Originals* is a good place to begin, since it contains all the themes that animate Merwin's later poetry. The passage is dominated by desire and wonder, by memories of a limitless, unspecified originary realm, and finally by a sense of failed (though not completely futile) knowledge. The speaker imag-ines entering or structuring a new imaginative space, domesticating an otherwise sublime realm, and finally standing on its threshold, neither driven out nor completely welcome, sensing only that some greater strength or wisdom lies beyond his reach:

> Weathered picket fences not much bigger than my knee stood around the vegetable beds, dusty but shining, and I admired them. I would have liked to have fences like that, by the house I imagined myself living in, as I would have liked to have a boat, and a horse. I thought I might be able to make fences like that, for a garden, if I were allowed to, and if I could find the right pieces of wood somewhere. I admired the bare straight walks around the outside of the fences. It would have been hard to judge the size of the garden because the paths led through the shadows of tall bushes, and beyond the bushes, and under the trees. One path at the end disappeared among the leaves and shadows. All of that was still the garden, and I could not tell how far it went. I had never seen a garden like that. I awoke to the realization that I had not known, until then, what gardens were really like. Everything that I had heard called by that name, including the narrow bits of yard outside our kitchen window at home, with its yellow irises and its hardy asters and its one rose, fell short of this, and retreated. They were all mementos of something or apologies for something, decorations or disguises. The one I was standing in was a real garden, not a corner or a border or a circle in a lawn, or a section of something else. Where it was it was the whole place. And real things to eat grew there. I scarcely arrived there and I did not know how long I would stay, and there was nothing for me to do in that garden. The sun shone straight down into the middle of the vegetable beds and held the leaves still. It had been summer for longer than I had known. (pp. 3–4)

As a representation of a child's construction of imaginative space and order, this passage strikes me as peerless. The psychological depth and the verbal simplicity (which, of course, is extremely artful) serve each other well, redeeming the ordinariness of experience and invoking just enough mythic overtones—the garden, the path, the "ordered" sun—to enlarge the metaphoric vehicles so that the personal and cosmological tenors are equated. Innocence has rarely been more knowingly represented, nor have origins often been at once this personal and this immemorial.

The next chapter in *Unframed Originals*, "Mary," also shows Merwin at his best in integrating originary experiences, which seem to have a mythic quality, with the axiological and characterological fixities that dominate a child's imagination. He says of his father's cousin, Mary, that "Naturally she could not be told anything." There is considerable tension in this simple diction, since throughout the book the child accepts what is presented as natural and inevitable, and thus as having a cosmic force, yet locates the source of the inevitability in workaday situations and ordinary family relations. (Merwin seems to be exploring the space between "ordinary" and "ordering.") Enough sociological details are given to convey the culture and ethos of late nineteenth- and early twentieth-century Presbyterian culture in northeastern America. These details then lead to a "mythic" revelation or concealment. Mary bears comparison with Dante Riordan in Joyce's *Portrait of the Artist*, especially in the casual and yet forceful impact she has on the child's sense of values and truths. Here is a paragraph where we can see part of this complex structuring and transformation, as Mary is shown performing a set of motherly functions and redraws the boy's understanding of intimacy and propriety:

> Some meaning of the word "naphtha" was inexplicably hers, and echoed the smell of her damp apron that reached below her knees, and of the duster on her head, and of her hands, long shapeless and rough, running from gray to orange. With those hands she tugged my clothes onto me and fastened them up, right or wrong, or pulled them off. Whatever she touched was the wrong size. When I was left with her and she gave me a bath, from the moment it was announced, it felt like a mistake that nobody within hearing could do anything about. The water was sure to be either too hot or too cold, and she could not hear what was said about it, nor hear it running when it should have stopped. The sound kept on. She looked crosser than when she was washing other things. The heavy hands gripped and rubbed and remained strangers. Washcloth into ears. Years later when it was my sister's turn she said Mary hurt. I had felt that, and had never got used to it, and yet the words startled me and did not sound right. I knew, as one knows a fact, that Mary had never been a child. She had always been exactly the same. Naturally she could not be told anything. There were things that were true in themselves that were not true when it came to her. (pp. 60–61)

Even in the small detail of "She looked crosser than when she was washing other things" we feel the spinster's fear of the body, her Protestant urge to chastise it and purify it at the same time. With the word "naphtha," a prominent laundry soap before detergents, the atmosphere of historical detail shades into an imaginative equation of clean clothes, clean bodies, and clean minds. The child's body is being objectified—almost treated like laundry—while at the same time a subjective dimension is opened into the habits and personality of another person. Under this pressure, words like "always," "never," and "naturally" combine a childlike innocence with an unquestioning adult solidity to produce a whole cosmogony of sensibility.

But the motifs here that recur frequently in Merwin's poetry are what interest me at the moment. I would name two and argue that they become the two major themes of Merwin's work. They are (1) a tendency toward a kind of rarified, second-degree allegory, which I will call the allegory allegorized, and (2) the disembodiment of the narrative agent, who is often like a figure from a quest myth. These two themes are closely linked and at times the distinctions between them are blurred by the intense, exploratory quality of Merwin's work and by the meditative mode that dominates his sensibility. This meditativeness underlies the verbs that open the quoted passage ("I admired," "I would have liked," "I imagined," "I thought I might be able") and it is poised between knowledge and action, between self-knowledge and self-concealment, between physical completion and disembodiment.

By the allegory allegorized I mean Merwin's use of a parablelike narrative in which plot and incident overshadow character and local color to suggest a philosophical or psychological truth that implicitly escapes all formulations, either discursive or narrative. Using allegory in the strict sense of saying one thing and meaning another, we can see this theme as Merwin's way of holding out some tale or incident as the trace of a profound truth to which it points, and then withdrawing the truth itself and pointing back instead to the narrative as the only available (yet insufficient) formulation. The tale allegorizes the truth, but the truth turns out to be a secret which can only be read as concealing something else, an allegory without an interpretable center. This theme can be epitomized by the sentence in the first paragraph quoted above that begins "I awoke to the realization that I had not known." Many of Merwin's poems lead up to a moment of realization that knowledge is something other than what the speaker had been searching for. In some of the poems, usually the clearest and to me the most central work of Merwin's canon, this diegesis, this leading up to and through an incident or string of incidents, is itself the central focus of the poem. It is at that point that a second degree allegory intervenes. The locus classicus of this gesture is the ending of "Air," the often-anthologized poem from *The Moving Target*, where remembering and forgetting cancel each other out, as do youth and age, wisdom and experience, and we're left with this revelation:

> This must be what I wanted to be doing,
> Walking at night between the two deserts,
> Singing.
>
> (*MT*, 50)

The irony of "must" here can be read in two ways, either as a concession to determinism and an acceptance of fate, or as a claim to complete autonomy. In either case the last word is virtually toneless; the singing is a form of whistling in the dark, a kind of self-concealed solipsistic indulgence. If we identify the singing with all the forms of lyric statement, then the poem says that poetry is either (or both) a song to one's self or the only sustaining cosmological force. What the poem offers is less a revelation than the suggestion that any revelation will prove hollow and the reverse of what we were seeking. But the response to this suggestion must be continued singing, or rather seeking revelation through lyric means.

"Air" ends with a participle, "singing," one that conveys an affirmation of the value of process over completion. At the same time the narrative diegesis apparently is resolved ("This *must* be . . ."), yet the only "answer" is yet more singing, more searching. The formulation of a goal in words serves to embody and disembody the consciousness of the questioner; as in "I awoke to the realization that I had not known," something is posited and dissolved at the same time. Such language problems put enormous pressure on Merwin's signifiers. He must pare down his language so as to drive further into the significance that lies behind every tale; yet the verbal compression also suggests a guilt at the inability to get even the simplest formulation to yield meaning. Merwin seems to love language and story-telling as much as he mistrusts it; if only he could use words to get past words, yet what but words could convey so appropriately our fallenness, our condemned pursuit of that toward which all the signs point? The failure of words to say all, yet their beauty (especially when they are self-denying) at showing what is lost: this is what the allegorized allegory embodies, as it encodes the secret knowledge that only further secrecy can be revealed.

In paring down language out of ascetic purity or guilt, Merwin writes allegories about the act of writing. The one-line "Elegy" reads: "Who would I show it to." The threat implied here is that any formulation or display in language betrays the truth of feeling, since the ideal listener is absent or already fully possessed of the meaning. Most of Merwin's poems about language, such as "Words" and "The Unwritten" (*WA*, 61 and 40), show that the struggle to write poems is endemic to language's fullness and its emptiness. When he says in "Provision" (*L*, 55) "What you do not have you find everywhere," we can either hear a claim that satisfaction is omnipresent or that desire is; the world answers to our needs, but only by shaping itself to mirror them or becoming their very gound. Even when he apparently means to be self-assuring, Merwin's words drift toward an always dispersed, always escaping meaning:

> There is nothing the matter with speech
> Just because it lent itself
> To my uses

> Of course there is nothing the matter with the stars
> It is my emptiness among them
> While they drift farther away in the invisible morning
>
> (*L*, 61)

The emptiness of the desiring speaker reflects back ironically on the reassurance about speech and undercuts it, and such emptiness colors all the poetry. The words in the poems are so colorless, as invisible as they are, because, like the sun hiding the stars, there is either too much light or no fixed realm of darkness against which we can always see meaning. We read back from Merwin's ascetic language to a consciousness that has either faced the demon of silence and drift or chosen to embody it. All the stories of the poems, all the allegorizing fables, achieve a kind of exhaustion and fullness by pointing on to some yet greater emptiness. This greater emptiness makes meaning possible, not by positing truth but by always suggesting the promise of it. Merwin continually slides his signified along a track that is always connected to, but just beyond any clear connection with, his signifiers.

Merwin's abstract allegories often end in the mood of the negative sublime. Typically, a natural power appears to coalesce into some overpowering force or presence, but instead the presence is felt most forcefully as absence or lack, and the saving distance of the true sublime is experienced as a swallowing abyss. In Kant's dynamic sublime, the proximate fearsomeness of nature precedes the moment of aesthetic insight, and then by knowing we are at a distance from such power, we experience sublime feelings. We know we can be overwhelmed by nature's power, and yet through our independence from nature we know we are safe from such power. Merwin inverts, or subverts, this dynamic stasis. In the quotation about the garden, notice how the "real garden" replaces the earlier versions of garden and thus becomes a version of the sublime: "Where it was it was the whole place." But this sudden fullness, this extensive power that outstrips comprehension ("It had been summer for longer than I had known"), though it confers a sense of reality and centeredness on the speaker, nevertheless leaves him incapacitated: "there was nothing for me to do in that garden." In "The Last One," from *The Lice*, the assumption that everything can be turned to use and made over into a human possession is slowly defeated by the persistence of the "shadow," which becomes a version of the absence that frustrates all human industry and intention. The ending of the poem relocates the shadow in those who would try to dominate or destroy it:

> It swallowed their shadows.
> Then it swallowed them too and they vanished.
> Well the others ran.
>
> The ones that were left went away to live if it would let them.
> They went as far as they could.
> The lucky ones with their shadows.
>
> (*L*, 12)

The diegetic resolution of the search for control or meaning leads back to the searchers themselves, and so what the "shadow" means is not to be located anywhere in the world, but only in the people who seek the meaning. The diegetic unfolding always loops back to a lyric stasis, rather than an achieved ecstasy or an entrance to some transcendence. Merwin is almost a Mallarméan poet, but in ways that are more psychological than linguistic. The Merwinian speaker, who is doing what he "must be doing," and the people he describes who "went as far as they could," are operating at the limits of endurance and comprehension. These limits seem all that are available in a world of deserts and shadows, and the singing we hear is at most a lyric murmur, a slight lilt just beyond the borders of despair and impotence.

The second extensive theme in Merwin's work is what I have called the disembodiment of the narrative agent. Disembodiment usually occurs figuratively, or as an impulse toward a disembodied state, because the seeker finds the world irremediably fallen, so that to be entangled in materiality is synonymous with evil. This impulse also occurs as a solution to a certain kind of blocked quest. Disembodiment allows the poet to suffer the pain of separation required of all questers and at the same time to gain access to a transcendent meaning open only to the spirit. This mediation occurs concisely in "Words" (WA, 61), which can be read as Merwin's version of Frost's famous epigram, "Fire and Ice." Here is the poem:

> When the pain of the world finds words
> they sound like joy
> and often we follow them
> with our feet of earth
> and learn them by heart
> but when the joy of the world finds words
> they are painful
> and often we turn away
> with our hands of water

The hands of water are a way of not grasping the joy of the world while at the same time capturing the desire to hold and fondle it. This poem can be read as Merwin's poetic, a poetic that inevitably turns one emotion into its opposite and then is left with only absence to celebrate. "The Unwritten" (WA, 40) begins with a conceit of the "words that have never been written" crouched inside the speaker's pencil. The unwritten words, which apparently express the realm of desire and knowledge that is "dark in the dark," are shown as having the potential to be bodied forth. But even then the words would be "hiding in the air," so "multitudes in days to come may walk through them / breathe them / be none the wiser." The revelation would be a concealment, the presence of the words still a form of disembodiment no more capable of seizing the world than are the "hands of water." "Hands of water" presents a consciousness that regards the body as necessary but insufficient.

In the opening paragraph of *Unframed Originals,* the child's earlier sense of yard and flowers falls short of the demanding and yet unobtainable archetypal image of the garden. Now that the replacement has occurred the earlier "bits" are "all mementos of something or apologies for something, decorations or disguises." The last two possibilities—decoration or disguise—look to cover up a bodily identity that is insufficient or a source of guilt. To decorate or disguise is to disembody by creating a bodily image that renders the primary body invisible. A like sort of disembodiment (through concentration on that which is beyond and yet attached to the body) occurs in the sentences "It would have been hard to judge the size of the garden because the paths led through the shadows of tall bushes, and beyond the bushes, and under the trees. . . . All of that was still the garden, and I could not tell how far it went." Physical identity is at once the way beyond itself and the impediment that prevents transcendence.

My difficulties with this aesthetic become clear in the context of the first five poems in *Writings to an Unfinished Accompaniment,* which form a sort of untitled suite best read as a self-contained and self-glossing set of texts. The group begins with an indefinite future vista ("years from now") and ends with a prehistoric past that stretches back before biological evolution ("Before the first cell / the sands"). These immense frames of time support a world of present human activity that is haunted by memories and transfixed by hope. All human projects are seen through a lens of oblivion or transcendence that renders details insignificant and turns hope into something furtive and numbing. Summer dominates the first three poems, and the last two are versions of a mythic landscape. But the season of summer is less a calendric or celestial period than it is the mythic idea of Summer, with its emphasis on fullness and momentary stasis. The poems form a matrix of mythic time and space, a small creation myth in which order emerges from emptiness and temporal sequence arises out of an immemorial sense of time. Ironically, however, the fullness of Summer's time becomes a sort of emptiness and the material space of a structured world is seen as erosive and dispersive.

The poem contrasts the alienation of the human with the purposiveness of the animal realm:

> Years from now
> someone will come upon a layer of birds
> and not know what he is listening for
>
> these are days
> when the beetles hurry through dry grass
> hiding pieces of light they have stolen
>   (WA, 3)

The human future lacks certainty, comprehension, or self-knowledge. Only the beetles are capable of some providence, however furtive and fragmentary. The second poem suggests that the human developed out of the material and will follow a predetermined devolution back to a merely geologic existence: "all the stones have been us / and will be again." This stonelike human origin and goal produces a nonknowledge, a form of blindness that is either the product of too much seeing or the culmination of growth at a point just beyond fullness.

> . . . remember waking with no face
> knowing that it was summer
> still
> when the witnesses
> day after day are blinded
> so that they will forget nothing
>   (WA, 4)

The source of vision is intense deprivation; the fullness of light entails a loss of the self.

The third poem presents an image of summer fullness as familiar and comforting: "High above us a chain of white buckets / full of old light going home." This echoes the beetles with their stolen "pieces of light," though here the light is above us and returning to its source and (presumably) away from us. The poem ends with a feeling of alienation, a sense of altered identity that lacks the restorative return of the light:

> now even the things that we do
> reach us after long journeys
> and we have changed
>   (WA, 5)

The quest-journey here is like the action of memory, the return of awareness after temporal separation, but without memory's sense of restoration, since our having become different means the return is more disruptive than integrative. Our disembodiment-as-stones and our search-and-finding that reveals only ignorance or lack enunciate the themes I mentioned earlier.

The two poems shift from predominately temporal images to spatial ones, though all five poems allude to a spatio-temporal matrix. In "The Distances" the empty desertlike sense of multidirectionality becomes a sign of our immortality, as the distances are described as

>   setting out from us
>   all of them setting out
>   from us
>   and none dies and none is forgotten
>   (WA, 6)

These imagined quests seem to be a source of fulfillment, since they continue to live and be remembered, as if the mythic template sustains and is kept alive by its many instances and the limitless desire from which it springs. But such a hopeful formulation is undercut by the poem's concluding image, and we get only unfulfilled longing and awkward positioning in the world's order:

>   and all over the world there are dams
>   lying on their backs
>   thinking of the sea

Though the poem seems to begin with felt absences turned to a form of achievement, it ends with a sense of impropriety and foolish longing. We are as unhoused by our desires as we are sustained by a mythic order which seeks to focus and preserve desire. The final poem equates the erosion of rocks with human suffering and sees the rocks returning to sand as an image of nihilistic obliteration. We can hear echoes of Shelley's "Ozymandias" in the poem's final im-

age, but we can also see a return, through pain and suffering, to a
prebiological order:

> Oh we have moved forward in pain
>
> what has broken off every rock
>
> have they each suffered
> each time
> wanting to stay
> have they not
>
> Before the first cell
> the sands
>
> (WA, 71)

The five poems are united by the metaphors of humans as stones,
light as fulfillment, and longing as journey, and these metaphors articulate an implicit myth. This myth claims that fulfillment imagined as summer is virtually the same as desolation figured as sand.
The mythic time of summer and the mythic space of a desert are
both full and empty; we are most ourselves when time stands still
and light floods our sight, revealing yet blinding. Our allegories always point somewhere else, and our bodies are always to be escaped.

Merwin's style is in many ways consonant with his vision, and in
saying this I mean to suggest that he is a highly successful writer.
Indeed, if you accept the apparent possession of an achieved style as
one of the hallmarks of literary excellence, then you will likely
value W. S. Merwin very highly among his contemporaries. But I feel
he has trapped himself in a mythic and psychological cul-de-sac
which makes his language increasingly flavorless, like the exhaustion of an irony that has hung on too long. His vision has some affinities with Beckett's, and his language has similar barrenness. But
Beckett's dramaturgy, his sense of scene and narrative, give his minimalist language a richness that is further strengthened by an irreducible lyricism lurking beneath the corrosive irony. And Beckett, of
course, is funny. His comic vision humanizes his tragedy. But Merwin's mythography doesn't fully realize just what Beckett's dramaturgy provides: a sense of an audience, a dialogue, even a dialectic,
between despair and renewal, comedy and tragedy. Merwin asks too
much of the lyric poem since he asks it to perform many of the functions of myth but without an anthropological love of detail and

locale, and without the obsessive sense of release and containment we associate with ritual. His special sense of irony leaves Merwin with a tonelessness in his language whereby phrases like "dams / lying on their backs" and "beetles . . . hiding pieces of light" are forced to convey nearly awesome mythic and emotional significance and yet often sound cute or precious. Themes such as disembodiment and the allegory allegorized require considerable innocence in order to be fully sincere, but not a childlike innocence.

Merwin's vision has real force and seriousness and even redemptive humanistic depth, but all too often his language is placeless, "unstapled" from the page, and unhoused anywhere except in a myth for which no one knows the ritual.[2] The risks of this tendency, which I believe seriously damages poems like those I analyzed from *Writings to an Unfinished Accompaniment*, are most apparent in the prose-poems of *The Miner's Pale Children* (1970) and *Houses and Travellers* (1977), where literary and mythical motifs abound but real experience is mostly absent.[3] This sort of blandly universalized narrative, with its faint surreal atmosphere and its parable structure, derives from the literary adaptation of myth begun after Frazer's *Golden Bough* and urged on by Eliot's "Ulysses, Order, and Myth." In verse forms or prose-poetry, its diverse practitioners are Russell Edon, Charles Simic, Gregory Orr, Mark Strand, William Matthews, and many others. Merwin's range of literary and mythic reference is broader and generally more subtle than these younger poets, and his melodies and his ear are often more sweetly tuned than theirs, but the project remains etiolated. I can honor the sensibility portrayed in Merwin's poetry and respect his moral and artistic integrity, but his most abstractly allegorized poems and prose are for me an aesthetic dead end.

NOTES

1. This essay was written with the generous support of a grant from the Rockefeller Foundation Humanities Program.

2. Alan Williamson has spoken of Merwin's "mistrust" of language, a mistrust he shares with other poets of his generation. Read under this rubric, Merwin's poetry can seem heroically spare and ethically stringent, and might even warrant comparison with, say, Benn or Celan. I find such a reading cogent but unconvincing, again because of such images as "beetles . . . hiding pieces of light," which strike me as neither spare nor visualizable

nor authentically expressive. Such images reveal the weakness of Merwin's rhetoric. The notion of "unstapling" the poem occurs as Merwin discusses punctuation (Ed Folsom and Cary Nelson, "'Fact Has Two Faces': An Interview with W. S. Merwin," *Iowa Review*, 13 [Winter 1982], 62), but he goes on to speak of the poem having "a sense of integrity and liberation that it did not have before." The passage is of great importance for Merwin's attempt to describe the origin of what he calls a set of "new rules" for lyric poetry.

3. I reviewed *Houses and Travellers* (*Georgia Review*, 32 [Fall 1978], 683–87) and will not repeat my strictures here, except to say that separating genuine myth from etiolated stereotypes remains one of the most difficult but important critical challenges. Glib manipulation of "mythy" motifs and images has become one of the mainstays of the rhetoric of contemporary lyric and will probably seem as false to later readers as Victorian moral uplift seems to us.

CHARLES ALTIERI

Situating Merwin's Poetry since 1970

W. S. Merwin's poetry since *The Moving Target* is not easy to assess. It certainly carries to an extreme the versions of Romanticism basic to deep image poetics, thus inviting criticisms like those of Robert Pinsky and James Atlas. For these defenders of civilization, Merwin's pursuit of vague resonance in silence and his obviously reductive vocabulary abandon the region of precise thinking and reduce human life to poetic sighs and warm emotions.[1] Such criticisms, however, ironically ignore Merwin's extremities. They apply perfectly to, say, the domesticated romanticism of William Stafford and his epigoni, but they do not address the extreme self-consciousness and careful staging by which Merwin asks us to reflect on his attitude before we subsume it under styles he is careful to reject. This many critics have seen. In fact Merwin has drawn more good criticism than most poets of his generation because many of us need alternatives to the models of mature discrimination projected by Atlas and Pinsky as poetry's resting place in its dotage. But then another danger emerges which threatens all sympathetic accounts of Romantic writers. Critics want to convince those with classical values, so they labor to place the poet within thematic terms that demonstrate how the poet in fact addresses perennial problems and has important things to say. Yet this too tends to underplay the extremes the poems insist on.

Domesticating Merwin is not simply a critic's problem. In *The Compass Flower* and *Finding the Islands* Merwin has domesticated himself, to almost universal dissatisfaction. As critics, however, we cannot be content simply with registering our reasons for our negative reaction. Ideally we should be able to construct a model which

159

derives the weakness from the strength. If we capture the distinctive force of his best poems—in themselves and, above all, as features of a dialectic (or, for the less pretentious, a conversation within his poetic career) we might also see how the achievements themselves motivate the more conventional romantic mode of his most recent work. I want to show here that neither the thematic nor the deconstructionist stance will take us far enough in relation to these questions.[2] Instead we need to attempt what I call a process of situating the poetry. Situating requires two basic critical acts. First we must create a context for the poems through which we can try to understand the probable intentions as serious and intelligent responses to representative human problems. Then we must show how the poem carries the motives so as to in fact exemplify qualities which become plausible or compelling possible responses to the problem. Here the critic must borrow from Heidegger the idea of treating poems literally as sites, as places where themes are carried in acts of mind and acts of mind introduce us to spaces where the imagination can explore new ways of recognizing and coming to terms with its basic demands. Merwin matters as a poet because he was the first American poet since Stevens, Eliot, and perhaps Roethke, to create a convincing space of reflection where the demands and powers of the imagination could not be absorbed within the same logic of description and feeling we might find in a radio call-in hour to a psychologist. Merwin's best work makes us think about how we can think and where we must place our sensibilities in order to align ourselves with what may be our deepest energies. Thematic analysis only gives us the content of thoughts, not the challenge and possible values offered by a stance and sequence of thinking. Emphasis on deconstructive energies, in contrast, preserves the importance of dramatic examples, but renounces the hope of anything more than a set of negative values on which to base its account of motives. One might say that a full situating of Merwin's poetry would explain both temptations—to theme and to deconstruction—as aspects of a struggle within the poetic thinking. Then it would show how the qualities of the thinking allow partial resolutions of the conflict. But the language of resolution must be tentative indeed, if not deconstructive, in order to account for the strange entrapment within positive values which so deadens Merwin's most recent poetry.

I propose to pursue my somewhat grandiose (Romantic) goals by concentrating on a single quest basic to the creation of the style of *The Moving Target* and then to the experiments which follow in the next two volumes. (How else defend Romanticism but by quest metaphors?) Lemuel states the key terms early in *The Moving Target:* "What do I have that is my own. . . . what is essential to me" that can "sustain me for my time in the desert" (*MT*, 8). Merwin goes on to give one of the best poetic maps of this desert I know by exploring the many forms of "Division, mother of pain" (*MT*, 53). For he makes disorientation and the gulf between what appears as self and what denies that appearance by its cries of need the central condition of his style. We must learn to dwell in an imaginative site where it is rewarding to ask whether this impersonal voice can be in fact mine, what it means to find identity where all the signs of my identity are lacking, and what one can encounter in those regions of the mind where the allegorical intelligence merges its logic with the surreal language of the unconscious. Such questions lead Merwin to structure *The Lice* and *The Carrier of Ladders* in terms of unresolveable tensions between two poles—one a renewed sense of a transpersonal presence released by the imagination's unmasking of traditional lyrical stances and the other an image of negation itself as the only undivided plenitude. After *The Carrier of Ladders* Merwin's stances almost reverse themselves, in what I take to be a paralyzing way. The activity of negation comes to appear in fact only an increasingly gimmicky rhetoric, so that the pursuit of absence turns on obvious manipulative devices which become all too present as the source of poetic effects. When the desire for poetic acts of mind, or poems becoming literal experiences, seems so contaminated by the rhetoric constructing them, Merwin tries to turn to a poetry of personal speech. But that model only reinforces his increasingly quiescent sense of presence, so that he loses much of the tension and strangeness of *The Lice* to become perhaps the gentle uncle of surrealist poetics.

I

In our traditions, with the controversial exception of the late Eliot, whom Merwin often echoes, selfhood is an affair of presence. One can feel himself integral when, like Robert Creeley, he achieves harmony with the concrete place where he stands and with the desires and objects also occupying or impinging on that place. The dream is

Whitman's though its manifestations vary: if one can gather and praise all that touches his consciousness in a given moment—either by a particularizing catalogue or through some symbolic or mythical field, he has overcome division and found at least a momentary home. For Merwin, however, the gross particulars usually mock any potential sense of essential reality. They are doomed to pass away and change, as are the moods and feelings they generate. This illusory present is more insubstantial than the darkness or painful sense of absence it replaces. Moreover, the language one uses to fix those particulars, or even to comfort oneself by lamenting their passing, eventually mocks him with its inadequacies and its absences ("My words are the garment of what I shall never be / Like the tucked sleeve of a one-armed boy" [L, 62]).

"The Cold before the Moonrise" marks the distance from any sense of a particular home which instigates Merwin's quest:

> It is too simple to turn to the sound
> Of frost stirring among its
> Stars like an animal asleep
> In the winter night
> And say I was born far from home
> If there is a place where this is the language may
> It be my country
>
> (L, 46)

The poem doesn't even consider the possibility of being at one with the natural scene (in part because the title indicates the constant pressure of change). It seeks instead, as the only possible harmony, a language capable of expressing his grief and division. But one cannot live in so simple a language, for language is as distant from him as he is from the particulars of the scene. Language will not allow us the consolation of defining absence in a specific form and therefore of controlling it. Instead self-consciousness about language only doubles the initial loss. We are as alienated from the gulf we would name as we are from the home we would possess. We have only traces of what drives us to the forms of expression it frustrates.

Now we face Merwin's version of what we might call the Beckett dilemma: to speak is absurd when all language must fail, but not to speak is to give way to a theatrical despair which in fact cheapens and misrepresents our condition by giving the illusion that there is a satisfying role we can play and that we have the power to play it. All we can do is keep circling the dilemma and listening to what we make of it and as it: "Absolute despair has no art. I imagine the writing of a poem, in whatever mode, still betrays the existence of hope, which is why poetry is more and more chary of the conscious mind, in our age. And what the poem manages to find hope for may be part of what it keeps trying to say" ("Notes", 272). As Charles Olson suggested, we must find out what lies on the other side of despair, if only—as Olson was too optimistic to add—because our names for despair place us already outside it. Merwin's best poems usually begin in this dilemma. If our typical despairing postures will not account for our art, what deeper, more enduring relations between humans and their world might an imagination reveal that scrutinized the condition. All the strategies of negation will be necessary if one is to keep attention focused on our metaphysical plight yet avoid any covertly self-congratulatory roles or submission to discrete particulars. Merwin is his own best critic on the shape his career must take once he has cast off his *Drunk in the Furnace:* "The focusing on one place in that way was deliberate, and it led me to see how limited the possibilities of that were, for me, then. Something else would be needed."[3] The poet can watch his own watching, so he in effect makes all the strategies of distancing both an end and a means. Only in a continual sense of departure is there any hope of discovering a home.

II

Merwin's basic form of distancing is the traditional *via negativa.* If negation is ever to transcend itself, plenitude must be approached "backwards." By defamiliarizing the senses we have not social truths but a stillness in which all our acts participate:

First you must know that the whole of the physical world floats in each of the senses at the same time. Each of them reveals to us a different aspect of the kingdom of change. But none of them reveals the unnameable stillness that unites them. At the heart of change it lies unseeing, unhearing, unfeeling, unchanging, holding within itself the beginning and the end. It is ours. It is our only possession. Yet we cannot take it into our hands, which change, nor see it with our eyes, which change. . . . None of the senses can come to it. Except backwards. . . .

Somewhere on the other side of that a voice is coming. We are
the voice. But we are each of those others. Yet the voice is
coming to us. That is what we are doing here. It has to pass
through us in order to reach us. It has to go through us without
pausing in order to be clear to us. Only in the senses can we
pause because only in the senses can we move. The stillness is
not in the senses but through them and the voice must come
through the stillness. Each in turn we must become transparent.
(*MPC*, 56–57)

In *The Moving Target*, Merwin spends the first two-thirds of the
volume carefully mapping the varieties of division before presenting
his more radical mystical projections. Roughly the first third elabo-
rates the premises driving Lemuel to his desperate quest for es-
sences. Lemuel is a marvelous example of Kenneth Burke's scene-act
ratio. Reduced by his social setting to the identity of a dog, he
can only state the essence he dreams of in terms already perverted.
His Stevensian capable hero is the wolf, the strongest form of self-
defining spirit he can imagine. Other speakers in the volume are
deprived even of this concreteness. Surrounding this poem are numerous others dramatizing alienated selves: "Home for Thanksgiving," for example, expresses a selfhood so tenuous it can be preserved only by sewing "himself in like money" and avoiding all
contact with human beings. Others like "Sire," "The Nails," and
"Acclimatization" render a condition of absence from the essential
self so profound it makes even problematic selfhood seem almost a
luxury. In "The Nails" the speaker seeks a central self he can offer in
love, but the refrain "it isn't as simple as that" renders an oppressive
self-reflexiveness, only euphemistically called *self*-consciousness.
"Alone like a key in a lock / Without what it takes to turn," the
lover cannot respond to the necessities of the moment:

> Winter will think back to your lit harvest
> For which there is no help, and the seed
> Of eloquence will open its wings
> When you are gone.
> But at this moment
> When the nails are kissing the fingers good-bye
> and my only
> Chance is bleeding from me,

> When my one chance is bleeding,
> For speaking either truth or comfort
> I have no more tongue than a wound.
>
> (*MT*, 19)

If he had no mouth, he would have no desire to speak and he would be free; there would be no nagging absence trying to complete the moment. But instead there remains a sense of potential which intensifies the unfulfilled desire. For a man, having a mouth implies having something to say, but that logic only metamorphoses the mouth into a wound—paradoxically deepened by its desire to be healed.

The second third of the volume turns in the opposite direction. If the voyage within produces only increasingly oppressive absences, the only hope to find what is essential lies outside the self, in contact with a vital present. However, the speakers usually cannot break through the categories of their own psyches to make contact with the fluctuating present. Division becomes a problem of knowledge, not of action as it had been in the first poems. We can remember "another time / When our hands met and the clocks struck / And we lived on the point of a needle, like angels" (*MT*, 34), but now we find it impossible even to remember what we knew, we are so far from "the days":

> It's the old story,
> Every morning something different is real.
> This place is no more than the nephew of itself,
> With these cats, this traffic, these
> Departures
> To which I have kept returning,
> Having tasted the apple of my eye,
> Saying perennially
> Here it is, the one and only,
> The beginning and the end.
> This time the dials have come with the hands and
> Suddenly I was never here before.
> Oh dust, oh dust, progress
> Is being made
>
> *MT*, 43)

We are the objects, not the subjects of progress, and are perplexed by Eliot's memory and desire:

> Coming late, as always,
> I try to remember what I almost heard.
> The light avoids my eye.
>
> How many times have I heard the locks close
> And the lark take the keys
> And hang them in heaven.
>
> (MT, 41)

The speaker "almost" hears what he desires. Its proximity makes him act. Yet he actually hears only symbolic reminders that what he desires remains absent from him. The speaker is tempted by the potential in the moment as another speaker was by having a tongue, but he fares no better. He ends up only with another wound, a fictive unknowable heaven which continues to generate desire ("how many times") but not to satisfy it. He is doomed to the shadowy absences created by fictive images—blocked by his own being (his faulty eye) from the fullness of "the light." "More and more / I get like shadows; I find out / how they hate" (MT, 37).

In that hatred, however, the shadow plays an important dialectical role—defining the quality of the light and the forms of relationship light has to the landscape and enabling Merwin's first efforts to make negation a vehicle of presence. Because its existence depends on an object which stands between it and the source of the light, the shadow testifies to the presence of a true source, even if it is condemned never to participate directly in that presence. And shadows create contrasts which make dramatically evident the many variations the light takes in its encounters with the landcape. Without shadow, or analogically without consciousness, there would be only a single unqualified and unappreciated mode of being. In addition, the shadow, like Snyder's mirror, offers us a backward transparent image of our own place within and without natural experience, thus offering one version of "unnameable stillness." By trying to inhabit one's own shadow one might dwell within what continually evades our representations. Shadow is the embodiment in landscape of the "suspended regard"—a function performed in the mind by memory and silence.

Memory, then, will play a crucial role in helping us glimpse that heaven where the keys are hidden. Memory is not captive within the present; in fact, as Augustine insists in his meditation on memory in the tenth book of the *Confessions,* it exists nowhere. Yet memory allows us to call from the present what matters, what has an essential relation to the self—who also exists nowhere yet is manifest as a desire for coherence and recurrence. Memory enters Merwin's world to bridge the gap so often evoked in the I/eye pun. The I is divided because it cannot trust the eye which links us to the world of process and the world of process is unknowable because the I's consciousness distorts what the eye sees. Memory preserves what recurs and hence seems important to both eye and I. Moreover, memory is impersonal, not only because it occupies no place but more importantly because in many ways it follows its own laws and does not serve the will. It is perhaps governed by the eye as much as by the I, and perhaps governed beyond them by a single power. Finally, memory is impersonal because like the shadow it is both particular and abstract: as a shadow changes form yet remains essentially the same when the direction of light changes, the memory recalls particular images, yet seems also to leave traces of basic recurrent patterns in its operation. (In another vocabulary, the memory is the place of the unconscious.) For Merwin, as for St. Augustine, memory is a vital key to "the singing beyond" (*MT,* 64) since it allows us access to a realm of being where the limited self and the contingent present merge into the grander transpersonal union:

> In this passage, and in much of Follain's prose, as well as in his poems, the regard is suspended, whether deliberately or helplessly and the complexity of its circumstance as the bearer of memory is clear. Who is the "I" who is thinking those exact things about the puddles and the shadows; and who recognizes that the shutter fastenings in the shape of busts of little people were wearing Renaissance feather bonnets? Is it the child of eleven or so, or the man who left when the war was over and has gone to Paris and the legal profession and the literary world? It is more than both: it is the suspended regard which they share; and the evocation of this "impersonal," receptive, but essentially unchanging gaze often occupies, in Follain's work, the place of the first person.
>
> It does so because memory has a special role in his writing. It is not simply a link between past and present, life and poetry. Memory, as distinct from the past it draws on, is what makes the past a key to the mystery that stays with us and does not change: the present.

Follain is deeply concerned with the mystery of the present—
the mystery which gives the recalled concrete details their form,
at once luminous and removed, when they are seen at last in
their places, as they seem to be in the best of his poems. This is
their value "in themselves." At the same time it is what gives
them the authority of parts of a rite, of an unchanging ceremony
heralding some inexorable splendor, over a ground of silence.
And for Jean Follain it is a fulfillment not only of a need for ceremony but of a fondness for the ceremonies, in which each detail, seen as itself, is an evocation of the processions of an immeasurable continuum.

And both the passage of time and the sense of the unchanging
show the details to be unique. Follain never regarded them otherwise—that is the child whom he did not betray.[4]

Merwin's analysis of Jean Follain might serve as the best description we have of Merwin's own sense of value. Memory is evoked in
the "suspended regard" whereby the impersonal occupies the place
of the I/eye, and in turn memory brings to the horizon of the present
a ground of silence or shadow that both allows particulars to stand
out and encloses them in a sense of "the immeasurable continuum"
which endures. "Daybreak" concludes *The Moving Target* with a
sense of what Merwin can "find hope for" by dramatizing just such a
perspective:

> Again this procession of the speechless
> Bringing me their words
> The future woke me with its silence
> I join the procession
> An open doorway
> Speaks for me
> Again
>
> (*MT*, 97)

The particulars here emerge only indirectly, since the poem takes
place within a consciousness reflecting on a scene. It might be the
last stanza of a meditative Romantic lyric. Merwin is deliberately
making the reader come to realize that the speechless bring words,
for as we try to fill out the poem and imagine how daybreak might
justify claims that it is a "procession" and an "open doorway," we
find ourselves recreating the scene from memory and working our

way out of the poem's reflective distance from what it describes. In effect, we are asked to fill the empty space created by a poem which itself offers a displaced consciousness. From that absence (both thematic and, in the reader, psychological) we come gradually to recognize a set of enduring relationships. Daybreak is a threshold moment where conflicting forces are tenuously balanced and where all the natural elements have important psychological and symbolic analogues. Here pale, bare, and almost absent light (seeming to appear without a source for the sun is not yet visible) reveals most clearly its dependence on darkness. The departing darkness literally creates the stark "procession" ritual in which the details of the present gradually become separate and emerge into their separate beings. But at daybreak, the particulars seem less individuals than part of the single pale light whereby the "silence" of the future retains its mystery and yet seems to call the speaker forth into its still plenitude. This union of speech and silence provides the analogue in consciousness to the merger of light and darkness; it makes possible one's "singing" "between the two deserts" (*MT*, 50). Moreover, daybreak is a recurrent phenomenon; it complements, evokes, and sustains memory's function of securing our confidence in duration. Waking can be a terribly frightening experience with the kind of cyclic consciousness echoed in the poem's own structural repetitions of "again." The final "again" seems the volume's response to Lemuel's prayer: what is essential is what can be accepted in its duration. The necessity of daybreak, like the necessity driving Merwin's speakers to their alienation, can be comforting because it makes us feel at one with those deepest rhythms of invisible being. And it is the traces of that invisible being, called up by one's sense of recurrence, which gives intellectual resonance to the sense of the scene as a "procession." A procession is a ritual, religious form—here for a natural experience—and a procession allows the individual both to be himself and to participate in a collective ritual force. The poem's structure enhances this meaning, for in the central line of the poem's seven-line cyclical form (balanced by the *agains*) the speaker takes up the burden and joins his subjective self to the actions of the entire scene. He realizes here what Merwin has defined as the essential condition of poetry—that it be "experience" not "action," not something that is "communal" and "may be shared with machines" but a moment of being "personal and inseparable from the whole" ("Notes," 270). Experience is the doorway to complete Being.

III

"Daybreak" provides the moment of the open doorway where process and recurrence, self and whole are reconciled, but it neither adequately dramatizes the scene nor explores the conditions and meaning of that reconciliation. Rather it echoes and fulfills other poems toward the end of *The Moving Target* which explore more fully why and how this moment of union with essential process can be satisfying. Recurrent process is the embodiment in nature of the fact of necessity, and necessity in turn is the concept by which memory restores man to his home in process. Necessity is the authentic force in man and nature underlying the illusory phenomena: "May I bow to Necessity, not / To her hirelings" (*l*, 25). So long as "Hope and grief are still our wings / . . . we cannot fly" (*L*, 4) because they provide illusions of freedom which mask the need to bow to necessity so that one may find the open doorway. The fictive world of human hopes and fears occupies consciousness without grounding it; we seek human reasons or aims for events in a world where "everything that does not need you is real" (*L*, 35). To experience that "real" we must destroy merely human desires and imaginative constructs.

Two poems best summarize how one comes to recognize necessity and how that recognition helps us find selfhood within the fundamental rhythms of natural being. "The Way to the River" is the easier and less successful because it ultimately relies on love—a phenomenon simply asserted by Merwin and hard to reconcile with most of his landscape. Conceptually love seems too easy, too traditionally an emblem of the union of the personal and the whole (since love is at the least potentially universal) to resolve displacements as disturbing as Merwin's despairing poems.[5] Nonetheless the poem connects love and necessity in some interesting ways. The goal of the poem is to achieve the contemporary version of paradise, to be able to say and to accept the words "Be here":

Be here the flies from the house of the mapmaker
Walk on our letters I can tell
And the days hang medals between us

I have lit our room with a glove of yours be
Here I turn
To your name and the hour remembers
Its one word
Now

Be here what can we
Do for the dead the footsteps full of money
I offer you what I have my
Poverty

To the city of wires I have brought home a handful
Of water I walk slowly
In front of me they are building the empty
Ages I see them reflected not for long
Be here I am no longer ashamed of time it is too brief hands
Have no names
I have passed it I know

> *Oh Necessity you with the face you with*
> *All the faces*

This is written on the back of everything

But we
Will read it together

(*MT,* 77)

To say "be here," one must reach the river, the reality of the present, and he must be willing to let it be, not to act upon it and transform it to satisfy his desires. Two attitudes make this possible. The first is "love," for love in Merwin is the opposite of desire; love accepts and dwells with. It brings no intentions to what it experiences and thus dwells with silence, not with names ("We say good-bye distance we are here / We can say it quietly who else is there / We can say it with silence our native tongue" [*MT,* 79]). The corollary of love then is the act of accepting one's poverty, an act which frees one from imposing desires on the present to make it fit certain dreams and thus allows one to see not how he differs from the river but what he shares with it. In this poem to accept one's poverty is to accept time ("I am no longer ashamed of time") and to recognize in a fresh way that "a great disorder is an order" and that change is our one condition of permanence.[6] Change is that face of Necessity which includes all its faces, a fact one can only learn when poverty deprives him of his hold on any of those specific faces. And change, like love, is both particular and universal; the hour's one word is "Now" because all time shares the qualities of presence and dissolution. So change as necessity can be seen as an absolute condition of being; that is, it becomes a kind of God informing a different, analogical book of nature. Those reduced by poverty to recognize that absolute can recognize as well how fully they share, and even more, participate in, the absolute condition of being. Merwin's poetry often borders on theology in both tone and theme precisely because he pursues such fundamental issues and seeks analogical religious solutions. Perhaps most important in this specific solution is its open-endedness; a sense of recurrence and continuity makes possible for the lovers a realistic dream of an open-ended yet structured future. Few religions can do more; without this vision of necessity and the concomitant sense of selfhood, Merwin's actors usually face a far more problematic sense of the void to come:

> I am the son of the future but she shows me only her
>   mourning veil
> I am the son of the future but my own father.
>   (CL, 92)

"For Now" presents a more extreme religious model for experiencing necessity; it dramatizes an Eliotic process of negative mysticism as the way to achieve a "Poverty" beyond even love. The title's dual meanings suggest the poem's basic strategy; "For Now" is a dedication to the reality of the moment, but is also a provisional statement of a strategy for acting within the flux to uncover more permanent qualities of that moment. To "come to myself" in an abiding present one must perform a provisional stripping of the self; he must reverse Whitman's self-expanding catalogues and say "goodbye" to all those mere "guests" of himself "expecting hosts" until he has achieved that poverty where he can recognize necessity. The abiding self, if there is one, is not in its possessions but in that consciousness (not necessarily a subjective one) which defines its being as what remains when all those possessions have been stripped away. (This is a secondary meaning of the poem's statement "Tell me what you see vanishing and I / will tell you who you are.") By its conclusion this negative "Song of Myself" demands the surrender of Merwin's and the speaker's most intimate and most often affirmed qualities, and there occurs a glimpse of what remains:

> Goodbye distance from whom I
> Borrow my eyes goodbye my voice
> In the monument of strangers goodbye to the sun
> Among the wings nailed to the windows goodbye
> My love
>
> You that return to me through the mountain of flags
> With my raven on your wrist
> You with the same breath
>
> Between death's republic and his kingdom
>
> (MT, 95)

The "You" who returns here is richly ambiguous: the pronoun is left undefined because the "You" sought throughout the poem ("You are not here will the earth last till you come") is essentially an ineffable presence knowable only when names are left behind, but it probably includes "My Love," the reader (since he comes back through the empty signifiers of the "mountain of flags"), and the speaker's essential self. All three in fact are now inseparable from that selfhood which on the level of necessity is a collective and unnameable one. This objectified mystery returns wearing on its wrist not a watch to measure time but a raven, a symbol of time experienced as the painful sum of the series of "goodbyes." With this bodily knowledge of time, the speaker now literally shares the same breath with the collective "you." Breath here suggests the achievement of ineffable knowledge, the speech beyond speech, and links that knowledge with the central force which is at once energy of life and experience of death. Our breathing is one of our deepest bodily experiences of what it means to exist in time; each inhalation necessary for life must be followed by an exhalation which is its own death.[7] The ancients were perhaps wiser than we (or Olson) realize in equating breath and spirit. Breath furthermore helps explain how we stand between death's "kingdom," which is the universal mastery of death over all that breathes, and his republic, where we die as we lived, each alone. Death's kingdom though is the stronger force and thus the poem's concluding image. At this nadir of selfhood, one recognizes how death, like change, is an absolute condition of being and hence a God we can know and participate in, without the mediation of fictive myths. And within this absolute, we are in a way reborn, for, as Merwin often reminds us, to be dying is to be immortal, to be united with a force which permeates all life.

It is not a very large jump from the ineffable presence of the "You" realized in poverty to the dramatic sense of darkness as source of true presence in "Finally," but the shift nonetheless sows the seeds for more complex and occasionally quite different meditations in *The Lice:*

> My dread, my ignorance, my
> Self, it is time. Your imminence
> Prowls the palms of my hands like sweat.
> Do not now, if I rise to welcome you,
> Make off like roads into the deep night.
> The dogs are dead at last, the locks toothless,
> The habits out of reach.
> I will not be false to you tonight.
>
> Come, no longer unthinkable. Let us share
> Understanding like a family name. Bring
> Integrity as a gift, something
> Which I had lost, which you found on the way.
> I will lay it beside us, the old knife,
> While we reach our conclusions.
>
> Come. As a man who hears a sound at the gate
> Opens the window and puts out the light
> The better to see out into the dark,
> Look, I put it out.
>
> (*MT,* 22)

The true self is his dread and his ignorance because it is incompatible with the easy habits and superficial qualities of the active life in time and in society. The true self calls from the darkness, and to come to it we must share that darkness. By putting out the light, our practical self no longer creates a shadow by standing between the light and the ground, but merges completely with the shadow and the kingdom of darkness which includes it. In effect, the speaker avoids the problem of finding the source of light by making absolute its antagonistic opposite. In the darkness, where the shadow need no longer hate, one finds a completeness impossible for the rational consciousness condemned to the tensions and oppositions of the daylight. Darkness here is the ontological analogue of the unconscious and of the furnace where the drunk finds the spirits necessary if he is to continue his song.

IV

"Finally" provides a dramatic basis for our returning once more to the topic of Merwin's style, in its pursuit of "something else" beyond what the poetry of the local in *The Drunk in the Furnace* could provide. The essence of that style is its negation of the light of ordinary experience. The rejection of punctuation is only a small part of its de-creating qualities, for at every opportunity that style breaks down expected connections—by exploding verbal clichés, by continually refusing normal continuities of logical, chronological, or dramatic development, and by rearranging the ordinary landscape into a psychological, surreal one. Merwin's fidelity to *symboliste* traditions is nowhere more evident than in his distrust of ordinary language; easy speech belongs to the world of drunks and presidents, censustakers, and wavers of flags. Ordinary language can rarely survive dislocation, because its function is to cover over ignorance, not to lead beyond itself into the mysteries of silence.[8] A student of mine summarized Merwin's style with the observation that a miner's children should be pale. But since Merwin cannot trust a poetics of place, he must base imaginative value on remaining pale, on denying roots in any place or even in dramatic contexts. We have seen how absence, like the shadow, helps define the enduring present, but we need now to see how that absence also provides access to realities only dimly suggested by the constraints of the natural order. The "something else" Merwin pursues is "the true source"[9] whose home is what Merwin has called "the great language" which poetry is always trying to speak:

> The demand is often for a substitute, a translation, and is regularly made by those who are poorly acquainted, or uncomfortable, with the original idiom. But the original seems more and more frequently to be, not a particular mode of poetry, but the great language itself, the vernacular of the imagination, that at one time was common to men. It is a tongue that is loosed in the service of immediate recognitions, and that in itself would make

it foreign in our period. For it conveys something of the unsoundable quality of experience and the hearing of it is a private matter, in an age in which the person and his senses are being lost in
the consumer, who does not know what he sees, hears, wants,
or is afraid of, until the voice of the institution has told him.
("Notes," 269–70)

Merwin had been fascinated by meditation on the "true source" in
his earliest volumes. But even strong poems like "The Annunciation"
treat origins in terms of a New Critical incarnational aesthetic:

> Only
> If I could remember, if I could only remember
> The way that word was, and the sound of it. Because
> There is that in me still that draws all that I am
> Backwards, as weeds are drawn down when the water
> Flows away; and if I could only shape
> And hear again that word and the way of it—
> But you must grow forward, and I know
> That I cannot. And yet it is there in me:
> As though if I could only remember
> The word, if I could make it with my breath
> It would be with me forever as it was
> Then in the beginning, when it was
> The end and the beginning, and the way
> They were one; and time and the things of falling
> Would not fall into emptiness but into
> The light, and the word tell the way of their falling
> Into the light forever, if I could remember
>   And make the word with my breath.
>   (GB, 39)

In his later work, on the other hand, memory is not primarily a
means for returning to an actual state of origins. And, more important, the breath functions primarily to unmake words by emphasizing the gulf between desire and its representation: "The beginning /
is broken / No wonder the addresses are torn" (L, 24). So poetry is
less an art of regathering fragments than of stationing oneself within
what fragments share.

Our best guide to this "poetics of absence" is Heidegger, the
modernist thinker who most fully resisted Christian incarnational
models. His essay on Trakl is his most appropriate work, because it
meditates on Trakl's figure of total alienation: "Something strange is

the soul on earth."[10] What, Heidegger asks, are the implications of this condition for the poet? His task is to accept his "apartness" as stranger and make of it the true site of poetry. By maintaining his distance from the world the poet preserves what is unborn in the nature of mortal man—a sense of being, quieter and more "stilling" than those who are at home in the world can know. The soul in its apartness also keeps alive a sense of pain and melancholy which is at once a tearing away from the things of the world and the way to acceptance. For pain is the "animator," the discontent which drives man to bring being out of concealment (Heidegger defines truth as *a-letheia*, out of forgetfulness) into the light shared by the soul, itself on fire in its pain. Heidegger's effulgent and evocative prose is difficult to summarize, but the following sentences should give some idea of the tone and themes of the piece:

> The language of the poetry whose site is in apartness answers to the home-coming of unborn mankind into the quiet beginning of its stiller nature.
> Because the language of this poetry speaks from the journey of apartness, it will always speak also of what it leaves behind in parting, and of that to which the departure submits. . . .
> The ambiguous tone of Trakl's poetry arises out of a gathering, that is out of a unison which, meant for itself alone, always remains unsayable. The ambiguity of this poetic saying is not lax imprecision, but rather the rigor of him who leaves what is as it is, who has entered into the "righteous vision" and now submits to it.

This concept of apartness—as the fidelity of the stranger to his necessary alienation and ultimately as the site in which being can be gathered—is basic to understanding Merwin's style with its impersonal "suspended regard." "That Biblical waif, ill at ease in time, the spirit" ("Notes," 270) can be known only in a silence or darkness echoed by poetic language. Merwin's later work denies the self-referential, autotelic qualities of language to pursue what he calls a kind of transparence in which the words are "in the way as little as possible" and seemed used up by the real.[11] Yet this transparence is an ambiguous one, for he wants language also to become "itself something you cannot catch hold of." These diaphanous words point beyond their vanishing to a silence only reached through transparence. Thus the language keeps pushing us out of time to the apartness where the apparently disembodied speaker dwells. There he can function as the shadow does in "The Last One" or darkness in "Finally"; he keeps alive a hope of the spirit ill at ease in time and allows a glimpse into the source or silence. The voice retains a cold dignity—justly proud of refusing to depend on things or "activity" and faithful to the great language.[12]

The voice of apartness exists somewhere between the echoes of speech in time and its absent source. And Merwin's work seen as a whole sustains this relationship by creating an elaborate system of echoes, so that the reader gradually feels his own apartness from each specific act of naming. Merwin's recurrent use of a basic vocabulary of images—knives, shadows, gloves, salt, ash, etc.—forces on the reader a sense that no specific instance of an image contains its complete meaning. If we compare Merwin's system of images with that of a poet like Yeats, the way they reinforce absence becomes clearer. Yeats, especially in his *Vision* years, wants the images to absorb the world, to reflect how style and personality can transform the flux and hold reality and justice in a single thought. In Yeats the repeated images function like a theological system, metaphorically reinforcing a universe of analogies. Merwin, though, uses repeated images not to systematize the world, but to tempt us with the possibility of system and of a single informing principle sustaining that system. He leads us beyond particulars, but leaves us lost in this new mental space. The system is never realized; the images are echoes of one another uttered by a biblical waif stranded in time, not the tools of a Promethean imagination reconstituting the real. Nonetheless, and this is the major point, the echoes perform a kind of religious function because as they thrust us into apartness, into an absence beyond the immediate dramatic reality one expects from a poem, they make evident to us how much we are creatures of absence by the very fact we can be taken in. If we too enter apartness, in effect we grant the claims upon us of that absence which is the central reality for consciousness in our time. Our salvation must lie in whatever formed silence we can realize in that apartness.

V

With *The Lice*, however, Merwin becomes so fully self-conscious about the implications in the apartness of his style that Heideggerean optimism seems too simple a perspective. The faith that within apartness one holds and gathers a numinous Being perhaps need not be rejected, but it must be tested and called into question. The epigraph to the volume cues us to this different, more problematic landscape: "All men are deceived by the appearances of things, even Homer himself, who was the wisest man in Greece; for he was deceived by boys catching lice: they said to him, 'What we have caught and what we have killed we have left behind, but what has escaped us we bring with us.'" While a moving target is a teleological image, a goal of desire difficult but not impossible to hit, the epigraph to *The Lice* suggests that even the desire to know is a privative state, a disturbance by lice of some primordial stillness. And more problematic yet grows the value of what we can know, for to know is to define that informing darkness and thus to mis-take its mystery. How simple we have been to overlook the possibility that the darkness invoked at the end of "Finally" might not be a positive essential self in tune with an active source of being. The darkness is precisely that—a darkness—perhaps a source of light to one who can preserve apartness, but perhaps also only prelude to the deeper darkness of nonbeing or the Void which might be the only true stillness. Absence may not be the means to a suprahuman fullness, but may be itself the only absolute worth pursuing:

I

Encouragement meant nothing

Inside it
The miners would continue to
Crawl out of their dark bodies
Extending the darkness making
It hollow
And how could they be rightly paid

Darkness gathered on the money
It lived in the dies the miners pursued it what
Was their reward

Some might bring flowers saying Nothing can last
Some anyway
Held out their whole lives in their glass hands

Sweeter than men till past the time
Some with a pure light burned but over

Their heads even theirs
Soot wrote on the ceiling
An unknown word

Shutting your eyes from the spectacle you
Saw not darkness but
Nothing

On which doors were opening . . .

III

At one stroke out of the ruin
All the watches went out and
The eyes disappeared like martins into their nests

I woke to the slamming of doors and got up naked
The old wind vanished and vanished but was still there
Everyone but the cold was gone for good

And the carol of the miners had just ended

                                                    (L, 20, 22)

The Moving Target sought to encounter "nothing that is not there,"
but The Lice, with its pervading concern for the reality of death and
the implications of that reality for human consciousness, seeks to
question "the nothing that is." The ultimate question in The Lice is
whether death can be seen as an absolute condition within and en-
closed by life and process or whether life is merely an inadequate
prelude to the ultimate void beyond all the songs of human miners
and only figured by death's occurrences in time.

To appreciate the tensions of The Lice we must oppose to the
Heideggerean voice it seeks to keep alive another, darker vision by
E. M. Cioran, a thinker indebted to Heidegger and sharing his hu-
morless, portentous tone.[13] Like Heidegger, Cioran sees apartness,
pain, and division as the indispensable means to a final homecoming, but for Cioran one comes home only by entering a more radical
apartness. He must renounce all desire and enter the plenitude of a
void that is "nothingness stripped of its negative aspects, nothingness transfigured." There is no return from nothingness to a deeper
sense of the Being that abides; the more apart one grows the more he
recognizes how all being—material objects and the thoughts and desires these objects engender in man—is sheer appearance doomed to
vanish. The only freedom is to create vanishing rather than be subject to it:

To undo our bonds, we must, in the future, refrain from adhering to anything whatever, anything but the nothing of freedom. . . . Ideally, we would be able to lose, without regrets all taste for beings and things, each day honoring some creature or object by renouncing it; thus making the rounds of appearances and dismissing each in turn, we would achieve a state of unremitting withdrawal, which is the very secret of joy. . . . To evade the intolerable, let us resort to distraction, to flight, let us seek a region in which no sensation deigns to assume a name, and no appetite to incarnate itself, let us win back the primordial repose, let us abolish, along with the past, odious memory but especially awareness, our immemorial enemy whose mission it is to leave us destitute, to wear us down.

The clearest analogue to Cioran's vision in *The Lice* is the poem "Divinities," an attempt by Merwin to return once more to theology and reimagine how man can conceive the absolute conditions of being:

> Having crowded once onto the threshold of mortality
> And not been chosen
> There is no freedom such as theirs
> That have no beginning
>
> The air itself is their memory
> A domain they cannot inhabit
> But from which they are never absent
>
> *What are you* they say *that simply exist*
> And the heavens and the earth bow to them
> Looking up from their choices
> Perishing
>
> All day and all night
> Everything that is mistaken worships them
> Even the dead sing them an unending hymn
>
> (*L*, 59)

The pure nonbeing of those without beginnings embodies a stillness and a necessity more profound than any to be found within process (Keats's dying and obscure gods are replaced by those never born). The dead sing a hymn to these divinities in reverence of an absolute self-sufficiency and eternity of loss which the dead only approximate. For the dead had a beginning, and thus suffered death and even after death were not free from the processes of decay and memory.

Only by imaginatively entering death, as Merwin does, can one even
approach the knowledge of the void. Death is something we carry
with us and can never catch, yet once we approach its reality life
becomes the shadow always escaping our grasp. "Looking East at
Night" beautifully renders this perspective:

> Death
> White hand
> The moths fly at in the darkness
>
> I took you for the moon rising
>
> Whose light then
> Do you reflect
>
> As though it came out of the roots of things
> This harvest pallor in which
>
> I have no shadow but myself
>
>   (L, 36)

The poem is almost the direct opposite of "Daybreak": here the dusk
is an open doorway out of life; its pale, expansive stillness quietly
mocks as it complements the glories of the sunset. The eastern sky
evokes death because its light seems at home in the encroaching
darkness; like death and the moon, it shines with reflected light. But
whose light does death reflect? The simplest answer is that death is a
reflection of man's individual consciousness (see L, 70), and this
answer helps explain why the individual self becomes the mind's
shadow in the last line. Selfhood blocks the mind from that lunar
light. On a deeper level, though, death is also a dim reflection of an
absolute nonbeing at "the roots of things" which uses death to harvest being unto itself. The self then is shadow not only because its
characteristic activities block the light, but because that light provides a radically new perspective on how insubstantial the self and
its body really are. The more one holds to the necessities of the
world the wider and deeper the shadow.

The omnipresence of death and the power of the void need not remain metaphysical abstractions. One of Merwin's more terrifying visions is his realization of how intensely modern life both participates in and actively pursues that void. What is our language, for
example, but a way of continually generating partial absences that
separate us from being: "My words are the garment of what I shall

never be / Like the tucked sleeve of a one-armed boy" (*L*, 62). We keep projecting words to capture a reality, yet we find in the end only more words and deeper doubts about our ability to capture experience. Because "the beginning / Is broken," "the addresses are torn" (*L*, 24); everything we describe in order to know requires always supplementary descriptions. Language tries to make things present, but leaves us only with an absence requiring more words, ad infinitum. And even when words do seem to catch hold of a reality, as the epigraph of *The Lice* reminds us, they kill it. In "Fly" (*L*, 73), Merwin realizes not only that having "believed too much in words" he killed the bird he tried to train, but also that he killed whatever part of himself ("so that is what I am") could have been united with the bird's natural sense of being.

If we only killed with words, however, nonbeing would still be essentially a metaphor and life more acceptable. The tragic irony, though, is that in our quest to make everything present and knowable on our terms we kill what there is to hold us to life. Hope in life must confront not only the abortive "why not" logic of rationalist activism (see "The Last One," *L*, 10) but the actual fact of a war destroying a nation, its countryside, and perhaps the future of all mankind:

When the forests have been destroyed their darkness remains
The ash the great walker follows the possessors
Forever
Nothing they will come to is real
Nor for long . . .

Overhead the seasons rock
They are paper bells
Calling to nothing living

The possessors move everywhere under Death their star
Like columns of smoke they advance into the shadows
Like thin flames with no light
They with no past
And fire their only future

(*L*, 63)

"For a Coming Extinction" (*L*, 68–69) follows the series of war poems in *The Lice* and ties their despair to Merwin's more metaphysical speculations on the void. The rationalist speaker asks the whale he is making extinct to remind "The End / That great god" "that it is we who are important." In asserting man's special place, he also reminds us of man's guilt as destroyer of his planet. More important than this basic irony, though, is the religious setting and the other poems in the volume that context calls up. For the consciousness here in his destructiveness is actually altering the gods we must pray to—from gods of life to gods of darkness and death. Making animals extinct is our "sacrifice" to that god we now invoke. And the irony ultimately doubles back on itself and the reader. For our immediate reaction is to want to destroy people who think like this speaker. Even on this practical level, then, apocalyptic destruction—psychically if not physically—comes to seem our one hope for salvation. Yet even in the midst of the despondent social poems near the end of *The Lice* Merwin finds in his fears a moral note that qualifies and redirects any ultimate surrender to the void. "If I were not human I would not be ashamed of anything" (*L*, 71) seems just one more statement of a consciousness desiring to erase itself into nonbeing. But it returns us and Merwin to a mode of necessity evident in other despairing moments. We are human, and being human condemns us not just to shameful deeds but to a desire to criticize and correct those deeds. A void sought in despair is an impossible paradox, for the very conditions generating despair keep alive also a sense of moral possibilities and a dream of fuller being. Not only does Merwin resist unjust war and the destruction of Nature, but he makes poems of that resistance. The poems, of course, may only attach one to a dying planet and actually increase the number and beauty of things that must die, but they also suggest the possibility of an abiding permanence—capable of providing an alternative to the void. It would be an exaggeration to claim that in *The Lice* Heidegger's vision of apartness ultimately prevails over Cioran's, but Heidegger's at least continues to survive. Language, for example, need not be only a process of supplementation: in the silence within the overlapping words trying to define and judge experience an informing presence might be taking shape:

> This silence coming at intervals out of the shell of names
> It must be all one person really coming at
> Different hours for the same thing
> If I could learn the word for yes it could teach me questions

I would see that it was itself every time and I would
Remember to say take it up like a hand
And go with it this is at last
Yourself

The child that will lead you

(L, 38)

And even death itself not only calls us to the void but gives us a vantage point from which to view and sing of the processes which
worship it:

I think all this is somewhere in myself
The cold room unlit before dawn
Containing a stillness such as attends death
And from a corner the sounds of a small bird trying
From time to time to fly a few beats in the dark
You would say it was dying it is immortal

(L, 48)

The bird sings both to and against death, and in his singing of his
own mortality he gives us a model for a form of immortality once
again within process.

The conflicting perspectives culminate in "Looking for Mushrooms at Sunrise," the volume's final poem. What hope Merwin can
derive from the volume's journey is embodied here, but it remains
qualified by the appeals of death and the void:

When it is not yet day
I am walking on centuries of dead chestnut leaves
In a place without grief
Though the oriole
Out of another life warns me
That I am awake

In the dark while the rain fell
The gold chanterelles pushed through a sleep that was not mine
Waking me
So that I came up the mountain to find them

Where they appear it seems I have been before
I recognize their haunts as though remembering
Another life

Where else am I walking even now
Looking for me

(*L*, 80)

The poem's final question casts us back on other questions raised along its way. What is it that calls him to the mushrooms—is it some common life-process they share which the morning wakes in him, or is it a deep participation in the blankness of death only imaged in "a sleep that was not mine"? What is the other life he remembers—an instinctive childlike sharing in natural growth or a state of nonbeing before life? Do the mushrooms live in or live off the darkness and the decaying chestnut leaves in which they thrive? Finally, does the final question suggest that the speaker envisions those incomplete and fragmented parts of himself participating in a natural process by which the living feed off the dead, or do these fragments seek the complete identity of nonbeing?

VI

Merwin's next two volumes are very difficult to cover properly. There are many respects in which we must see *The Carrier of Ladders* and *Writings to an Unfinished Accompaniment* as providing a thematic climax to the project initiated by *The Moving Target*. They incorporate all the negation in his preceding work while mapping a form of plenitude based on ideas of necessity and process. It would be melodramatic to say that he overcomes the appeal of the void. Rather he finesses it, recognizing that the pursuit of absence entails endless regress and division, even if there one finds a form of authentic being. The price for this form of authenticity is too great; one cannot uphold any moral vision except an ascetic purity and one cannot experience bonds to other selves or to even the forms of presence one pursues. Conversely, to the extent one needs such visions and connections one must doubt whether the negative way in fact fulfills our energies. So Merwin tries to find in change and necessity within natural process an alternative ground to endless self-reflection. In natural process the force producing absence is always in fact present as something beyond the self that endures and allows identification with it even as the specific contents of the self and its processes continue subject to destruction. This shift in emphasis allows him to return to many of the themes of *The Moving Target*, now with a much less nervous and desperate attitude. The lines become shorter and more confident than in the preceding books; the language grows less surreal and epigrammatic, more concrete and rooted in dramatic contexts, and the surreal landscape becomes less dislocating, more firmly articulated as a metaphoric structure. These stylistic shifts all echo the dominant thematic goal of the volume—to reach that moment when the bearer of the dead and the carrier of ladders (the characters in the epigraph) share the same essential starting point, a point within process where necessity grounds and supports the poet's "ladders": "And what is wisdom if it is not / now / in the loss that has not left this place" (CL, 8).

These "developments," however, leave Merwin in a difficult position. Faith may not be so helpful for a poet. Even here, where the imaginative acts remain richly suggestive, there is a marked lessening of dramatic pressure on individual poems. The poems have a timeless peace that makes them indistinguishable. Instead of feeling that Merwin has a project of questioning the world, I begin to think he has only a rhetoric for giving a new bottle to old, and somewhat sour, Romantic wine. As he reaches a vision he can affirm as both true and liveable, he also paints himself into the poetic corner he called The Compass Flower and seems unable to escape in Finding the Islands. I want here to trace through The Carrier of Ladders the basic terms of what will lead to the loss of force in The Compass Flower as Merwin takes stock of what is now permitted to him by his achievements.

The opening three poems of The Carrier of Ladders provide a model for the dialectic of division and the undivided in that volume and make clear how wisdom and a sense of unity are possible only by a total commitment to where we are. The opening poem, "Plane," takes Merwin's familiar journey and extends the idea of departure to metaphysical dimensions. The speaker's lucid self-objectification dramatically enhances the division he describes:

> and with my mind infinitely divided and hopeless
> like a stockyard seen from above
> and my will like a withered body muffled
> in qualifications until it has no shape
> I bleed in my place
>
> where is no
> vision of the essential nakedness of the gods

nor of that
nakedness the seamless garment of heaven

nor of any other
nakedness
                                                    (CL, 3)

The succeeding poems try to envision conditions of selfhood capable of participating in that nakedness:

Maybe I will come
to where I am one
and find
I have been waiting there
as a new
year finds the song of the nuthatch
                        (CL, 19)

"Teachers" dramatizes the rediscovery of childhood vision where
voyage is not departure but the recognition of oneself on the way:

but I say to myself you are not a child now
if the night is long remember your unimportance
sleep

then toward morning I dream of the first words
of books of voyages
sure tellings that did not start by justifying

yet at one time it seems
had taught me
                                        (CL, 4)

One overcomes division within the self by refusing to define that self
from outside, by not desiring justification from imaginative projections of the future or rational analyses of the effects of the past. Like
the process itself, one is justified by the fact one is here. The next
poem, "The Owl," projects what being undivided might mean in
terms of interpersonal relationships. The speaker of the poem is
caught in his own self-conscious reflections and unable to love or
even to recognize the reality of one who loves him ("You are never
'there'"). She is not "there" hidden in protective "woods" ("woulds")
because she is so intensely "here" in possession of her own voice and
asking to be known in more immediate, intuitive ways. Love for her

is a total commitment "without hope / or need of it," and thus a complete expression of her own unjustifiable necessity.

Absolute light and absolute darkness are the two modes within natural process which allow one to envision the undivided as an aspect of necessity and thus to have a model for the self. Daybreak and Merwin's symbolic birds again in "The Birds on the Morning of Going" provide one pole of this vision:

> If I can say yes I
> must say it to this
> and now
> trying to remember what the present
> can bless with
> which I know
>
> from all other ages how little has come to me
> that is breath
> and nothing that is you
>
> now I can see
> I have been carrying this
> fear
> the length of my life asking *Is this*
> *its place*
> bringing it here
>
> to the singing
> of these brightening birds
>
> they are neither dead nor unborn
>
> a life opens it opens it is
> breaking
> does it find occasions for
> every grief of its childhood
> before it will have
> done
>
> oh my love here even the night turns back
> (*CL*, 33; see also *CL*, 32, 75, 113)

Literally, the night turns back because of the absolute intensity of the morning, but on the metaphoric level the darkness that is beaten back is the questions he tries to impose on the scene. The light is its own answer and will not brook human impositions asking for justification and seeking through reflective consciousness to impose on the scene more than it needs or can bear. And in other poems the intensity of night is perhaps even closer to an absolute necessity of presence. "February" presents night's most evocative message, "*I know nothing / learn of me*" (*CL*, 51). The night returns us to Merwin's earlier meditations on death as an essential emptiness, but that emptiness is itself a recurrent part of process. We need not imagine that emptiness as another, absent reality; it is "here," so much here in fact one need not learn *from* it, but *of* it. The undivided can only be known when one surrenders the whole referential model of learning from things. Through emphatic knowledge of "the first darkness" there need no longer be "a single prayer and it is not for men" (*L*, 43):

> Maybe he does not even have to exist
> to exist in departures
> then the first darkness falls
> even there a shining is flowing from all the stones
> though the eyes are not yet made that can see it
> saying Blessed
> are ye
>
> (*CL*, 124)

Although man may now be a part of the prayer and be able to bless the darkness, he still does not have the "eyes" to understand it. There is a human analogue to the undivided, but it exists for the most part only as the single statement rendered in a "Memory of Spring": "The first composer / could hear only what he could write" (*CL*, 115). The composer does not write what he hears; that would be merely imitation. But whatever imagination encountered this first spring found only what it put there. Reception and creation were one and the same act, voice and name a single reality with no sense of an absent Logos. But how restore in time what only that memory of the title now preserves. The one possibility is to reach out toward the self-contained fullness of a moment and to perceive within that moment traces of the great language which first composed it for consciousness. "In the Time of the Blossoms," Merwin's triumphant conclusion to *The Carrier of Ladders*, brings together all his work and rewards the sufferings of his determined apartness with a gathering of the poet into the presence of all being:

> Ash tree
> sacred to her who sails in

> from the one sea
> all over you leaf skeletons
> fine as sparrow bones
> stream out motionless
> on white heaven
> staves of one
> unbreathed music
> Sing to me
>
> (CL, 138)

The scene, with its repeated "ones," presents a natural moment which reconciles many of those divisions which permeate Merwin's work. The "leaf skeletons fine as sparrow bones" of the ash tree in bloom remind us of how deeply death participates even in the fullest moments of natural blossoming. And like Yeats's chestnut tree, the ash reconciles flux and stasis as the blossoms balance in the wind and seem to multiply in their composed plenitude. The ash tree evokes a kind of "mythological present" reenacting that moment preserved within the memory of the great language when the tree was conceived as a sacred, mythic phenomenon. The landscape not only speaks as an open doorway but preserves those dimensions of imaginative speech invested in it by generations of men. The goddess here "who sails in from the one sea" is Nemesis: "The ash tree was one of the goddess's seasonal disguises, and an important one to her pastoral devotees, because of its association with thunderstorms and with the lambing month, the third of the sacral year."[14] The tree is symbol of fertility, but also of the dangers of fertility. The ash tree was thought to draw lightning and thus was associated with the Furies (who are Ash-nymphs) in their dual roles as figures of divine judgment and as bringers of rain. The fullness of life is never far from the realities of death and judgment, but it is precisely this fact which makes worship authentic and awe-full and which allows man's religious imagination to appreciate so fully these moments when life balances and transcends the death it carries with it. The tree's motionless motion and balance of life and death allow us to see its participation in a cosmic music—now unbreathed because it transcends the life-and-death rhythm of breathing and far surpasses in its gathering power the mere words we make out of that breathing. The speaker is no longer maker, tormented by his own inadequate breath, but once again an open doorway accepting his role as mediator of that music from visual appearance into fuller states of awareness.

The last line of the poem is the first to mention the poet, for he
is at once peripheral to the scene's fullness and the necessary completion of it if that fullness is to be known. The poet is once again
objectified, but not in the terrifying objectifications of the self-
consciousness in the volume's opening poem. His objectification is
now the condition of his homecoming, at one with necessity and
plenitude.

This triumphant moment, however, remains only a moment within
flux. There is no assurance even within the poem that the poet can
translate his passive receptiveness into a principle of recurrent activity. The unbreathed music can sing to him, but his own songs require breath and the problematic division between living and dying
each breath entails. Merwin's triumph here is less a solution than a
successful mode of dissolution which can ground and comfort the
terror of the way. It establishes the chance of a momentary harmony
which justifies a quest one cannot begin by justifying. In retrospect,
"In the Time of the Blossoms" allows us to see what has been involved
in the moments of stasis experienced through light and through darkness. The silences of *The Lice* can, at least at times, merge into the
creative silence of a unity with natural being. Even the more despondent poems in seasons other than spring (like "Third Psalm: The
September Vision," "Late Night in Autumn," "February," and "Ban-
ishment in Winter") achieve a kind of harmony with that process, precisely in and through the despondency they share with the
landscape:

> I am the son of untruth but I have seen the children in Paradise
>   walking in pairs each hand in hand with himself . . .
> I am the son of ruins already among us but at moments I have
>   found hope beyond doubt beyond desert beyond reason and
>   such that I have prayed O wounds come back from death
>   and be healed . . .
> I am the son of love for which parent the blood gropes in dread
>   as though it were naked and for which cause the sun hangs
>   in a cage of light
>   and we are his pains
>   (CL, 96)

VII

Merwin has had perhaps too many such moments. The more one repeats this sense of presence, the more it begins to appear a perma-

nent condition of experience. And these lyric poems become less moments of discovery than examples of a faith. This latter condition constitutes the poetic world of *The Compass Flower* and *Finding the Islands*. As Merwin becomes increasingly convinced of presence as a perennial feature of experience, his poems appear increasingly to lack the dramatic presence we find in moments of discovery. His major work depended on a rhetoric which seemed to embody a process of withdrawing the mind from ordinary realities. Absence as an initial condition of language led to hard-won glimpses of deeper forms of presence. When *The Compass Flower* seems capable of dwelling in immediate perceptible presences or direct, loving relations with other human beings, the rhetoric of absence seems only an affectation, a way of denying the true, simple, and available sources of value. Several poems in *Writings to an Unfinished Accompaniment* mark this shift by allowing the stylistic negation and taut surreal logic to seem only elaborate gestures. *The Compass Flower* tries to transcend the gesture, to make language fully present as speech and as an act of naming perceptions. But in the process it deprives Merwin's poetry of its tension, its life, and its possible significance as an attitude. In saving his soul, Merwin is risking the loss of poetic immortality.

I cannot here give an elaborate defense of my charges. Merwin's limited sphere of concerns can become tedious even when we are discussing good poems. And when the poems in question are widely acknowledged as weak, there is little point to extensive readings. What matters is simply finding how, and perhaps why, the poetry becomes enervated. I think one example should suffice—the poem "The Fig Tree," which invites comparison to "In the Time of the Blossoms":

> Against the south wall of a monastery
> where it catches the first sun
> a fig tree a shadowy fig tree
> stands by the door
> all around the flowing trunk
> suckers grow
> it is against
> the law of the church to pull them out
> nobody remembers why
> tree roots older than the monastery
>   (*CF*, 87)

Merwin has not lost his structural skill. Indeed the problem derives largely from his too thorough control. His poem on the ash tree employed delicately rendered physical perception in order to celebrate a moment of perception which linked natural process to the mythic response of the great language. Here we find the same sense of time, but there is little delicacy of perception and no urgent pressure from the desire that the scene sing for the poet. Here relaxed perception suffices to satisfy all lyric demands, so the process of poetic thinking seems simply a casual process of observation and relaxed thought.

Merwin does not relax his skill, but neither does he make the skill a self-reflexive process of spelling out a site the mind can occupy. Rather the skill simply realizes connections he wants us to take as latent. "The Fig Tree" gains what power it has by overcoming a traditional contrast between the church and pagan thought. The tree combines two powers, or two different models of origin, which give it a mythic force: it embodies the principle of immediate flowing life and it offers a virtually timeless sense of duration. Because its roots are older than the monastery, a glimpse of it catching the first sun leads one to reflect on how even the church, perhaps even all cultural orders, can acknowledge powers driven by far greater and deeper laws. Natural forces both structure time and emerge in moments that transcend its regularities because they have the full sense of appearance we take as contrary to law. But it is as testimony to immanent laws that the particulars so capture the first light.

All the details cohere, but they do so so quietly and with such unassuming composure that it is hard to care very much about them. There is no need to ask them to sing because there is no pressure on the poem for that kind of intensity. Intensity seems in this world a cheap evasion of deep and natural order. Yet, as one sees perhaps most clearly in the effects of Wordsworth's quite similar integrations of pagan roots and church custom, the denial of intensity has disastrous poetic consequences. On the simplest level, Merwin's cadences go slack; there is no pain to impart force and obsessional qualities to the abstracted line units. Now Merwin offers something like personal speech instead of the bare impersonal regard of an abstracted voice. He simplifies his earlier juxtapositional style, while keeping the sense of spare notational elements as building blocks. But without tension and without distance, the remnants of *The Moving Target* style seem extremely limited. They lack movement, and they preserve enough of the old absence to make a speaking voice seem enervated and without distinctive qualities. Merwin wants to have his person while at the same time absorbing the person into larger processes. He gets both only by making each seem bland enough to deserve the other.

If we approach these issues from a more abstract stance, we can begin to see how Merwin at his most confident finally becomes an emblem for the failure of much contemporary poetry. "The Fig Tree" is a descriptive poem. The only voice in the poem is a recording presence which offers a narrative eliciting a quiet sense of wonder. The wonder itself belongs to silence. The poem need not describe the reaction, only prepare the way and then efface itself. Poetry becomes a distanced witness but dare not become an icon trying to carry in itself the qualities it points to. Merwin needs this ascesis because he sees his earlier rhetoric as part of the problem rather than part of the solution. Like many of his peers looking back on what now seems the spiritual excesses of our desires to invent a society which would not destroy Vietnam, Merwin needs an escape from the self-staging elicited by elaborate poetic rhetoric. His rhetoric of impersonality proved doubly destructive: it in fact trapped him in a personal style he had to live in like a glove (even now as he tries to escape it), and it in part created as acts of projection the very absences and self-divisions he then had to resolve through it. A style which becomes an elaborate mechanism for abstracting oneself from perception will demand increasingly abstract, elaborate, and slippery forms of resolution. If poetry is to create ways of engaging values immanent in the world, it must allow direct speech and action within an ordinary world. But how then does poetry keep from itself turning ordinary, from proving its salvational force by its dullness, or at best quiet acceptance. Merwin's descriptive voice denies elaborate rhetoric in order to align poetry with forms of enduring presence one can live by. But life comes in slack cadences. If we call this art, we in fact create another, perhaps deeper absence in life because we force ourselves to live without the more intense, momentary presences of rhetorical afflatus as it divides us from ourselves and forces us to dream of imaginative spaces where no one but the imaginary, ideal selves can hope to live. I do not speak of fantasy, but of ritualized versions of the power and pains one finds in empiricial experience. It may be wise to reject desires to inhabit such worlds, but then one probably ought not hope to dignify one's alternatives by writing lyric poems that de-scribe them. The gulf between that and the forms of intense presence possible in self-conscious lyrical states demeans both art and life.

NOTES

1. I somewhat overstate p. 70 of James Atlas, "Diminishing Returns: The Writings of W. S. Merwin," in *American Poetry since 1960: Some Critical Perspectives*, ed. Robert B. Shaw (Cheadle Hulme: Carcanet Press, 1973). For Pinsky's arguments, see *The Situation of Poetry* (Princeton: Princeton University Press, 1976), pp. 93–94, 164–65.

2. For the first alternative, the thematic, see Cheri Davis, *W. S. Merwin* (Boston: Twayne, 1981), Carol Kyle, "A Riddle for the New Year: Affirmation in W. S. Merwin," *Modern Poetry Studies*, 4 (Winter 1973), 288–303, and Anthony Libby, "W. S. Merwin and the Nothing That Is," *Contemporary Literature*, 16 (1975), 19–40. Once one chooses themes as one's focus, one cannot escape the debate as to whether Merwin is affirmative or negative. For the second view, of Merwin's negations as what I loosely call the de-construction of themes, see Cary Nelson's essay on Merwin in the present volume. Much of what I will have to say is intended to oppose this very in-telligent study. Nelson can make Merwin his hero because he gives "our his-tory its most frightening voice" through his refusal of all it can offer. In his failure speaks the emptiness of our history. However, I think significant po-etry ought not reflect history but provide alternatives to it. I think Merwin at his best does that. I should finally mention the good discussion of Merwin in Evan Watkins, *The Critical Act* (New Haven: Yale University Press, 1978), pp. 224–36, who manages to make negation a form of knowing without my ponderous contexts.

3. Frank MacShane, "A Portrait of W. S. Merwin," *Shenandoah*, 21 (Win-ter 1970), 7.

4. I quote from Merwin, "Poems by Jean Follain," *Atlantic Monthly*, 224 (Feb. 1968), 77.

5. For what love means to Merwin see also *MT*, 78–79, 36–38; *L*, 62; and the closing groups of poems in each of his three earliest volumes.

6. The idea of change as necessity is central in Howard's fine discussion of Merwin in his *Alone with America*.

7. For this sense of breathing I am indebted to Richard Howard's lecture, "The Art of Erasure."

8. For Heidegger's distinction see his *Being and Time*, trans. John Mac-Quarrie and Edward Robinson (New York: Harper, 1962), pp. 204–15. To be more exact we might define Merwin's sense of authentic speech as a focused silence created by language on the verge of disappearing. Sheer silence is a surrender to the blindness of the gods or the temptation to passivity de-monically offered by "Things" (*MT*, 12).

9. Merwin in MacShane, "Portrait of W. S. Merwin," p. 7.

10. Martin Heidegger, "Language in the Poem," in *The Way to Language*, trans. Peter Hertz (New York: Harper and Row, 1971), 159–98. The discussion here is based primarily on pp. 180–95 and I quote pp. 191, 191–92, 192.

11. "An Interview with W. S. Merwin," *Road Apple Review*, 1 (Spring 1969), 36.

12. Merwin's use of startling metaphors or "conceits" is a powerful way of forcing us to recognize both the "apartness" of language and the way its freedom from the logic of particulars allows it to penetrate the silences where Being lies. A similar and suggestive effect is created in "The Wave" (*L*, 25–26) where Merwin shifts from a repeated past tense ("I inhabited") used to describe his memory of experiences passing away to a present when he turns to language. See also "Things" (*MT*, 12) and "Watchers" (*L*, 77) for the horror attendant on his fears that one might lose the absence of "apartness" and surrender to the materiality of things or to a landscape cleared of hiding places for eyes to watch us out of the darkness.

13. I use here Cioran's essay "Encounter with the Void" in *Hudson Review*, 23 (1970), 37–49. I quote below pp. 43, 39, 41.

14. Robert Graves, *The Greek Myths* (New York: Braziller, 1957), pp. 126–27. I also use his discussion on p. 38. It is important to notice here how Merwin's themes and scene are essentially the same as in "Daybreak," but he includes the scene within the poem (it is a more trustworthy presence than the process of mind) and, more important, includes the "great language."

WALTER KALAIDJIAN

Linguistic Mirages:
Language and Landscape
in W. S. Merwin's Later Poetry

Preserve my tongue and I will bless you again and again
("Lemuel's Blessing," *MT*, 8)

Read out of context, this psalmic motto seems addressed to a metaphysical presence beyond the rhetorical limits of Merwin's verse. It
beckons us toward an originary, transcendent source prior to language. Regardless of who is speaking—whether it is the poet entering into a covenant or his totemic Other bestowing a command-
ment—the poem's numinous tongue bespeaks a world charged with
the aura of unmediated presence. Yet does Merwin intend this invocation of "otherness" to be an authentic sacrament—celebrating a
guardian spirit he has compared to the "nagual" of primitive worship?[1] Elsewhere in the same poem he prays: "let the memory of
tongues not unnerve me so that I stumble or quake" (*MT*, 7). Here,
evoking the logos is unmanageably paradoxical: to purge language of
its secular history you must enter the fateful dialogue of its babbling
tongues.

From Merwin's *Moving Target* (1963) to his *Opening the Hand*
(1983), this turn toward textuality is a characteristic maneuver—one
that undercuts the logocentric truth of poetic utterance, leaving it
dismembered. "My words," he writes in a famous simile, "are the
garment of what I shall never be / Like the tucked sleeve of a one-
armed boy" (*L*, 62). As vestments of loss, such lines are severed from
any referential meaning beyond the brief drama of their own unravel-

ing. Words fail to embody the poet's phenomenological encounters with Being-as-presence. Instead, as in Jacques Derrida's metaphor, language is a "fabric of signs" tucked back on its own absence of signified meaning. Enacting that disillusionment with language's phenomenological function is Merwin's paradigmatic later project.

Like Roethke and Wright, Merwin's initial verse was in highly crafted closed forms—work that won the 1952 Yale Younger Poets Award for *A Mask for Janus*. This early recognition was Merwin's entrée into a literary establishment whose aesthetic tastes were determined by Eliot and the American New Critics. In the fifties, Rich, Merwin, and Wright all emerged as significant poets by publishing their first books with Yale, tailoring their formidable verbal talents to suit New Criticism's demand for technically difficult, learnedly allusive, and ironic formal lyrics. By the sixties, of course, all three had abandoned this style, turning instead to the deep image surrealism that enabled Roethke and Bly to adopt a more emotive poetics.

Resembling Wright's experiments with colloquial idioms, Merwin's poetry moves beyond Bly's subjective imagery toward the same minimalist dialogue with silence that finally stifles Wright's inventiveness. Merwin, however, courts absence in a different way. Unlike Wright's poetry, Merwin's does not depend on registering an authentic authorial presence. Merwin instead speaks to an absence at the heart of language, thereby reducing lyric expression to a rhetorical effect. Calling the phenomenological poetics of Roethke, Wright, Bly, and Rich into crisis, Merwin initiates the closure of voiced presence in the contemporary American lyric.

Yet Merwin nonetheless sometimes gestures toward an almost Heideggerean vision of language's humanistic, even metaphysical, function, while he resists what Heidegger describes as the inauthentic, everyday use of language as an instrument of public communication.[2] In contrast to this linguistic commodification, the poet's discontinuous and indeterminate syntax "destroys" his imagery's representational closure. That destruction of the image's decidable meaning preserves an uncanny quality of "otherness" in Merwin's best poems. Merwin's aesthetic, which evokes the unfamiliar, the ambiguous, the strange, resembles Heidegger's phenomenology of disclosure as *a-letheia*—a temporal process that brings beings into an openness of illumination *and* concealment: "Truth is un-truth, insofar as there belongs to it the reservoir of the not-yet-revealed, the un-uncovered, in the sense of concealment. In unconcealedness, as truth, there occurs also the other 'un-' of a double restraint or refusal. Truth essentially occurs as such in the opposition of lighting and double concealing. Truth is the primal strife in which, always in some particular way, the open region is won within which everything stands and from which everything withholds itself and withdraws itself as a being."[3]

In Heidegger's terms, the poet (as a "messenger," "shepherd," "neighbor," or "guardian" of Being) leads us authentically into language, the "house" of Being, a "dwelling" that is also a "region" of thought—a "coming into the nearness of distance." Derrida, of course, identifies a substantial vestige of metaphysics in this model.[4] "With respect to the metaphysics of presence and logocentrism," Derrida writes, Heidegger's work "is at once contained within it and transgresses it."[5] Derrida would complete (and so displace) Heidegger's "transgression" of Western metaphysics by supplementing "destructive" thinking with "deconstructive" writing—a textual practice Derrida describes as l'écriture, trace, différance, supplement, and hymen. Derrida's critical turn toward textuality, moving beyond Heidegger's identification of language with Being-as-presence, parallels Merwin's later poetic. Merwin often undermines the authenticity of his phenomenological landscapes by exposing their grounding in fictive textual production. His aesthetic moves toward that threshold where experience is appropriated by language. There the world is transfigured by the word's symbolic order—its self-referential system of differential signs.

Merwin enacts his ambivalent vision of language—as either a medium of phenomenological disclosure or a wholly structured system of linguistic codes—through two traditional metaphoric landscapes. The postmodern metropolis, on the one hand, is the site of the Word's secular traffic in material signification; there "ciphers wake and evil / Gets itself the face of the norm / And contrives cities" (L, 34). The city is a modern Babel, where "Division the mother of pain" (MT, 53) proliferates in infinite verbal differences. This vision of the Word's fall from ideal presence into an inscribed text of division recalls Saussure's argument that "in language there are only differences without positive terms."[6] Signified meaning, instead of being a privileged origin, is merely the product of a systematic relation of signifiers. Poetry is just one more echo in the endless feedback of "tongues being divided" (*CL*, 107), and the poet's identity is called into radical crisis. No longer prior to language, the experience of selfhood is displaced by the divided Word and can only be possessed as a site of contradiction. Appropriated by a cultural matrix of colliding messages, subjectivity is reduced to a metaphoric contraption: "I am the son of division but the nails the wires the hasps the bolts / the locks the traps the wrapping that hold me together are / part of the inheritance" (*CL*, 97).

Within language's labyrinth of division, however, Merwin finds pastoral enclaves where words bestow an improbable grace. "This must be what I wanted to be doing," Merwin realizes in one such moment, "Walking at night between the two deserts, / Singing" (*MT*, 50). To utter this song despite language's division is to imagine dwelling within a pastoral myth that harmonizes self and world. Like Eliot's Tiresias, Merwin wanders "between two lives"—one of fragmentation, the other of mythic unity. Merwin's pastoral, however, represents a more personal desire for presence. However transient, ironic, or mute, Merwin's pastoral makes devotional gestures toward a purged landscape where "the grass had its own language" (*L*, 5). Yet that "other," more "natural" language can only be uttered negatively, through its difference from the rhetoric of the city. Constituted by that dialectical tension, Merwin's poetry rigorously resists a phenomenological transfiguration of the language of the city:

> Once once and once
> In the same city I was born
> Asking what shall I say
>   (*L*, 32)

Throughout the later poetry this image of birth as a kind of aphasia before language's city of words emerges as an unavoidable rite of estrangement. He writes:

> I would never have thought I would be born here
>   . . .
> With my grief on your bridges with my voice
> In your stones what is your name
>   (*MT*, 62)

The desire to name—to master reality through the Word—has already been claimed by language, into whose history we are born too late. To enter language is to be inscribed by discursive forces already set in motion. In *The Lice*, Merwin represents the assault of that "memory of tongues" with the myth of "The Hydra": "The Hydra calls me but I am used to it / It calls me Everybody / But I know my name and do not answer" (*L*, 5). The dilemma here is unresolvable; to offer his name as a rejoinder to the hydra would only give it another mouth. To be born out of silence into the city of names is to be inscribed, paradoxically, among the traces of its dead: "But you the dead / Once you go into those names / You go on you never / Hesitate / You go on" (*L*, 5). No longer a point of origin for or bearer of spiritual essence, one's personal voice dissolves into the sedimented, textual history:[7]

> Where do the hours of a city begin and end
> among so many
> the limits rising
> and setting each time in each body
> in a city how many hands of timepieces
> must be counting the hours
> clicking at a given moment
> numbering insects into machines to be codified
> calculating newsprint in the days of the living
> all together they are not infinite
> any more than the ignored patience
> of rubber tires day and night
> or the dumbness of wheels or the wires of passions
>
> where is the horizon the avenue has not reached it
> reaching and reaching lying palm upward
> exposing the places where blood is given or let
> at night the veins of the sleepers remember trees
> countless sleepers the hours of trees
> the uncounted hours the leaves in the dark
> by day the light of the streets is the color of arms kept covered
> and of much purpose
> again at night the lights of the streets play on ceilings
> they brush across walls
> of room after unlit room hung with pictures
> of the youth of the world
>
> (*CF*, 29)

This astonishing poem advances the Blakean critique of the city as a wholly "charter'd" locale. For Merwin, the production, quantification, and encoding of reality into cultural "limits" is a hellish spectacle. The hours of the metropolis, "numbering insects into machines to be codified," "are not infinite" but fallen. Merwin's personification of inanimate things—"the ignored patience / of rubber tires," "the dumbness of wheels"—subverts such Cartesian binaries as subjectivity/objectivity, the inwardness of consciousness/the outwardness of things, spiritual essence/material substance, and mind/body. Merwin's surreal city disrupts any mimetic grounding in referentiality by exposing such divisions as culturally produced fictions, categories within the text of bourgeois capitalism's myth of the individual. In "The Counting Houses" the strategy is hyperbolic. Merwin expands what he calls "the habitual and customary referentiality which is dulled and blunted and exterior" to acknowledge fully and thereby exhaust its tragic potential.[8] The poet's seemingly emotive experience of the city actually is made possible by his linguistic response to the "codified" transformations of its symbolic systems.

In stanza 1 the "ignored patience" of this verbal metropolis becomes excruciating. "Reaching and reaching lying palm upward," the urban landscape strains toward some transcendent horizon of the *civitas dei*. Yet that gesture only reopens the wounds of its mortality, "exposing the places where blood is given or let." That collective crucifixion, however, yields a redemptive vision of the "countless sleepers the hours of trees / the uncounted hours the leaves in the dark." Merwin's pastoral dream cannot be embodied, of course, except in these provisional textual pleasures. Even there the phenomenal utopia is only a fleeting linguistic difference bounded by the language of the street. Moreover, the irony of Merwin's final lines immobilizes any privileged world of beauty and truth. In the poem's closing metaphor, aesthetic representation itself suspends the youthful immediacy of the image—the duration of its "uncounted hours"—by reducing art to artifact. The unregenerate space of the avenue returns as the architecture of the counting house now becomes the cryptic gallery of art. Here, ghostly street lights "brush across walls / of room after unlit room hung with pictures / of the youth of the world." Ultimately, this is a metaphor for Merwin's anxiety about the material mediations of verbal representation. Any Romantic faith in a world of ideal meaning existing prior to language is radically suspect. Youth here is merely a text.

History's temporal gravity is spatialized again as architecture in this uncanny portrait of "St. Vincent's":

its bricks by day a French red under
cross facing south
blown-up neo-classical facades the tall
dark openings between columns at
the dawn of history
exploded into many windows
in a mortised face

(CF, 34)

Gazing into the hospital's "mortised face" of time, we ourselves are
viewed fatefully from the "dark openings" of "the dawn of history."
Yet the wall's blank, unreadable surface expresses only the void of its
hollowed visage. Like this shadowy facade and the half-illumined
labyrinth of "The Counting Houses," Merwin's later verse is a chiar-
oscuro of indeterminacy. His recent work resembles an extended web
of fragments, a palimpsest, where what can be read is either never
entire or a dialogic effect of other utterances it simultaneously reveals and effaces.[9]

Yet if there is a wholeness to Merwin's later work, it resists the
symbolic depth of the high modernism of Yeats or Eliot. Unlike
Yeats's reliance on A Vision's esoteric myth of history or Eliot's
Christian orthodoxy, Merwin's project rejects the closure of master
narratives. Although individual images can catalyze extended readings of other poems, Merwin's text invites a plural, anarchic play of
meanings. In addition to his ambiguous syntax and his abandonment
of punctuation,[10] he has conceived the form of the later poetry against
a background of what critics have described either positively as silence, transparence, numinous presence, or negatively as void, abyss,
distance, death, failure, and apocalyptic chaos.[11] However hopeful or
despairing past readings of Merwin's "otherness" have been, most
mystify and valorize his work with an appeal to phenomenological
experience.[12] Stephen Spender, for example, points to the "animis-
tic" quality of the verse, while Denis Donoghue says the poetry uses
a "natural" rather than "rhetorical" syntax.[13] Donoghue argues that,
in contrast to the fragmented and eruptive language that Roland
Barthes finds in modernism, Merwin attempts a "natural" syntax in
which "relations between one thing and another are given."[14] Yet
Merwin often invokes his characteristic diction, or the silence of his
lacunas and erasures, not so much to create a mystified world of
"natural" presence, but more to exploit a compositional resource.

His strategy is to bracket out the final status of his poetry's "otherness" in order to exploit it discursively. Merwin's verbal mastery is precisely that uncanny deployment of silence, nothingness, and distance to render invisible, paradoxically, any trace of phenomenological determination.[15]

The Romantic hope, of course, is that a luminous spirituality will inspire the poet's words with an ideal transparence; yet for Merwin that plenitude is merely a linguistic effect. Moreover, his pastoral landscapes which seem to lead beyond writing are nevertheless thoroughly rhetorical. Though Merwin might want to efface his medium to voice the immediacy of experience, the materiality of language is never transparent: "it never is the experience, it is something else."[16] That admission, however, need not be a source of regret. That there are no exits from Merwin's city of signifiers to a pastoral world of ideal meaning is at once tragic and liberating. Merwin discovers a tragic joy in overcoming the burden of the Word's history through momentary acts of verbal displacement. Because his poems are willed in spite of the Word's fall from unmediated presence, their vistas at times seem to open onto landscapes that possess a kind of phenomenal grace. Each, however, is finally a linguistic mirage.

The urban locale of "The Child," for example, is first the site of Merwin's alienation, but it is displaced by a qualified image of hope that describes the poet's rebirth into language:

Then there are the stories and after a while I think something
Else must connect them besides just this me
I regard myself starting the search turning
Corners in remembered metropoli
I pass skins withering in gardens that I see now
Are not familiar
And I have lost even the thread I thought I had

(L, 37)

In memory's metropolis the search for meaning leads only deeper into a narrative labyrinth of loss and bewilderment. The city's "stories" become gardens of withering skins whose ciphers, as in "The Counting Houses," are "not familiar" but wholly estranged. Nevertheless, if as a poet Merwin could be "consistent even in destitution," he claims, "the world would be revealed" (L, 37). The poem's final lines enact that disclosure as the birth of silence:

This silence coming at intervals out of the shell of names
It must be all one person really coming at
Different hours for the same thing
If I could learn the word for yes it could teach me questions
I would see that it was itself every time and I would
Remember to say take it up like a hand
And go with it this is at last
Yourself

The child that will lead you

                                                              (L, 38)

This nativity recalls Eliot's depiction of Christ as logos in "Gerontion": "The word within a word, unable to speak a word; / Swaddled
with darkness."[17] Yet unlike Eliot's poem—whose meaning is in-
formed by allusions to the biblical narrative of Christ's birth, crucifixion, and resurrection—Merwin's "silence" here is relatively indeterminate. Merwin's "word/child," though revealed, is not entirely
revelatory. Not only is his hope conditional on learning "the word for
yes" but his imagery describes an unsettling simulacrum of division. Merwin's "verse/child" is uncanny because it is both "yourself" and "other." It mirrors the poet's temporal displacement from
all his other fictional selves who are "coming at / Different hours for
the same thing." Because they "must be all one person," they can
only offer each other their common, unfulfilled arrivals in language.
In that destitution—the city's infinite regression—Merwin recognizes himself as the child of language. The child comes forth but not
necessarily as an iconic emissary of hope.

Throughout the later poetry Merwin returns to that paradox of incarnation: "I am the son of the future," he writes in Carrier, "but she
shows me only her mourning veil / I am the son of the future but my
own father" (CL, 92). "The Day" (WA, 14) seems to speak directly to
the ending of "The Child" as if it were a coda meant to crystallize
the poet's fascination with incarnation as repetition:

If you could take the day by the hand
even now and say Come Father
calling it by your own name
it might rise in its blindness with all
its knuckles and curtains
and open the eyes it was born with

                                                    (WA, 14)

Sharing the same "knuckles and curtains" of the flesh, the names "father" and "child" become synonymous. The final image of birth is at once an epiphanic and grotesque recognition.

Any critical reading that attempts to inform Merwin's aesthetic with an idealized vision of hope misreads the tone of poignancy throughout his later poems. In Carol Kyle's reading of "The Child," for example, Merwin's thread imagery becomes a trope representing the "connection" between self and environment. Surrealism, for Kyle, is Merwin's way of spinning a unified vision out of the apparent fragments of modern experience: "Surrealism in Merwin's poetry," she writes, "is much more than a technique: it is a large, affirmative vision, optimistic in the connections among all things."[18] In Kyle's reading the "technique" of discourse, again, is in the service of some larger, disembodied "vision" of experience. But Merwin's surrealism is inscribed with the omnipresent "division" of language itself. Merwin consistently distances his poetry from that kind of absolute appeal to visionary experience. The thread in "The Child" leads only endlessly through the decentered maze of discourse. Merwin's use of this same trope in "The Thread" from *The Carrier of Ladders* traces even more darkly the poet's passage through the archives of the Word:

> Unrolling the black thread
> through the tunnel
> you come to the wide wall
> of shoes
> the soles standing
> out in the air you breathe
> crowded from side to side
> floor to ceiling
> and no names
> and no door
> and the bodies
> stacked before them like bottles
> generation upon
> generation
> upon generation
> with their threads
> asleep in their hands
> and the tunnel is full
> of their bodies
> from there
> all the way to the end of the mountain

the beginning of time
the light of day
the bird
and you are unrolling
the Sibyll's song
that is trying to reach her
beyond your dead
(*CL*, 121)

In "Lemuel's Blessing" the poet trembles before "the memory of tongues." Here in "The Thread," unrolling the "Sibyll's song" is hopelessly detoured by history's dead. The poet's Orphic quest out of the tunnel's underworld is thwarted by the sheer density of time's victims. This graphic vision of history as mortality invokes a claustrophobic image of time as Holocaust.[19] There, Merwin recognizes himself among the anonymous citizens of death's ghetto.[20] Even the thread of language, which might connect him to the descending dove of the Holy Ghost, belongs to the Sibyll—a grotesque reminder of Petronius's Sibyl at Cumae. Merwin's muse "beyond your dead" is herself the personification of the unregenerate Word—an immortal yet decrepit spinster. In "Sibyl" the poet addresses his muse with the same sense of tragic irony: "Your whole age sits between what you hear / and what you write." Contending against the moment's fateful unraveling, the poet races to outdistance memory: "the same wind that tells you everything at once / unstitches your memory / you try to write faster than the thread is pulled" (*WA*, 53). Inspired by that divine wind—*that ruach*—one would envision a world wholly transparent. Yet for Merwin the clarity of that "correspondent breeze" does not disclose an absolute presence, but an omnipresent nothingness. To survive, he must frantically pace himself against the memory of his own vacancy. Moreover, his verse must be manufactured in the sweatshop of language, whose history is a random tapestry of discursive practices. Often, for Merwin, poetry itself becomes an alienated medium whose "stitching" everywhere seems to violate experience. At these times, the city becomes the locale for the poet's urgent sense of crisis in vocation: "the nine village tailors fear / their thread if not their needles if not / their needles in everything and it is / here this is New York" (*CL*, 83–84).

Merwin has called New York the archetypal city; there he works through his anxiety about language's mediation of "everything."[21] In "Island City," a more recent poem from *Finding the Islands*, a startling image of the city's cacophony personifies the reduction of poetry's voice to secular noise:

> Pile of box houses
> with wires on every side
> and box voices and box dogs
>
> Around a corner
> somebody who's a city
> pounds all day on a tin door
> (FI, 22)

The "box voice" of poetry—its verbal medium—can never wholly transfigure the limits of its linguistic artifice. Moreover, because words are our only entrances to presence, they bestow merely a provisional authenticity to our experience of the world. Mistaking language for reality, for Merwin, is the greatest kind of victimization. In another urban poem, "The Widow," Merwin indicts that consciousness unknowingly determined by the imagery of cultural functionalism:

> You confide
> In images in things that can be
> Represented which is their dimension you
> Require them you say This
> Is real and you do not fall down and moan
>
> Not seeing the irony in the air
>
> Everything that does not need you is real
> (L, 34–35)

Indeed, the poet would also collapse under his own discursive fictions if he believed in the need for anything beyond their pseudo-reality. Aware of his investment in the representations of language, however, Merwin voices the Word's inscribed indifference at the heart of "everything." That acknowledgment of despair, paradoxically, is a source of celebration. By unhinging referentiality, Merwin's vision of the city's mobile linguistic transformations becomes, finally, ecstatic:

> the stone city in
> the river has changed and of course
> the river
> and all words even those unread in
> envelopes

all those shining cars vanished
after them entire roads gone like kite strings
incalculable records' print grown finer
just the names at that followed by smoke of numbers
and high buildings turned to glass in
other air oh one clear day

(CF, 33)

Merwin's Heraclitean affirmation of "all words" becomes pastoral
by invoking an infinite semiotic transaction quite void of human
agency. That vision of linguistic free play becomes openly bucolic in
"The Well":

Under the stone sky the water
waits
with all its songs inside it
the immortal
it sang once
it will sing again
the days
walk across the stone in heaven
unseen as planets at noon
while the water
watches the same night

Echoes come in like swallows
calling to it
it answers without moving
but in echoes
not in its voice
they do not say what it is
only where

It is a city to which many travellers
came with clear minds
having left everything even
heaven
to sit in the dark praying as one silence
for the resurrection

(CL, 37)

Each of these images is impenetrable to our knowing. We could
never hope to master the infinite patience of this strange landscape.
The stone sky and waiting water mirror one another in the common
countenance of an absolute stasis. For Merwin, the infinite regress of

that eternal regard becomes totally "other," as language—the "voice" of the well's dark pool. The well is pregnant with "all its songs" and there is the assurance that "it sang once / it will sing again." Yet those "immortal" hymns were never meant for us. Our desire to possess that collective voice, to receive baptism into some essence of the Word's symbolic order, is inevitably refracted as an echo of deferral. The well's voice "answers without moving" because it was never there other than as surface—a limitless layering of echoes devoid of depth or essential meaning. Here, of course, we have come full circle to Merwin's initial depiction of Babel's "memory of tongues." Now, however, the poet enters that city of language as a pilgrim to a New Jerusalem. Like the "many travellers" who have "left everything even / heaven / to sit in the dark praying as one silence," the poet has abandoned desire for experience unmediated by language. Yet, the city's redemptive dwelling is infested, ultimately, by the unfulfilled irony of messianic desire—an all-too-human anticipation which Merwin, like Beckett, finds absurd.

In Merwin's most recent work the mobility of water and words describes a confluence of pastoral and urban settings. Woven into the fabric of each country scene is the same verbal trace that shuttles through the urban tapestry:

> beside me the hissing
> cataract plunged into the trees
> holding on I moved closer
> left foot on a rock in the water
> right foot on a rock in deeper water
> at the edge of the fall
> then from under the weight of my right foot
> came a voice like a small bell singing
> over and over one clear treble
> syllable.
>
> (*OH*, 81–82)

In this bucolic baptism, set in the tropical mountains of Hawaii where Merwin now spends half the year, we find the same immersion into language as in this verbal descent through a New York rainstorm:

> here are the faces the faces
> the cool leaves still lucent before summer
> the voices

I am home before the lights come on
home when the thunder begins after dark
and the rain in the streets at night
while the iron train again
rumbles under the sidewalk
long cans full of lights and
unseen faces disappearing
in my mind

many travelling behind the same headline
saying second
IRA hunger striker dies
in British hands in Ireland

                                                              (OH, 50)

To step into this urban world is to enter into the dark flux of its
"words flowing under the place of the avenue." But that descent
allows the poet to return to a new dwelling within the "known music" of the city's urban voices: "most beautiful / of cities and most
empty / pure avenue behind the words of friends / and the known
music" (OH, 51).

The "music" of Merwin's latest two volumes, Finding the Islands
(1982) and Opening the Hand (1983), is "known" in the same terms
as in the earlier volumes—through its double mediation of the poet's
experience. In either its urban or pastoral mode, Merwin's most recent verse can at once disclose a dwelling of phenomenological plenitude, one hospitable to human desire, while systematically frag-
menting it. In Finding, plenitude takes precedence. Here, the poet's
names provide entrances to everything language had failed to provide or only promised in The Moving Target, The Lice, Writings, and
The Compass Flower. These frank, erotic lyrics depict a love conceived in a language of assured simplicity. No longer hollowed by division, the poet calls forth an intimate unity: "We tell each other a
language," he writes, "and it breathes / between us" (FI, 51). At times
his words lead his readers into that shared life: "Our names surrounded / by a heart / entwine in the dark" (FI, 55). More often,
though, they become entirely elusive: "If I were to talk of you / how
would anyone know what the words meant" (FI, 66). Indeed, Finding
aims to possess a voice that moves beyond langauge into a wholly
ineffable world, yet, paradoxically, abides there uttering its name:
"For each voiceless flower," the poet promises, "there is a voice

among / the absent flowers" (*FI*, 7). Again, Merwin's pastoral mode gestures toward a threshold of presence just beyond the poet's words:

> In your voice the rain
> is finding its way to the stream
> above the sea
>
> (*FI*, 62)

> Gray voice
> nuthatch after sunset
> nothing to call it
>
> (*FI*, 10)

> Some of the mayflies
> drift on into hot June
> without their names
>
> (*FI*, 5)

> Once you leave
> you have a name
> you can't remember
>
> (*FI*, 34)

Each of these three-line lyrics, Merwin has said, embodies a discrete poetic form: "complete as a small, if not the smallest unit." Together they exist "in relation to each other."[22] What draws them into a larger continuity, however, is not a conscious authorial intention, which Merwin rejects, but precisely that unknown source of forceful "otherness"—what he has called "the teacher who is not dead, the world of silence."[23] That paradox of Being, which resides in all creation but only as an invisible Other, *is* the poet's forgotten name— an absence that reminds him of the world's "islands" of phenomenological plentitude.

In *Opening the Hand* the silence of that "one word for all the trees ever seen / and their lifetimes" (*FI*, 11) becomes deafening, just as the poet's need to speak its name becomes more insistent: "if I could take one voice / with me it would be / the sound I hear everyday" (*OH*, 24). That omnipresent sound—what Heidegger would describe as the "call" of Being—summons the poet to a more authentically conceived world.[24] Yet its communication lacks message or judgment; its clearing is obscure. The "one word" of silence teaches us of the authentic only by resisting the threshold of meaning. Consequently, Merwin's dialogue with that voice has led him to a kind of

attentive passivity. Hearing, wondering, looking are the representative terms of Merwin's witnessing here. Indeed, the syntax of his
title, Opening the Hand, like Finding the Islands, suggests an ongoing phenomenological process—an unfolding gesture of commitment to the Other. Typically, openness to experience is rendered as a
mode of perception. Here, the poet's listening and seeing fuse the
silence of person and planet into a single dwelling:

> By now you have envisaged
> . . .
> the fire on the beach
> through the endless hours of sunset
> and have held the sound of the north dome
> of the planet turning
> gazing constantly at the sun
> the lull of the lakes at that
> time the hum of the surfaces
> the breath of woods
> bird voices clattering
> through the sleepless light
> of the sun at midnight
> and your long shadow walking
> on the still water
>
> that is what you go on seeing
> at that latitude
> as the water turns silent and then
> begins to tremble
>
> (OH, 63)

Implied in the tone of Merwin's last word, "tremble," however, is the
risk accompanying "that latitude" of pastoral vision. In "The Middle
of Summer," listening to each turn of the planet's "north dome" reminds him of time's winter.

While love's fulfillment was Merwin's subject in Finding, time,
aging, and death qualify the pastoral optimism of Opening, particularly in the troubled ruminations of section 1 that work through the
loss of the poet's father. The dream images of the father in "The
Oars" and "Sunset Water," the psychic presentiments of his death in
"The Waving of a Hand" and "Strawberries," the play of imagination
and memory of "Sun and Rain" and "The Houses" culminate in "Apparitions." There simply "opening the hand" reminds the poet of the

past's uncanny persistence in the present—of his bodily inheritance of a familial likeness. But if Merwin—like Keats in "This Living Hand"—were to open his hand to us in a final blessing, it might, I think, be the volume's last poem, "The Black Jewel":

> In the dark
> there is only the sound of the cricket
>
> south wind in the leaves
> is the cricket
> so is the surf on the shore
> and the barking across the valley
>
> the cricket never sleeps
> the whole cricket is the pupil of one eye
> it can run it can leap it can fly
> in its back the moon
> crosses the night
>
> there is only the one cricket
> when I listen
>
> the cricket lives in the unlit ground
> in the roots
> out of the wind
> it has only the one sound
>
> before I could talk
> I heard the cricket
> under the house
> then I remembered summer
>
> mice too and the blind lightning
> are born hearing the cricket
> dying they hear it
> bodies of light turn listening to the cricket
> the cricket is neither alive nor dead
> the death of the cricket
> is still the cricket
> in the bare room the luck of the cricket
> echoes
>
> (OH, 83)

"The Black Jewel" is Merwin's consummate articulation of that unnameable but unifying syllable which he has struggled to speak as early as "The Child" and as recently as "Summer Canyon," "Green

Island," "Dark Side," "After a Storm," and "Hearing." Yet his metaphoric rendering of that logos here bristles with deceptions. Its crys-
tal is "black" because the cricket voices an alienating universal. Ultimately, the cricket's sound describes the same mediating role of
figurative displacement that Merwin experiences through language's
demonic incarnation as division. The poet's metaphoric chain of as-
sociative images—"south wind in the leaves," "surf on the shore,"
"barking across the valley"—mobilizes a process of verbal substitution that is devoid of meaning precisely because it is conceived
against the cricket's unfathomable dark. In stanza 3 the poet's entire
experience, which is "only the sound of the cricket," endures now as
the wakeful vigilance of an estranged consciousness. The unity of
the "whole cricket" is a radically anti-platonic version of God's om-
niscient witnessing. Unlike earlier, Romantic mystifications of this
visionary image—for example Emerson's "transparent eyeball" in
"Nature" or Shelley's "Hymn to Apollo"—Merwin's omnipresent
"pupil" reflects a more Dionysian, earthbound spectacle reminiscent of Yeats in "Tom the Lunatic."[25] The cricket's eye, through
which Merwin would imagine a plenitude of phenomenological
presence, resists that visionary drive to become sheer surface. The
compositional quality of Merwin's line—"it can run it can leap it
can fly"—in its contracted textures mimics the material particulars
of nature. Yet the poet can also dilate his imagery to engulf us in an
unsettling distance: "in its back the moon / crosses the night."

Crystallized in "The Black Jewel" is Merwin's sense of the void behind each of the world's surfaces. Hearing the "one cricket," Merwin
enters its subterranean dwelling "in the unlit ground / in the roots."
There, the poet's journey "under the house" leads him into a deeper
listening to that "one sound" whose unity permeates the night's
jewel as an omnipresent silence. This demonic dimension of the
world's oneness transforms the poet through its "blind lightning."
Although lightning traditionally signals spiritual liberation, here its
force is discharged, again, as the black thunder of the cricket's unknowable voice. Its dark Word involves both "mice" and "bodies of
light" in a common incarnate fate, where all opposites collapse into
the same abyss. There, the poet discovers the source of his own speaking to be deathless: "the cricket is neither alive nor dead / the death of
the cricket / is still the cricket." The cricket's voice "echoes" beyond
life and death in the "breathless mouth" of language itself.

Although Merwin's most recent two volumes gesture toward a pastoral vision of phenomenological experience, each line is, finally, a "black jewel" compressed from the discursive sedimentation of other texts. Not even *Finding*'s most candid and spontaneous love lyrics escape that rhetorical grounding. Indeed, Merwin has known this truth about language throughout his career: every seemingly essential utterance is already split by the Word's polysemy. "It would be very difficult and very rare," he has said, "to make a poem out of pure anger, or out of pure anything. Even love poems are seldom made out of pure love. Actually, they're made out of words, so all of the paradoxes that are built into any phrase come into it. Pure anger would just be a scream."[26] It is this divorce of the Word from both essential meaning and authorial delimitation which makes the poet wary of language's representational function. Merwin's verbal medium, even in his pastoral love lyrics, can become a kind of threat to the phenomenological dwelling he would envision:

> Across the mountain I see you
> across the crater
> we live on
>
> you avoid the words
> about you
> like a mountain goat
>
> (*FI*, 57)

Words can become sources of redemption for Merwin—insofar as they open ways that lead to the phenomenological disclosure of the world. Yet the poet's language itself can become a demonic force, one that reifies that envisioned world as a wholly codified text. Just as Merwin's pastoral "island" is bombarded by the urban present— "Young deer standing in headlights / in ditch below cliff / cars coming both ways" (*FI*, 10)—so, the poet's "other" life is often in the way of the Word's more mobile and mechanistic autonomy, "in the way of language":

> Something continues and I don't know what to call it
> though the language is full of suggestions
> in the way of language
>   but they are all anonymous
> (*OH*, 67)

Merwin always finds himself "in the way of language" in this dual sense: simultaneously led to encounter a subjective, pastoral life and named as object by the city's text. Moreover, this double conception of language advances his poetry beyond both the more Romantic aesthetics of place in a poet like Theodore Roethke and the "subjective or deep" imagery of phenomenological surrealism in Robert Bly's and James Wright's "emotive" verse.

In these urban and pastoral moments we could easily oversimplify Merwin's complex play of landscapes by reducing them to a rigid binarism. We could group, on the one hand, images describing natural innocence, seasonal renewal, and a subjective phenomenology of bucolic presence. On the other hand, we could set off locales which are marred by our industrial apocalypse, determined by a totalitarian quantification of time and space, and blighted by the loss of a genuine cultural and communal inheritance. We could even assign each setting a particular idiom. Indeed, Merwin himself in "Notes for a Preface" tends to oppose what he calls "the great language itself, the vernacular of the imagination" to "the voice of the institution" in which "the person and senses are being lost in the consumer, who does not know what he sees, hears, wants, or is afraid of."[27] The problem in such an essentialist reduction, however, would be the temptation to resolve that tension by privileging the voice of imagination as an empowering term lending a transcendent legitimacy to Merwin's work. In fact, Merwin's poetic practice resists that kind of Romantic synthesis. Because Merwin is aware of language's mediation of all imaginative vision, he allows pastoral utterance and the discourse of the city to coexist and even to become reversible idioms within one continuous text. This kind of fusion not only happens in the final, urban image in "The Well," for example, but also at the end of "In Autumn." There, nature's arbor becomes another anticipation of a New Jerusalem: "The lights are going on in the leaves nothing to do with evening / Those are cities / Where I had hoped to live" (L, 41). Moreover, Merwin will often yoke his country and urban images for telling, surrealistic effects: "Hay in and a cow sick / the unwatched television / flickers on his face" (FI, 36).

It is within the Word's symbolic order, finally, and not in some ineffable phenomenology of numinous experience, that Merwin creates a forceful, postmodern aesthetic. Moreover, his text's dialectical exchange of country and city landscapes reveals the poet's fundamental ambivalence toward that contemporary practice of writing. Language, as in "Words from a Totem Animal," can trap us in the artificial limits of linguistic representation: "I stumble when I remember how it was / with one foot / one foot still in a name" (*CL*, 17). But poetry can become an Orphic force through which we are led into the rebirth of language:

> it is true that in
> our language deaths are to be heard
> at any moment through the talk
> pacing their wooden rooms jarring
> the dried flowers
> but they have forgotten who they are
> and our voices in their heads waken
> childhoods in other tongues
>
> (*CL*, 56)

If Merwin is possessed by a vision of apocalypse—what one reviewer has called "the agony of a generation which knows itself to be the last"—he also speaks from what Auden named (in his preface to *A Mask for Janus*) "the other side of disaster."[28] In almost any of the later poems we can trace Merwin's imaginative shuttle between these two almost archetypal landscapes. Indeed, one of his techniques is to make the sense of individual images oscillate so rapidly between these two alternatives that whole poems enact their fusion. Both moments coalesce into a single discursive practice—a landscape of verbal differences whose settings are reversible. The double edge of Merwin's faith in and suspicion of that dwelling of names cuts through each of his powerful images. His paradoxical understanding of language and its landscapes informs each utterance with both an assertion of the Word's "strange land" and a questioning of its "heaven" of tongues:

> the prophecies waking without names in
> strange lands on unborn tongues those syllables
> resurrected staring is that heaven
>
> (*CL*, 87)

NOTES

1. Paul Carroll, *The Poem in Its Skin* (Chicago: Big Table, 1968), p. 143.

2. See Martin Heidegger, "Letter on Humanism" in Martin Heidegger, *Basic Writings*, ed. David Farrell Krell (New York: Harper and Row, 1977), p. 197; Paul A. Bové, *Destructive Poetics* (New York: Columbia University

Press, 1980); William V. Spanos, "Heidegger, Kierkegaard, and the Hermeneutic Circle: Towards a Postmodern Theory of Interpretation," in *Martin Heidegger and the Question of Literature: Towards a Postmodern Literary Hermeneutics*, ed. William V. Spanos (Bloomington: Indiana University Press, 1979).

3. Martin Heidegger, "The Origin of the Work of Art," in Heidegger, *Basic Writings*, p. 180.

4. It is, of course, in Heidegger's valorization of speech over writing—his description of discourse as "saying," "keeping silent," "hearing the peal of stillness," etc.—that Derrida uncovers the trace of metaphysics it is Heidegger's project to overcome. See Martin Heidegger, *Being and Time*, trans. John MacQuarrie and Edward Robinson (New York: Harper and Row, 1962), pp. 203–10; Heidegger, "Letter on Humanism," pp. 210, 213, 221; Martin Heidegger, "Language," in *Poetry, Language, Thought*, trans. Albert Hofstadter (New York: Harper and Row, 1971), pp. 206–10; Martin Heidegger, "Conversation on a Country Path about Thinking," in *Discourse on Thinking*, trans. John M. Anderson and E. Hans Freund (New York: Harper and Row, 1966), p. 68.

5. Jacques Derrida, *Of Grammatology*, trans. Gayatri Chakravorty Spivak (Baltimore: Johns Hopkins University Press, 1976), p. 22. For other discussions of Derrida's relationship to Heidegger see: Joseph N. Riddel, "From Heidegger to Derrida to Chance: Doubling and (Poetic) Language," *Boundary 2*, 4, no. 2 (1976), 571–92; Frances C. Ferguson, "Reading Heidegger: Jacques Derrida and Paul de Man," *Boundary 2*, 4, no. 2 (1976), 593–610; Bové, *Destructive Poetics*; David Couzens Hoy, "Forgetting the Text: Derrida's Critiques of Heidegger," in *The Question of Textuality*, ed. William V. Spanos, Paul A. Bové, and Daniel O'Hara (Bloomington: Indiana University Press, 1982); Rodolphe Gasché, "Joining the Text: From Heidegger to Derrida," in *The Yale Critics: Deconstruction in America*, ed. Jonathan Arac, Wlad Godzich, and Wallace Martin (Minneapolis: University of Minnesota Press, 1983); Vincent Leitch, *Deconstructive Criticism* (New York: Columbia University Press, 1983).

6. Derrida's radical extension of Saussure to critique all "transcendental signified" meaning has helped to shed new light on Merwin's poetry in two recent essays. The most rigorous Derridean reading of Merwin's career to date is Cary Nelson's "The Resources of Failure: W. S. Merwin's Deconstructive Career," which observes: "To speak these words is to experience an uneasiness that cannot be resolved; yet the poet who speaks them may appear, paradoxically, as Jacques Derrida has come to be viewed in contemporary criticism, the master of irresolution. The challenge Merwin sets himself in his best work is to occupy exactly that position—to become the anonymous American figure who announces the harmonizing dissolution of the language" (p. 79). Again, in Charles Altieri's chapter we find a similar Derridean moment: "Man keeps projecting words to capture a reality, yet he finds in the end only more words and deeper doubts about his ability to capture experience. For language is no longer referential, but, as Jacques Derrida puts

it, a process of 'supplementation'. . . . Language tries to make things present, but it leaves only an absence requiring more words, ad infinitum" (*Enlarging the Temple*, p. 219).

7. "[T]he author does not precede the work, he is a certain functional principle by which, in our culture, one limits, excludes, and chooses; in short, by which one impedes the free circulation, the free manipulation, the free composition, decomposition, and recomposition of fictions." Michel Foucault, "What Is an Author?" in *Textual Strategies: Perspectives in Post-Structural Criticism*, ed. Josué V. Harari (Ithaca: Cornell University Press, 1979), p. 159. See also, Roland Barthes, "The Death of the Author," in *Image, Music, Text*, trans. Stephen Heath (London: Fontana, 1977).

8. Ed Folsom and Cary Nelson, " 'Fact Has Two Faces': An Interview with W. S. Merwin," *Iowa Review*, 13 (Winter 1982), p. 51.

9. The "whole work," Merwin has said, "is one large book, because there is a more or less audible voice running through everything. At least I would like to think that one's work becomes a coherent project eventually, that poems are not merely disparate pieces with no place in the whole." Folsom and Nelson, "Interview," p. 33.

10. Dating from *The Moving Target* Merwin has abandoned punctuation in order to exploit syntactic ambiguity. This rhetorical strategy, according to Jarold Ramsey, invites the reader into a plural act of interpretation: "The reader is thereby forced to attend to the semantic movements of the verse very closely and open-mindedly; without the formal syntactic signals of commas, periods, question-marks to simplify things for him, he generally has several possible meanings opening before him at once." "Continuities of W. S. Merwin," p. 25. In addition, the dramatic quality of engagement which these lines demand transforms Merwin's poems into verbal objects, which seem to have an almost autonomous aesthetic life: "Punctuation," Merwin has said, "nails the poem down on the page; when you don't use it the poem becomes more a thing in itself, at once more transparent and more actual." "A Portrait of W. S. Merwin" (interview with Frank MacShane), *Shenandoah*, 21 (Winter 1970), 12.

11. Indeed, Merwin's text so invites these kinds of phenomenological readings of his "otherness" that it is the major preoccupation of most of his critics. John Vogelsang, for example, views this experience of silence as the redemptive telos which Merwin's verse attempts to voice. For Vogelsang, Merwin's poetry becomes "an art of recognition, an art that conveys the unsoundable quality of experience, the silence and the divine, in the sounding human voice." "Toward the Great Language: W. S. Merwin," *Modern Poetry Studies*, 3, no. 3 (1972), 9. Charles Altieri's reading of Merwin, though qualified by a Derridean skepticism, gestures toward a logocentric vision: "These diaphanous words point beyond their vanishing to a silence only reached through transparence. Thus the language keeps pushing one out of time to the apartness where the apparently disembodied speaker dwells. There he can function as the shadow does in 'The Last One' or darkness in 'Finally'; he keeps alive a hope of the spirit ill at ease in time and allows a glimpse

into the source or silence," pp. 177–78. In contrast, I find Anthony Libby's discussion of nothingness less hopeful, yet still mystified: "With unusual specificity Merwin locates the emptiness that receives mystical truth at the heart of the experience of the various senses, but truth remains as unattainable as it is immediate. . . . Like acts of magic, many of these visions compel belief as they resist explication." "W. S. Merwin and the Nothing That Is," *Contemporary Literature,* 16 (1975), 35, 25. In his illuminating contrast of Merwin and Whitman, L. Edwin Folsom resists that mystification of the void as truth: "It is not a creative void that Merwin faces, not something he expands into and absorbs; rather it is a destructive void which opens its dark abyss, ready to swallow the poet and all of life with him." "Approaches and Removals: W. S. Merwin's Encounter with Whitman's America," *Shenandoah,* 29 (Spring 1978), 66.

12. For two notable exceptions, see the quotations from Altieri and Nelson in n. 6.

13. Stephen Spender, "Can Poetry Be Reviewed?" *New York Review of Books,* Sept. 20, 1973, p. 10. Denis Donoghue, "Objects Solitary and Terrible," *New York Review of Books,* June 6, 1968, p. 22.

14. Donoghue, "Objects," p. 22. See also Roland Barthes, "Is There Any Poetic Writing," in *Writing Degree Zero,* trans. Annette Lavers and Colin Smith (New York: Hill and Wang, 1978).

15. Moreover, in his own discussions of his verse, Merwin suggests an almost inevitable, even fated quality to his writing's rhetorical base. For example, concerning Whitman's rhetorical excesses, Merwin has said: "When you're trying to avoid that one kind of rhetoric, of course you're developing a different kind of rhetoric." Folsom and Nelson, "Interview," p. 36.

16. MacShane, "Portrait," p. 12.

17. T. S. Eliot, *The Complete Poems and Plays 1909–1950* (New York: Harcourt, Brace, 1962), p. 21.

18. Carol Kyle, "A Riddle for the New Year: Affirmation in W. S. Merwin," *Modern Poetry Studies,* 4 (Winter 1973), 296.

19. This image becomes even more repulsive as a war souvenir in "The Dachau Shoe," *MPC,* 15–16.

20. Unspoken but implied here is Eliot's haunting question: "After such knowledge what forgiveness?" (Eliot, *Complete Poems,* p. 22). Unlike Eliot with his faith in God's redemptive Word, however, Merwin remains with those who have "no names" because they are irrevocably displaced from "the beginning of time / the light of day / the bird."

21. Merwin described New York as the "archetypal city" in a prefatory remark to his reading of "The River of Bees" during his performance as part of the Fall 1982 Literary Festival sponsored by Southern Methodist University, Dallas, Texas.

22. Folsom and Nelson, "Interview," p. 44.

23. Ibid., p. 43.

24. Martin Heidegger, *Being and Time,* pp. 317–25.

25. Whatever stands in field or flood,
     Bird, Beast, fish or man,

Mare or stallion, cock or hen,
Stands in God's unchanging eye
In all the vigour of its blood

William Butler Yeats, "Tom the Lunatic," in *The Variorum Edition of the Poems of W. B. Yeats*, ed. Peter Allt and Russell K. Alspach (New York: Macmillan, 1965), p. 529.

26. Folsom and Nelson, "Interview," p. 41.

27. W. S. Merwin, "Notes for a Preface," in *The Distinctive Voice*, ed. William F. Martz (Glenview, Ill.: Scott, Foresman, and Co., 1966), pp. 269–70.

28. Laurence Lieberman, "Recent Poetry in Review: Risks and Faiths," *Yale Review*, 57 (Summer 1968), 597. W. H. Auden, Preface to *A Mask for Janus* (New Haven: Yale University Press, 1952).

ED FOLSOM

"I Have Been a Long Time in a Strange Country": W. S. Merwin and America

We have learned to talk about W. S. Merwin's poetry as if it were distant, foreign, alien. "The Writing on the Void," "The Dwelling of Disappearance," "The Struggle with Absence," "The Resources of Failure," "Waiting for the End," "A Poetry of Darkness," "Alien Voices," "W. S. Merwin and the Nothing That Is"—on and on sound the dark silent names we have given to our commentaries on his work. And for good reason: Merwin's vision often has amounted to a cold stare; his voice often has hovered on edges of silence. It has become a critical commonplace to refer to his career as a translator as somehow at the source of his distance and alienation: he is a poet often literally listening to dead voices, in languages not his own, getting his light from distant stars which have already vanished, aware that his own work too will outlast him, and when he dies, "the silence will set out / Tireless traveller / Like the beam of a lightless star" (*L*, 58). The image many readers have of Merwin, reinforced by the paragraph-summary of his life at the back of all his books, is of a wanderer, an exile, living in Majorca, Portugal, France, England, Mexico, translating from French, Spanish, Russian, Japanese, Chinese, Greek, Sanskrit, farther and farther back, adrift in time and displaced in space. (G. S. Fraser even sees him as a critical exile, who "would have had far wider fame in another period, perhaps in another country.")[1] His early formalistic poems, steeped in myth, felt "classical" to readers experiencing the increasing howl of the 1950s, and his sparse and unpunctuated poems in the 1960s felt as if European surrealism had somehow injected itself into the very structures of his poems, breaking his form open—but open only in a newly constrained way. So when Merwin talked of his evolving "open forms," he did not sound at all like the exuberant poets with whom we usually associate that phrase: "What are here called open forms," said Merwin, "are in some concerns the strictest." The "freedom" that accompanied his open forms was attenuated, estranged, and his talk about it was cryptic: "The 'freedom' that precedes strict forms and the 'freedom' that follows them are not necessarily much alike. Then there is the 'freedom' that accompanies poetry at a distance and occasionally joins it, often without being recognized."[2]

This sparse open form with its restricted freedom came to sound for many readers prophetic, cold, a voice from beyond the human realm; Stephen Spender noted in 1973 that "It is as though things write their own poems through Merwin."[3] From *The Moving Target* (1963) through *Writings to an Unfinished Accompaniment* (1973), Merwin's voice maintained its distance, the poems defamiliarizing us with the world that the words tried to align themselves with. It was as if Merwin the translator were coercing us into an activity of translation from a language we only dimly recalled, the words looking familiar, but sounding oddly foreign in their shattered syntax and puzzling new juxtaposition. It was not easy to interpret the beams from these lightless poems, but many readers were entranced by them nonetheless.

Beginning with *The Compass Flower* (1977), and continuing through *Finding the Islands* (1982) and *Opening the Hand* (1983), the elusive and attenuated "freedom" that Merwin had seen accompanying his poems at a distance seemed suddenly to hover much closer by, altering his form again but more remarkably altering the order and relation of words. Dark, dimly perceived landscapes of absence dawned peopled, full, lit. Love was expressed openly; cynicism and cold anger were transformed into a lighter, often playful irony. The taut unfamiliar strings of words became familiar, relaxed, occasionally slack. The poems were often longer, filling more of the page. The tight fist was opening, and the new light revealed landscapes we knew: it was almost as if we had learned the language for these poems too easily, or as if we had known it all along. Many readers who had thrived on deciphering the runelike inscriptions of *The Lice* felt that they had to invent all the difficulties in order to talk about the recent work. Critics who were comfortable with their dark titles found little to celebrate in the newer poems, though the poems themselves of course celebrated a great deal.

The light of these new poems illuminates Merwin's pattern of return; they may seem a radical departure from his earlier work, but their subjects and tone have in fact been there in various guises all along. One thing the poems return to is Merwin's own past. Amidst all the talk of foreign languages and foreign places, it is easy to lose sight of Merwin's upbringing in Union City, New Jersey, and in Scranton, Pennsylvania, and his long family history along the Allegheny near Pittsburgh. It may be surprising to hear Merwin, in his first interview (in the mid-1950s), express this localized desire: "I want to go back to Pennsylvania, and write about it—poems—plays—stories—everything. Pennsylvania is where I come from."[4] *Unframed Originals* (1982) is part of that going back, a mixture of story and autobiography focusing on his childhood and ancestry in Pennsylvania and New Jersey. The cast of family characters—his stern Presbyterian-minister father, Aunt Alma, Old Jake, John D.—and family towns like Rimer were already appearing in poems in the mid-1950s (some collected in *The Drunk in the Furnace*, others still uncollected) and have continued to appear on through *Opening the Hand*, which begins with a series of poems that correspond to scenes in *Unframed Originals* (one poem, "Unknown Forbear," even describes the photograph that appears on the cover of *Unframed Originals*). As we cast back through Merwin's books given the insights we gain in *Unframed Originals*, we find family poems where we had not seen them before, and much of what seemed alien and distant begins to seem instead troubling and close: prophecy and cryptic comments now sometimes collapse into remarkable expressions of family experiences. Even vaguely allegorical-sounding poems like "The Church" and "The Old Room" in *The Carrier of Ladders* become clarified and grounded in Merwin's autobiographical and very American past. His career begins to feel much more placed and personal, much more concerned with family and national myths than with universal myths.

So in Merwin's most recently published interview, the interviewer remarks on Merwin's large collection of books on American history; Merwin confirms his fascination with the subject, "especially the 1890s," which is, he says, "one of the real turning points in American history" when Coxey's Army, "the first protest army," marched on Washington: "The whole great dream of the frontier had come to an end. . . . There was no longer any West for a man to go to, not in the old sense. It ended. The buffalo had been killed off, the Indians had been rounded up, mostly—none of this destructive afflatus was going to work anymore; it wasn't the answer. Doing such things was an anachronism. And so we had the first petitioning groups walk on the White House lawn. This wasn't treated as anything of great importance, but I think it was a crucial moment."[5] The march of Jacob Coxey (1854–1951), leading a few hundred unemployed men from Massillon, Ohio, through Pennsylvania to the Capitol in 1894 in order to urge economic reform following the Panic of 1893, turns out, surprisingly, to have fascinated Merwin for a long time. In 1959 he applied for a fellowship to write "a narrative poem, of some length, set in the United States in the early 1890s and based on the march of Coxey's Army." The poem would have followed the march from its inception through to Coxey's arrest: "The story, to me, represents a profoundly significant gesture in the history of America and the Western World," wrote Merwin in his application statement, "a shift of frontiers and the search for new ones." He proposed to return from France to the United States in 1960 and retrace the march, wandering through Pennsylvania where his own history shared a ground with Coxey's. He said he had been working on the project for three years, and had been fascinated with it "for much longer than that." In 1960 he undertook a "grueling reading tour" in America in order to have "a chance to dig up some facts on my Coxey project."[6]

We can probably be thankful that Merwin devoted the next years to *The Lice* instead of to his epic on Coxey's Army, but it is important to note his desire at this time to write a long and distinctly "American" poem. He had just published *The Drunk in the Furnace* with its concluding section of autobiographical poems, and it seems clear he was now looking for ways to ground his poetry in his own land. During the early 1950s he had written radio and television scripts for the BBC and had been telling some classic American stories: Hawthorne's "Dr. Heidegger's Experiment" and Twain's *Huckleberry Finn* were two of his scripts. Telling these stories kept him in touch with the country that he had temporarily left. In the late 1950s he wrote two original full-length plays set in America: *A Peacock at the Door*, about a murder breaking the clean patterns of a

small nineteenth-century Pennsylvania town, and *The Gilded West,*
a play about Buffalo Bill and the "Wild West." Clearly American cultural myths and Merwin's own Pennsylvania family legends were
very much on his mind. Recently Merwin recalled his desire, in the
1950s, to return to America: "I got very homesick. It wasn't a matter
of approving of what was happening at home, it was just a matter of
hearing your own language. Lowell has a line in one of his poems,
when *he* was living in England those last years, about one of his trips
back to New York. He said, 'At least I don't have the feeling that I'm
growing deaf,' which is something I felt for several years."[7]

In 1957 Merwin's ambivalent affection for America worked itself into a poem called "After Some Years," which has remained
uncollected:

> I have been a long time in a strange country.
> The natives have been kind, in their weird climate,
> Receiving me among them as one of themselves.
> Their virtues are different from ours, and in some ways
> Superior. I have lost the sense
> Of absurdity regarding many of their odd customs.
> I get their wry lingo tangled up with my own.
> Maybe you have to go far away
> To learn where it is that names you. The fruits here
> Are excellent; better than at home.
> I can no longer taste them. I would be glad
> To be standing in a drab city of my recollection
> Where no one but newsboys would name this place
> And they mispronouncing. I hope I may
> Before too long. Before the speech here has become
> Natural to me, even more so
> Than the tongue I was born to, before these
> Sights cease to be foreign and are more familiar
> Than any I can recall. And while I
> Can still clearly remember that at home too the world
> Is made of strangers. For I do not wish
> To head back into an expectation
> Of anything better than is there, and struggling
> With some illusion, find my own place
> Is as far away as ever. But it should be
> Soon. Already I defend hotly
> Certain of our indefensible faults,

Resent being reminded; already in my mind
Our language becomes freighted with a richness
No common tongue could offer, while the mountains
Are like nowhere on earth, and the wide rivers.[8]

The poem is a striking love song, a call to extricate himself from the
Circe-like enticements of the foreign natives in a land where he
would never be fully native, but a land where, if he stayed, his own
native attachments to America would atrophy. He was anxious to get
home, then, to stop the process of having America and American English become foreign to him, to return to the place that named him,
to the tongue he was born to, to the scenes that nurtured him. The
rhythm of the poem enacts the entanglement of his speech, how
"their wry lingo [got] tangled up with my own." Slipping in and out
of iambics ("I hope I may / Before too long. Before the speech here
has become / Natural to me . . ."), shifting from stilted syntax to
simple expression, the poem seems written on the edge between two
styles: the formal and high-toned one about to be discarded, the
more colloquial but still restrained one about to be (re)embraced. His
return from Europe would involve a linguistic as well as a geographi-
cal journey.

Merwin kept a journal recording his "Flight Home" in 1956, his
first visit to America since he had departed seven years previously. In
the journal he struggles with his attachment to America; he "wanted
to stay in America" even before he left ("Why go to Europe when I
knew so little of America?"). "I know just how much, and in what
ways I'm fond of Europe," he noted, "but I don't know what I felt
about America." He is aware that he had created fictions and fan-
tasies about America while he was living in Europe: "I expect to be
immensely relieved to be able to abandon the fiction entirely, and let
the real thing take over." He is, he says, ready to be honest and critical, sustained by his love for his native place: "Let me find . . . a hard
eye, proud of having no mercy, needing none, for the thing it loves."
And he goes on to contrast the way Europeans regard their home
places with the way Americans must regard theirs:

I suppose it would be simpler to say that they have loved their
place for generations, centuries; and know it, without having to
make a fuss about it. Whereas, by comparison, we begin as a
loveless people. Generation after generation having cared little

Notebook pages (1960s).

for the place. Our fathers began by caring little enough about
Europe so that they could leave it. We've used the place, wasted
it. It has made us prodigal, restless. And we are attached to it in
still-raw ways that we aren't aware of, most often. We ought to
know that we couldn't hate it as fiercely as we do sometimes
without there being something honest in our attachment to it.
But there is always the sense of surprise, of inarticulate awk-
wardness, at discovering that the name for what you feel is love.[9]

The ambivalence Merwin expresses here nicely captures the tone toward America that he would employ throughout his career: a disgust
for what we've done to this continent in the name of America, a surprise at the depth of attachment he feels for the place. The journal
captures the central importance for Merwin of the idea of America,
of what his native place can mean for him.

Merwin's return to America, then, was not a simple embrace, but
the beginning of a long struggle with things American. He wanted to
be not just an American-born poet, but an American poet in the full
sense of the term, using his poetry to probe the peculiarly American
ways of viewing the world. He would define himself by resisting certain elements in the American tradition, embracing others, and helping define a new American tone. In 1970 he expressed his dilemma
this way, revealing by the nature of his concerns just how distant
from an American tradition he had come to feel: "I have sometimes
puzzled over the possibility of being an American poet (but what else
could I be—I've never wanted to be anything else), and certainly the
search for a way of writing about what America *is*, in my lifetime,
is a perennial siren. But not, I think, in any way that's obviously
Whitmanesque."[10]

Merwin's struggle with Whitman and the Whitman tradition would
become central to his poetic development. Whitman's definition of
the American poet, and his embodiment of and enthusiasm for the
absorptive and appropriating American attitude, would be what Merwin would define himself *against*. He would associate himself instead with other elements of the American tradition; he has expressed admiration for poets as diverse as Thomas Dudley, Emerson,
Whittier, Jones Very, and Melville,[11] but it is finally Thoreau whom
he sets up in a polar opposition to Whitman: "I've suspected for a
long time that an American poet's sympathy would tend to go either
toward Whitman or toward Thoreau, not toward both."[12] For Mer-

win, "Thoreau is really the main one that I go back to." He serves
Merwin as an affectionate presence in the American tradition: "I feel
grateful to Thoreau in a way. He's been a companion" (Folsom and
Nelson, "Interview," p. 34). When asked what drew him to Thoreau,
Merwin responded:

> I suppose the way in which he meant "In wilderness is the pre-
> servation of the world" for one thing. Or the recognition that
> the human can not exist independently in a natural void; what-
> ever the alienation is that we feel from the natural world, we are
> *not* in fact alienated, so we cannot base our self-righteousness
> on that difference. We're part of that whole thing. And the way
> Thoreau, very differently from Whitman, even in a paragraph
> takes his own perception and develops it into a deeper and
> deeper way of seeing something—the actual seeing in Thoreau
> is one of the things that draws me to him. I think that Thoreau
> saw in a way that nobody had quite seen before; it was American
> in that sense. (Folsom and Nelson, "Interview," p. 33)

Thoreau's penetrating (rather than absorptive) vision, his insistence
on a humility before the natural world which we are a part of, bonds
Merwin to him, and the Thoreauvian attention to day-to-day details
of living in the natural world, his penetrating attachment to the
place he lives his life in, is part of what marks Merwin's poetry from
The Compass Flower on. His home in Hawaii (which he built) works
for him much like the Walden cabin did for Thoreau; it is an extension of himself, a modest exfoliation of his needs, a center from
which he can observe his environment, measure the quality of the
land and of his life, remain somewhat isolated and aloof from human
society (though close enough so he can visit). Even Merwin's minimalist, sparse three-line form that he began employing as early as
The Moving Target and developed fully in *Asian Figures* and *Finding
the Islands*, a form that insists on close attention to brief moments,
derives in part (as he tells us in the foreword to *Asian Figures*) from
Thoreau, whose aphoristic sentences often embody Merwin's "urge
to be self-contained, to be whole."[13] Thoreau, too, often stands behind what have seemed to many readers the incongruous pastoral
moments that have punctuated Merwin's poetry even during its
bleakest periods.

If Merwin's Hawaiian (and earlier rural French) pastoral images
resonate with Thoreau's work, his evocations of New York City echo

Whitman. Merwin is as ambivalent about New York—where he spends part of each year—as he is about all of America: "I don't altogether understand my relationship with that place. . . . I think that New York is an incredibly destructive place, but I love it in some strange way. . . . If I could figure it out, I probably would never bother to go back again."[14] Because he can't figure it out, he keeps writing poems about it, about "the most beautiful / of cities and most empty," the city where he can admire the "amber light" and sigh "I am home," but where he knows simultaneously that murder and destruction and empty noise are in control, the city where "we all sleep high off the ground," its soaring glass towers the manifestation of the separation from earth, from nature, that the city has fostered (OH, 50–51). While his tone is certainly different than Whitman's, Merwin's sense of New York as a source of both creative and destructive energies is similar to Whitman's vision of Mannahatta. Both *The Compass Flower* and *Opening the Hand* balance New York poems with Hawaii poems, poems about the chaotic present of America and poems capturing moments of quiet affection away from the chaotic present, though the dichotomy is not simple: Hawaii has been invaded by the same manipulative and destructive forces that created present-day New York (see "Questions to Tourists Stopped by a Pineapple Field," OH, 43–45), and New York still can afford vestige memories of something more sustaining (see "The Fields," OH, 56).

In those New York poems where we do feel some vestigial affection, Merwin comes as close as he ever will come to being Whitmanesque, celebrating as did Whitman the specificity of the urban present. "St. Vincent's," a long poem in *The Compass Flower*, was, Merwin says, "a deliberate attempt to practice something closer to the tradition of Williams and Whitman." What he admires about that tradition is "the ease of address, the immediacy of the use of historical circumstance, which sometimes I would very much like to have been able to use more familiarly myself" (Folsom and Nelson, "Interview," p. 49), but he is aware that his own sense of the impenetrability of facts ("one is always looking at the outside of facts") will never allow him to easily absorb the world as named things into his poetry.

If he admires the ease of Whitman's address, though, he is deeply troubled by all that follows from that ease: "I've tried over the years to come to terms with Whitman, but I don't think I've ever really succeeded." While he finds power and beauty in Whitman, "the positivism and the American optimism disturb me." Whitman's is "not a poetry that develops in a musical or intellectual sense." Too trusting in facts, in things, Whitman's poetry for Merwin "doesn't move on and take a growing form—it repeats and finds more and more detail":

> "That bothers me, but in particular it's his rhetorical insistence on an optimistic stance, which can be quite wonderful as a statement of momentary emotion, but as a world view and as a program for confronting existence it bothered me when I was eighteen and bothers me now. It makes me extremely uneasy when he talks about the American expansion and the feeling of manifest destiny in a voice of wonder. I keep thinking about the buffalo, about the Indians, and about the species that are being rendered extinct. Whitman's momentary, rather sentimental view just wipes these things out as though they were of no importance. There's a cultural and what you might call a specietal chauvinism involved." (Folsom and Nelson, "Interview," pp. 30–31)

We can hear in these comments the echoes of Merwin's earlier fascination with Coxey's Army, with the march that represented for Merwin the reversal of the "great dream of the frontier" ("The buffalo had been killed off, the Indians had been rounded up, mostly—none of this destructive afflatus was going to work anymore"). Whitman is, for Merwin, the poet of the destructive American afflatus, whose windy rhetoric enacts the arrogating, accumulating process of American history: Whitman, Merwin says, is "basically a rhetorical poet . . . : you decide on a stance and then you bring in material to flesh out that stance, to give details to your position. . . . The stance is basically *there;* so much of the poetry simply adds detail to it" (Folsom and Nelson, "Interview," p. 32). Merwin's once-projected American epic on Coxey, then, would have told one story of the depressing results of the Whitmanian optimism, of the western-moving absorptive American myth. Merwin says he has occasionally found himself occupying Whitman's position, the poet speaking of and to America, but feels obligated to communicate a very different message than Whitman did. At the core of his cold prophecies of ecological and apocalyptic doom in *The Lice,* for example, is his revulsion at "the great phoney myth of the 'winning of the West'—it was the *destruction* of the West." He wants to force us to re-see our national myths, to see that the Virgin Land, American Adam, Whitmanic heroic American process "*was* heroic, but it was heroic in an incredibly cramped and vicious way. People did suffer and were magnificent, but they were broken and cruel, and in the long run incredibly destructive, irreversibly destructive. What we've done to this continent is something *unbelievable*—to think that one species could do this in a hundred years" (Folsom and Nelson, "Interview," p. 39). The poem on Coxey's Army would no doubt have explored the suffering, cruelty, and destructiveness deriving from the American dream, but his attention turned from Coxey's Army to *The Lice* and *The Carrier of Ladders*, and we can see now that those books develop his American concerns, form pieces of an American epic. They offer an image of America that realigns, alters, even reverses crucial aspects of our deeply held common myths about ourselves and about the enterprise of our country. In *The Lice* Merwin answers Whitman; his sparsity and soberness—his doubts about the value of America—temper and shadow Whitman's exuberance and enthusiasm over the American creation. In *The Carrier of Ladders*, Merwin includes an American sequence of poems, not an epic but a powerful short group of poems that probes the American psyche, descending in time (through "this feeling of inhabiting a palimpsest" [Folsom and Nelson, "Interview," p. 38]) to discover what America was, in order to face and assume the guilt of the destructive American expansion across the continent, to invoke the vanished native and face the implications of his absence.

The Lice is Merwin's anti-song of the self. Here, instead of the Whitmanian self expanding and absorbing everything, naming it in an ecstasy of union, we find a self stripped of meaning, unable to expand, in a landscape that refuses to unite with the self, refuses to be assimilated, in a place alien and unnameable. *The Lice* opens with "The Animals," a poem about a ruined American Adam who, like Whitman, would like to turn and live with and name the animals, but who finds that there are none left to name: "And myself tracking over empty ground / Animals I never saw / I with no voice / Remembering names to invent for them / Will any come back will one" (*L*, 3). This self becomes voiceless, as the things he would use his voice to describe disappear; a barren landscape is all that remains, and the poet's stripped, barren words reflect it. Instead of expanding his senses like Whitman, and intensifying his touch, sight, hearing, so that he could contain the multitudes around him, Merwin's senses, as in "Some Last Questions," crumble and fade, become useless: "What are the feet / A. Thumbs left after the auction / . . . What is the tongue / A. The black coat that fell off the wall / With sleeves trying to say something." All that is left is silence, "As though it had a right to more." The self is dying, its head returning to "ash" in the withering flames of the twentieth century (*L*, 6).

Whitman found the expanding American creation and the American landscape to be perfectly suited to his voice; the American poet would, he said in "By Blue Ontario's Shore," make America's "cities, beginnings, events, diversities, wars, vocal in him, / . . . its rivers, lakes, bays, embouchure in him."[15] But Merwin wanders rootless in this land, searching for a new landscape that might reflect the self and be rendered in his language: "If there is a place where this is the language may / It be my country" (*L*, 46). Unlike Whitman, whose song defined and named himself, whose expanding country reflected his expanding self, Merwin's self seems distantly apart from what he finds to name and from his words themselves: "my words are the garment of what I shall never be . . ." (*L*, 62).

Let's recall briefly just what part of Whitman's "American optimism" Merwin finds so disturbing. Whitman viewed the making of America as a vast artistic project, a development, expansion, and purification of the original ideals on which the country was founded (he dated his poems using 1776 as year one); he imagined the American bard leading his people across the continent, "enacting today the grandest arts, poems, etc., by beating up the wilderness into fertile farms," and he saw the obliteration of the virgin wilderness as a musical creation ("Fingers of the organist skipping staccato over the keys of a great organ," the "crackling blows of axes sounding musically driven by strong arms, / . . . there in the redwood forests dense"), with the white race infusing the Western "blank" with meaning as it came to life in the new imposed forms, "the unoccupied surface ripening." There were no regrets as Whitman/America went about "Clearing the ground for broad humanity, the true America." In "Song of the Redwood Tree," Whitman imagined the "Voice of a mighty dying tree"—one of the last on the continent—chanting its "deathchant"; its song was a suspiciously joyous abdication to the white race that was destroying it: "For a superber race, they too to grandly fill their time, / For them we abdicate, in them ourselves ye forest kings!" Whitman offers a catalogue of Western natural beauty that is being displaced by "America," and instead of lamenting the loss, claims that the natural beauty will not ever be lost, rather will become part of the conquering white race: "To be in them absorb'd, assimilated."

We have already seen what Merwin thinks of these views. The vast absurdity of claiming that we can "absorb" a wilderness (and the native race that lived there) while we systematically exterminate it is one of Merwin's most essential American concerns; we play tricks with language that come back to destroy us. This is one source of Merwin's distrust of language, and particularly of the rhetorical and flowing language of Whitman.

So in *The Lice* Merwin imitates Whitman in order to parody him and reject his vision of America. Like Whitman, he faces a void and seeks a new language to describe it, but the void he encounters is not the Western "blank" that Whitman joyously entered into, not a hopeful place for future imposition of form, but instead is the final void, the vast and empty destruction of the continent that America has resulted in: "The End" (L, 68). The hopes he had for his return to America in the 1950s now seem lost, and his native land seems more and more alien; "Whenever I Go There," he says,

> In new rocks new insects are sitting
> With the lights off
> And once more I remember that the beginning
>
> Is broken
>
> (L, 24)

The continent is paved over with rocklike apartments, its citizens a mindless infestation, and "the beginning"—the conceptual ideas of the country, the beliefs in life and liberty for all—is shattered into an empty reality. In 1970, when Merwin refused to sign a loyalty oath affirming his support of the Constitution of the United States, he justified his act by stating how abused the Constitution had become, how it had been twisted by those in power to make it say what it never meant; our present had become so severed from the ideals of the past that we could no longer be sure what we were being asked to be faithful to: "I cannot believe that the framers of the Constitution of the United States meant it to be a humiliating experience to be an American citizen. . . . It seems to me, in my position as an or-

dinary, relatively helpless citizen who has never sought public office, that I could not better support the Constitution of the United
States—whatever about it I respect and whatever its authors meant
to protect—than by refusing to sign a statement which is clearly a
small legislative outrage against individual liberty, perpetuated in its
name."[16] If America had a noble inception, something went horri-
fyingly wrong in its execution, and "the beginning / Is broken."

"The Last One" is Merwin's most direct response to Whitman; it
views America's westering creation as both a genesis and an apocalypse: a beginning followed by a quick end. The poem is filled with
imagery of Genesis, but it describes an anti-creation, and of the
books in the Bible, Revelation is "the last one." Here again we have
the American Adam (and Eve) who blithely decide to begin to cut
into the virgin wilderness; Whitman's grand ideals of a new race are
reduced to an empty "why not":

Well they'd made up their minds to be everywhere because why not.
Everywhere was theirs because they thought so.
                              . . .
In the middle of stones they made up their minds.
They started to cut.

                                                                (L, 10)

With a sense of meaningless manifest destiny, "they cut everything
because why not." Suddenly the whole American westering process,
as it does in Whitman (see "Facing West from California's Shores"),
comes to a halt at the Pacific Ocean: "Well cutting everything they
came to the water." The wilderness has been laid to waste; of a
whole continent of trees, now "there was one left standing. / They
would cut it tomorrow they went away." In Merwin's vision the final
tree, unlike Whitman's last dying redwood, sings no praise to the
axe-bearing men who chop it down. Instead, with a strange combination of biblical solemnity and monster-movie horror,

   The night gathered in the last branches.
   The shadow of the night gathered in the shadow on the water.
   The night and the shadow put on the same head.
   And it said Now.

The men come in the morning and cut the last tree down, but when
"They took it away its shadow stayed on the water." Bothered by this
turn of events, man tries all of his ingenious ways to rid himself of

the shadow: shining a light on it, covering it up, exploding it, and sending smoke up between the shadow and the sun. But all of this is to no avail; the shadow remains, and then it begins growing. "That was one day," announces the poet in an echo of the Genesis-creation which here indicates the beginning of the end. Man continues his efforts to eradicate the shadow as it grows onto the land, but the shadow, as it touches man, seems immediately to de-evolve him; he moves from the machine age to an age of primitive tools back to an age before tools:

> They started to scrape the shadow with machines.
> When it touched the machines it stayed on them.
> They started to beat the shadow with sticks.
> Where it touched the sticks it stayed on them.
> They started to beat the shadow with hands.
> Where it touched the hands it stayed on them.
> That was another day.
>
> (*L*, 11)

Then the shadow—a dark, all-devouring blob—grows on and on, like some anti-Whitmanian force (reversing Whitman's American expansion into and absorption of nature), which now expands into and absorbs (or obliterates) man: "Then it swallowed them too and they vanished." Only a few "lucky ones with their shadows" remain, having run away "as far as they could" (*L*, 10–12).

This poem, says Harvey Gross, "dramatizes nature's revenge against men."[17] It is, as Jarold Ramsey says, "an ecological version of the apocalypse."[18] But it is not *nature* gaining her revenge so much as nature's *shadow*—a hollow, dark force of non-nature, of obliterated nature, a dark, nonpalpable reminder of what used to be. It is the lack of nature that creeps back over the continent, obliterating man. It is the exhaustion of natural resources that causes the machines to cease functioning and leads man back to a primitive state, forced once again to use sticks and his hands, because there is no energy left for his machines. As so often in *The Lice*, Merwin here personifies emptiness or nothing; the Nothing of destroyed nature is what will kill man, finally; Americans think they have conquered the wilderness, only to find that No-Wilderness will conquer them. This poem demonstrates the anti-creation of America; the movement here is from west to east as the poem of America is erased, the creation of America wiped out, and nothing is left, finally, but barren, empty,

lifeless land. There is no sense of hope further west in the Far East
(no "Passage to India" as there was for the later Whitman); the only
faint hope is in the few chastened men who escape with their shadows, left to gnaw the crust of the earth in some remote corner of the
ruined country. But their shadows are part of the larger shadow; we
all are in complicity. Merwin, speaking of this poem, said, "I'm reminded of the line in the psalm, 'Yea they despised the pleasant
land.' The pleasant land was themselves" (Folsom and Nelson, "Interview," p. 55).

Later in *The Lice*, Merwin looks at America's continued attempts
to expand westward by going to Vietnam. In "The Asians Dying," the
same process of de-creation is described as Americans destroy another wilderness in the Far East: "When the forests have been destroyed their darkness remains / The ash the great walker follows the
possessors / Forever." Creating a nothingness, an obliteration, behind them, the Americans push on toward infinite new Wests: "Pain
the horizon / Remains." In Merwin's vision, the Americans are guided
not by a Whitmanian ideal, but only by "Death their star," which
leads the "possessors . . . everywhere" (*L*, 63). Even if Americans
seek to complete Columbus's original goal to voyage to the Far East,
suggests Merwin, they will only lay it waste, too.

And so Merwin, in "The Widow," examines the possibility of a
world without men. The widow is the virgin land, the wilderness
She, now envisioned as alone due to the death of her domineering
mate, the American He. And she seems to get along very nicely
without him. Here, says Anthony Libby, "the earth is defined not as
man's great mother but as the only survivor of an ancient union with
man that long ago ended in opposition."[19] And Merwin envisions the
widow Earth serenely carrying on her cycles of life in the absence
of man:

> How easily the ripe grain
> Leaves the husk
> At the simple turning of the planet
>
> There is no season
> That requires us
>
> (*L*, 34)

It is only the man-made impositions on nature that are fragile, that
will fade; life itself goes on smoothly without man's aid: "Everything that does not need you is real / The Widow does not / Hear you

and your cry is numberless" (*L*, 34–35). This is, as Libby notes, an "existential denial of men: 'numberless,' we simply do not count." It is better for life, ultimately (suggests Merwin), to leave the earth a widow, rid of men, than to leave her dead, along with man.

Throughout *The Lice,* Merwin's soul tries to fly, to transcend, to surge ahead like a Whitmanian soul, but the future is dead now; we are preparing "For a Coming Extinction" (*L*, 68), and so Whitman's spirit is gone—"The tall spirit who lodged here has / Left already"— and the spirit of the new poet is wingless; it cannot fly or transcend; there is no future to soar into, nothing to expand into and name:

> But when you look forward
> With your dirty knuckles and the wingless
> Bird on your shoulder
> What can you write
>
>   (*L*, 17)

The bird/soul tries, but can find no opening, no hope; "somewhere in myself," writes Merwin, "from a corner [come] the sounds of a small bird trying / From time to time to fly a few beats in the dark" (*L*, 48). When the bird does leave its "Life on my shoulder" and tries to fly, it kills itself in the futile effort: "you had to thresh out your breath in the spiked rafters" (*L*, 72).

The self in these poems is infested with lice, with diseased things it cannot find and kill and so must carry with it. Whitman's self sought to contain all, to embody past, present, future; Merwin's self seeks to contain nothing, to empty itself of a dead past ("The thermometers out of the mouths of the corpses" [*L*, 17]), a shattered present, and a dead and destructive future ("The fist is coming out of the egg" [*L*, 17]). Memory is no virtue for Merwin here, for he seeks to break off from a meaningless past. As for what is to come: "We are the echo of the future"; "we were not born to survive / Only to live" (*L*, 33). Our popping H-bombs are only a faint echo of the vast future apocalypse, which man will not survive. Not to repossess the past, then, is to be in total darkness, but at least free; the need here—and it is the opposite of Whitman's need—is to *empty* the self, to find a new void within, and then to listen and learn from the silence of a de-created history: "Now all my teachers are dead except silence / . . . I cannot call upon words" (*L*, 50).

Whitman describes the self in "Song of Myself": "There is that in me—I do not know what it is—but I know it is in me. / It is not chaos or death—it is form, union, plan—it is eternal life—it is Happiness." This kind of affirmation vanishes in Merwin's anti-song; he finds himself "in life as in a strange garment." The American self/poem/country has ended its expansion and begun its inevitable diminishment. The signs are on the pages themselves: Whitman's poems expand and flow, Merwin's poems are fragments, remnants. "Song of Myself" ends confidently, sure of the self, looking outward toward ever-expanding journeys even in death: "If you want me again look for me under your boot-soles. . . . / Missing me one place search another, / I stop somewhere waiting for you." *The Lice* ends in a muted echo of these last words, with the Merwin-self divided, unsure, tentative: "Where else am I walking even now / Looking for me" (*L*, 80).

In *The Carrier of Ladders* Merwin joins writers like William Carlos Williams (*In the American Grain*), Hart Crane (in *The Bridge*), Theodore Roethke (in "North American Sequence"), and Gary Snyder (in *Turtle Island*) in attempting an imaginative descent to the American past, to probe beneath the layered creation of America to face the lost native. For Whitman, the American direction was west and to the future; for twentieth-century American poets, the direction has become, more and more, down—through the layers of what America is and has been—and to the past. In "The Lake," Merwin approaches his descent, which finally occurs in the American sequence of poems ("The Approaches" through "The Removal"—a group he conceived of as a distinct series). "Did you exist / ever," he asks, as he gets in a boat and sails out in a lake, where he senses how immense the distance below him is to where the Indian (perhaps) exists; the poet is on the surface layer of a continental palimpsest, on the flood of America that has covered (or perhaps obliterated) the native cultures; he looks far down, under, to the past:

> I lay there
> looking down while the mist was torn
> looking down
> where
> was the Indian village
> said to be drowned here
>
> one glimpse and I would have hung
> fixed in its sky
>
> (*CL*, 30)

He is, as he hovers on the surface of the water in the present, the dead Indian's future; he hangs in the Indian's sky only when the Indian's present is past; there are no natives left in the drowned village (if, indeed, it is still there) to look to the watery sky to see the white man in their future, the new creation that would cover them.

In "The Approaches," the poet sets out on his imaginative journey to the past, and is deceived in his first glimpse of the Indian, but wanders aimlessly on, hoping to find signs of the past: "I say I may never / get there but should get / closer and hear the sound / seeing figures I go toward them waving / they make off / birds / no one to guide me / afraid / to the warm ruins" (CL, 42). In "Lackawanna," the poet begins in Pennsylvania in his boyhood, and begins to question the black river that seems to flow from within himself: "Where you begin / in me / I have never seen." The river becomes associated with the past, with American history: "and through the night the dead drifted down you / all the dead / what was found later no one / could recognize." The poet had been "told to be afraid" of entering that dark river, but at the end of the poem, he takes the plunge, entering the flow of history: "I wake black to the knees / so it has happened / I have set foot in you / both feet / Jordan / too long I was ashamed / at a distance" (CL, 44–45). He enters the river of history that takes him "to the warm ruins / Canaan" (CL, 42), the promised land of the pre-Americanized land (Hart Crane, too, in his descent to the American past in The Bridge, associated the virgin land with the "Promised Land").

"Other Travellers to the River" included William Bartram, botanist, painter, ornithologist, and writer whose Travels (1791) helped inculcate the idea of the Noble Savage in the white man's mind; the poet, like all sojourners to the past wilderness that Bartram described, can only see the wilderness through his eyes, his words—we can only see his formations of what was there: "William Bartram how many / have appeared in their sleep / climbing like flames into / your eyes." But as those merging with Bartram imaginatively stand at the Mississippi, "gazing out over the sire of waters / with night behind them / in the east," the darkness overtakes them; the night in the east expands westward and "they would wake not remembering." Meanwhile the river of history is "bearing off its empty flower again," inexorably carrying away to the dim past any hope of a glimpse of the wilderness, or of the native who is forever retreating west, forever engulfed in the descending eastern night before he can be apprehended (*CL*, 46). Our early descriptions of the land, voicing its vast silences in English syllables, were the first step in appropriating the land.

Moving further westward in his imagination, Merwin looks at "The Trail into Kansas"; he tries to merge with the westering settlers to get a glimpse of the virgin land, but "The early wagons left no sign." He does find a "line pressed in the grass *we were here*" (wagon wheel ruts tracing the American journey), and he begins to sense what it was like to enter the new land. The journey is torturous, but the settlers hoped that they would "heal / there," in the West, land of hope. As they journey, they sense they are watched, but their movement is inexorable, and they have no fear; the natives are no threat now, for in Whitman-like progression they continually vanish as the frontier pushes westward: "we know we are / watched but there is no danger / nothing that lives waits for us / nothing is eternal." (Their confident words, ironically, include them; they too, as we have seen in "The Last One," will vanish in an equally inexorable anti-progression.) These Americans are immigrants—"guided from scattered wombs"—who go about "choosing choosing / which foot to put down." With no affection for the land or the natives they displace, they dig in: "we are like wells moving / over the prairie / a blindness a hollow cold source / will any be happy to see us / in the new home." No one, of course, will be there to meet or greet them; the natives will helplessly disappear as the white Americans approach. Merwin, in his merger with the frontier settler, then, senses the Indian watching, but still cannot find him, see him (*CL*, 47).

In "Western Country," Merwin senses "the exiles," the natives moving west in hope they can live, not realizing that the ultimate West they head for is death: "I watch the exiles / their stride / stayed by their antique faith that no one / can die in exile / when all that is true is that death is not exile." The Indian has appeared finally, but only to disappear. Merwin finds no regeneration in his descent to the past; his chilled, exhausted voice rises in anger as he watches the dispossession: "and I know what moves the long / files stretching into the mountains," he says: "my countrymen are more cruel than their stars" (*CL*, 48). They follow vague goals, hopes, "each man with his gun," as they take over the western country. In "The Removal," dedicated "to the endless tribe," Merwin sees the natives as

"The Homeless"; they are "the echoes [that] move in files [one step ahead of the "long files" of the white settlers] / their faces / have been lost / . . . tongues from lost languages" (CL, 60). And the Americans destroy not just the native, but the native's mother, the land itself; they ravage the wilderness She that had supported the Indian: "the tree has been cut / on which we were leaves." There are now only remnants; Merwin finds "A Survivor" who carries on the old ways on a reservation, but he is just a vestige: "the old speech / is still in its country / dead" (CL, 61; see, too, an earlier poem, "The Native" [DF, 252–53], a portrayal of the poverty to which the native is reduced in "that abandoned land in the punished / North"). The white man takes all the fertile land: "They leave us the empty roads" (CL, 58). Merwin, like Gary Snyder, begins to sense the ghost of the Indian haunting the memory of the white man: "We move among them / doubly invisible." But Merwin finds no hope of actually resurrecting those ghosts: "when we have gone they say we are with them forever" (CL, 58). Toward the end of this sequence, as in this poem, Merwin's voice has merged with the Indian; again like Snyder, he speaks ("we") from the Indian's perspective. But unlike Snyder's native perspective, Merwin's voice comes to us faintly, from a distant, irretrievable past, not from an angry present.

America is firmly in control of the continent now: "the president of lies quotes the voice / of God / . . . the president of loyalty recommends / blindness to the blind." And the continental network of American communication says nothing of worth: "silence the messenger runs through the vast lands / with a black mouth / open" (CL, 57). America talks (boastfully) only of itself, ignoring the "deaths" that "are to be heard / at any moment" in "our language" (CL, 56); "there is only one subject / but he is repeated / tirelessly" (CL, 57). Andrew Jackson, who supported and directed the vast removal of southeastern tribes to the Far West in the 1830s, is one of the "presidents of lies," deceiving the Indians as they are forced to migrate into hardship. So, in "Homeland," Merwin offers an Indian-like curse on Jackson as the native homeland is seen divided and desecrated by the white man's boundaries and sense of property: "all the barbed wire of the west / in its veins." And, finally (in an imagistic revenge of nature on the white man/vampire who has sucked the vitality from the land), "the sun goes down / driving a stake / through the black heart of Andrew Jackson" (CL, 50). Merwin portrays some of Jackson's work in "The Crossing of the Removed," as Indians cross the Mississippi River to their barren new homes (Merwin may be recalling the Choctaw migration from Mississippi [1831] where many natives died in freezing weather crossing over to Arkansas); as they cross, they vanish: "At the bottom of the river / black ribbons cross under / . . . on the far side the the ribbons come out / invisible" (CL, 61).

John Wesley Powell, the one-armed explorer, becomes the emblem for Merwin of the white man's movement into the wilderness. Powell, a geologist and geographer, led the Geologic Survey (1881–94) that mapped out the West, imposed American lines upon the wilderness; it was while he was issuing these maps that Frederick Jackson Turner announced the closing of the frontier, the end of wilderness. All America, suggests Merwin, was a one-armed explorer: "The one-armed explorer / could touch only half of the country." His other arm—the missing one—was "his scout" that reached into the wilderness but "sent back no message / from where it had reached / with no lines in its palm." Like the lines on Powell's many maps, the hand he kept on the eastern side of the frontier was familiar, known, lined, visible. But no white man knew the western side of the frontier; like an invisible hand, it was unlined, unmapped, unknown, unseen. So, as Powell "groped on / for the virgin land," he could never find it; like his missing hand, he sensed it was there, but when he reached for it, he found only his real hand again; in seeking the virgin land, he only "found where it had been" (CL, 49). (Merwin had been working with this notion since Green with Beasts, where, in "The Wilderness," he finds "Remoteness is its own secret," and no matter how far into the "horizon's virginity" we penetrate, "We are where we always were" [GB, 140].) Powell touched the wilderness only to have it disappear, to have it become known at the very touch, to be fused to the American creation. The "virgin half," the half Powell could never really touch, could be sensed only with the missing hand, the hand of the imagination. So Merwin, in this sequence, tries to touch the virgin land, lost now in time and space, with the "missing hand" of his imagination, for no actual descent is possible. But as he moves the imagined hand west into the past, he at first can find only "the dead guarding the invisible / each presenting its message / I know nothing / learn of me" (CL, 51). The natives beckon him, but, dead, they can offer no help, no real knowledge; their extinction guards the invisible wilderness that Merwin cannot touch. The sequence ends with an Indian woman, a widow, captured by the whites; she is stripped of her land and her compatriots; she is mingled in marriage with the white man so that "everywhere I leave / one white footprint." And from here, the procession moves quickly to its inevitable end: "at last they are gone / filing on in vacant rooms" (CL, 62).

Merwin's descent ends here; the vacant rooms of the natives' death are vacant rooms in himself, too, as the Indian disappears from his imagination and he returns to the present. Unlike Gary Snyder in *Turtle Island*, Merwin does not return to the present replenished with native ways; he returns only with an affirmation of American destructiveness, of man's stupidity and inhumanity, and of an irreplaceable emptiness lying beneath this continent. But in taking this archetypal American journey, in responding to the Whitman/American traditions and myths as starkly as he does in *The Lice*, Merwin places himself firmly in the tradition of American poetry.

At the heart of the American sequence in *Carrier* is a poem that joins Merwin's personal memory with an archetypal memory: "Huckleberry Woman" tells of a "Foreign voice woman" who emerges from the Pennsylvania landscape of his youth ("you climbed the mountain in back of the house / . . . before day you put on / the bent back like the hill"). She is an immigrant, distant from Merwin's own sense of experienced reality ("of unnamed origins nothing / to do with what I was taught"). Merwin now recalls the woman as "remote from anything I was allowed contact with" and sees her as "another representative of that existence which the Indians too bespoke"; he says he "was in awe of her." She used to pick huckleberries in the hills and then "come down the alley in the early mornings calling 'Awkleberries! Awkleberries!' with a wash-tub full of them on her head."[20] One morning she spilled the whole tub in the alley. Her speechless cry of "loss loss the grieving" joins the young Merwin to her, and she becomes a "key / unlocking the presence / of the unlighted river / under the mountains" (CL, 52). She unites him with an experience of the land and of emotion beyond spoken words, beyond the ways he had been taught to hear and respond. She is part of his American journey and of his personal journey to descend below the old traditions of knowing and appropriating. "Huckleberry

Woman," then, with its fusion of personal memory and American myth, anticipates the struggles with and descents into his intensely personal and distinctly American past—descents that occupy much of *Unframed Originals* and *Opening the Hand*. Merwin's long and troubling journey home from a strange country continues.

NOTES

1. G. S. Fraser, "The Magicians," *Partisan Review*, Winter 1971–72, p. 475.
2. W. S. Merwin, "On Open Form," in Stephen Berg and Robert Mezey, eds., *Naked Poetry* (Indianapolis: Bobbs Merrill, 1969), pp. 271–72.
3. Stephen Spender, "Can Poetry Be Reviewed?" *New York Review of Books*, Sept. 20, 1973, p. 12.
4. "Interview for *Audience*," in W. S. Merwin Archive, University of Illinois Library, University of Illinois at Urbana-Champaign, MSS 2/13, #16.
5. Michael Clifton, "W. S. Merwin: An Interview," *American Poetry Review*, 12 (July/Aug. 1983), 22.
6. The grant application is in the W. S. Merwin Archive, University of Illinois Library, MSS 2/13. The comment about the reading tour is in a letter to Arthur Mizener, Dec. 12, 1960, also in the Merwin Archive.
7. Clifton, "Merwin: Interview," p. 18.
8. W. S. Merwin, "After Some Years," *Harper's*, 214 (June 1957), 45.
9. W. S. Merwin, "Flight Home," *Paris Review*, no. 17 (Winter 1958), 128, 135–36.
10. Frank MacShane, "A Portrait of W. S. Merwin," *Shenandoah*, 21 (Winter 1970), 7.
11. W. S. Merwin, "Anthology Pieces," *Poetry*, 81 (Jan. 1953), 261–64.
12. Ed Folsom and Cary Nelson, "'Fact Has Two Faces': An Interview with W. S. Merwin," *Iowa Review*, 13 (Winter 1982), 34. Further references to this interview are incorporated into the text.
13. W. S. Merwin, "Foreword," *Asian Figures* (New York: Atheneum, 1973), p. i. For more of Merwin's views on Thoreau, see Richard Jackson, "Unnaming the Myths," *Acts of Mind* (Tuscaloosa: University of Alabama Press, 1983), p. 51; Jack Myers and Michael Simms, "Possibilities of the Unknown: Conversations with W. S. Merwin," *Southwest Review*, 68 (Spring 1983), 171.
14. Clifton, "Merwin: Interview," pp. 17, 22.
15. Quotations from Whitman's poetry are from Harold W. Boldgett and Sculley Bradley, eds., *Leaves of Grass: Comprehensive Reader's Edition* (New York: New York University Press, 1965), pp. 184, 206–210, 344.
16. W. S. Merwin, "On Being Loyal," *New York Review of Books*, Nov. 19, 1970, p. 17.

17. Harvey Gross, "The Writing on the Void: The Poetry of W. S. Merwin," *Iowa Review*, 1 (Summer 1970), 103.

18. Jarold Ramsey, "The Continuities of W. S. Merwin," p. 30.

19. Anthony Libby, "W. S. Merwin and the Nothing That Is," *Contemporary Literature*, 16 (Winter 1975), 20.

20. W. S. Merwin to Ed Folsom, Apr. 25, 1981.

THOMAS B. BYERS

The Present Voices:
W. S. Merwin since 1970

In three extraordinary volumes of poetry produced in the 1960s—*The Moving Target* (1963), *The Lice* (1967), and *The Carrier of Ladders* (1970)—W. S. Merwin established himself as a major postmodern poet. The voice he developed then defined itself by opposition to the poetics of Ralph Waldo Emerson and Walt Whitman, the two great proponents of the American poet as a culture-hero who "stands on the center" and "is emperor in his own right" by virtue of being the Orphic "sayer" and Adamic "namer" of the universe.[1] In rebellion against this imperial figure, Merwin wrote what L. Edwin Folsom has called "an anti-song of the self,"[2] characterized by a radical distrust of speech as presence or as an instrument of transcendence. He expressed this distrust in a surreal, oddly impersonal, allegorical iconography which I have elsewhere claimed "attempts to reflect the *inability* to generate presence, and which denies the concrete physicality of things [as named in poems] in favor of their shadows, their echoes, their multiple connotations," so as to "decompose the customarily felt unity" of our perceptions.[3]

Since then, however, Merwin has changed again. The bleak power of his work in the sixties has ironically confronted him with the very urge which impelled the great transcendentalist projects: the need to break with tradition and habit in order to overcome alienation and fulfill an instinctual (erotic) desire for presence. It seems highly unlikely that Merwin would or could ever fully reverse himself, renounce his critique of transcendentalism, or speak in a voice of Whitmanic afflatus. As he himself says in his recent *Iowa Review* interview, "obviously I can't believe that I'm ever going to be in the center of that [Whitmanian] tradition; I don't share any of the original assumptions."[4] On the other hand, there is considerable evidence that, beginning with *Writings to an Unfinished Accompaniment* (1973), he has been engaged in completing a more or less dialectical relation to his transcendentalist precursors, by moving toward a synthesis of their theory and practice with his own critique and rejection of them in the sixties. I propose to examine three aspects of this movement: first, the articulation of the need for it and of its direction in *Writings* and some other texts; second, the revealingly problematic solution attempted in the nature and love poetry of *The Compass Flower* (1977) and *Finding the Islands* (1982); third, the proposition of more promising directions, apparent in some parts of *The Compass Flower* and the poet's most recent collection, *Opening the Hand* (1983).

KNOWING THIS CHANGE

Writings in large part continues the concerns and mode of the volumes immediately preceding it. For instance, it opens with a short sequence which allegorically confronts our fall from unity to "Division, mother of pain" (*MT*, 53), and our consequent tendency to destroy nature. In such poems as "At the Same Time," "Spring," "Ash," "In the Life of the Dust," "The War," "The Water of the Suns" (*WA*, 37, 42, 51, 73–74, 82, 83) metaphysics and social criticism coalesce in a jeremiad now familiar precisely because of its originality and power in the sixties books. Moreover, these poems deploy many of the peculiarly disembodied icons previously developed: doors, birds, glass, clouds, eyes, hair, ash, dust, statues, wings, water, stone, feet, bells, fire, veins. This continuity presents a problem, however, for if much of *Writings* seems accomplished enough, much of its accomplishment seems already to have been implied—and largely attained—in earlier work. Had poems such as those mentioned seemed to extend the themes or develop the poetic voice significantly, they might have been hailed as part of a mature—even a great—creative outpouring. But in fact many readers found them repetitious, and a little slack by comparison to their predecessors. And even today the later book still seems to lack the degree of internal coherence and development that had made the three prior ones seem something more than mere collections. Thus around the time of *Writings* one began to hear the charge that Merwin had become too successful and had lost his self-critical edge—that critical acclaim and regular appearances in the *New Yorker* had made him complacent.[5]

Perhaps these claims hold some truth; in any case I agree in general with the widespread view that nothing Merwin has done before or since is any more original or fully realized or significant than the sixties books. Nonetheless, in hindsight I also believe that the dissatisfaction with *Writings* resulted partly from the complacent expectations and limited perceptions of readers who so quickly recognized its continuities that we failed to sense its differences. For the volume as a whole *reassesses* as much as it consolidates precedent work. None of Merwin's books is more self-consciously concerned with its relation to tradition and habit, to precursors and especially to his own prior achievements.

This reassessment reflects a career crisis rooted in the very problems felt by readers. Merwin himself explicitly recognizes that the mode which had made him a leading poet of his time might be nearing exhaustion. He is confronted by something congruent to what Harold Bloom, discussing the anxiety of modern poets before their poetic "fathers," calls "the embarrassments of a tradition grown too wealthy to need anything more," and perhaps even by the "fear that no proper work remains for him to perform."[6] While this poet's need to break with his own past suggests no more than a rough analogy to the outline of Bloom's theory of influence, two factors strengthen the analogy. First, as we shall see, Merwin's crisis may indeed include an Oedipal component. Second, the poems of *Writings* and *The Compass Flower* in particular reveal not only a new project and a shift in Merwin's attitude toward certain precursors, but also a revision of specific tropes from some of his earlier poems.

Merwin's awareness of his situation surfaces in a complaint entitled "Habits" (*WA*, 28), saying that they "go on handing me around." They control his poetic resources in memory and dreams, and even more important, the organs—eyes and tongue—of that dual "power to receive and to impart" which Emerson identifies as the poet's special gift.[7] Even worse, the habits use his tongue "to tell me / that they're me"—to constitute and define his identity in their terms. Moreover, "they lend me most of my ears to hear them," and thus rule not only the self-critical faculty of the ear as monitor, but the poet's whole capacity to listen to his muse.

Another personification, "the man called Old Flag" (*WA*, 23), defines the vision and tone of these habits. He is dominated by bitterness and grief, and is finally the poet himself at the height of the phase now nearing its end. His "hollow sleeves" recall a stunning image of language as absence from *The Lice*: "My words are the garment of what I shall never be / Like the tucked sleeve of a one-armed boy" (*L*, 62). When the speaker tries to break from the older mode, he is thwarted by his uncontrollable allegiance to its flag: "my words might be his dogs"; they "have never forgotten" him, "and they run to him laughing / . . . / they dance at his feet as though / before a throne." "Old Flag" is the very sort of imperious master criticized in such works as "Caesar" (*L*, 19) or "The Fountain" (*MPC*, 36–45). He turns the poet's own words into the dog who "wears servility / In his tail like a banner" (*MT*, 6). Merwin began his great phase of the sixties by rejecting this creature in favor of his own totem, Christopher Smart's "'wolf, which is a dog without a master'" (see "Lemuel's Blessing," *MT*, 6–8). But by *Writings* the wolf has been domesticated.

The rebellious urges quelled by "Old Flag" are all for speech: "I want," says the speaker, "to tell of the laughing throne / and of how all the straw in the world / records the sounds of dancing," and "to speak of the sweet light / on a grassy shore." His subjects are to be laughter, unity, natural plenitude; his tone optative. And especially in the image of light and grass, he seems to long for a new faith in language as representation, taken literally as re-present-ation, or naming as renewal of presence.

Whitman, who claims to "call any thing back again when I desire it,"[8] is our tradition's most extreme exponent of this faith. And here Merwin does take some steps toward reconciliation with him. The title figure of "Old Flag" transforms an intertext from "Song of Myself," 6. There the speaker's first response to the child's question *"What is the grass?"* is "I guess it must be the flag of my disposition, out of hopeful green stuff woven." Sad and bitter, the flag of Merwin's disposition seems older—both more traditional and oppressive and more exhausted—than his precursor's, and in rejecting his own, Merwin favors something much closer to its Whitmanian opposite. The relation is clinched when, in the "sweet light / on a grassy shore" desired by Merwin, we hear the subdued echo of the grass and the sunrise on the beach where Whitman attained his mystical-erotic epiphanies ("Song of Myself," 5 and 24).

These attainments suggest what at bottom draws Merwin away

from his own austerity and toward Whitman: the call of Eros. In *The Lice* Merwin showed the dangers of a bonding instinct so intense that it leads us to try to abolish difference by absorbing everything. Reinterpreting love, he emphasized respect for the integrity and dignity of the other. Hence he severely restrained the self and its speech, allowing the latter to aspire only to the preparation of silence. By "The Piper" (*CL*, 28–29), he finally felt he had come "to know what I cannot say"—to know that he could not speak presence. And hence he declared himself "almost ready to learn" what could only come after these limits had been discovered.

However, "To the Rain" (*WA*, 95) takes a key turn:

> hem of the garment
> do not wait
> until I can love all that I am to know
> for maybe that will never be
>
> touch me this time
> let me love what I cannot know
> as the man born blind may love color
> until all that he loves
> fills him with color

The new course is plotted in the crucial substitution of "touch me" for the Piper's "teach me." The speaker rejects the sublimation of knowing, with its self-discipline and delay of fulfillment, in favor of present contact. And in doing so he manifests at once a profound recognition of his own temperamental limits and a dramatic change in the value he places on erotic imagination. The simile here compares Merwin as lover to a man "born blind," innately incapable of the knowledge of another that love and sight normally bestow. But it also suggests that by being physically and emotionally touched, he may be filled with that which his incapacity has denied him. His alienation can be overcome by "blind" love.

Significantly, the blind man's filling is clearly not a literal but a symbolic process. By loving color, he may know it despite its physical absence from him. The analogous process for the poet is to love plenitude—and even more, to love his imaginative representations of that plenitude which is not literally present to him. The "blind neighbor" who once "required of me a description of darkness" (which the poet could not provide [*L*, 30]), has been replaced by the poet himself as blind seer, imaginatively capable of (ful)filling him-self. To admit this possibility is to admit precisely what Whitman proclaimed and Merwin renounced in him: the belief in verbal repre-sentation as the poet's enactment of erotic bonding, overcoming dif-ference, alienation, absence.[9]

Merwin's blind man recalls a similar figure in Theodore Roethke's "Journey to the Interior," from his late, lovely "North American Sequence":

> As a blind man, lifting a curtain, knows it is morning,
> I know this change:
> On one side of silence there is no smile;
> But when I breathe with the birds,
> The spirit of wrath becomes the spirit of blessing,
> And the dead begin from their dark to sing in my sleep.[10]

Merwin swerves from this, just as he does from his own "Piper," in that love, not knowing, has become the crux for him. In addition, he turns his attention more to life than to the dead. But otherwise Roethke's lines might equally apply to the younger poet. As he emerges on the other side of the silence so grimly sought in the six-ties books, he moves tonally from "the spirit of wrath" to that of blessing. And his "breath[ing] with the birds" no longer marks a sur-render of speech, but rather a desire to achieve "the presence of sing-ing" which he attributes in a prose piece to the "Birds at Noon" (*HT*, 205–6). This colorful, creative singing "makes the whole tree light up" and "makes morning."

"Birds at Noon" comes near the end of *Houses and Travellers*, in a sequence considerably more personal and descriptive, less abstract and allegorical, than most of this book or the earlier *Miner's Pale Children*. It signals a change carried much further both in *Opening the Hand* and in the poet's indispensable third volume of prose, *Un-framed Originals*, made up (as the subtitle tells us) of recollections of his past. Despite the dust jacket's warning that the book tells rela-tively little about the author himself, what is amazing in comparison to all his earlier work is how *much* it reveals—not only of exqui-sitely observed, if often bleak, concrete details (many of which are clearly the sources of particular poems), but of his childhood feel-ings, and his adult judgments. The opening piece, "Tomatoes," alone tells more than ever before about the home life in which his consciousness was formed: the Calvinist rectitude and prohibitions, the disapproval of intimacy, the "angry and capriciously punitive" behavior of his minister father (UO, 48), the child's "feeling [of] grief inextricably tangled with my own unexpected and unconvincing goodness" when his father would try to "be pals" with him. This pact would be sealed with a gift "such as a card printed with the Ten Commandments, the names of the Books of the Bible, the Apostles' Creed and the Lord's Prayer" (UO, 49).

The heart of the piece is the opposition of freedom and openness to repression. The former are embodied in the boy's paternal grandfather, who tells him "You can eat them [the tomatoes of the title] right now" and "You just help yourself, if you see anything you want." His father, on the other hand, charges him to "let them alone. Don't touch anything," and makes it clear that this is what it means for him to "be a good boy" (UO, 5–6). The forbidding of the fruit parallels the denial of relationship between grandfather and grandson, for Merwin saw the old man only this one time. An alcoholic, the grandfather was persona non grata to Merwin's father; the purpose of the single visit was the father's successful effort to get grandfather to sign himself into an old men's home, and leave his low house in the garden where the tomatoes grew (UO, 7).

As Merwin discloses his regret and resentment at the truncation of this relationship, he also partially exorcises the powerful ghost of a "shaming . . . hurtful" father (UO, 176), whose constant messages were restriction and self-control, and of whose approval the boy never felt sure ("He seldom addressed himself to me," says the author in the next piece; "maybe I embarrassed him" [UO, 59]). This exorcism takes on profound significance in light of the parallels between the Merwin of the sixties and the Calvinist spirit: the personal reserve; the ontological guilt and self-condemnation; the sense of original separation and nostalgia for lost wholeness; the distrust of language and of (Whitmanian) erotic impulses. Even the poet's powerful ecological warnings may descend in part from his father's constant strictures against touching anything.[11] In The Carrier of Ladders he identifies himself explicitly as "the son of the future but my own father" (CL, 92). Hence "the man called Old Flag" (WA, 23), who blocks the door of affirmative speech, is not only the poet himself, but his father in him; his "hollow sleeves" recall the sleeves of that worthy's preaching robe (see UO, 109), and the poet's words which "might be his [Old Flag's] dogs" match with the father's fin-

gers when, in "Apparitions," (*OH*, 15–16), they "stand forth one by
one   obedient as dogs / so the scissors could cut."

By contrast, the freer, more loving grandfather, dressed in white
clothes and straw hat, but whose face his grandson cannot recall
(*UO*, 57), perhaps takes on the lineaments of the ancestor-poet previously anathematized for his intoxication on his own speech—Walt
Whitman. This identification is strengthened by the images of "Unknown Forbear" (*OH*, 28), a poem which refers to the photograph reproduced on the dust cover of *Unframed Originals*, and whose title
figure seems identifiable (either literally or by association) with the
grandfather as he is described in that volume. Like Whitman in various photographs from his later years, the forbear is "in his dark suit /
and white beard." The "mullein" and "green bank" of his surroundings recall sections 5 and 2 of "Song of Myself." And the "pine tree"
may be descended from the "fragrant pines" of "When Lilacs Last in
the Dooryard Bloom'd," especially since Merwin's "painted / picket
fence" with its ungated opening seems to echo the "white-wash'd
palings" which demarcate Whitman's dooryard. Perhaps, finally, the
"laughing throne" in "Old Flag" is reserved for grandfather Whitman, the "Laughing Philosopher."[12]

MOVING THE TARGET

The two most favored objects of the Eros for which the poet turned
from his father are nature and a woman. In Merwin's translation
of a thirteenth-century Persian poet, they meet inside the self as
moon-*anima:*

> Within you there is such a moon
> that even the sun in the sky
>
> shouts again and again I am
> yours to command
> I am your slave
>
> Like Moses look for that moon
> in your heart
>
> look for your joy
> through your own window[13]

Merwin's career since *Writings* obeys these imperatives, and three
nature poems from *The Compass Flower* embody the change in attitudes and poetics necessary to his compliance.

In "Working into Autumn" (*CF*, 45), the window is open, and the speaker sees his joy in a natural plenitude onto which he plans to launch his house/body as an ark. However, the rain has ended, and hence the ark (never mentioned by name) becomes not a vehicle for flight from the spirit of wrath, but a container for the blessing of the poet's new covenant with nature. The open window focuses this text's rewriting of the first poem in *The Lice* (*L*, 3), whose speaker lives "behind windows" which are clearly barriers. He has never seen the Animals, and he holds only the most tentative hope that "one" of them may "come back," show itself, and promise to meet him again. "Working into Autumn" may be that meeting, for in it hens, jays, and mosquitoes are in full view (the latter almost touching him), and the window is no longer barrier, but potential passage. The return desired in the earlier poem has been realized: "where I remained the distance came to me."[14]

In a companion poem, "September Plowing" (*CF*, 44), nature's secrets are disclosed in "the autumn light // that brings everything back in one hand / the light again of beginnings / the amber appearing as amber." In this apparent recovery of origins, substance and quality (color), reality and appearance, even signified and signifier are one. New confidence in perception and language accompanies and enables new openness in the poet's perennial love of nature. "I consider life after life as treasures," he says, and these treasures are not buried or taboo, but are rather *pleasures* in their plenitude, as "on all sides the dark oak woods leap up and shine." Their enjoyment need no longer be constrained by the ecological necessity of repressing the self to preserve difference; now the love can forge erotic bonds. And recalling such change later in "The Waters" (*OH*, 3), the poet clearly recognizes it as a recovery not only of nature but of his emotional and sensual self: "joys and griefs I had not thought were mine // woke in this body's altering dream."

Hence the shift in allegiances evinced in "A Contemporary" (*CF*, 15), whose sifting of tradition links it to the poems from *Writings* discussed earlier. It opens by renouncing T. S. Eliot, whose tropes and tone had figured prominently in Merwin's work from the start: "What if I came down now out of these / solid dark clouds that build up against the mountain / day after day with no rain in them." From this wasteland imagery the poet turns to "a garden in the south"— the country of Eros—to "live . . . as one blade [one of many leaves] of grass." In so doing, he fuses Whitman's organic transcendence of death with his own previous urge to escape the bonds of names and of the ego:

> I would be green with white roots
> feel worms touch my feet as a bounty
> have no name and no fear
> turn naturally to the light
> know how to spend the day and night
> climbing out of myself
> all my life

By at once descending from the clouds and ascending from (while still rooted in) "myself," the poet would come closer than ever to *transcending* not the world, but his own alienation. Then "sun would shine through me," and "all" would be "my life." And thus he would become much more a contemporary of those of his fellow poets who reject modernism in favor of a revised but renewed romanticism. He would approach the affirmative strain of what Charles Altieri calls the *"immanentist* vision," one of whose principles is that the poet becomes part of the field.[15]

Hence Merwin's turn from abstraction and allegory to increasing reliance on the personal observation and representational imagery of a lyric "I." As *Unframed Originals* displays this change in the prose, *The Compass Flower, Finding the Islands,* and *Opening the Hand* do so in the verse. Regrettably, these changes do not guarantee first-rate poetry. And though Merwin remains one of our most important poets, his stock does seem to have fallen a bit lately. One reason is simply that the less successful efforts are easier to censure now. Poems in the sixties mode might seem too abstract and unspecific, or too unconnected and demanding.[16] But even in these, one might sense mystery similar to that of the mode's successes, and hence wonder if the problem was in part one's own. When the newer work goes wrong, the failings seem much more certain. No doubt this difference simply reflects the canons of poetic taste in our time, but such matters as sentimentality, excessive modification, or overt lack of control strike us as (at times painfully) obvious.

Consider, for instance, "Spring Equinox Full Moon" (*CF*, 59–60). Parts of this poem, particularly its last stanza, are quite likeable. However, the first stanza's "thighs slender sunset shining shores" seem overmodified, and the adjectives serve not so much to change the nouns as to create a sonorous musical effect for its own sake. The "closed eyes of every creature / sepia and amber days" of stanza 3 bathe the poem in a somnolent nostalgia more autumnal than springlike. In fact, a great many of the love poems are set in an autumn twilight which tends to sentimentalize and enervate their erotic charge. The "fruit nakedness / morsel breasts / melon navel" of the lover's body seem overripe, and when coupled with the nostalgic ambience, their orality hints at regression. "Melon navel" in particular seems so unfitting as to be almost ludicrous. Finally, another passage exposes a lapse in Merwin's usually firm control over the ambiguous syntax created by his elimination of punctuation: "untraceable fine sounds / passing as on a face / feet first drops of rain on a mountain." These lines make sense when read as two parallel noun phrases, with "sounds" the subject of the first, and "feet" that of the second, followed by the "drops of rain" as a figure for them. However, given the rhythmic pattern of the first two lines and the absence of punctuation, we may be inclined to read "feet first" as an iamb, semantically the opposite of "head first," and modifying the preceding "sounds / passing as on a face." But this reading makes no sense, and in fact makes the lines seem silly. The reader probably shares the responsibility for excluding this reading, but Merwin has seldom before allowed such rhythmic and syntactic enticements to what seems finally so inappropriate.

Other poems offer various examples of uncontrolled resonances. In "Islands" (CF, 64), the speaker's confession that "all my life I have wanted to touch your ankle" verges on foot-fetishism, and "I beach myself on you" unhappily makes the speaker sound like a whale. "Warm Pastures" (FI, 30–33) closes with the following tercet: "I wake touching her / and lie still to listen / to the warm night." The only unusual verbal effect here is the synaesthesia of listening to warmth, and this unfortunately echoes the title of what may be our time's most popular book of sentimental schlock poetry—Rod McKuen's Listen to the Warm. If the context were more ironic, the line might seem a savage self-undercutting. But such is not the decorum of "Warm Pastures." Rather, the echo fits all too well with the rather prevalent sentimental tendency of Finding the Islands.

This tendency is of a piece with a certain exhibitionism and pride in sexual possession:

> Nobody in the world
> knows how you
> smell to me
>
> ———
>
> I hold your toes and your ankles
> kiss the backs of your knees
> draw them apart
>
> ———
>
> Through the hours of the day
> I carry in my mouth
> the taste of you
>
> ———
>
> My tongue follows
> the smooth sides
> of each of your folds
>   (*FI*, 51–52)

I don't wish to dwell on these; other readers may like them better than I do, and *Finding the Islands* certainly offers many passages which I find more successful. But reading these lines I feel like a voyeur—and without the distance and choice in the matter necessary for the guilty pleasure of that experience.

What seems missing is poetic tact; we simply expect more control, particularly in explicitly sexual poetry.[17] Its absence signals not only the present shedding of erotic and poetic inhibitions, but the painful intensity of restraint they imposed in the past. "Late I came / to the joy of this," the poet admits (*FI*, 44), and "You began our love / with flowers I / had never heard of" (*FI*, 62). In addition, the tactlessness seems more explicable in light of how much is at stake. For the love relationship in *Finding the Islands* offers salvation from some very specific problems of the sixties. Now the self can grasp a present other: "I have reached for your hand / and found it" (*FI*, 43). His journey, which earlier could only hope to avoid stasis and reach the edge of a silent other world, now has an earthly, attainable end: "I travel on and on / until there is only you / my homeland and morning" (*FI*, 45). Even transcendence ("climbing across"), once out of the question for this poet, seems possible in the love encounter: "Meeting we stood on a small bridge / with the world / flowing under us"

(*FI*, 46). He owes his new love of the world to his beloved: "Yours is the radiance / you say is mine since you met me" (*FI*, 44); "By now whatever / I see is lovely / seems a reflection of you" (*FI*, 53). Language, once an instrument of division, is now shared: "it breathes / between us" (*FI*, 51), and the very rhythms of his speech are born in their unity: "Our breath has mingled / for so many years / it moves as one" (*FI*, 53). Finally, erotically knowing the beloved opens the possibility of knowing the right names, and using them to invoke presence: "I call you with my body / that knows your one name" (*FI*, 55).

Given all this, the poet refuses to set boundaries or impose tight controls on the emergent language of his love. He must be honest to his emotions, even if this means that sometimes he "Starts too near / ever to / arrive" (*FI*, 36). And the sexual component is central, for it is the heart of his discovery of presence. Thus he may view the control now being relinquished as belonging to the impersonal, alienated tradition of Eliot, of his father, of his own sixties voice. As Cary Nelson points out, Merwin has long had "a sense of guilt about formal accomplishment. He is one of the very few good poets to consider aesthetic satisfaction not the highest of all emotions." But even his "meticulous care in deconstructing his poems"[18] in the sixties was a way of formally having one's cake and eating it too—of controlling the destruction of names. The solution in *Finding the Islands* is quite different; here he names much more straightforwardly, representationally—even naively. Instead of giving us "less and less in his poetry,"[19] he gives us more than we want, and demands not so much interpretation as acceptance. For us, as for him in "To the Rain," loving, not knowing, is to take priority.

Of course, the problem is that we may refuse. Our era holds no canon of taste more tenaciously than the ban on uncontrolled sentimentality. Moreover, while aesthetic satisfaction may well not be the highest emotion of all, we generally prize it as the definitive value *in art*. And although it might be possible to defend Merwin's transgressions as encoding a serious challenge to our standards and definitions, I suspect most readers would find this defense sophistical in the absence of specific evidence of self-reflexivity, and would tend instead simply to judge the poems as flawed.

Nonetheless, both Merwin's artlessness and his new confidence in representational imagery help define his particular version of a move paralleled by Yeats's descent from *The Tower* to the "foul rag-and-bone shop of the heart," Stevens's from the supreme fiction to *The Rock*, Williams's from *Paterson* to "The Desert Music" and *Journey to Love*. Having articulated a complex personal mythology, the poet responds to a late flowering of desire by returning from the intricacies of his own consciousness to contact with earth. Newly enamored with "the hum of the surfaces" (*OH*, 63), he becomes more than ever, in J. Hillis Miller's term, a "poet of reality."[20] However, there is always also some continuity from the mature to the late phase, and in Merwin this continuity generates an interesting tension. For his myth in the sixties is actually an anti-myth, a dismantling of faith in human constructs, and especially in the poet's power of right naming. His supreme fiction is an articulation of silence. In effect, he undermines his own practice, so powerfully that we resist any later attempt to undo what was done—or to do what was undone—in the middle phase. So, in fact, does he. Thus even when he turns from a critique of naming to a desire for it, it remains problematic.

The overuse of modifiers, already mentioned in another connection, focuses the problem. Consider this extreme example from "Summer Canyon": "Gray rocks darken / wet bronze pine bark echoes jay shriek / across tall rainy yellow grass" (*FI*, 11). Of the fifteen words which compose this scene, eight are adjectives; once again we are given too much, rather than too little. Creative writing students are often told to cut every adjective that merely describes an object, rather than transforming it; the principle is that one must trust nouns and verbs to convey a scene's essentials. Desperately as he may want to be a nature poet, Merwin lacks that trust in names—and in his own perceptions—necessary to simple representation.[21] In a sense his distrust seems honorable and even truthful; it is ironic that we tend to judge his description as too artificial—as striving too hard for artistic effect—when in fact it may be less so than the stripped description of the imagist tradition. Merwin exposes imagism's illusions, by reminding us that description is never transparent, always dependent on artifice and mediation. Regrettably, however, poetry in this simple form cannot easily bear such ideological weight; without stronger cues we resist the notion that such a text's value lies in its thwarting of the desire it expresses—that it's good poetry because it's bad description. Hence Cary Nelson's judgment that when "Merwin attempts to write positively about love and nature," he simply "regularly fails."[22]

CHARITY'S HOMECOMING

But there are other, more interesting veins in Merwin's recent work. If the excesses of *Finding the Islands* result from the opening to erotic desire, other texts deal in a more complex way with the release of other repressed material. As explained earlier, the poems of the sixties make Merwin sound like a secular version of his Calvinist father. In hindsight, their nearly complete repressions of self and speech, however culturally fitting and aesthetically sound, may also be seen as a reaction-formation against the son's hostility toward the father. Only since the deaths (in the 1970s) of both his parents has Merwin seemed to feel both the need and the freedom to confront in print his feelings toward them. A major theme of *Unframed Originals*, this confrontation is also central to the sequence of poems which begins *Opening the Hand*.

In these texts, the filial hostility finds voice and the author asserts his superiority, on his own terms, to Merwin, Sr. Thus in "The Houses" (*OH*, 11–14), the son's poetic recovery of the vision of the houses stands as a rebellious triumph over the father's oppressiveness in general, and particularly over the strictures he placed on the imagination when "he warn[ed] the son not to tell stories" (*OH*, 12). "The Oars" (*OH*, 4) tells how the father, when young

> . . . sat in a rowboat
> with its end on the bank   below the house
> holding onto the oars   while the trains roared past
> until it was time for him   to get up and go

His passivity, his timidity in not leaving the shore, his mere waiting for the time to be up contrast sharply with the son's history, both in life and in poems, of setting out, journeying, taking risks (see, for example, "Provision" [*L*, 55], "Huckleberry Woman" [*CL*, 52–53], "The Arrival" and "Island" [*CF*, 9, 82], etc.).

Similarly, "Sunset Water" (*OH*, 5) is founded on the contrasting relationships of father and son to nature:

How white my father looked   in the water
all his life he swam   doggie paddle
holding hurried breaths   steering an embarrassed smile

long after he has gone I rock   in smooth waves near the
   edge of the sea
at the foot of a hill   I never saw before
or so I imagine   as the sun is setting
sharp evening birds   and voices of children
echo each other   across the water

one by one the red waves   out of themselves reach
   through me

While the father seems pale and timid, and clearly out of his element, the son is at home in the water. He rides its rhythms, and accepts and values both the newness and the beauty of the scene. There is even a hint, in "or so I imagine," of a realization that his harmony with nature in fact constitutes a return to a forgotten (womblike) origin. And at the end he is reached and permeated by the other which extends itself to him.

But what gives this poem a beauty beyond (or even in spite of) its self-assertion against the father is the undercurrent of tenderness for him—both for his vulnerability and for the momentary, childlike pleasure he reveals, almost in spite of himself, in his "embarrassed smile." Other feelings which conflict with the antagonism and complicate the sequence both emotionally and stylistically are disclosed in poems such as "The Waving of a Hand" and "Strawberries" (*OH*, 6, 7), both of which concern dreams and dreamlike materials connected with the father's death and the son's sense of loss. These might best be described as "haunting," in more than one sense. In "Sun and Rain" (*OH*, 10), the flow of animals and the coming of rain figure the speaker's flood of emotion as he recalls the day his mother

. . . told me of seeing my father   alive for the last time
and he waved her back from the door   as she was leaving
took her hand   for a while and said
nothing

The combination of the father's beckoning gesture (which requires the opening of his hand) with his silence makes the scene doubly poignant; the dying man at once reveals his dependence and love and, in a nonfulfillment of the moment, is unable to articulate them. Given the emphatic position of "nothing," there is a hint that this inability manifests a general failure of character, yet this hint supplements, rather than canceling, the pathos of the gesture and the situation.

The sequence also goes beyond sympathy to implicate the poet himself, both in deeper bonds than he might have expected to discover or admit, and in responsibility for resistance to love and opening. In "Apparitions" (*OH*, 15–16), what may seem at first another Oedipal self-assertion, this time particularly of the son's (and the mother's) superior competence and independence, is profoundly complicated by the realization that the apparitions of his parents' hands are superimposed on the speaker's own. Even though he claims toward the end that his hands, as he usually sees them, "are nobody's children," the poem's real discovery is that they *are*, in part, the hands of his parents. This discovery also leads to a reassessment of the father's hands, which now look better than they did when they "had no comeliness / that I could recognize   when I yet supposed / that they were his alone." And in one of the most painful poems in Merwin's recent work, "Yesterday" (*OH*, 20–21), the speaker recounts a friend's confession of how he walked out on his father the last time they saw one another. Catching the son looking at his watch, the father "said you know I would like you to stay / and talk with me," but also offered the son an out: " . . . maybe / you have important work you are doing / or maybe you should be seeing / somebody I don't want to keep you." The son took the opening, and "got up and left him then / you know // though there was nowhere I had to go / and nothing I had to do." While the confessor is explicitly not the poet/speaker, the poem is full of ambiguities of audience and address; hence we come away with the sense that speaker and friend are disturbingly similar, that the speaker tells the story because of these similarities, and even that the friend may be a fiction, a defensive displacement, whereby the speaker can at once confess his behavior, and yet partially avoid the full brunt of the guilt it generates.

The self-implication surfaces again in "Son" (*OH*, 9), one of the sequence's most complex poems. It opens with a tender memory of the mother's goodbye to the dead father, and of the latter's funeral. Then it tells how the speaker moved to a new landscape, where his efforts to protect his privacy convey a hint of defensiveness: when "everyone there asked me / who I was   I asked them who they were." The remainder of the poem seems at first to be merely a rather sanctimonious criticism of the natives of the place for their barbaric behavior toward the mysteries of nature:

> at that time I found the cave   under the mountain
> drawings still on the walls   carved fragments in the dirt
> all my days I spent there   groping in the floor
> but some who came from nearby   were wrecking the place
>   for a game
> garbage through holes overhead   broken cars dead animals
> in the evenings they rolled huge rocks   down to smash the
>   roof
> nothing I could do   kept them from it for long
>
> the old story   the old story
>
> and in the mornings the cave   full of new daylight

A closer look at these lines, however, suggests a somewhat different understanding of "the old story"; what seems a lament against the insensitivity of others is revealed to be in part the narrator's own story as fiction or lie, another defense mechanism against internal failings, another effort to shift the blame.

This revelation is triggered by contemplation of the cave as a symbol of the speaker's unconscious, with its fragmented, partially erased symbols and messages. Then we see the speaker's exploration of it as not only methodologically crude, but more than a little obsessive, and the account of the "attacks" by others on it, which seems both likely and horrible enough if it is a literal cave, begins to seem paranoid, and a bit self-indulgent. The speaker seems to be lamenting the failure of his own defenses, and blaming others for "dumping on him" and thus wrecking his psyche. The very junk he resists may even be more his own than he has realized—the "broken cars" his own poetic vehicles, the "dead animals" the detritus of his preoccupation in the sixties with animals as symbols. By the end, then, the coming of "new daylight" into the cave may be not the violation the speaker would have us take it to be, but rather an illuminating opening of his consciousness to the world, in spite of his resistance. In this light, however interesting or even necessary the plumbing of his own unconscious may be to him, it implicates him in another resistance to Eros: he has cut himself off from any bonds to the human community, which (though it is in many ways corrupt) has a claim on him nonetheless.

This reading leads us to consideration of Merwin's other most productive recent vein. This vein combines his cultural critique with an effort to bond with others and rejoin the community, and at its best also combines representation with those "essential doubts about our epistemology" which Nelson finds necessary to his success.[23] In poems such as "The Coin," "Assembly," or "The Fountain" (CF, 75, 85, 92), the greed that turns nature into commodity coincides with a more positive sense of human vitality, and of an occasional connection between human activity and natural beauty. In "The Fountain," the "old woman . . . / who sells tickets for sex shows" also acts generously toward "her family and their friends / many of whom she did not even know." She gives them "a party / in her kitchen," and there reveals a side still committed to craft work and in touch with natural bounty. She "served everybody / yellow cakes and meringues / made from her own eggs," and she takes pride in disclosing (as an epiphany to her guests) her hidden but ongoing relation to nature: "look she said and opened the back door / to show the hens in the evening light / scratching around the fountain."

This small, unpretentious portrait of a surprisingly complex and ambiguous subject is not easy to bring off—or to discuss—without overinflating it. But for me it has the tact missing in some of the poems discussed earlier. It unfolds both a clear sense of how modern economic conditions bind us to corruption, and also a generosity of spirit and an appreciation—even a tinge of very quiet awe—before the persistence of relatedness.

Hence this new vein suggests more ambivalence about the human, and particularly a greater willingness to value human beings and their activities, than are to be found in the antihumanist poems of the sixties. These directions are most apparent in the poems of The Compass Flower and Opening the Hand which treat urban settings. Such settings would have been anathema to the primitivist ecological poet of The Lice, and the more recent poems have not lost sight of the reasons why. They portray the horrors of the city, and the degree to which it cuts us off from each other and from nature. The colloquial voice of "Happens Every Day" (OH, 52), reports a particularly absurd and frustrating street theft which is made possible by the total disconnectedness and detachment of the passersby. In "Coming Back in the Spring" (OH, 50), "the print [of subway riders' newspapers] turns to the day's killings / around the planet" as the train passes under scenes of urban death and devastation. The whole place "is an emergency," and the poem ends with a powerful image of our separation from earth: "we all sleep high off the ground."

But on the other hand, in this poem Merwin realizes and admits that in the city "I am home." Echoing Pound's vision of the crowd's beauty "In a Station of the Metro," he sees "the faces the faces / the cool leaves still lucent before summer." And he declares New York to be the "most beautiful of cities." Possibilities of defense against the emergency are suggested in "groups" whose greater safety allows them to "walk more slowly" than lone pedestrians or even couples, and in "the white tower beyond Union Square" which "is lit up blue and white" like an emergency vehicle responding to a call for help. The name of the square emphasizes that human community is a source of value in an artificial environment, just as it is for the men of "The Quoit" (OH, 62), who come together on the ominously undermined land for their game. Here, as in "The Cart" (OH, 25– 26), our activity seems rootless; we go "round over nothing." But nonetheless it may give pleasure, and part of the pleasure comes from the sense that in such motion we are recognized even by passing strangers. Indeed, as another fine city poem, "The Rock" (CF, 28–29), reminds us, "when we can love it happens here too." Moreover, this latter poem suggests that even though the link is overlaid and concealed, the city remains grounded on the bedrock of nature. So indeed do we, who still "hear . . . under the breath the stone." And because "at night the veins of the sleepers remember trees," we decorate our rooms "with pictures / of the youth of the world." Such pictures exemplify our limited but distinctly human ability to re-present what might otherwise remain completly lost to us. If being human alienates us, it also offers some unique capacities for compensation.

In "St. Vincent's" (CF, 34–36), a speaker who has "lived daily and with / eyes open and ears to hear / these years across from St. Vincent's Hospital" (in Manhattan) piles up images of it even as he admits how little he has really attended to it. He records the arriving ambulances which he and other passersby have ignored, the "mountains" of garbage, the "molded containers" either of "meals from a meal factory" or "specimens for laboratory / examination sealed at the prescribed temperatures / either way closed delivery," and the "faces staring from above / crutches or tubular clamps." But he has also seen "the building drift moonlit through geraniums," "the nurses

ray out through / arterial streets," "internes blocks away / on doorsteps one foot in the door," and

> . . . visitors talking in wind on each corner
> while the lights changed and
> hot dogs were handed over at the curb
> in the middle of afternoon
> mustard ketchup onions and relish

Whatever the horrors of the institution, it is also an active part—
even, perhaps, the heart—of the neighborhood's life.

As a result, the speaker's ignorance ("on what floor do they have /
anything"), his flippant questions ("do they have an incinerator / what
for / how warm do they believe they have to maintain the air / in
there"), and his Eliotic alienation turn back on him to reveal his ne-
glect as a moral failing. He has been a witness, but an inadequately
involved or committed one. His closing query, "who was St. Vincent,"
becomes at once a compelling question about forgotten origins,
and—in its answer—an implicit but intense self-criticism. For St.
Vincent was (is) precisely the patron saint of works of charity—from
caritas, or love as "unselfish concern that freely accepts another in
loyalty and seeks his good" (*Webster's Seventh New Collegiate Dictionary*). He also founded the Daughters of Charity, one of the first
female orders to move from the cloister out into the world to do good
works; in this poem the nurses who "ray out" from the hospital recall them. This love and engagement are precisely what the speaker
has lacked, and what Merwin rejected in the harsher poems of the
sixties, where he chose instead to "celebrate . . . our distance from
men" (*L*, 56). Now as he closes this distance, he must heed Emerson's
prescription for satisfying "all the demands of the spirit. Love is as
much its demand as perception."[24]

One final example from *Opening the Hand* reveals the new strain
at its best. "The Fields" (*OH*, 56) at first seems merely a rather con-
descending criticism of an ethnic street festival whose participants
lack firsthand knowledge of their origins. They cook stuffed cabbages, sauerkraut, potato dumplings "as those dishes were cooked
on deep / misty plains among the sounds of horses / beside fields of
black earth on the other side of the globe." But they lack the depth of
emotion their ancestors felt both at losing this past, and at being reminded of it, "recognized by the steam of sauerkraut" after "long
journeys" to the "strange coasts" of a new world. Hence the festival

seems empty, for in a world "where everybody is now" and no one
truly knows the past, the descendants

> . . . sing of places they have not known
> they dance in new costumes under the windows
> in the smell of cabbages from fields
> nobody has seen.

At first their singing seems a trivialization of its subject, and the
force of this criticism is not to be lost. But the last line carries a crucial complication. If *nobody* has seen this past, how does it make
itself felt in the poem? How but in the visual imagery of a poet who
not only has not seen it, but who is not even linked by heritage to
the tradition embodied in the smells and the music? His poem is not
only "the music / of what they do not remember," but of what he has
never known intimately enough even to forget. Hence the poet becomes an ironic version of Emerson's representative man, the scribe
for the absence implicit in the group's nonvision. He "sees and
handles that which others dream of,"[25] but which no *body*—including his own—has seen. He is, then, simply the most vivid dreamer.
So if others do violence to the past in an illusory commemoration of
it, then he is the most culpable of all.

This irony, by snaring the speaker who has tried to remain at a distance, above the scene, changes our whole sense of the poem, and
forces us back into it. And on reconsidering the care taken with the
cakes, the "gaz[ing] down onto the sleep of of stuffed cabbages" as
though they were babies, the playing of music, the singing and dancing, can we not read these activities as expressing and celebrating
that very "love [of] what I cannot know" which the speaker so ear-
nestly desired in "To the Rain"? If the past is now irrevocably past, it
is also as present as it can ever be—necessarily "in new costumes,"
necessarily re-covered rather than recovered, but nonetheless built
upon. Here the earlier "What We Are Named for" (sic; *MPC*, 132),
provides a gloss:

> To say what or where we came from has nothing to do with
> what or where we came from. We do not come from there any
> more. . . .
> And yet sometimes it is our only way of pointing to who we
> are.

The use of "we" signifies that collective knowledge is the issue. In
"The Fields," to say that nobody has seen the origins is also to say

that no *one* has seen them; they are remembered or imagined only in a group consciousness whose cohesion appears in the traditional symbol of the dance. And the poet as representative is at least as much the receiver of this group vision as the giver of it. Thus he depends upon others, [26] and joins in a community where all remain alienated from origins and hence somewhat diminished, where the dance goes round over nothing, but where everybody *is now*—both in the present and constitutive of it as the newest of the title's "Fields." Hence the poem balances bonding with grief, representation with epistemological complication. Its mode is not by any means Orphic naming or transcendent affirmation, but neither is it totally self-decreating allegory or bitter alienation from humanity. It reminds us that, for good or ill, "only in the present are the voices" (WA, 108).

Near the end of his essay on Merwin, Cary Nelson warns against criticism's tendency to "capitulate . . . in its final pages, by finding affirmation in the most bleak of modern works; it is part of the impulse to socialize the experience of reading literature." Though this tendency seems to me a descendant of tragedy's urge to reunit the community even through horror and grief, I agree that we must resist "a criticism that glibly seeks visions of democratic communality in poems devoted to moments of self-extinction or visions of collective dread." [27] On the other hand, such resistance should not prevent the recognition that in the last several years both Merwin's tone and the whole weight of his vision has shifted, at least for now. Hence I end with "The Fields" precisely because its ambiguous affirmation of communal possibilities rooted in negations and absences seems to me an extraordinary achievement, and an alternative to the more facile affirmations and the aesthetic problems that mar many of the nature and love poems. Whether Merwin will continue to mine this communal vein productively remains to be seen. But whatever he does next seems bound to compel our interest, for he continues to prove that his is one of the most various, productive, and demanding poetic gifts ever to "come and be given" (WA, 122).

NOTES

1. Ralph Waldo Emerson, "The Poet," in *Selections from Ralph Waldo Emerson*, ed. Stephen E. Whicher (Boston: Houghton Mifflin, 1957), p. 224. All subsequent Emerson citations refer to this volume.

2. L. Edwin Folsom, "Approaches and Removals: W. S. Merwin's Encounter with Whitman's America," *Shenandoah*, 29 (Spring 1978), 60.

3. Thomas B. Byers, "Believing Too Much in Words: W. S. Merwin and the Whitman Heritage," *Missouri Review*, 3 (Winter 1980), 87, 88.

4. Ed Folsom and Cary Nelson, "'Fact Has Two Faces': An Interview with W. S. Merwin," *Iowa Review*, 13 (Winter 1982), 49.

5. For a suggestion that Merwin has had his own doubts about the self-critical capacity, see his poetic account of a conversation with John Berryman (*OH*, 65–66):

> I asked how can you ever be sure
> that what you write is really
> any good at all and he said you can't
>
> you can't you can never be sure
> you die without knowing
> whether anything you wrote was any good
> if you have to be sure don't write

6. Harold Bloom, *The Anxiety of Influence* (New York: Oxford University Press, 1973), pp. 21, 148.

7. Emerson, "The Poet," p. 224.

8. Whitman, "Song of Myself," 30. This and all subsequent Whitman citations refer to the deathbed edition of 1891-92.

9. In *Opening the Hand*, Merwin recalls receiving fatherly instruction in this belief from John Berryman, who here stands in for the Whitman he loved:

> he said the great presence
> that permitted everything and transmuted it
> in poetry was passion
> passion was genius . . .

10. Theodore Roethke, "Journey to the Interior," in *The Far Field* (Garden City, N.Y.: Doubleday, 1964), p. 21.

11. Consider especially the toolbox which Merwin as a child received from his father, but was not allowed to open by himself. The "most solemnly prohibited [tool], and the one that my father most admired and praised, was a hatchet" (*UO*, 105); contrast "The Last One" (*L*, 10–12) and "Unchopping a Tree" (*MPC*, 85–88). Note also that the child preferred the spirit level (*UO*, 105).

12. For more on Merwin's ambivalence toward Whitman, see Folsom and Nelson, "Interview," pp. 30–35, 49. On p. 32 he emphasizes his continuing misgivings, but declares himself "very anxious not to be unfair" to Whitman, who seems to him "obviously a wonderful and generous human being" with "a quite incredible and original gift, equally incredible power."

13. W. S. Merwin and Talat Sait Halman, trans., "What Is the Whirling Dance," by Rumi, *American Poetry Review*, 7 (Jan./Feb. 1978), 3. Merwin's translations continue to trace his interests and affinities. Thus in the "Preface" to W. S. Merwin and J. Moussaieff Masson, trans., *The Pea-*

cock's Egg: Love Poems from Ancient India (San Francisco: North Point Press, 1981), p. vii, Masson reveals that Merwin selected the poems, and "No deliberate effort was made to select poems thematically, but to our surprise almost all of those chosen were love poems, hence the title of this book."

14. Further realizations of the relationship desired in "The Animals" occur in "The Waters" (*OH*, 3) where "there were lives that turned and appeared to wait / and I went toward them looking," and in "Hearing" (*OH*, 81–82), where "a voice" from nature comes "like a small bell singing / over and over one clear treble / syllable."

15. See Charles Altieri, *Enlarging the Temple: New Directions in American Poetry during the 1960s* (Lewisburg, Pa: Bucknell University Press, 1979), pp. 17, 18, and passim.

16. See Helen Vendler, "W. S. Merwin," in *Part of Nature, Part of Us: Modern American Poets* (Cambridge, Mass.: Harvard University Press, 1980), pp. 233–36, and Cary Nelson, "Resources of Failure," p. 89.

17. At times the lover has a saving sense of humor about his eagerness: "I like to walk behind you / to watch and remember / and look forward" (*FI*, 41). Or he can use a cliché with a comic combination of subtlety and audacity: "As we move together on your old bed / they are lighting fuses / for the new year" (*FI*, 44). But such moments are unfortunately rare.

18. Nelson, "Resources of Failure," p. 110.

19. Ibid., p. 111.

20. See J. Hillis Miller, *Poets of Reality: Six Twentieth-Century Writers* (1965; rpt. New York: Atheneum, 1969), passim. The danger in this analogy is that Merwin, born in 1927, is still significantly younger than were the other poets in their later phase. I don't want to rush him into premature old age, but the pattern does seem to apply, especially given the relatively colloquial and anecdotal, nonallegorical voice of *Opening the Hand*. Note also the references to lateness which permeate *Finding the Islands* (see, for instance, pp. 34–37, 43–45, 63–64, 70–71).

21. This uncertainty reaches all the way back to his childhood feelings about the flowers "etched into the frosted glass" of his family's front door: "there was something about them that I could never quite believe nor quite disbelieve" (*UO*, 58). It may also help account for the autumnal twilight of the nature and love poems; the air rarely clears completely for him. Even when he finds himself erotically awakened to the world, the awakening remains part of "this body's altering *dream*" (*OH*, 3, emphasis added).

22. Nelson, "Resources of Failure," p. 113. However, Nelson's "regularly" should not be taken to mean "invariably." All three of the most recent books contain successful poems on these themes. For a particularly lovely example, see "A Birthday" (*OH*, 67).

23. Nelson, "Resources of Failure," p. 113.

24. Emerson, "Nature," p. 55. See also Merwin's discussion of "St Vincent's" with Folsom and Nelson in "Interview," pp. 48–50, where the poet says, among other things, that "the poem was a deliberate attempt to practice something closer to the tradition of Williams and Whitman."

25. Emerson, "The Poet," p. 224.

26. This dependence is reinforced in "James" (*OH*, 64), where the news that his friend James Wright is dying causes the poet to forget the name of some flowers. In this poem, at least, both relation to nature and right naming hinge on human relationships.

27. Nelson, "Resources of Failure," p. 115.

EDWARD BRUNNER

Opening the Hand:
The Variable Caesura and
the Family Poems

In 1977, W. S. Merwin began to publish poems with a feature quite
uncommon in its own right, largely untried by his contemporaries,
and without precedent in his own work: a distinctive pause in the
approximate middle of each line, as in "Tidal Lagoon":[1]

> From the edge of the bare reef   in the afternoon
> children who can't swim   fling themselves forward calling
> and disappear for a moment   in the long mirror
> that contains the reflections   of the mountains

The caesura was a unit in Anglo-Saxon verse as well as French and
Spanish medieval romances and epics, poetry Merwin had translated
but with the impact of the pause minimized.[2] Moreover, this was
oral poetry, marked by conspicuous alliteration, while Merwin's
work resembles straightforward discourse. "Tidal Lagoon," for example, could be an ordinary prose sentence. In the English heroic
line, there is often a pause after the first two or three beats, enforced
by the syntax and always at the end of a word boundary. Yet such a
pause rarely calls attention to itself; related to the line-break, itself
a relatively modest unit in blank verse, it sets up a subtle counter-
rhythm within the iambic line. But Merwin's caesura is a dramatic
interruption, and his poetry is not in blank verse.

After briefly considering how other recent poets have used this
technique, I want to move into a rather technical analysis of Merwin's

use of the caesura in *Opening the Hand*. My concern, however, is not merely technical, since, as I will attempt to show, the hesitations and reversals created by the caesura help us to understand the ambivalent emotions that structure the powerful family poems in *Opening the Hand*. Indeed, when the caesura is abandoned in the book, as I shall argue in the second half of the essay, it signals a quite different kind of poetry, one more open to the voices of other people.

A few of Merwin's contemporaries have used a similar technique. Beginning with *Buckdancer's Choice* (1966), James Dickey interrupted long lines with one or more internal pauses. But the division regularly falls at a natural point in the syntax, reinforcing the line's speech rhythms. By contrast, Merwin regularly places his pause close to the middle of the line; once it has occurred, he uses it throughout the poem, while Dickey lets the device fall at the beginning, near the end, or not at all. Dickey explains that he first used the pause with two poems of "madness, death and violent affirmation" to convey "thought when it associates rapidly . . . in successive shocks, rests, word-bursts."[3] For him, the pause hastens the pace of the line, creating a swift momentum that suggests a mind under pressure. Merwin's pause, by contrast, often slows down the poem; like a barrier, it quells momentum.

Since *Leaflets* (1969), Adrienne Rich occasionally uses an internal pause in place of punctuation or to stress a phrase. Again, the device comes and goes according to syntax:

> There are days when housework seems the only
> outlet   old funnel I've poured caldrons through
> old servitude   In grief and fury bending
> to the accustomed tasks   the vacuum cleaner plowing
> realms of dust   . the mirror scoured   grey webs
> behind framed photographs   brushed away[4]

Rich's caesura is a punctuating device, and later in this poem, when she wants to speak freely to the reader, she drops it. By contrast, Merwin's caesura is a continuing constraint, one frequently at odds with speech rhythms:

> A guest at Thanksgiving   said And You've got
> a green water tower   with a blue two painted on it
> (*OH*, 37)

Merwin's caesura suggests that what may seem transparently clear may contain an element of obscurity.

Merwin himself has discussed his caesura only briefly, referring to it as "my 'broken back' line, the two-part line." His gingerly comments are distinctly impersonal, emphatically historical. The "old Middle English line" has been "overlaid" by "Italianate iambic pentameter," and "the caesura in the iambic pentameter line is like the ghost of the old Middle English line asserting itself all the time, saying I'm here all the time."[5] But what of the caesura as Merwin is using it, outside blank verse? The question is addressed only in this reserved conclusion: "If you take up something that is like a continuation of it, it seems a little stiff, but it can do things that iambic pentameter probably can't."[6]

Merwin may be so reserved, however, because he has expanded his enthusiasm on the virtues of observing the line-break, the importance of which is paramount to him. "One of the danger signs of recent verse," he states, is "the demise of the clarity of the line." So important is the line that he urged students in a workshop to examine carefully why a line stopped as it did in their work, even "at the risk of losing a great deal of spontaneity": "there are two things that a line is doing—it's making a rhythm of its own by means of stopping where it does; and unless you're doing it wrong, unless it's working against you and you've lost it, lost this *line*, it's making a continuity of movement and making a rhythm within a continuity . . . at the same time."[7] Though the line pauses when it ends, it also continues as part of the stanza or the whole poem. Yet one of these two inevitably dominates, a pattern that produces expectation. Will the line primarily pause or continue?

Merwin's unwillingness to elaborate on the "'broken back' line" indicates that he has no specific theory behind its use. Indeed, the variable caesura may be a variant on the unit that truly excites him, the line-break. The variable caesura introduces additional line-breaks into the poem, breaks that may or may not be as strong as those at the end of the line. Their strength, in fact, needs to be weighed each time. Most important, these pauses create additional movements that enhance the poem by allowing meanings to develop: "I think of stopping at a given point as a rhythmical gesture, and also as a gesture of meaning—because when you stop, if the rhythm is working, it is going to have an effect on the meaning, particulary if you're not

punctuating. But it's important to stop in such a way that the stop
has something to do with impetus. It keeps the motion of the poem
going, both in terms of sound, rhythm, and in terms of meaning."[8]
Though he is speaking of the line-break, his words apply to the caesura, for it is also a stop that keeps husbanding its own momentum,
a pause which promises to continue. It would appear that use of the
caesura is a phase in Merwin's development rather than an enduring
stylistic trait, a phase perhaps reflecting a need to write a poetry of
greater intricacy.

Generally speaking, the briefer the poem the more important the
caesura. "Tidal Lagoon" is an example of the way the caesura and the
line-break, in vying for authority, can provide a drama essential to
the poem:

From the edge of the bare reef   in the afternoon
children who can't swim   fling themselves forward calling
and disappear for a moment   in the long mirror
that contains the reflections   of the mountains

                                                              (*OH*, 36)

In each line, what happens after the caesura is in keeping with what
happened before it; but what happens after the line-break is unexpected. The caesura is more neutral, reflecting whatever occurs in
the line, while the line-break is disruptive, actively redirecting the
poem's movement. There is no reason to expect the abrupt swerve
after line 1, for the caesura leads to a bland prepositional phrase, "in
the afternoon," that suggests a placid scene. Then it turns out that
the reef is dotted with "children who can't swim." The caesura in
line 2 enhances this new drama, as the children "fling themselves
forward calling." But the next line break shifts the poem again;
instead of calling out in fear (which is what we would anticipate),
the children simply disappear for a moment into water that is profoundly placid, a "long mirror." Predictably, the caesura in line 3
signals no abrupt change. However, we have come to expect surprises from the line-break, and if line 3 recomposes itself into stillness, we might expect some twist at the line-break. When that twist
does not occur, when the profound calm remains, we feel relief and
surprise, even a deepening stillness, as the reflections of the mountains recompose themselves.

In "Tidal Lagoon" the minor authority of the caesura is played off against the major authority of the line-break to create anticipations that the poet can either affirm or deny. Yet other examples are less predictable, since the caesura challenges the line-break. Its activity in "Green Water Tower" is unpredictable, as Merwin signals at the outset by placing it in such a way that provocatively denies it is a pause only for speaking effect:

A guest at Thanksgiving   said And You've got
a green water tower   with a blue two painted on it

it is there at the edge of the woods   on the hill to the east
at night it flattens   into the black profile of trees
clouds bloom from behind it   moonlight climbs through them
to the sound of pouring   far inside

in an east wind we wake hearing it   wondering where it is
above it the sky grows pale   white sun emerges
the green tower swells   in rings of shadow
day comes   we drink and stand listening

                                                              (OH, 37)

The caesura never settles into a comfortable pattern. In line 3, for example, is there a full stop after "woods" or "east"? No answer emerges, and the question poses no problem since the reader glides easily in either direction. But the effect has been to undermine the authority of the line-break where one might anticipate the full stop to occur. In line 5, the opening half of the line, "clouds bloom from behind it," comes to a full stop; the closing half, "moonlight climbs through them," sets out as though it were also to stop, but it spills over to the sixth line. Which has more authority, the caesura or the line-break? The caesura sets in motion syntactical patterns that may or may not develop; at times growing more authoritative than the line-break, it creates a profusion of possibilities. Merwin encourages this confusion to resolve it in his final stanza. Beginning in line 8, he links a series of full sentences by emphasizing color, progressing from pale sky to white sun to green tower. Out of this progression emerges a sensual splendor as the poem turns toward encircling rings of shadow and emerging day, when colors are held together in contrast to their shadows.

"Green Water Tower" is, admittedly, a delicate rather than a complex poem. From its flat, anecdotal beginning, Merwin ultimately weaves together the man-made and the natural, integrating the tower back into the surroundings from which, in the opening lines, it was once so rudely withdrawn. By using the caesura's potential for mischief, then turning to create an orchestration from that same potential, he recovers his lost poise. As the needs of the poem require, so the caesura operates; its unpredictability distinguishes it from Dickey's pause, which isolates clusters of intense imagery, or Rich's pause, which heightens the rhythms of speech.

If an awareness of the caesura helps illuminate a relatively simple poem, will it shed light on a work that seems oblique almost to the point of obscurity? "The Oars" is notable for its air of sheer privacy:

> My father was born   in a house by a river
> nobody knows   the color of the water
> already seeds had set   in the summer weeds
> the house needed paint   but nobody will see
>
> after the century turned   he sat in a rowboat
> with its end on the bank   below the house
> holding onto the oars   while the trains roared past
> until it was time for him   to get up and go
>
> (*OH*, 4)

Merwin deliberately aborts what might have been a delicate turn from line 1 to line 2. It seems likely that "nobody knows" will refer to the house by the river; but as the second line makes clear, "the color of the water" is what "nobody knows." The pivoting relation between these two lines is withdrawn as soon as it is offered, and the first stanza resolutely truncates each line as a full sentence. This restriction helps explain why line 3 is so affecting: the possibilities implicit in the new seeds have already set, locked in a battle for survival with the undergrowth. There will be no wanton flowering here. In turn, this suggests that the general air of dereliction in the fourth line—"the house needed paint"—stems not from poverty so much as an attitude of deprivation. The setting is barren because the persons within it withhold their attention from it. The house needs paint because no one will see that it is starved for color, just as nobody knows the color of the water because no one has ever cared to look at it.

The poem is steeped in a profound sorrow. Consider the portrait of his father: with one end of the boat still on the riverbank and his hands on the oars, about him the century turns and trains roar past;

he is going nowhere, or nowhere he wishes to go. By itself this seems less a portrait than a critical caricature. Merwin retrieves it by the way he redirects our reading. Based on the pattern in the first stanza, one expects line 5 to end in a full stop. But the sentence continues through all four lines. As it persists beyond line-break after line-break, the sentence evokes a willingness to press against the sluggish torpor of the opening stanza, even as the scene described—a man elaborately fixed in one spot—denies that movement. Because of these mingling oppositions, Merwin's portrait of his father eludes caricature. Though the portrait is still, it is not static. If anything, it is tense and rigid, like an object held by conflicting forces.

Merwin's poems of his family can employ the internal movements created by the caesura just because they are dominated by profoundly mixed feelings. In "Sun and Rain," for example, the last halves of the lines in the first stanza form around prepositional phrases, leaving an effect of thoughts trailing off listlessly. Introducing clauses in the last halves of the lines in the second stanza, Merwin then can move out of his despair and toward a present both radiant and somber, a mingling of sun and rain:

> Opening the book   at a bright window
> above a wide pasture   after five years
> I find I am still standing   on a stone bridge
> looking down with my mother   at dusk into a river
> hearing the currents as hers   in her lifetime
>
> now it comes to me   that that was the day
> she told me of seeing my father   alive for the last time
> and he waved her back from the door   as she was leaving
> took her hand   for a while and said
> nothing
>
>   at some signal
> in a band of sunlight all the black cows   flow down the
>   pasture together
> to turn uphill and stand   as the dark rain touches them
>   (*OH*, 10)

The unfolding of "Sun and Rain" resembles "Green Water Tower" as the poem moves beyond a static introduction toward a dynamic, complex ending. But the transformations in "Green Water Tower" are primarily aesthetic, while those in "Sun and Rain" are noticeably urgent. The darkness in the first stanza is near to overwhelming as Merwin turns away from "a bright window" to a setting "at dusk" and is drawn into a memory of two persons looking down into an inexorable current. The prepositional phrases evoke a downward dissolution, as if the poem were unraveling itself. Against this emerges the saving gesture in the next stanza—hands held out for another and clinging for a long moment on the edge of death. The strength in that gesture is kept up in the forthright clauses which now activate the ends of lines. And this leads in turn to the present, with the movement of the creatures who "turn uphill" in "a band of sunlight" and stand "as the dark rain" which "touches" as the hands of his father and mother once touched. The rain is a gift arriving much as his father's gesture was a gift arriving to his mother; it holds that gesture alive and recovers it in the present.

A similar kind of gesture dominates the opening of "Son," but this is primarily a poem of grief and anger and despair—emotions expressed without simply yielding to any of them. The deep mourning that courses through the poem, almost helplessly, is never released:

As the shadow closed   on the face once my father's
three times leaning forward   far off she called
Good night in a whisper   from before I was born
later through the burial   a wren went on singing

then it was that I left   for the coast to live
a single long mountain   close to the shore
from it the sun rose   and everyone there asked me
who I was   I asked them who they were

at that time I found the cave   under the mountain
drawings still on the walls   carved fragments in the dirt
all my days I spent there   groping in the floor
but some who came from nearby   were wrecking the place
   for a game
garbage through holes overhead   broken cars dead animals
in the evenings they rolled huge rocks   down to smash the
   roof
nothing that I could do   kept them from it for long

the old story   the old story

and in the mornings the cave   full of new daylight

                                                      (*OH*, 9)

SUN AND RAIN

Opening the book   at a bright window
above a ~~broad~~ pasture   after five years
~~I as I see that I am full~~ standing   on the stone ~~bridge~~ bridge
looking down with my mother   at dusk into the river
hearing the current as hers   ~~then~~ in her lifetime

~~now later~~ it comes to me   /that ~~was~~ the ~~same~~ day
she told me of seeing my father   alive for the last time
~~and how~~ he waved her back from the door   as she ~~was~~ leaving
~~and~~ took her hand ~~for a moment~~   ~~without saying anything~~

all the black cows   flow down the pasture together
to turn uphill and stand   as the dark rain touches them

Merwin's typed, second draft of "Sun and Rain." The manuscripts demonstrate
that the caesura was built into these poems from the earliest drafts in pencil.

The pain of mourning is that one knows so much but is unable to act, since no change is meaningful enough to alter what is unalterable. And as one returns to a regular life, sensing a rhythm that is larger than private feelings, one's own actions seem increasingly futile. The bitter truth here is that life continues: the cave is full of new daylight, a fact foreshadowed by the wren that kept on singing during the burial. That rhythm proceeds despite the opposite urge in the poem toward oblivion, withdrawal, destruction.

Merwin spells out the mourner's deep reluctance to accept consolation in a particularly harrowing way: the poem steadily moves away from intricacy, but as it grows apparently simpler, the value of what it is moving away from increases. The poem's most complex moment unfolds in the first three lines, a moment whose wonder is broken by the sound of the wren singing. This stanza is, in fact, too complex to follow clearly until the second half of the third line when the source of the whispered "*Good night*" is identified. The series of gestures—reaching out three times, recalling a voice from another time, both new and identifiable as a voice of the past— mingle beauty and strength with pain, acceptance, and love. After that, everything is blunt. Each line tends toward a full stop. What enjambment exists is minor. Events march forward in rigid precision. (The forward connection is clearly stated with "then it was" and "at that time" and the unusual feature of beginning one line with "but" and another with "and.") This directness is an escape from pain which, paradoxically, keeps the painfulness the poet feels intact. Indeed, the bluntness emphasizes the originality of the opening lines. The option for intricate turns is always present; each line carries its caesura. But it is never exercised. The wonderful gesture at the beginning of the poem grows increasingly remote, increasingly unlikely ever to be duplicated; at the same time, its value increases enormously. Unlike "Sun and Rain," then, in which the poem composes a moment of consolation out of a series of dramatic turns, "Son" remains a painful experience.

The great advantage of the variable caesura is that it can foster what might be called an accessible complexity. It can create increased movements on the level of the individual line, while organizing those movements into larger, overall patterns which can serve as a guide to them. Especially in the family poems in the first part of section 1, the caesura is virtually essential because it both creates and contains a high degree of complexity. These personal poems are open to misunderstanding, hesitation, and bafflement; but the caesura can encourage the exploration of such hidden intricacy by allowing a way for it to flourish in each line, while also holding forth the possibility of a larger pattern that makes a work still intensely personal but accessible, not simply a collection of wrenching turns.

II

The sudden disappearance of the caesura midway through section 1 of *Opening the Hand* is one of the most dramatic events in the volume. It vanishes again in the shift from section 2 to section 3. Of the eighteen poems in section 2, fourteen feature the caesura, while of the twenty poems in section 3, only three use it, and in two of them ("Birthday" and "Direction") it is sometimes there, sometimes not. Why would Merwin drop the device at all, or in such a way as to call attention to those poems without it? One answer may be that the caesura, instead of being a device freely chosen, is an event demanded by a certain kind of poetry. When that poetry is no longer relevant, the caesura ceases to exist.

This answer is supported by the arrangement of poems in section 1. Poems in the first half center on Merwin's father and mother, with a crucial emphasis on his father's death; by contrast, poems in the second half focus on his aunt ("Birdie"), on himself as a child ("The Burnt Child"), on his sister and him as children ("The Cart"), and on a family member in a photograph reproduced on the cover of *Unframed Originals* ("Unknown Forbear"). The poems in the first half respond to a somber occasion; marked by a deep personal involvement, scored with upheaval and uncertainty, they virtually demand subtle shifts. But the poems in the second half are usually fluent and even straightforward. Neither absorbed in detail nor tangled in their predecessors' discords, to them the caesura would be a handicap.

The absence of the caesura signals a new kind of poetry. To mark the change, Merwin places "The Houses" as a transitional poem; it has an odd, new format unlike anything else in the book. After the initial three-line stanza, each stanza increases by one line until the central twelve-line stanza, after which each stanza decreases by one line until the final three-line stanza. The circular format brings together two incidents separated by years and indicates that little has changed. As a child, Merwin comes on a house while wandering in the woods; later, when he tries to show the house to his father, it is no longer there. The incident is repeated years later, when Merwin is visiting property his father just purchased; roaming around, he spots another house, but when he inquires about it, his father insists no such house exists. The story has the unsettling lucidity of a dream. The father and son cannot share their feelings; what exists for one is not only invisible to the other but, more harrowingly, what exists when the son is by himself actually vanishes when he tries to share it with his father. The image of the house recalls a tranquil stability that is beyond this pair, who cannot agree on even the most elementary things.

That Merwin acknowledges this profound disparity is a sign for change in these family poems, for at the base of his previous work is a compulsive desire to reach out to a father he is trying to understand even as that understanding arrives too late. To move beyond this absorption, one needs to recover a wider perspective, and the perspective in "The House," from a distance of perhaps forty years, underscores their fundamental separateness. When the incident duplicates itself years later, it suggests that the past is no longer fluid, as it had been at an earlier stage in the family poems, but fixed, completed. The poem's dream-format permits this knowledge to emerge as though Merwin were a helpless spectator to it. The remorseless addition and subtraction of the format is almost the opposite of the caesura poems, with their poet intricately involved in shaping his work.

What gives the past an air of stillness and lingering mystery is that all its unanswered questions remain both unfinished and complete; they are never to be answered. This is central to "Unknown Forbear," a poem to the man in the *Unframed Originals* photograph. Even though Merwin does not know the man, the man himself "appeared to know where he was / whose porch that was" and "who had opened the windows." The man may have known the answers to the questions that swirl around the poem, but Merwin knows these questions will remain unanswered. Accepting this is the burden of the poem. The touch of singsong in the lines, though the off-rhymes are barely noticeable since they hinge on the commonest words

("was," "whose," and "house," for example), suggests the poem's circular movement, turning about its subject but never grasping it.
Merwin himself can find no entrance into his subject; the effect is
like pausing before a glass barrier as an observer.

A striking characteristic of the poems without a caesura is that, in
contrast to those with the caesura, they are dominated by the sound
of individual human voices. Even "Unknown Forbear," the quietest
of poems, begins as Merwin imagines a voice calling offstage:

> Somebody who knew him
> ninety years ago
> called him by a name
> he answered to
> come out now they said to him
> onto the porch and stand
> right there
>
> (OH, 28)

Though Merwin cannot hear the name (which is in keeping with the
impenetrable barrier of the past that he is accepting), he can imagine
the act of calling, and his ability to imagine that suddenly animates
the photograph. No such opportunities occur in the caesura poems.
Voices are reduced to murmurs, and significant communication is
often carried by gesture. In "Sunset Water" the sounds of children are
heard, but indistinctly, as echoes across water. The most important
action in "The Waving of a Hand" is introduced by a gesture, accompanied by spectators who are speechless, and followed by a conversation that goes unreported. In "A Pause by the Water" Merwin anticipates breaking his isolation by meeting "the muffled couple"

> who have been coming here   every year for years
> soon we will eat our fish   in the lighted room
> and later they will show me   pictures of children
>
> (OH, 8)

Again the emphasis is on gesture, on showing rather than speaking;
the voices of the "muffled couple" remain inaudible.

The lack of strong individual voices in these poems gives an extraordinary power to the one voice that can be heard clearly; to be
able to speak at all becomes an event of some magnitude in an atmosphere where voices are reduced to murmurs and where feelings

are so deep they can only be carried by gestures. Thus the larger significance of the moment narrated by Merwin's mother in "Sun and Rain"—

> and he waved her back from the door   as she was leaving
> took her hand   for a while and said
> nothing
>
> (*OH*, 10)

—is that she was strong enough to relate the incident. She finds the words to tell of a moment profound enough to overwhelm any effort to speak. At moments, Merwin is unsure himself how to respond to her display of strength. In "Strawberries," for example, on the day of his father's death, Merwin tells of a vision in which he saw two wagons appear, one leaving a valley with "no driver," "carrying a casket," another carrying two kinds of berries. At night he dreams of things gone wrong, the water in the shower "running brackish," and an insect (of a kind he had seen his father kill) climbing his bathroom walls. When he wakes, his mother suggests a shower and offers strawberries for breakfast. If this coincidence signals a bond, it also portrays a strength of character in her that may be beyond him: what are to him foreboding, nightmare images, she assimilates into daylight routine. As a response to the father's death, it is both comforting and disarming. She is seen as accepting his death, even as her son questions how she can do so. It recalls the father's habit of suppressing true feelings.

In "Son," his mother speaks directly, in the most beautiful and most distraught moment in the sequence:

> three times leaning forward   far off she called
> *Good night* in a whisper   from before I was born
> later through the burial   a wren went on singing

These are the only words spoken directly in the first half of section 1, they are addressed to another who may not be able to hear them, they draw on a strange new voice from a remote past, and they exclude Merwin himself.

It seems that when a voice is heard it carries such a complex of emotions that it is almost unbearable: it is surely accurate to say that Merwin only hears the words spoken by the person he trusts the most. The sound of a trusted voice, gradually growing more distinct, appearing in poems midway through the group, indicates his effort to move beyond the withdrawal of mourning. The proliferation of voices in the second half of section 1 marks an emergence from withdrawal, an emergence that coincides with the abandonment of the caesura.

The ease with which poems move, after the midway point in section 1 and after the caesura is dropped, provides considerable relief. It is as though human speech itself provides a sustaining support new to the poem, and as Merwin moves away from his isolation, he hears the sound of voices with new delight and sensitivity. He talks about this in "Talking" and relishes his own surprised laughter. In "After a Storm" he states that "if I could take one voice / with me it would be / the sound I hear every day." Ending "The Family," he holds out the promise of speaking the names of the farmer's children as a way of enforcing the reality of a scene that may seem too purely idyllic.

The poem richest in voices is "Birdie":

> how many times you may have been born
> as my father's other sisters would say
> in your bawdy nobody is interested
> in things like that in the family
>
> somebody wrote down though that you was
> born one time on April 20
> 1874 so that my grandmother
> at that occasion was thirteen and the hardest thing
> to believe in that account as I think of it
> is that she was ever thirteen years old
> the way we grew up to hide things from each other
>
> (OH, 17)

Even when he is looking at a written transcript, he hears the sound of a distinctive voice, a voice that leads him suddenly to chime in as a chorus. This blending of voices recurs throughout the poem, as in the previous stanza where the speech of his father's other sisters, with its dark mispronunciation of "body," is cut off by an elder talking to an inquisitive child: "nobody is interested / in things like that in our family." Birdie, however, is interested in things of the body, which others find bawdy, and it is no surprise that she is regarded as an error by other family members. Her recorded birthdate is a mistake (or as Merwin states it, again recalling actual speech: "everybody knew / that you / was nothing but a mistake in / the writing"). To the family she remains a wanton outsider, though the innocence of her adventuresomeness takes their measure. Raucous, ebullient, exuberant, she is a reminder of a liveliness that did exist once; like Merwin's unknown forebear, she is a mystery, but one that centers on how so lively a person emerged from such a repressed family. In a passage which also appears in the prose of *Unframed Originals*, Merwin contrasts her free and easy manner with that of his own father and other family members:

> inviting all them so unexpected
> and not heard of for so long your own mother
> younger brother younger sisters new nephew
> to breakfast laughing and waving your hands
>
> with all the rings and them not listening
> saying they was in a hurry to drive farther
> and see the family and you going on
> telling them everything there was to eat [9]
>   (*OH*, 18)

Birdie rises to the occasion which was "so unexpected" while the rest of the family sticks steadily to the track. She is prepared to greet the family that is before her; they keep looking for the family elsewhere (in a manner guaranteed to scatter it further). She offers the largesse of her hospitality while they don't even listen. "Birdie" is more than a statement of critical contrast, however, largely because of Merwin's emphasis on the unknown: how did she turn out so differently? If this question circles the poem, it is notable that Merwin never tries to answer it, but he delights in the revived memory of her presence. Bringing voices forward instead of suppressing matters darkly, she is a kind of tutelary spirit to the rest of the family poems. While Merwin never duplicates her exuberance himself, her spirit is present in "The Cart," an amusingly quirky poem in which he recalls riding with his sister on a handmade merry-go-round.

It should be clear that the strength required for Birdie's voice to be heard, and for Birdie to speak, is an order of strength radically less than for Merwin's mother. But to be able to speak at all in difficult situations remains a value affirmed not just in the family poems but elsewhere in *Opening the Hand.* It is the value, for example, at the center of the two strongest poems in section 3, "Ali" and "Berryman." Beyond the simple details of "Ali," which relate the story of a dog too frail to live, a dog adopted by Merwin and his companion, there is the awareness that one has a deep responsibility to speak for those who have no speech. In mourning Ali, he also recognizes that his own care lengthened the creature's life, just as he acknowledges the joy in his life which came from caring for the creature. And as he speaks for Ali, he also speaks for that part of himself which cannot speak of his own losses. In caring for the creature, he is in some way caring for himself, perhaps forgiving himself for being unable to speak in other contexts.

With "Berryman," Merwin's primary achievement, as in "Birdie," is to capture the sound of another voice, to reproduce even a certain rumbling portentousness, as if Berryman had been consciously addressing a wider audience. But the power Berryman manifests has to do with speaking into an unknown void. At the end of the poem, in reply to Merwin's question "how can you ever be sure / that what you write is really / any good,"

> he said you can't
>
>> you can't you can never be sure
>> you die without knowing
>> whether anything you wrote was any good
>> if you have to be sure don't write
>>> (*OH, 66*)

Given these concerns, one poem that emerges as central in *Opening the Hand* is "Yesterday." It is the one poem in which the father speaks directly and at some length, relating his last words. Though it is not written with the caesura, it uses repeated phrases with a similar effect: they become persistent pauses that disjoin the poem's progress, shifting its movement, recalling it to another dimension. Centering directly on the problem of speaking in a situation in which it is impossible to speak, the poem also suggests that the speech which does occur is tainted. Yet its users are tacitly aware of that fact, accept it, and almost render it benign. Merwin himself fails to rise to the occasion; he falters and turns away, though in the writing of the poem, he speaks directly to this failure.

The courage required to write "Yesterday" is marked by the effort of summoning the final speech of his father, a speech which involves both father and son in falsehoods. Quite simply, his father offers him the opportunity to break off what will be their last visit together:

>   he
>   said you know I would like you to stay
>   and talk with me
>
>   oh yes I say
>
>   but if you are busy he said
>   I don't want you to feel that you
>   have to
>   just because I'm here
>
>   I say nothing
>   (OH, 20)

When his father presses the point, Merwin takes the offer:

>   and I got up and left him then
>   you know
>
>   though there was nowhere I had to go
>   and nothing I had to do
>   (OH, 21)

In first readings, this abrupt breakoff seems appalling, and the poem presents itself as a bare confession of remorse and guilt. Merwin abandons his father, after an interchange in which his father is actually encouraging him to stay. Later readings, however, raise disturbing questions. Why is his father so indirect, even manipulative? Did his father wish to encourage the withdrawal? Why portray him in so apparently negative a light?

These questions are partly answered. Framing the poem is the commentary of a friend who takes a conventional position, chastising Merwin for his flaws. "My friend says I was not a good son," he writes, "you understand / I say yes I understand." This position seems clearly an error, the easy judgment of an outsider who was not there. At one point Merwin sharply corrects his friend's words: "he says the last time I went to see my father / I say the last time I saw my father / / he says the last time I saw my father." Yet this is also the viewpoint the father cultivates in relation to his son. That conventional position, which believes it knows what is proper, lies be-

hind the interchange of father and son—a distant interchange as
stylized as a minuet, though one in which each one is waiting for the
other to make the move that will break through the surface. The
friend's remote detachment reminds Merwin of his relationship with
his father; Merwin's replies to his friend, indeed, directly parallel his
polite replies to his father: "I say yes I understand . . . oh yes I say."
They are non-replies, not true speech but nods of the head and tokens
of withdrawal that allow the other person to go on speaking while
Merwin plunges into unshareable thoughts:

> even when I was living in the same city he says
> maybe I would go there once
> a month or maybe even less
> I say oh yes
>
> (OH, 20)

Drawing the parallel, as Merwin does in writing this poem, is an act
of true speaking, an act exposing the falsity as well as the necessity
of his other acts. That is the courage of this poem, which reveals the
cowardice of the actors in it, cowardice entangling them all in this
occasion. The knowledge weighs down the entire poem, captured in
the reiterated "you know" and "you understand" which function like
a ponderous understanding that cannot be escaped. At the end, it is
even ambiguous whether Merwin is leaving his father or leaving his
friend:

> I look out the window
> my friend is older than I am
> he says and I told my father it was so
> and I got up and left him then
> you know
>
> (OH, 21)

Though he has left them both, at the same time he can never leave
them, can never cease hearing them, held as they all are in this
moment. One listens in amazement to Merwin reliving this experience, and one comes back to all the moments in his own life when
words could have been spoken but were not. A poem like this, which
speaks of all the barriers that exist between persons, and speaks of
them in such a way that no barriers are left between the poet and his
readers, is the most impressive achievement in Opening the Hand—

a volume named well, for in it Merwin opens his hand and reveals himself more fully than in any other of his works.

NOTES

1. Originally published between 1977 and 1981 in journals, the poems featuring the caesura were collected in *Opening the Hand.*

2. The publishing format of the translation of the *Poem of the Cid* differs from edition to edition. In the paperback by the New American Library, the presence of the caesura is noted by printing the second half of the line one space below the first stop. The Modern Library reprint (in *Medieval Epics*), however, signals the caesura with a four- or five-em gap in the line itself, as in "Tidal Lagoon."

3. James Dickey, Preface to *Falling, May Day Sermon and Other Poems* (Middletown, Conn.: Wesleyan University Press, 1981), p. viii.

4. Adrienne Rich, "Coast to Coast," *A Wild Patience Has Taken Me This Far* (New York: W. W. Norton, 1981), p. 6. In *Garbage Wars* (New York: Atheneum, 1970), Donald Finkel uses a similar kind of caesura as a semicolon, reinforcing the syntax; as with Rich, it appears in many poems, but always as an adjunct to heighten the voice of the poet.

5. Ed Folsom and Cary Nelson, "'Fact Has Two Faces': Interview with W. S. Merwin," *Iowa Review*, 13 (Winter, 1982), 62.

6. Ibid., p. 63.

7. Ibid., p. 60.

8. Ibid., p. 61.

9. The incident of this visit is told in more detail in *Unframed Originals*, pp. 50–53.

MICHAEL GREER AND
CARY NELSON

"St. Vincent's":
The Biography of a Poem

The textual history of "St Vincent's" includes five different texts—a
brief, abandoned poem ("Night opposite St. Vincent's") a first handwritten draft of "St Vincent's" on one densely packed page, a second
handwritten draft on three pages, a first typewritten version of the
poem, and finally, the poem as it appears in *The Compass Flower*. We
have reproduced only the first three of these texts here, followed in
each case by our typed transcriptions, since the first typewritten
draft of the poem, except for a key deletion that we will describe, is
very close to the final published version. Our aim is both to make a
representative set of Merwin manuscripts available to his readers
and to point out some of the major features of his revising process.
All of the holograph pages reproduced here were written in pencil.
"Night opposite St. Vincent's" is, as it happens, one of the more difficult manuscripts in the archive to read, since, unlike "St Vincent's,"
it was written with a very soft pencil. Merwin has, however, helped
us decipher some phrases we were unable to read.

"Night opposite St. Vincent's," though essentially an unfinished
fragment, does give us Merwin's preliminary effort at a poem on the
subject of the hospital across the street from his apartment. He
opens this text quite differently, describing primarily the space in
which he writes, as it is lit by the world outside his window, rather
than St. Vincent's itself. Almost no elements of this perspective
make their way overtly into the final poem. "I have seen," he writes

in the published poem, "the building drift moonlit through geraniums," but the act of seeing is essentially neutral. Yet the scene of
writing in "St. Vincent's," is, in an oblique and more uneasy sense, a
simulacrum of what can be known about the hospital across the
street.

Throughout the sequence of revisions, the issue is never simply
one of improving the quality of individual lines or canceling passages
of lesser quality. As with "The Complaint of My Family," Merwin
often drops passages of considerable power, presumably because they
are not true to the kind of poem he is impelled to write. Thus the
drafts sometimes present us with alternate, rejected images of what
the poem might have been. It also seems that Merwin is willing to
entertain a more self-expressive, openly intimate writing practice in
drafts than he is in finished poems. Consider this passage in the first
draft of "St Vincent's," which recalls the personal reference removed
in revising "Caesar":

> someone is in pain a knife is moving
> and somewhere a trumpet is sounding
> it is I it is I

Except for the phrase "a knife is moving," the passage is almost immediately canceled. The end of the next draft includes the lines "the
edge of the knife is moving through / minutes lights veins," but
these lines are also canceled. Merwin thus at first openly identifies
with a patient, a surgeon, and a trumpet giving witness, but these
overt identifications are soon eliminated.

In general Merwin seems more inclined in the drafts (than in the
final version) to speculate about what happens inside the hospital.
"On what floor do they have the operating theaters / delivery rooms /
emergency rooms / projection rooms for X-rays," he asks in a passage
from the first draft. These lines survive intact until the first typewritten draft, where they are struck out and revised to read "On
what floor do they have / anything." Similarly, in "Night opposite St.
Vincent's" he comments that "across the street" some are dying and
many are "awake about beginnings." In the first draft of "St Vincent's" he notes that "While I was watching the building some / inside it were conversing with death." This section is heavily revised,
both here and in the next draft, and becomes the sixth stanza of the
first typewritten draft:

Merwin's holograph manuscript of "Night opposite St. Vincent's," an unfinished first effort at a poem about the hospital.

Night Opposite St. Vincent's

All night the lights of cars are reflected on the blue ceiling

I can write without light

When the moon is new it will rise over the hospital
                     full
light and shade black against window grille

twined with begonia and coleus

street light on shelves of books poster of Mozart
_____
across the street

        few cars on the Avenue at last

past the door of the casuality ward

[illeg.] across the street some arrive dying

and many are arrive awake about beginnings
    _____

Sounds like she dropped it
    _____

writing by feel

    _____

face leaves

A typed transcription (by C. N. and M. G.) of "Night opposite St. Vincent's."

> while I have stood watching that building
> blood inside it
> has been negotiating hand voice scream
> in particular
> a solitary brain remembered every window
> it had ever seen
> breaths have arrived each alone out of
> the dark waters there behind the walls
> but not a name of any of them did I hear

Having typed out this stanza, Merwin draws a line through it, thereby eliminating the last passage about the patients in the hospital.

In the process he also severely curtails what is a strong but blocked intersubjective component in the first two drafts. By the final poem, he meets only the faces of people on the street, having cut passages speculating about unseen faces in the hospital itself. "While I watch," he writes in a passage canceled in the second draft, "eyes are open inside the windows." In the printed poem the building has become obdurate and unknowable; he is seen only by its "mortised face." Indeed, the first two drafts had a certain visionary fusion of self, other, and material substance at their center. A passage from the first draft suggests that a single space subsumes all the watching at work in the poem:

> we have floated together on the waters
> that building and I
> and around us the whole city on the flood

In the second draft the second line becomes "that building and I a mind," but this evocation of a transpersonal mental space is eliminated in the same draft. There is still a certain copresence of self and other in the final poem, but it no longer holds out the possibility of intersubjective communication. The look exchanged with St. Vincent's is now a neutral one, more in keeping with those dark openings between the columns in the building's facade; in the second draft Merwin adds a line telling us that the face of St. Vincent's exposes us to "the dawn of history," an image that empties the present of everything but its impossible originary moment. In the process of revision the self too has lost its empathic status, acquiring instead the unknowable materiality of the building across the street. "And who was St Vincent," the poem's final line, occurs in the first

draft as a recurrent refrain that serves in part as a compositional resource. "Who are they / who are we / who was St Vincent," Merwin
asks, then cancels the passage. By the final version, these questions
are covered by the single question about the hospital's name.

The poem's basic structure is, in fact, established in the first holograph manuscript, but the poem expands with a series of passages
drawn back into the stanzas from the margins of the page. The drafts
in general are striking for the way their appearance suggests the asso-
ciative power of the images Merwin first records. More graphically
than the printed version can demonstrate, the first draft gives us a
poetic of the open field whose semiosis is contingent and fluid,
whose referentiality is as much to memory, perception, and the pro-
ductivity of writing as to St. Vincent's itself.

"St. Vincent's" was not, however, the end of the process. Merwin
remained interested in the very images he had edited out of the drafts
and, in 1984, published "Night above the Avenue," a poem whose
opening lines recall the abandoned "Night opposite St. Vincent's":

> The whole time that I have lived here
> at every moment somebody
> has been at the point of birth
> behind a window across the street
> and somebody behind a window
> across the street
> has been at the point of death

The "dark interiors / of their bodies," he continues, "have been
opened to lights / and they have waited bleeding . . . unseen by each
other we have been transformed." Obviously the fascination with
the interior of the hospital and the metaphors of transformation, rejected in the revision of "St. Vincent's," have stayed with him. The
concluding line may now seem to evoke the plural, ever unstable,
textuality of these multiple drafts: "and I have wakened in a wind of
messages."

St. Vincent's

Merwin's first draft of "St. Vincent's."

St Vincent's

I search ~~through~~ among
~~What~~ What these eyes light on and these
ears go out to as
into rain clouds that rose over the city
on the first of the year ~~and~~ where
~~are they now~~ have they got to now
~~now~~ in the same ~~year~~ month
    daily with eyes open and ears to hear
    there   & years
and ~~so~~ I have lived ~~for many~~ months ∧across from ~~&~~
St Vincent's Hospital

French ~~red~~ bricks under the cross facing west and
the blown up neo classic facades the ~~great~~ tall
~~tall~~ dark openings between columns
exploded into many windows in a brick face
    have

not even when the sirens
stop
nearer

inside it the ambulances ~~were~~ unloaded
frequently frequently the sirens ————— screaming through traffic blocks away up
ago I learned not to hear them   Seventh Avenue long
inside that face they \unloaded   ambulance
    ~~unloaded~~ the sirens almost
they have been unloaded ~~are~~   they
    always
    —————— they turn they ~~have~~ turned to back in
    are two   —a few ~~have~~ stayed to look and
    passers-by
At night there ~~were several~~ blue windows   neither did I
on the top floor has
in which a bright blue light burned all night
~~many~~
~~every~~ nights when most of the others are out
on what floor do they have the operating theaters
~~the~~ delivery rooms
~~the~~ emergency rooms
~~the~~ projection rooms for X-rays

    some
    was
While I'watching the building ~~someone~~
  inside it were ~~dealing~~ ~~neg dealing~~ conversing
  ~~was born in it~~ ~~it was talking~~ with death in particular
  ~~particular~~ ———— negotiating
~~and so was I~~ ~~someone~~ was remembering all the windows that hand that voice that scream

and who was St Vincent

When do they wash
nor anyone washing the windows
nor looking out

I watched it at Christmas
and at New Year

~~Someone was born~~ arrived out of the ~~unborn~~
~~waters~~
Which are ~~which is~~ there behind the walls
but ~~and~~ not a name of them ~~did I know~~ have I heard ~~and I might have been~~

though
~~yet not~~
we have floated together on the waters
that building and ~~through them~~
~~around~~
and ~~beyond~~ us the whole city ~~at~~ — ~~on~~ the flood
~~and to us winter illeg.~~

I have seen ~~it~~ moonlit through geraniums ~~climbing~~
the hospital
late at ~~on~~ nights when the trucks were few
the moon past the full
parts of
Those upper windows ~~with~~ in the ~~moonlit~~ sky for hours
~~I have watched them take out the garbage~~
In the morning
piling up mountains of ~~black green~~ plastic bags white

I have ~~watched~~ seen the nurses ray out through the streets
seen
In the evening I have noticed
green
black   teams
~~seen~~ interns on doorsteps blocks away
I have come upon
seen the men in gloves taking out the garbage at all
hours

I have seen ~~them~~ catch fire and ~~seen watched~~ the ~~smoke steam~~
studied   cloud
~~people~~ and the fire-engines at the ends of the jets of the hoses
as near as that
and

covered   stacked
~~the~~ plastic trays are ~~unloaded~~ inside
a delivery entrance on Twelfth Street
they may be meals from a meal factory in made
up as for long journeys by
plane
or specimens for laboratory examination
~~in cold or~~ chilled and packed cold
either way
delivery

met   stiff   the red beacons pounding and pounding
have ~~seen staring frightened~~ faces above crutches or ~~faces not~~
the engines ~~pump thumping~~
/tubular clamps
out for a walking along the sidewalk
wheelchairs turtling
~~.~~ wind

~~I saw them and I heard them day after day~~
~~and I knew them less than~~ they were not in the papers
~~and I knew them less than the news in the paper I scarcely read~~   Jan 17 1974
I see the smoke rise from those chimneys
do they have an incinerator   how warm do they keep
~~what does it do what~~ for   that air
visitors talking about visits in the ~~cold~~ on the corner
some of the windows appear to be covered with tin
reflected
while the lights change and   ~~but it may be the light~~
~~someone is in pain~~ a knife is moving
are handed over   at   still   coming and going
~~hot-dogs~~ ~~are sold on~~ the curb in the middle of the afternoon
~~and somewhere a trumpet is sounding~~
I ~~imagine always~~ imagine bees ~~coming~~
ether and police going somewhere   ~~it is I it is I~~
~~and going~~ on the sills
mustard ketchup and relish
who are they
who are we
minutes   who was St Vincent
~~words~~
through ~~filles~~ lights ~~blood~~ veins   —— who was St. Vincent
fluids
and ~~others~~ are watching
~~what is there to the be seen~~ whatever there is to see

A typed transcription (by M. G.) of Merwin's first draft of "St. Vincent's."

The second draft of "St. Vincent's."

St Vincent's

~~I search among what these~~
~~These eyes keep lighting on and these~~
~~listening through~~
~~ears keep beyond~~
Thinking of rain clouds that rose over the city
on the first of the year

~~and considering~~
~~I consider~~ in the same month I consider
that I have lived daily and with
eyes open and ears to hear   these ~~months and~~ years
across from St Vincent's Hospital
whose roof
above ~~which~~ those clouds rose
~~clouds appeared~~
                                    — ~~these eyes keep lighting on~~
bricks by day a French red under
~~the~~ cross facing south
blown up neo classic facades the tall
dark openings between columns at
the dawn of history
exploded into many windows
                -ised
in a mortered face

inside it
the ambulances have unloaded   after ~~the~~
frequently frequently sirens'
howling nearer through ~~the~~ traffic ~~blocks away~~ up
Seventh Avenue long
ago I learned not to hear them

which-way-is-the-head

at night two long blue ⌐and one short one
windows on the top floor
burn all night me
many nights when most of the others are out
on what floor do they have the operating theaters
theaters the delivery rooms the
emergency rooms
the X-ray projection rooms
rooms

while when
every-time-that   have stood
while I was watching that building some
side
the-[illeg]-night   a blood
inside-it-were-dealing-with-looking at one a single-body 'inside it
near-death-in-particular-night
has-been-were-been
body-was negotiating-that hand that voice that scream
a-in-a-skull-eye   in particular
under-an-under brain was seeing
body was remembering every window
single one some remembering
a sole
          dark or light it had ever seen saw
                    each above
          breaths and a spirit arriving out of the the
                                        the dark   the
          directionless directionless waters behind there behind those walls
                              the   did
          but not a name of them all have I heard
              a of any

A typed transcription (by M. G.) of the second draft of "St. Vincent's."

The second draft of "St. Vincent's" (cont.).

                                           have
                       ~~yet and~~
and   ~~though we have~~ floated together ~~on the waters~~
                       ~~roof~~
                       ~~that building and I a mind~~ I
         ~~and around us the whole city on~~ building-lined ~~structure in~~
         ~~In the cloud~~ I have seen the ~~drifting~~ facade moonlit through geraniums
                                                        drift

late at night when the trucks were few
~~the~~ moon just past the full
~~those~~ upper windows parts of the sky as long /as I looked
         I watched it at Christmas and New Year
                       I have
early in ~~in~~ the morning ~~have~~ seen the nurses ray out through ~~the streets veined~~ arterial
         streets ~~in~~
in the evening have noticed internes
blocks away on doorsteps ~~leaving saying good-bye~~ one foot ~~in a sill~~ in the door
I have come upon
                                           all hours

the men in gloves taking out the garbage at ~~all hours~~
~~all he~~ piling up mountians of   with much
plastic bags white strata /green intermixed and
black
I have seen them
catch fire studied the cloud
at the ends of the jets of the hoses
the fire engines as near as that
red beacons and ~~throbbing~~

I ~~filed molded plastic trays~~
I have noted ~~covered plastic trays~~ stacked outside
a delivery entrance on Twelfth Street
whether meals from a meal factory made up with these
mummified
~~up to as with those set out~~ peeked for long journeys by plane
or specimens for laboratory
examination ~~sealed~~ sealed
~~analysis chilled and packed~~ at the proper temperatures
either way ~~hundred~~
closed delivery

and   ~~I have~~ met faces staring from
           above crutches or tubular clamps
           out for ~~a walk~~ tentative walk
           wheel chairs turtling
           heard visitors talking in the wind on ~~the~~ each corner
           while the lights changed and
           hot dogs were handed over at the curb
           in the middle of the afternoon
           mustard ketchup onions and relish and laundry
           and police smelling of ether ~~going~~ ~~were~~
~~at the se~~ were going back

                    all
           and I knew them less than
~~they were not in~~ the papers of our days
smoke rises from the chimneys do they have an incinerator
what for   believe they the
how warm do they have to keep ~~that~~ air
~~inside~~ there some of the windows appear
~~a few~~ ~~several~~ made of
           several to be ~~covered with~~ tin
           but it may be the light reflected

A typed transcription (by M. G.) of the second draft of "St. Vincent's" (cont.).

The second draft of "St. Vincent's" (cont.).

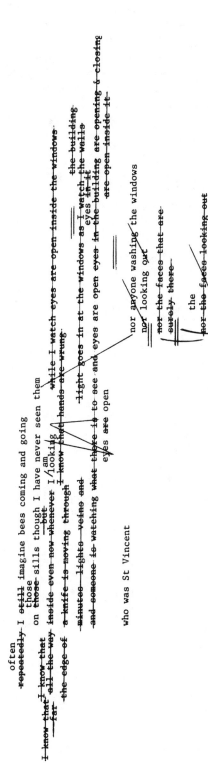

A typed transcription (by M. G.) of the second draft of "St. Vincent's" (cont.).

W. S. Merwin's Other Career: The Manuscript Archive at the University of Illinois

THE ARCHIVE

After an extended period of evaluation and a preliminary cataloguing, Merwin's manuscripts—contained in eighteen rather large boxes— were acquired by the University of Illinois at Urbana-Champaign in July of 1984. Merwin's translation manuscripts, contained in four cartons, were purchased in 1982. Both groups of manuscripts are part of the collection of the Rare Book Room and are available for use by qualified scholars. A full description of the contents of the archive would require a book-length manuscript. As part of *this* book, how-ever, we do want to identify the main categories of manuscripts and point to some representative highlights, so that other scholars know what resources the archive offers. Merwin retains the literary rights to the archive, but quotation in scholarly publications (within the limits of "fair use") is permissible.

The manuscripts cover a period beginning in the mid-1940s and extending to the early 1980s. They include much of Merwin's un-published work from his student days at Princeton, the notes for and drafts of his published poetry, prose, and translations, and an extraor-dinary amount of unpublished poetry, prose, and drama from all pe-riods of Merwin's career. Archives of this sort, presenting a complete record of almost forty years of active writing and revision, are very rare. They should interest not only students of contemporary writ-ing but also anyone interested in the creative process.

The total effect of these manuscripts is to force us to distinguish between Merwin's public career—shaped by what he published—and his more private career as a writer. The publications are clearly only part of the story, for one cannot now realistically choose to ignore the unpublished work. For example, can one now say that Merwin only began to write prose about his own family and his Pennsylvania background in the late 1970s, when the manuscripts reveal that he was writing prose resembling *Unframed Originals* (1982) in the 1950s? Did Merwin only begin to write specifically political poetry in the 1960s? That is when he began to publish such poetry, but he was writing it at Princeton in the 1940s. One perspective identifies the changes in his publications with his whole person; another perspective recognizes that the publications represent choices about a public identity that does not wholly match the writing he actually did.

UNPUBLISHED PROSE

Yesterday—17th December 1954—saw one of the most terrifying things I have ever seen. Walking in Camden Town lighted by the incredible faces, like chunks of peat lighted and walking and arranging their delights in their way. Walking past the Gaumont cinema, looked across the street through the slow-moving traffic and at a butcher's window. A metal bar hung by metal stirrups from the ceiling; on the bar a row of hooks, and on each hook a cut of meat, for Christmas. Raw. And the whole thing, bar, hooks, cuts and all, being swayed slowly back and forth by an electric mechanism, at the speed of a pendulum of a grandfather's clock. The chunks of meat swaying like a multiple clock, alive and raw, among those dead faces. The motion was the past. It was like a high voltage going up my spine.

[journal entry]

There is a surprising amount of unpublished prose in the archive, beginning with an essay on Donne and metaphysical poetry that Merwin wrote while a student at Princeton, moving through early unpublished pieces on Lorca and journal entries (as above) from the 1950s, and concluding with individual unpublished essays from the 1960s and later. One takes particular note, for example, of "A Recollection of Stones," a striking autobiographical narrative, of an essay on Milton that Merwin presented at a conference in the 1960s but never published, and of "A Progress Report, or The New Cock Robin," a satirical essay on ecology very much in the style of "A New Right Arm." There are also a number of autobiographical fragments.

One of the more surprising of these is an unassuming black composition book; in addition to holograph drafts of some of Merwin's early book reviews, it contains a thirty-page handwritten manuscript titled "View from the Palisades," an unpublished piece that describes some of Merwin's childhood and college experiences and concludes with a long description of one Father Feeny preaching on Boston Common. Internal evidence, including a reference to "the late Senator McCarthy," makes it possible to date "View from the Palisades" as having been written either late in 1957 or early in 1958. Although it was never published, the prose is generally polished, in part because Merwin often rewrote individual paragraphs several times before proceeding. Of Merwin's published work, *Unframed Originals* most clearly resembles "View from the Palisades." Indeed, there are several pages where the two texts overlap. Most of the material here, however, is new. Readers will note that the second paragraph below covers some of the same material as the opening pages of "The Skyline" in *Unframed Originals*, though the tone here is more ironic and the details are elaborated differently. The recollections recorded in "View from the Palisades" have an edge of wit that probably draws on Merwin's uneasy proximity to some of the events he describes. It was to take him more than twenty more years to achieve the more meditative tone of *Unframed Originals*. A few paragraphs will give something of the flavor of the earlier manuscript:

> A child could have been born and come of age in the time since we had moved away from Union City: twenty-two years. . . . I went back to Union City a few times when I was sixteen during my first term at Princeton, in the last year of the war. It was summer: Princeton was on a war-time schedule, with a summer term.

> On Palisade Avenue are the Protestant churches of Union City. The first a modest gothic house of worship, the color of sooty cement, with bright varnished doors and a stained glass window like dirty hard candy, showing the Good Shepherd. Farther along is the Baptist Church, in colonial red-brick, and opposite stood my father's church, the biggest of the three: a yellow-brick edifice with two brown doors needing paint, a rose window, and a

precariously high steeple. Over the window was a cross full of light bulbs; the weekly church bulletins, under the name of the church, said "The church with the illuminated cross." The quotation marks puzzled me, since my father admitted that nobody really called the church that. The cross was not lighted often: usually at least one of the bulbs was burned out, and it was hard to replace them up there. My father was the first minister in the neighborhood to put a glass-fronted bulletin board in front of the church, with posters in it, changed once a week, depicting the Light of the World, or Suffer the Little Children; the Baptists, across the street, quickly adopted the idea. In the '30s the congregation shrank until the church was too large for them. The church building, in the language of church administration, is called "the plant"; the congregation failed to make enough money to keep their plant in repair. Cracks and patches of damp grew on the walls; the iron stairs around on either side that led to the basement rusted until they were unsafe. The congregation had sold their previous plant, a neoclassic building on Fourth Street, to Jews, for a synagogue; now they refused a handsome offer from the Catholics for this one. This, it seemed to them, was a chance of being the church militant, possibly their last one. They saw themselves fighting a rear-guard action and the principle they were defending was their own undemonstrable supremacy, a lost cause, and a bitter one, and the defendants fought among themselves until they reached a stalemate. Years later the place was sold, for less than a fifth of what the Catholics had offered, to be used as a warehouse. It was pulled down a few years after the war.

Up at the top of the avenue, around the reservoir, there are streets of identical low gray houses. . . . In a second floor of one of them, facing the reservoir, had lived a Miss Fitzgerald, genteel, thin, and very nearly young; and before that she had occupied a second floor in a street where some businesses were stuccoed white and were lived in by rich Italians. At that address my sister and I had started being taken to elocution lessons; and from the time that Miss Fitzgerald moved until she married, we went once a week to the street facing the reservoir. We went in a gaggle of a dozen or so children, and half as many mothers; I imagine Miss Fitzgerald had one price for private students and another price, at so much a head, for a class. The lessons were strained but not unpleasant gatherings. The mothers gave their authority into the nervous keeping of Miss Fitzgerald, and went and sat in her dark dining-room with its two curtained stained-glass windows. The pupils sat around the front room, out of their sight, and said their pieces in turn, caught each others' eyes, made faces, giggled, poked and kicked each other. Miss Fitzgerald's only disciplinary weapon was a shocked sadness which she would turn on us, and sometimes it worked, and the rest of the pupils would turn their own self-righteous scorn on the worst offender, and then outdo each other in priggish good conduct, until the lacey tastefulness of the occasion touched off the giggles again. We liked Miss Fitzgerald; but it is not effective to be shocked too often. It was never effective when one particular boy, the smallest, was feeling obstreperous. He was too young to be touched by Miss Fitzgerald's helpless disappointment in him, but it was not only that. Everybody else, by then, knew better than to be disappointed in him. He never learned his pieces, and they were no worse than the poems about pines and flowers that the girls had, or the T. A. Daley and Edgar A. Guest that I was given. He was a malicious, sudden child; once he came up behind some of us with a railroad spike and nearly killed us with it, and several years later when a game of Cops-and-Robbers was flagging, he got his father's policeman's revolver out of the house and shot one of the other boys.

LETTERS

As a person who has, by choice, often lived without a telephone, but who has nonetheless maintained relationships with friends and editors throughout the world, Merwin has of necessity been a voluminous correspondent. Most of his letters remain in the possession of his original correspondents; however, the archive does include many letters written to Merwin and a number of his own letters of which he retained carbons.

Since it is Merwin's habit often to use the reverse side of letters he receives as writing paper, and since he saved most of the drafts of his own writing, the record here of the letters Merwin received is very large indeed. They provide, for example, an unusually complete record of his dealings with editors at journals and publishing houses, including explanations of acceptances and rejections, requests for revision, and discussions of current and future projects. In some cases, this enables us to establish that Merwin was, at various points, interested in publishing some of the unpublished works in the archive, including a long narrative poem on Don Quixote and his play "Darkling Child."

One segment of Merwin's correspondence is largely complete in the collection—his twenty-year correspondence with his editor and designer at Atheneum, Harry Ford. Mr. Ford kindly contributed this whole correspondence to the archive. Their letters often deal with a variety of matters, both minor and substantive. Consider, for example, Merwin's Aug. 26, 1976, comments on the significance of the cover design proposed for *The Compass Flower:*

> I think of the compass flower, insofar as it has any specific botanical reference, as being not only the rose but also the lotus, and it's interesting how close some of the drawings of the more simple, species roses (and even the single roses of York and Lancaster, the varieties of both of which are known) are to some of the more abstract drawings of the lotus. I think what I mean, principally, is that I'd be a bit disappointed if there were a flower in the design that was too *exclusively* a rose, though of course if there is one the suggestion of a rose would belong to it.

In this letter (Apr. 8, 1967) Merwin records his continuing ambivalence about critical writing, an ambivalence that has touched his own prose as well:

> Having been brought up on the New Critics, one of whom (if he was one, superb maverick that he really seems to have been), Blackmur, exerted himself to see that I really got as much education as I seemed capable of getting, I've steadily avoided it (criticism) for twenty years, with only odd exceptions—Blackmur himself being one. I'd say Burke was another but I often don't think I know what he's talking about and realize I put off finishing his last two books, very respectfully, but very long too. What I'm saying is that having been toothed on the quarterlies I was not left with the feeling that criticism was anything that was going to help me or do more than sandbag my own efforts; I'd not expected to find in it confirmations, excitements, suggestions that had to do with my own hopes of making sense with words.

This passage (from a letter of Oct. 24, 1967) describes his thoughts as he contemplates gathering together the very different kinds of translations he has done:

> One point comes up, arising out of the different kinds of translation (the different sorts of approach, over twenty years begin to surprise even me, but it's not that). A lot of the poems, of course,

come from the languages I can read, like French and Spanish; but there are quite a lot too, from Welsh, Chinese, Kabylian, Arabic, Roumanian, etc., for which I've obviously used a prior translation into (usually) French or Spanish. When possible I've used several versions. What do you think about listing sources? I started to, and now I begin to hesitate. It seems that in a book where all sorts of approaches to translation exist side by side, and all sorts of periods and languages, one isn't attempting the kind of collection of translations that's served, by a bi-lingual edition. And isn't the noting of sources a development of the same principle? Would it be as well, for instance, not to say, in each case "from a literal version" (as in the case of the Vietnamese poems) or "from a French translation by ———" in others, but to explain the whole case briefly in a prefatory note?

Other letters discuss the contents and arrangements of individual books, the viability of particular writing projects, and, frequently, Merwin's intentions behind specific decisions. The letters also give considerable insight into how Merwin lives and how he responds to his environment. Before he had built his house on Maui, he described himself, in a letter of June 12, 1980, as

A transient with a view out the window to my right, of the rest of the little valley running down the last quarter mile or so to the sea-cliffs, the bottom of it full of the green and red clouds that are the tops of big mango trees, and only three roofs half-showing through the trees, between here and the sea, in a big landscape. Out the sliding glass doors in front of me are the tops of the mangoes themselves. An owl lives in them, and Chinese thrushes and white-eyes and cardinals and finches. Sometimes frigate birds sail over. It's quiet. The breeze down here, the birds, occasionally the sound of rain in the trees, are all that's to be heard, most of the time. Somebody along the ridge has a peacock that screams in the distance.

Another group of Merwin's letters, acquired separately but included in the archive, are a series of letters written to Arthur Mizener from 1950 to 1960. Merwin writes about meetings with other literary figures, about writing projects in progress (some of which were never published), and about his future plans. In a letter of Feb. 5, 1957, he comments on a relatively unproductive period: "I've been going through a lengthy spell of disliking poetry, mine in particular, and everybody else's for good or bad measure, for the past couple of

months, and have written only a few poems since October. This sort
of thing happens, and I don't think it's a bad thing, as long as it
doesn't set in permanently. On short terms I think it's what is called
'cleansing.' Anyhow, in my case [it] leads to a general overhaul and
tightening up."

THE PULITZER PRIZE

Merwin was awarded the Pulitzer Prize for poetry in 1971. In June of
that year he published a brief statement in the *New York Review of
Books*, commenting that "after years of the news from southeast Asia
and the commentary from Washington" he was "too conscious of
being an American to accept public congratulation with good grace,
or to welcome it except as an occasion for expressing openly a shame
which many Americans feel." He asked that the prize money be divided equally "between Alan Blanchard . . . a painter who was blinded
by a police weapon in California while he was watching American
events from a roof, at a distance—and the Draft Resistance."

The archive provides considerably more information about Merwin's decision. In one way, the story begins much earlier, with the
statement Merwin appended to his poem "Graduation: Princeton
1947" that registers his uneasiness at being associated with public
occasions at significant historical moments. At the least, Merwin
implies that public rituals, whatever their ostensible function, always serve at the same time to commemorate the society at large.
The poet who participates in such ceremonies may reasonably feel
responsible to make a more socially pertinent act of witness. Merwin's decision about the Pulitzer Prize is also consistent with a
number of political essays he has published over the years, some of
which are not widely known.

The archive reveals that Merwin was troubled about the symbolism of the prize some months earlier. He had heard that winter
that he might receive the award and wrote to Harry Ford, his editor at
Atheneum, on Feb. 5, 1971:

I find the whole prize business more than a little embarrassing.
The pleasures involved are either second-hand-pleasure in other
peoples' pleasure—or else they cut across the institution itself
and arise in spite of it: from the fact that Richard and the other
judges wanted to place a mark of their esteem on what I've done.
Oh, it's not the moment to spoil your pleasure or theirs with a

grumble about what I feel with regard to the institution of prizes and awards, and with public gratulations of all kinds, above all at a time when the Institution that is our historical circumstance as a whole gives us no grounds for anything but shame.

The motives here are clearly personal as well as political. In any case, Merwin tried to steel himself for the behavior the literary community, wishing to believe that art was separate from and untainted by history, would want from him. On Feb. 22 he wrote to Ford again, promising "I am not going to say anything more, stuffy and so forth, about prizes." But in April, Merwin sent Ford a short note, asking him to forward a long statement (some seven hundred words) about the award to the *New York Review of Books* or *The Nation*. He talks at some length about the private nature of real honor and then addresses the Pulitzer Prize in the context of current history, arguing that it is "a national institution," that even though the "trustees are not the Pentagon . . . the award is part of the present establishment's gratulatory mechanism." Where, Merwin asks, in 1971 can an American institution obtain honor to distribute? He closes with a detailed explanation of how he wanted the prize money to be distributed.

Ford wrote back immediately, refusing to forward the statement and urging Merwin not to print it. Ford felt it was unwarranted to see the occasion as political and the prizes as in any way official. He felt, moreover, that he could not be involved in Merwin's action. Perhaps feeling that a short statement would be less likely to be misinterpreted, perhaps suspecting that the longer statement indulged his own feelings too much, Merwin wrote and published a shorter notice. The archive, however, includes the original (unpublished) statement.

There are two more chapters to this story. W. H. Auden, who had accepted Merwin's first book for Yale and written a foreword for it, wrote to the *New York Review* objecting to Merwin's action; Merwin wrote a letter of reply. Finally, the archive reveals that Merwin was later himself invited to serve as a judge for the Pulitzer Prize; he declined.

DRAMA

The image of Merwin as a poet, translator, and writer of prose is so firmly fixed by now that relatively few people remember that he also wrote several plays in the 1950s. Similarly, it is not often mentioned

that Merwin published twenty-three book reviews between 1949 and
1961, one each in 1965, 1966, 1968, and 1972, and none thereafter until 1983. Both these kinds of writing occupied a significant part of
Merwin's life for a period of time before he abandoned them. Merwin
clearly thought of himself as both a poet and a playwright in the
late 1950s. Standard bibliographies mention three plays: "Darkling
Child" (with Dido Milroy), "Favor Island," and "The Gilded West,"
each of which was produced at least once. The first act of "Favor Island" was later published, but the rest of the play is unpublished;
neither of the others has been available in any form. The subject
matter of these plays is often surprising. Here is the prologue to
"The Gilded West":

> The curtain rises on a panorama, or a bit of panorama, represent-
> ing a rather spectacular landscape of the Old West. Shots ring
> out, echo, build up into volleys. Then there is the sound of a
> bugle from far away, then more shots and the sound of horses
> galloping. There is what appears to be a gauze curtain across the
> front of the panorama, and the shadows of galloping horsemen
> flash across it. The shots continue, recede.
>
> A light is switched on, on-stage, and the gauze curtain is seen
> to be a tent wall of Wm. F. Cody's private quarters on the grounds
> of his Wild West Show. The tent contains a leather-covered but-
> toned lounge, or chaise-lounge, one or more wicker arm-chairs,
> at least one chair and possibly a stool or bench made of steers'
> horns . . . and Buffalo Bill's show regalia. . . .
>
> When the light goes on in the tent the panorama goes dim,
> almost invisible, and during the first few minutes of the action
> it disappears. The Doctor, Donald McPherson, a Scot around
> forty, comes on with his black bag and his sleeves rolled up, fol-
> lowed by "The Kid," Joe Comstock, a rather jowly man, also
> around forty, in shirt sleeves, vest and derby hat. The Doctor
> walks over to the saddle and starts examining it. There is another
> volley of shots; they pay no attention; The Kid idles around and
> addresses the Doctor.

Even less well known is that some of Merwin's dramatic work that
was never performed in the theater, such as "The Pageant of Cain," a
verse masque, was in fact produced on BBC radio in the 1950s. Merwin also did a children's play, "Rumpelstiltskin," for BBC television.

All of these plays are available for study in the archive. Thus the
archive can be used to reconstruct a whole portion of Merwin's ca-

A notebook with Merwin's notes on a rehearsal of *Favor Island*.

reer that has been essentially unknown until now. What is more striking to learn, however, is that Merwin also wrote a number of other plays that were never produced in any form—including, among others, "A Peacock at the Door," "Shadows of Horses," "The Wood of Women," "The Case of the Convert," and "A Maggot in Bedford." Here is the prologue to "A Peacock at the Door":

> (As the curtain rises there is the sound of someone plucking absently but repeatedly on the same string of a harp.
>
> The stage represents the summer parlor of the Chapman house, in Andalusia, Pennsylvania, in May 1832; and, on one side of it, the front porch, and on the other the kitchen stoop and outer door. The house was built in 1827, a substantial and handsome place of some local importance. In the parlor there is a wide doorway into the front hall, and the bottom of the front stairs is plainly visible. There is another door in the parlor, leading into the kitchen.
>
> The room has a slightly improvised look. It is used as a schoolroom all winter, and there are vestiges of that use still in evidence: a black-board on one wall, with a map-roll above it. Certain pieces of more elegant furniture have been moved into it, notably a graceful chaise-lounge, and a harp.
>
> At the moment it is shortly after sunset. The shutters of the parlor and kitchen windows are closed.
>
> In the parlor are Mrs. Lucretia Chapman and her daughter Lucretia (Lucy), both in travelling clothes: cloaks and bonnets. Lucretia is a handsome, strong-featured woman in her early forties; Lucy is a girl of sixteen or seventeen, dressed to look several years younger. Lucy is fingering the harp as she peers through a crack in the shutters. Her mother is seated.)

Nowhere in the extensive literature about Merwin are any of these plays mentioned. Their presence in the archive makes it possible to argue for a much greater place for dramatic writing in Merwin's work during the 1950s. Of course Merwin did not publish these plays, so they are not part of his public career; some, indeed, are clearly unfinished. Some would now be likely to be judged unsuccessful, a position Merwin himself would probably share. So part of their interest will be to help us understand how a highly successful poet might find another medium—the theater—an inhospitable one. *A Peacock at the Door*, for example, is torn between highly symbolic or operatic versus realist impulses, and, I would argue, fails as a result.

Some of the difficulties with Merwin's plays were noted in a letter he received from Frances Ferguson in the 1950s:

> I think the Cain masque has possibilities, especially in the kind of language you have worked out for it. The first monologue seems to me to be the best thing in the whole piece: it is very handsome, melodious, and speakable. The good thing about the language in general is that it is pretty colloquial yet capable of lyric development. That is hard to achieve, and of course one must have that kind of language for any kind of poetic drama. . . . But, as you know, I tend to believe that the language is not the basic problem—or at least it is no more than one way by which to approach the real difficulties of poetic drama. Story, plot, and the rhythmic scheme of the whole—'the relation of part to part, and of each part to the whole'—are more important in drama than in lyric verse. To say nothing of characterization, its distance from realism, its flatness or roundness, etc. In those matters your touch is far less sure. The whole thing would benefit very much from cutting. It would also do better as a radio-drama than as a stage-piece—the visual effects would add little, and they are often not thought-out at all. Music would help.

EARLY POEMS

The archive contains approximately three hundred unpublished poems from the earliest period of Merwin's career, beginning while he was still a student and extending through the period when he wrote his first book. No doubt the single most valuable portion of this part of the collection is a tan box marked "Oct. 1946–June 1948." This box contains the largest group of poems predating the poems to be collected in *A Mask for Janus,* and I believe they will require us to reevaluate the shape of Merwin's career. I expected these poems to be early versions of the elegant, dark romanticism of his first books, but they are not. They are, to be sure, often rather mannered, but their tone and subject matter are not at all what one might anticipate. In many ways these early poems are closer to the powerful, negative poems Merwin wrote during the Vietnam War than to the poems he published during the 1950s.

The 1946–48 manuscripts establish Merwin's characteristically
bleak perspective, dethroning the originary claims of his first books.
"No one could make the dark be still," Merwin writes in "In Time of
Destruction," a poem dedicated to "the young men of my generation
who have died by violence." Similarly, he dedicates "Graduation:
Princeton, 1947," the unpublished poem he read at the 1947 Princeton graduation, to "those who are not graduating with our classes,
because they are dead" and appends a remarkable note to the graduation committee that requested the poem: "if the requisite sentiments and unqualified optimism are nowhere to be found in the
poem, that is so merely because I could nowhere find them in myself, looking upon the occasion as I do with little optimism for the
future." Clearly, a rather specific sense of historical futility is at
work here, one prompted by the slaughter of World War II. Indeed
there are other poems with specific historical references. Their titles
include "The Glove and the Floor (A commentary on the Streets of
Warsaw)," "Variation on a Theme Concerning A Gauntlet Picked up
in the Streets of Prague 1946," and "For a Flier Killed in the Recent
Destruction." But, as in *The Lice,* this dark mood also extends to
nature, which offers neither consolation nor salvation. "Past the
bleared pane fields drown," he writes in "Breakfast Piece: Feb. 1948,"
and continues a few lines later by observing that the "wind's language cannot say / Why I should not let my hands / Hang down like
the clock's hands." If anything, nature is a model for inaction.

Many of these poems, predictably, are unfinished. Others were
clearly written by a young poet at the very start of his career, ar-
guably even before his career began. Yet many of the poems include
passages of force and originality that make genuine additions to our
understanding of Merwin's work:

> As one remembers sleep I know I have stood
> Hours in sand till shoes and hands are loose
> As soaked weeds, floated pebbles; the strong tide has fled
> Leaving me bare as washed bone, weak as words.
>   ["1947"]

> From her corked and curving blood
> She straightened open and ran away.
>   ["Death of an Old Widow"]

Hamlet is the story of a man who doubts the ultimate worth of the things on which he believed.

If Shakespeare were no good the course would be no good.

Whose beard blows in fifty directions
Is coming apart at the shadows.

Concerning the uses of an alien
The old jacked woodlum with
the sickle
Is ignorant of the asunder darkness
And patriarchal sun

The old gentleman with
the well kept
In the wandering darkness
proclamation

The rain descending asunder,
Tired over the plum blossoms,
Over the weighty shoulders of old
Who holds sickles, the rain running under
The ominous feet of the stranger like
Undermines a sand stream
not thin his shadow,
the rain Swallows the plum blossoms at a snatch,
Holding itself forth as handsel of God
Supplies a surrogate music for the old
Scrapes thin the delicate word of the
silence.
The old alien with the sickle-heavy arms,
Ignorant of rain as a toast is innocent
of a catch,
Watches the disordered rain arrive,
Fragments whose souls do not live
where they lived.
The old men with his beard
Flowing in fifty directions
Is coming apart at the shadows.

Notebook pages (1940s).

The leaking sea hung its death on our hill.
There was nothing left but water.
No one could make the dark be still.
The fish were drowned under slaughter.
                    ["In Time of Destruction"]

(Now my sleep revokes its tides)
        ["Breakfast Piece: Feb. 1948"]

Suffice it to say that Merwin's shift from an elegant and confident romanticism needs to be rethought. *The Drunk in the Furnace*, and particularly *The Moving Target*, are no longer the first major change in his tone and subject matter. The first, at least for those who have the opportunity to examine these manuscripts, took place between 1948 and the time when he began writing *A Mask for Janus*.

WRITING AS REVISION

Since Merwin has saved drafts of all of his work since the 1940s, the archive documents the revising process throughout his career. It will take some time before we can make broad generalizations about how Merwin revises manuscripts, but we can comment on some isolated examples.

To begin with, some general observations: In addition to writing on the backs of letters and envelopes he receives in the mail, Merwin also sometimes uses the reverse side of his own earlier manuscripts, though generally only after the individual poems have been collected into a book. Until then, he keeps a penciled record of journal submissions on the reverse side of typed, completed poems. After a book has been published, however, he sometimes, in effect, writes the next book on the back of the previous one. This rather palimsestic writing practice must, one would think, involve more than a desire to conserve paper. The way the manuscripts were saved—essentially filling envelopes with them after work on a project was completed— suggests that Merwin does not return to consult old manuscripts. He seems inclined rather to divest himself of his past as he proceeds, a judgment supported by the fact that, once a book is assembled, he does not keep careful records of the poems he published in journals but chose not to collect in book form.

LOST SONG

Some of the writing jumps up
some of the coats breathe
some of the sirens were sick
some of the mountains are hollow
some of the curtas smelled
some of the rain was salt
some of the days were glass
some of the neighbors are holes
some of the wishes gasp

whose feet
carry me home

"Lost Song," an unfinished, unpublished poem of the 1960s. Merwin later used the surrounding space to make fragmentary notes for other possible poems.

In addition to drafts of individual works, Merwin also regularly carries small pocket notebooks in which he writes phrases, lines, and stanzas as they come to mind. There are also many full-size sheets of paper filled with individual lines, images, and stanzas, many of which never make their way into individual poems. This is clearly a continuing part of the compositional environment for him, rather than a consistent first stage of composition. Frequently, these jottings are a way of ringing changes on words that have particular resonance for him.

The amount of revision Merwin does varies considerably with individual works. Clearly, sometimes short poems will come to him in relatively finished form. At other times, even short poems will be elaborately revised. The drafts of "The Drunk in the Furnace," the title poem of Merwin's 1960 collection, include fifty versions of the opening stanza. "Epitaph" occurs in the manuscripts as a forty-one-line poem. The final version, published in *The Dancing Bears*, is only four lines long. Recalling Pound's reworking of "In a Station of the Metro," the final version of "Epitaph" is in a sense the epitaph of its earlier drafts. Titles also sometimes change. One dramatic case is *The Lice*, which Merwin titled *The Glass Towers* when he first gathered the poems together in book form. *Writings to an Unfinished Accompaniment* began as *Pieces to an Unfinished Music* and then became *Words to an Unfinished Accompaniment*. "December among the Vanished" was first titled "Shelter among the Vanished"; the title change helped remove, or at least make uncertain, any sense of shelter in the poem. "Hydra" (the later poem of this title) was first titled "You, the Dead." "The Gardens of Zuñi" was first "Discoverer" and then "Forerunner."

"Caesar" provides a good example of how revision for Merwin can involve working with a few key lines. He seems more likely in revising to push a line toward compressed ambiguity than to disambiguate. In the first version of the poem, the speaker waits "at the glass doors"; these become more vatic "doors of ice" in the next version. Merwin temporarily revises "I look out the window" to "I look out the funeral parlor window," a version that is much more limited and referential, but he drops this alternative immediately. Most dramatically, "I hear them shouting Caesar Caesar and for me of course," becomes, through a series of revisions, "I hear the cry go up for him

Caesar Caesar," which removes the bald statement of personal complicity and instead leaves the status of the speaker unresolved.

The general configuration of the pages of revision also varies considerably. "Caesar" is an orderly sequence of drafts. "The Complaint of My Family," on the other hand, an uncollected poem published in the *Evergreen Review* in 1965, involves a reshuffling of lines and modifiers. Along the way images are developed in a number of alternative contexts, many of which are abandoned. In the drafts there are "white houses," "white photographs," and the family is described as "all white they are all the same"; only the white photographs make it into the final version. A number of interesting lines are dropped: "Up my grandmother's spine bent like an accident / They still marched with their messages," "I collect the symptoms under the / Eyes of the crooked doctors," and "Were there ever any keys to their hands" are among the lines eliminated. All these passages, however, can now be counted, after the fact of the published poem, as phenomenological extensions of it. They amplify its resonance and deepen the cluster of associations at its core. Cut from the poem, they are now again part of its textuality.

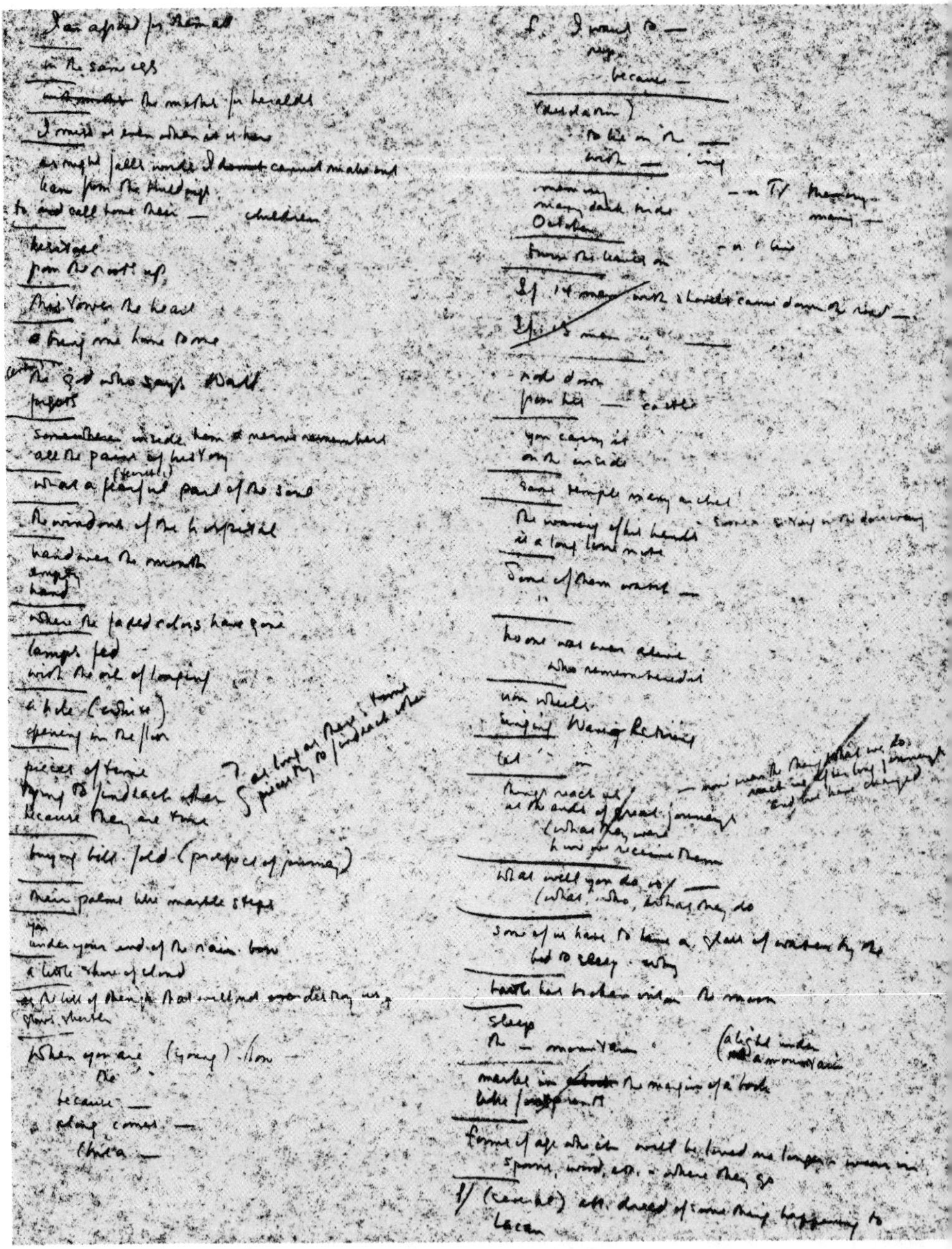

A page of notes (from the 1960s).

am afraid for them all

the same egg

~~th moths~~ the moths for heralds

miss it even when it is here

night falls words I do not cannot make out
ean from the buildings
d call home their _ children

esitate
rom the roots up

his tower the heart

oring me home to me

en)
e god who says Wait
orgets

~~somewhere~~ inside him a nerve remembered
ll the pains of history

——   (terrible)
hat a fearful part of the soul

ne windows of the hospital

and over the mouth
mpty
and

here the faded colors have gone

amps fed
ith the oil of longing

hole (white)
pening in the floor

ieces of time
rying to find each other
ecause they are time

uying bill-fold (prospect of journey)

heir palms like marble steps

ou
nder your end of the rain bow

little shore of cloud

s the list of things that will not ~~eve~~ destroy us
rows shorter

hen you are   (young) -
        the '
    because
    along comes
    (but a

*as long as there's time
pieces try to find each other*

Typed transcription (by C. N.) of the preceding page of notes.

---

f.   I want to ——
      rep.
        because ——

(   ) .
      to lie in the ___
      with __ ing

memory   T/ memory
many dark   many —
October   or I live
turn the leaves on

If 14 ~~men~~ with a shovel came down the road —— .
~~If~~ 15 men   "   ——   "

rode down
from his _ castle

you carry it
on the inside

same temple many arches
                someone sitting in the doorway

the waving of his hands
is a long line

Some of them   ——
    "

no one was ever alive
    who remembered it

iron wheels
singing Wa   Ret

let '' in

*-now even the things that we do
reach us after long journeys
and we have changed*

things reach us
at the ends of great journeys
    (what they were
     how we receive them

What will you do w/ ——
    (what, who, what they do

some of us have to have a glass of water by the
    bed to sleep - why

        has broken into the moon

sleep   (a light under
the - mountain   a mountain

marks in ~~a book~~ the margins of a book
like footprints

forms of age which will be lived no longer - wear in
    sp   , wood, etc. - where they go

/ (several) abt. dread of something happening to
        Lacan

Holograph manuscripts of two versions of "Caesar" (a third is very close to the final version as collected in *The Lice*).

The uni

The uniform I have to respect says

The uniform

My shoes are dying and as I wait at the glass doors

I hear them shouting Caesar Caesar and ~~for me of course~~

But when I look out the ~~window funeral parlor~~ window

I see only the flatlands ~~and the slowly and the slow~~

~~And the windmills slowly vanishing. And the windmill~~

~~slow Vanishing of the windmills~~

~~The centuries~~

~~And~~

And the slow Vanishing of the windmills the centuries

Draining the deep fields

The thug on duty says what would you change

He takes the emptiness out of the vases

And holds it up to examine

And it is evening

With the rain beginning to fall forever

One by one

He calls night out of the teeth

And at last I take up my duty

Wheeling the president past banks of flowers

Hoping he's dead

And at the doors of ice

Caesar

My shoes ~~are~~ go dying and as I wait at the glass doors

~~Caesar Caesar~~

But when I ~~go to~~ look out the window I see only the flatlands
And the slow vanishing of the windmills
Centuries draining the deep fields

This is still my country
The thug on duty says What would you change
He looks at his watch ~~and~~ lifts emptiness out of the vases
~~And~~ And holds it up to examine

\#\# And it is evening
With the rain beginning to fall forever

One by one he calls night out of the teeth
And at last I take up
My duty

Wheeling the president past banks of flowers
Past the ~~silent dust~~ feet of stairs
Hoping he's dead

Mar 21   1963

Typed transcriptions (by M. G. and C. N.) of Merwin's drafts of "Caesar."

Holograph manuscripts of "The Complaint of My Family," an uncollected poem published in the *Evergreen Review* in 1965.

The Complaint of My Family

I thought I ~~was~~ had got so I could ~~tell~~ the symptoms and I was making a collection
The locked elbows of ~~my~~ my aunts gripping their purses over empty breasts
It's not that after all   The aunts —   collection of symptoms

~~The aunts~~

~~The~~ I collect the symptoms under the
Eyes of the crooked doctors.

The complaint of my family rides in the locked elbows
Of my aunts gripping their purses in the house
Over empty breasts

Up my grandmother's spine bent like an accident
They still marched with their messages

Typed transcriptions (by C. N.) of Merwin's drafts of "The Complaint of My Family."

The Complaint of my Family

Of the truth of the photographs the decision
the reader to decide
But nowhere is the complaint of any family more...

...they are the same...
...here is where...

Even in each other there houses the silence of the women...

Even in each other there houses the silence of the women...

Holograph manuscripts of "The Complaint of My Family," an uncollected poem published in the *Evergreen Review* in 1965.

The Complaint of My Family

Even in each other's houses the elbows of the women
Locking purses over empty breasts
And the men in their hats recounting never is when their curtains
blow
How many thieves are buried in sand

On the backs of the photographs the diseases
Are written in dust
But nowhere is the complaint of my family named

face   forbears
~~My family of sand~~ They are all the same/my ~~family~~ of sand
~~My family~~ ~~My family of sand~~ my family of white photographs
never is when ——— ~~curtains~~
~~Their curtains blow~~ Their curtains blow

Even in each others houses the elbows of the women
~~The elbows of the women~~ Lock purses over empty breasts
All around them the tags of the packages hang still
~~The men in their hats~~ The men in their hats say again
How many thieves are buried in sand

On the backs of the photographs the diseases
Are written in dust
But nowhere is the complaint of my family named

They are all the same face my forbears of sand
My family of white photographs

never is when their curtains blow

Even in each others houses the elbows of the women
Lock purses over empty breasts
~~All around them~~
On all sides   The blank tags of the packages hang still
        ~~And~~ The men in their hats say again
        How many thieves are buried in sand

Typed transcriptions (by C. N.) of Merwin's drafts of "The Complaint of My Family."

On the backs of the photographs the drawings
The mountains to level
But therefore is the complaint of many (mainly women)

Its truth has rested in — there ... must harden
hide the mountains of maize that made soul
they friends of God

They are all which they are all the same
They know nothing

Holograph manuscripts of "The Complaint of My Family."

On the backs of the photographs the diseases
Are written in dust
But Nowhere is the complaint of my family named

Its breath has rocked in in these white neat houses
Like the motions of water that mark sand
My family of sand

They are all white they are all the same
They know nothing

On the backs of the photographs the diseases
~~The diseases~~ Are written in dust
But nowhere is the complaint of my family named

They are all the same my family of sand
My family of white photographs
~~Elbows of the women locked purses over~~

They thought it would be
Stolen from them ~~they~~
What was it

Were there ever any keys to their hands

                                                many
                              How/thieves are buried in sand

                              each other's
                         in ~~their own~~ houses
                    Even ~~indoors~~ (the elbows of the women
                    Locked purses over empty breasts

                    _____

                    ~~What shall I do now go home~~

Typed transcriptions (by C. N.) of Merwin's drafts of "The Complaint of My Family."

The Complaint of My Family

On the backs of the photographs the diseases
Are written in dust
But nowhere
Is the complaint of my family named

They are all the same face
My forbears of sand
My family of white photographs

Never
Is when their curtains blow

Even in each others houses
The elbows of the women
Lock purses over empty breasts

On all sides the blank tags
Of the packages hang still

The men in hats say again
How many thieves
Are buried in sand

"The Complaint of My Family" as it appeared in the *Evergreen Review.*

APPENDIX 2

Merwin Manuscripts in Other Collections

As various libraries acquire archives of other modern and contemporary poets, translators, publishers, and directors, additional manuscripts by or about Merwin inevitably turn up in their collections. This appendix will not list all Merwin holdings, since many libraries have only two or three letters or a tape of a reading, but rather identify the strengths of some collections of particular interest. The Lilly Library at Indiana University, for example, has the producers' copies of several of Merwin's BBC radio scripts, some of which are heavily annotated with production notes; their holdings include bound directors' scripts for "The Pageant of Cain," "Favor Island," "Poems by Pablo Neruda translated and read by W. S. Merwin," and "New Poems by W. S. Merwin" (1962). (The BBC reference library itself, of course, has extensive records of Merwin's work with the BBC, though their collection is regrettably not open to the public.) It is Merwin's letters that turn up most frequently in those archives that are open to researchers. The poetry collection at the State University of New York at Buffalo, for example, has thirty-two letters by Merwin, including twenty-one to George Hitchcock (1965–74). The interest of the letters in different archives varies considerably; many involve arranging details of visits and readings and negotiations with publishers, but some of the letters have considerable literary substance. Others are helpful in answering specific questions. Among the sixteen letters at the Pennsylvania State University are ten written to Tambimuttu (1956–57) that demonstrate Merwin's interest in publishing *The Ark of Silence*, a poetry and prose bestiary.

The Humanities Research Center at the University of Texas at

Austin has twenty-four letters by Merwin, including an important series of fourteen letters to Phillip Vaudrin at Alfred A. Knopf, discussing both the American edition of *Green with Beasts* and other prospective projects.[1] These letters describe Merwin's extensive work on an unpublished autobiography in 1954–55 and explain the existence of a number of autobiographical fragments in the University of Illinois archive. The key passages from Merwin's letters to Vaudrin follow:

> I've been chivvied into writing a book of autobiographical prose, by the way, which I hope to have finished by spring. . . . Do you think such a project might interest you? (Oct. 30, 1954)

> As for the book of prose—it's an autobiography until the beginning of 1952, when I seemed to be at several crucial points—beginnings—at the same time, the roots of all of them going a long way back. It was suggested to me at the time by Longmans here in London, with an offer of an advance and subsistence if I needed it, till it was finished, but I refused then because of fixed aversions to writing autobiography, ditto for writing prose, and because they would not commit themselves to doing the poems too, and because I had too much else to do. So I'm not committed to them, though they may still inquire, and would like to do the book.
>
> I started it toward the end of September—I've roughly two hundred pages of draft so far. The prose is not strictly naturalistic, but a texture whose intensity changes as it goes. I should think it would be a book of around 400 pages; I'd like to think I could have the draft complete by the end of the year, but I probably won't, and it will take me probably as many months again to do the re-writing, cutting, shaping in many places, etc. (Nov. 13, 1954)

> The autobiographical thing is pushing on—getting on for 85,000, but it will take a good bit of overhauling. And probably a good bit of cutting too! I'll certainly let you know what happens about it, and any developments with publishers over here. I'm still hoping to finish it by spring because I've got a lot of other things on my plate and don't fancy spending forever crooning over me, as I was, is, or might. (Dec. 3, 1954)

> As for the prose book—the autobiographical thing—it's very improbable, for reasons that would make an interminable and very boring letter, that I'll finish it in the near future. I mean in

the next two years or so. It goes without saying that anyone who does the poems gets first go on the prose book (or anything else) if it's finished and they're at all interested, but I couldn't as things go at the moment have it any more definite than that. I came to the decision not to finish it for the time being after three months of writing and deliberation, and I think for various reasons it would be bad for me to even try to go on with it now. I hope that doesn't leave you feeling that I've let you down, because I didn't mean to. (Jan. 13, 1955)[2]

The real reasons for dropping the autobiography for the present can be summarized simply: Constant Autobiographobia always, from the time such a scheme was first bruited, Hatred of prose and of narcissism—feeling that it was wrong, that I should be *making* something, and inability to find a mode which would satisfy these two without hurting other people. Which, after three honest months (well, as honest as months ever are) and 300 pages I couldn't, so I cut my losses. No, I imagine there's nothing lost, and perhaps I can even use bits of it. But maybe you can see why I won't commit myself to it either way, even to myself, for the present. (Jan. 25, 1955)

Among the ninety-five Merwin letters held by the Lilly Library are nine written to Ezra Pound (from 1946 to 1953), twenty-one to Mark Strand (1967–81), and twenty-seven to Galway Kinnell (1953–79).

In the first letter to Pound (Sept. 12, 1946), Merwin introduces himself as a senior at Princeton who will be studying with Blackmur and Berryman the following year. He expresses sympathy for Pound's situation, invites permission to correspond, and asks Pound to recommend introductory volumes on Provençal. By the following year, he arranges to visit Pound at St. Elizabeth's. Here is Merwin's letter of Mar. 27, 1947:

Dear EP,
Writing an essay on your work—will talk it over with you in a wk. or two when I come to see you.—Is it possible to republish "Certain Noble Plays etc"? If so, & I can find someone who will do it, will you help me get it through? Would you approve? Reading Fenollosa. He has been greatly ignored. I feel grateful for him. (to him). Still keep Herbert by as a guide in some things. Stanzaic technique—I shall learn stanzas—apply much of your strength, clarity, delicacy. Rhythms—am learning much from

Langland after I manage to pull off layers of redundant erudition. Do you know Amdur's essay on you? Not as sympathetic as I but juster than most.

Points (mine) center about "revolution of the word." No one has studied Fenollosa. Much good poetry being written but he still has things to teach. Especially *verbs, verbs, verb,*—reductio ad simplex and the atomically concrete! Still with Langland for rhythm, Herbert for some details of org. technique, you, Fenollosa for diction & org. of imagery & a delicacy of attitude, coming from who knows where I may be able to evolve a *style.* Something different from H. W. Longfellow at any rate.—
Leave for Wash. April 3—See you sometime thereafter.

The topics in the remaining letters range widely. Frequently, as in this passage from a Sept. 27, 1947, letter, Merwin, who was only twenty years old at the time, comments on other writers:

Find this enormous craze over the Dickinson woman somewhat far-fetched. Her best stuff extremely interesting, but as to whether it constitutes a body of work of any value, or whether the few poems which we have that are really fine are any better than fine poems struck off by an enormously intelligent woman half by chance in writing innumerable pieces of utter nonsense, is something which appears very dubious to me. Berryman said you appear to have read Lowell and w/some interest—(any really would be more than I had expected, re Lowell's place in Miltonic trad.) At best I should have expected you to "have recognized an energy which you believed to be wrongly directed"—believed it to be so, insofar as yr. Confucian ethical relativism, general horror of positivism, and persistent refusal to (happily) do anything more hostile than encourage the younger generation, would permit . . . I believe Lowell's achievement to date to be of astonishingly large proportions, am continuously elated to find poetry of this sort and caliber possible, whether or not it is in my own direction.

In the same letter, Merwin comments on some of his thinking on other current issues: "Have been trying all summer to explain that Freud and modern psychol. are to a very large extent a social phenomenon as well as scientific, i.e. that they represent the bourgeoisie's attempt at a scientific apologia for itself." And, as one would expect, he comments on his own writing—"Poetry coming: have been writing at least 15–30 lines a day for over a year. Since I write in tight stanzas work takes longer & need not always be as many lines as free verse" (May 4, 1947); "have written something every day—try to take two or three hours in the afternoon. Technique keeps at a steady lift, I believe" (Sept. 27, 1947)—and sends his own manuscripts: "I hate to keep dumping my coals on Newcastle—but you are my only key to a world where I hope I belong but whose doors keep disappearing" (Apr. 22, 1953). At one point the strain in the relationship breaks through: "Oh Hell—how am I ever to know how to say things to you. I am always wondering as to your interests, and my capacities in their directions. Whereas the thing to do probably is to forget all about them . . ." (Sept. 27, 1947).

Pound was also clearly a focus for Merwin's own ambivalence about America, a theme surfacing in his early correspondence and unpublished poetry and continuing throughout his work: "America with its great denial of cultural values is a strange & horrible experiment—seeing how long a lead ball held together by bank notes can fall in a vacuum before it innocently hits the bottom and breaks open" (Merwin to Pound, May 14, 1947). Some twenty years later, the other half of the ambivalence comes through in letters to Mark Strand and Howard McCord, the latter a group of four letters at the University of Delaware library. Merwin is writing from France, discussing the difficulties of earning money and contemplating a trip home: "I sympathize with you at the University. . . . Nobody's way of avoiding it is ideal, evidently. I managed by writing for the BBC and living cheaply in England; then living cheaply in the country in France & growing what we consume, but the trouble with the latter is that I'm not in our horrible country, & in the end it matters" (Merwin to Strand, Jan. 15, 1968). A few months earlier, Merwin had expressed similar sentiments to McCord: "The only country that finally gets at me is our own strange place, and I mean the place too, the continent, though most of the parts of it that have spoken to me longest are now unrecognizable" (Oct. 24, 1967). And shortly thereafter:

The news of course is appalling. I find it, though, harder to be *out* of the country when it's as bad as this. I say that, & remember that what finally made me think I wanted to live elsewhere, year 'round, for some good long time, was the general man-in-the-street behaviors at the time of the Cuban missile crisis in late '62. . . . And we left the following spring. The problem, you see, is that we have a roof over our heads here, that we love; an ancient farm, in beautiful country above the river. . . . But it's in the wrong country—or what has become that . . . it seems unbelievable that it will soon be six years since my last round of protest, protest writing. . . . "Ten years gone by in a dream in this country of Yang-Tcheou." But not quite. (Merwin to Strand, Jan. 27, 1968)

A short time later Merwin is in New York: "The awfulness in the papers—well, perhaps I owe it to my education to look. . . . And everything set in the bright cold, in streets lined with the day's uncollected garbage. It all seems not like something new or different (and I am so frighteningly at home 2 minutes after I set foot in the place, after however long) so much as like an ill-concealed self emerging at last" (Merwin to Strand, Feb. 7, 1968). Within two years, these internal promptings, recorded in letters that sometimes read like an autobiographical journal, would generate several public actions. Merwin would publish "On Being Loyal" and "On Being Awarded the Pulitzer Prize" in the *New York Review of Books*, the first a statement refusing to sign a loyalty oath, the second giving his Pulitzer Prize money to the draft resistance and to a painter wounded during a demonstration.

Throughout the correspondence with other poets, Merwin also regularly comments on their own work. Inevitably, his aim is partly to give support and encouragement, but he does mark differences with their projects when these differences are important to him. Consider the opening paragraphs of a 1947 letter to Pound:

Have been re-reading "Personae." How can I thank you enough. A peculiar, almost mystic, affinity with Keats has all day amounted with me almost to an obsession. Personae crushes the grape against my palate.

There is in words as you use them in "Personae" (I confess I cannot like the Cantos nearly as well—I do not believe their sheer poetic *magic*, that element of perpetual and delicious surprise, approach that of Personae with the same power nor ring true as it does) a feeling of utter delight which is almost Greek and no one in English but Chaucer has organized *swift* poetic movement as you have and still keep it clear, delicate, chaste.

Writing to thank Kinnell for sending him *Flower Herding on Mount Monadnock* (published in 1964), Merwin effects largely the same balance: "It contains what for me are certainly the best poems you've written, and I think the ones I like best in it are very good indeed, and some of them intensely close and moving. Emma Lazarus, most of what you write about the harbor this time (I never liked the Ave C. poem as much as I wanted to) the Buddhist of Altitudes, for example, the last, in particular, of the Poems of Night." Some years earlier, Kinnell had requested a fellowship recommendation from Merwin to continue his work on Villon. Merwin, writing on Mar. 7, 1956, suggests that his name will not carry much weight, reconfirms his general willingness to support Kinnell, but reports his discomfort with this particular project, in the process defining some of his own attitudes toward translation:

> Anyway, I wouldn't be the person to pronounce on these matters because I'm hardly objective. I guess you'll remember that when you told me about this project I said that I felt Villon was untranslatable, which is not a very good viewpoint to approach your translations from, I imagine. That's one point of bias. Another is simply that they're not the *kind* of translations I can really judge at all objectively because they're a kind of translation I disapprove of: I mean the sort of wildly colloquial rendition of something like Villon. I know all the arguments in favor of this way of doing it but I never liked the result.

Merwin's most remarkable letter of commentary and evaluation among this group was written on Dec. 26, 1970. Kinnell had sent him a draft version of *The Book of Nightmares* and Merwin returned a three-page, single-spaced set of specific suggested revisions. Comparing this letter with the drafts of *The Book of Nightmares* (also at the Lilly Library) and with the published version of the book shows that Kinnell took many of Merwin's suggestions but rejected others. Here are the general remarks that frame Merwin's specific recommendations:

> I think that, as a whole, it's a magnificent and moving work . . . I still like best, I think, the sections I liked best on first reading them: "The Hen Flower" above all, and the last section. For the rest, you've been struggling too long with the same sense of the work . . . to be surprised at my saying that I think it's still

uneven, and that parts of it don't work for me. The besetting
danger of the whole work, as it strikes me, is sentimentality. . . .
My emotional reponse to it apart (insofar as that is possible) it
seems to me, where I think it's dominant, to weaken the passage
and the work as a whole, by a sort of begging of the affective
question. The danger is increased by the deliberate choice of
some of the dramatic settings for different sections, in which
much of the emotional response is assumed in the subject itself—the recurrent poor old man, some of the passages about the
two children, some of the Blue Juniata section, for instance. . . .
[Merwin's list of specific suggestions, some two single-spaced
pages in length, occurs here.] . . . I'll say again that, with all
these particular objections, the book itself is one I'm grateful
for—its existence—and one that moves me both in itself, and
because it's been *possible* for someone as close to me in several
respects—time, for the very least of them. The ambition of the
work in itself is something that heartens and delights me, and
your voice, at its best (which I think of as "The Porcupine,"
"The Hen Flower," "The Bear," in that order, I think) I listen to
with as much response and admiration as to that of anyone of
our age.

Finally, it would be to display a complete absence of any self-
reflective capacity to close without acknowledging Merwin's considerable ambivalence about archival work. There are numerous
comments about this in letters at Buffalo and Illinois, generally in
response to requests from libraries to deposit his papers there, but
one passage in an Aug. 7, 1964, letter to Mona Van Duyn (from
among fourteen letters by Merwin in the Washington University
Collection)[3] is particularly clear:

I really have a sort of aversion, partly superstitious I imagine and
partly all sorts of heaven knows what, to turning over what papers there are to any institution. I don't think I'm gambling on
stocks going up, because I don't think I really believe in the
stocks at all. I don't think and can't be put to think that such
drafts as Robert Graves persuaded me years ago not to destroy as
I was doing, are of value to anybody. I won't destroy them (or
haven't so far) because I know they might fetch a little when we
needed it, but I so dislike the idea of manilla faces poring over
everything that I've seen fit to reject, and working it up, that I
really just sort of compost it. Anyway it's all in an attic in London and we never go there.

NOTES

1. As part of its archive of Knopf material, Texas has a number of other items relevant to Merwin, including the internal readers' reports on *Green with Beasts*.

2. Merwin inadvertently dated this letter 1954.

3. The Special Collections division of the Washington University Library includes another archive of potential interest to Merwin scholars—Tom Clark's Naropa archive, that is, the material he gathered during his two-year investigation of the Naropa Institute in Boulder. Much of the investigation focused on the incident at a 1975 Halloween party when Merwin was forcibly brought before Chogyam Trungpa for a violent public encounter. (See bibliography entries under Tom Clark, Peter Marin, Ed Sanders, Eliot Weinberger, and Robert Woods, as well as Merwin's "Letter from William S. Merwin to Investigative Poetry Group," 1980.) The archive includes Clark's correspondence, drafts of his publications about Naropa, copies of other publications on Naropa, and such materials as the tapes of Clark's interview with Allen Ginsberg. A detailed register is available from the Curator of Manuscripts at Washington.

Bibliography

WORKS BY MERWIN

BOOKS OF POEMS

A Mask for Janus. New Haven: Yale University Press, and London: Oxford University Press, 1952.
The Dancing Bears. New Haven: Yale University Press, 1954.
Green with Beasts. New York: Knopf, and London: Hart-Davis, 1956.
The Drunk in the Furnace. New York: Macmillan, and London: Hart-Davis, 1960.
The Moving Target. New York: Atheneum, 1963, and London: Hart-Davis, 1967.
The Lice. New York: Atheneum, 1967, and London: Hart-Davis, 1969.
Three Poems. New York: Phoenix Book Shop, 1968. [126 copies printed. Poems reprinted in *The Carrier of Ladders.*]
Animae. San Francisco: Kayak, 1969. [Poems from *The Moving Target, The Lice,* and *The Carrier of Ladders,* but arranged in a new way. Drawings by Lyn Schroeder.]
The Carrier of Ladders. New York: Atheneum, 1970.
Signs: A Poem. Iowa City: Stone Wall Press, 1971. [200 copies printed. Decorations by A. D. Moore. Originally printed in *The Carrier of Ladders.*]
Writings to an Unfinished Accompaniment. New York: Atheneum, 1973.
The First Four Books of Poems. New York: Atheneum, 1975. [Reprints *A Mask for Janus, The Dancing Bears, Green with Beasts,* and *The Drunk in the Furnace.*]
Three Poems. Honolulu: Petronium Press, 1975. [75 copies printed. Linocuts by Steve Shrader. Poems reprinted in *The Compass Flower.*]
The Compass Flower. New York: Atheneum, 1977.
Feathers from the Hill. Iowa City: Windhover Press, 1978. [270 copies printed. Reprinted in *Finding the Islands.*]
Finding the Islands. San Francisco: North Point, 1982.
Opening the Hand. New York: Atheneum, 1983.

UNCOLLECTED POETRY

"On John Donne." *Nassau Literary Magazine,* 105 (Dec. 1946), 30.

"Variation on the Gothic Spiral." *Poetry,* 71 (Mar. 1948), 304.

"Love in the Old House." *Hudson Review,* 1 (Winter 1949), 522–25. [Also appeared in *Listener,* 46 (July 5, 1951), 19.]

"Three Sonnets about a Theme" ("Now save the restive air that lifts and runs"; "Those sloped fields three years covered with the sea"; "I trace a dark lie mastering the wall"); "Equinox"; "Dirge." *Perspective,* 4 (Winter 1951), 23–25. [The second sonnet, "Those sloped fields," also appeared in *Listener,* 45 (May 10, 1951), 761.]

"Riddle Me." *Listener,* 45 (Apr. 12, 1951), 572.

"Alba." *Perspective,* 5 (Winter 1952), 44–46.

"Flamenco." *Listener,* 48 (July 24, 1952), 147.

"Cabo Da Roca"; "Dance." *Quarterly Review of Literature,* 6, no. 4 (1952), 363–66.

"Poem" ("White dove, unless the wind too much abuse you"). *Listener,* 49 (Apr. 9, 1953), 603.

"Toro." *Poetry,* 83 (Nov. 1953), 72–74. [Also in *Listener,* 52 (July 1, 1954), 17; and in *New Pocket Anthology of American Verse,* edited by Oscar Williams. Cleveland: World, 1955, pp. 351–52.]

"Spider." *Poetry,* 83 (Mar. 1954), 320–22.

"Cormorants"; "The Hydra." *Botteghe Oscure,* 13 (Apr. 1954), 286–90. ["Cormorants" also appeared in *Harper's Bazaar,* Apr. 1956, p. 194.]

"Catching Leaves in the Autumn." *Sewanee Review,* 62 (Summer 1954), 451–53.

"Hunting Song." *Listener,* 52 (Aug. 12, 1954), 249. [Also in *Harper's Bazaar,* Apr. 1956, p. 194.]

"Bear"; "Camel." *Poetry,* 85 (Jan. 1955), 214–19. ["Camel" is also in *New Pocket Anthology of American Verse,* edited by Oscar Williams. Cleveland: World, 1955, pp. 353–55.]

"Several Distiches about an Occasion." *Hudson Review,* 8 (Spring 1955), 97–98.

"The Other Tree." *Poetry,* 86 (July 1955), 228–29. [Also in *Listener,* 54 (Sept. 1, 1955), 330; and in *Best Poems of 1956: Borestone Mountain Poetry Awards 1957,* edited by Robert T. Moore. Stanford: Stanford University Press, 1957, pp. 65–66.]

"Sow." *Paris Review,* no. 11 (Winter 1955), 70–71.

"Eclipse of the Moon." *Audience,* 4, nos. 3–4 (1956), 9.

"Snail"; "Leopard." *Sewanee Review,* 64 (Winter 1956), 120–24.

"The Soul's Rich Idleness"; "Northeast October." *Poetry London-New York,* 1 (Winter 1956), 33–34.

"Corps de Ballet." *Poetry,* 87 (Mar. 1956), 325–27.

"Faces and Landscapes." *Nation,* 182 (Apr. 14, 1956), 308.

"Toad." *Listen,* 2 (Summer 1956), 14–15.

"The Nine Days of Creation." *Kenyon Review,* 18 (Summer 1956), 367–69.

"The Fish Hawk." *Botteghe Oscure*, 18 (Sept. 1956), 238–39.

"In the Light of Autumn." *Nation*, 183 (Sept. 29, 1956), 272.

"Campaign Note." *Nation*, 183 (Dec. 1, 1956), 482.

"Luzerne Street Looking West," *Hudson Review*, 9 (Winter 1956–57), 509–10.

"Whaler"; "Mercy." *Poetry*, 89 (Mar. 1957), 346–47.

"Uncle Cal." *Nation*, 184 (Mar. 2, 1957), 190.

"The Miner"; "A Wit in Age"; "Coal Barges." *Kenyon Review*, 19 (Spring 1957), 195–96.

"After Some Years." *Harper's*, 214 (June 1957), 45. [Also in *Best Poems of 1957: Borestone Mountain Poetry Awards 1958*, edited by Robert T. Moore. Stanford: Stanford University Press, 1958, p. 59.]

"Rimer, Penna." *Harper's*, 215 (Nov. 1957), 72.

"Prologue at Midnight." *Nation*, 186 (Feb. 22, 1958), 164.

"Aunt Alma"; "Nothing New." *Paris Review*, no. 18 (Spring 1958), 90–92.

"Birthday." *Nation*, 186 (Apr. 26, 1958), 367.

"The Survivors." *New Republic*, 138 (June 16, 1958), 20.

"Lost Voices." *Nation*, 188 (Feb. 14, 1959), 143.

"Winter Evening: London." *Harper's*, 219 (Dec. 1959), 40.

"On a Sacrifice of Darkness." *Poets and the Past*, edited by Dore Ashton. New York: André Emmerich Gallery, 1959, p. 36.

"Pedigrees." *Nation*, 191 (Nov. 12, 1960), 371.

"Tribute." *Nation*, 193 (Dec. 23, 1961), 516–17.

"Despair"; "Foreign Summer." *Poetry*, 99 (Jan. 1962), 206, 209. [Also in *American Poems: A Contemporary Collection*, edited by Jascha F. Kessler. Carbondale: Southern Illinois Press, 1964, p. 56, p. 58.]

"Map"; "Revelation"; "Horizons"; "Arrival"; "Star." *Chelsea*, no. 11 (Mar. 1962), 24–25.

"Views from the High Camp." *Contemporary American Poetry*, edited by Donald Hall. Baltimore: Penguin Books, 1962, p. 161.

"Among the Eyes," *Poetry*, 104 (Sept. 1964), 344.

"As the Dark Snow Continues to Fall"; "The Complaint of My Family." *Evergreen Review*, 9 (Mar. 1965), 50.

"The Garden." *KAYAK*, no. 4 (1965), 20.

"Esther." *Poetry*, 113 (Dec. 1968), 149–50.

"The Last Woman of Brunat." *Quarterly Review of Literature*, 16, nos. 1–2 (1969), 145–47.

"The Arm." *Chelsea*, no. 28 (Aug. 1970), 99.

"The Borrowers." *Nation*, 211 (Oct. 19, 1970), 378. [Also in *Antaeus*, no. 6, (Summer 1972), 66.]

"Falls"; "Elder Brother." *Quarterly Review of Literature*, 18, nos. 1–2 (1972), 127–34.

"Speakers of the Word for Heaven." *Atlantic Monthly*, 231 (Feb. 1973), 52.

"The Fowler"; "Attention"; "In Winter Silence." *Harper's*, 246 (June 1973), 58–59.

"Journal." *Mundus Artium*, 6, no. 1 (1973), 91.

"The Tree of the Heirs." *Mundus Artium*, 6, no. 2 (1973), 113.
"A Root." *Field*, no. 10 (Spring 1974), 5.
"Demonstration." *Paris Review*, no. 58 (Summer 1974), 131–32.
"Stairs." *Georgia Review*, 29 (Spring 1975), 61–62.
"White Fox"; "Another Parting." *Georgia Review*, 30 (Spring 1976), 32–33.
"Days." *Paris Review*, no. 66 (Summer 1976), 17.
"Eclipses"; "Rock Pool." *KAYAK*, no. 43 (Oct. 1976), 5. (As Edward Brunner
    pointed out to us, lines 14, 15, and 17 of "Rock Pool" are revised and
    used as the sixth tercet of "Turning to You" in *Finding the Islands*.)
"Days." *Paris Review*, no. 66 (Summer 1976), 17.
"Late Spring"; "West Wall." *Antaeus*, no. 52 (Spring 1984), 128–29.
"The First Year." *New Yorker*, 60 (May 7, 1984), 48.
"The Sound of the Light." *New Yorker*, 60 (Sept. 24, 1984), 48.
"Summer '82." *New Yorker*, 60 (Oct. 22, 1984), 44.
"Native Trees," "Night above the Avenue," "Mementos," "Sky in Septem-
    ber." *Iowa Review*, 14 (Fall 1984), 1–4.
"Now Renting." *New Yorker*, 61 (Jan. 28, 1985), 26.
"Anniversary on the Island." *Memphis State Review*, 5 (Spring 1985), 4.
"Glasses." *New Yorker*, 61 (May 20, 1985), 40.
"Before Us." *Grand Street*, 4 (Spring 1985), 83–84.
"Touching the Tree." *Grand Street*, 4 (Summer 1985), 82.
"The Salt Pond." *New Yorker*, 61 (Sept. 23, 1985), 34.
"Koa." *Antaeus* (Autumn 1985), 131–34.
"Shadow Passing." *Grand Street*, 5 (Autumn 1985), 40.
"After School." *New Yorker*, 61 (Dec. 2, 1985), 48.
"Notes from a Journey." *Grand Street*, 5 (Winter 1986), 22–25.

(On a few occasions, Merwin has changed the titles of poems between their
periodical publication and their publication in books. Usually these changes
are very minor, but one may be of special note: "Variation on a Line by
Emerson" in *A Mask for Janus* originally appeared in *Mandrake*, 2 (Spring–
Summer 1952), 149–50, as "Variation on a Line by Bryant"; the following
year, in a review in *Poetry*, Merwin admitted, "I find I have spent several
years in the unfortunate delusion that Bryant and not Emerson was the
author of *The Rhodora*." See *Poetry*, 81 (Jan. 1953), 262.)

PROSE

A New Right Arm. Oshkosh: Road Runner Press, 1970. [Reprints "A New
    Right Arm" from *Kulchur*, 3 (Autumn 1963), 3–16.]
The Miner's Pale Children. New York: Atheneum, 1970.
Houses and Travellers. New York: Atheneum, 1977.
Mary. Brooklyn: Jordan Davies, n.d. [1982]. [175 copies printed. Reprinted in
    Unframed Originals.]
Unframed Originals. New York: Atheneum, 1982.
Regions of Memory: Uncollected Prose, edited by Ed Folsom and Cary
    Nelson. Urbana: University of Illinois Press, 1987.

UNCOLLECTED PROSE

[Items marked with an asterisk are reprinted in W. S. Merwin, *Regions of Memory: Uncollected Prose*, edited by Ed Folsom and Cary Nelson.]

* "John." *Perspective*, 2 (Spring 1949), 133–40. [Story.]

"The Neo-Classic Drama." *Hudson Review*, 2 (Summer 1949), 259–300. [Review of Martin Turnell, *The Classical Moment*.]

"The Religious Poet." *Adam International Review*, no. 238 (1953), 73–78. [Essay on Dylan Thomas's poetry.]

"Anthology Pieces." *Poetry*, 81 (Jan. 1953), 261–64. [Review of Louis Untermeyer, ed., *Early American Poets*.]

"Four British Poets." *Kenyon Review*, 15 (Summer 1953), 461–76. [Review of W. S. Rodgers, *Europa and the Bull*; Kathleen Raine, *The Year One*; Edwin Muir, *Collected Poems*; Louis MacNeice, *The Burnt Offering*.]

"The Translation of Verse." *Kenyon Review*, 16 (Summer 1954), 497–505. [Review of Frederick Bliss Luquiens, trans., *The Song of Roland*; Leonard Bacon, trans., *The Lusiads of Camoens*; William C. Atkinson, trans., *The Lusiads of Camoens*; Roy Campbell, trans., *Poems of St. John of the Cross*.]

"Without the Reality of Music." *Poetry*, 88 (Apr. 1956), 48–52. [Review of Hugh MacDiarmid, *In Memoriam James Joyce*.]

"Romantic Distrust." *New York Times Book Review*, Jan. 27, 1957, p. 14. [Review of *Collected Poems of Kathleen Raine*.]

"He Can Be Funny, Too." *New York Times Book Review*, Mar. 17, 1957, p. 33. [Review of Kingsley Amis, *A Case of Samples: Poems 1946–1956*.]

"Urbanity and Grace." *New York Times Book Review*, May 26, 1957, pp. 6, 28. [Review of Howard Moss, *A Swimmer in the Air*; David Louis Posner, *The Deserted Altar*; Laurie Lee, *My Many-Coated Man*; Thomas Merton, *Strange Islands*.]

"A Fierce Horror of Romanticism." *New York Times Book Review*, July 21, 1957, p. 10. [Review of Yvor Winters, *The Function of Criticism*.]

"Into the Present, Poets of Our Youth." *New York Times Book Review*, July 28, 1957, p. 5. [Review of Alfred Noyes, *A Letter to Lucian*; Siegfried Sassoon, *Sequences*.]

"Something of His Own to Say." *New York Times Book Review*, Oct. 6, 1957, p. 43. [Review of Ted Hughes, *The Hawk in the Rain*.]

"Humanity in Decline." *New York Times Book Review*, Feb. 2, 1958, p. 5. [Review of Roy Fuller, *Brutus's Orchard*; Brian Giles, *A Dead Sparrow*; Christopher Hussall, *The Red Leaf*; Quentin Stevenson, *The Succession*.]

"Macready and the Bowery B'hoys." *Nation*, 187 (July 5, 1958), 114–15. [Review of Richard Moody, *The Astor Place Riot*.]

"Through the Blur of Pain." *Nation*, 187 (Aug. 16, 1958), 74–75. [Review of Albert Camus, *Exile and the Kingdom*.]

"The Identity of Keats." *Nation*, 187 (Sept. 6, 1958), 114–15. [Review of *The Letters of John Keats*.]

368 Bibliography

"Ecology, or the Art of Survival." *Nation*, 187 (Nov. 15, 1958), 361–62.
[Review of Ludlow Griscom, Alexander Sprunt, Jr., *The Warblers of America*; Guy Mountfort, *Wild Paradise*.]
"The Ark of Silence." *Western Review*, 23 (Autumn 1958), 75–82. [Prose bestiary to accompany his animal poems.]
* "Flight Home." *Paris Review*, no. 17 (Winter 1958), 126–36. [Journal entries.]
"Pool of Desperation." *Nation*, 188 (Jan. 31, 1959), 103–5. [Review of Christopher Hibbert, *King Mab*; Christopher Hibbert, *The Road to Tyburn*; Dorothy Marshall, *English People in the Eighteenth Century*.]
"Laughter and the Cage." *Nation*, 188 (Feb. 28, 1959), 190–91. [Review of Brendan Behan, *Borstal Boy*.]
"The Sense of a Decision." *Nation*, 189 (Nov. 21, 1959), 382–83. [Review of George R. Stewart, *Pickett's Charge*.]
"Introduction." *Poem of the Cid*. New York: New American Library, 1959, pp. vii–xxxiv. [Reprinted in *Medieval Epics*. New York: Modern Library, 1963, pp. 443–66. Historical/critical essay.]
* "Letter from Aldermaston." *Nation*, 190 (May 7, 1960), 408–10. [Personal essay about nuclear disarmament march.]
"Among the Rats." *Nation*, 191 (Nov. 5, 1960), 351–52. [Review of Jules Roy, *La Guerre d'Algerie*.]
"Art and Ornithology." *Nation*, 193 (Aug. 12, 1961), 82–83. [Review of Thomas Sadler Roberts, *Bird Portraits in Color*; Henry Marion Hall, *A Gathering of Shore Birds*; Crawford H. Greenewalt, *Hummingbirds*.]
"The Relevance of Some Russians." *Nation*, 193 (Sept. 23, 1961), 182–84. [Review of Franco Venturi, *Roots of Revolution*.]
"Bedeviled by Friends." *Nation*, 193 (Nov. 4, 1961), 355–56. [Review of Doris Langley Moore, *The Late Lord Byron*.]
"Introduction." *Some Spanish Ballads*. New York: Abelard-Schuman, 1961, pp. 11–20. [Literary/historical essay about Spanish *romances*.]
[Brief comment about "In the Night Fields"]. *Poet's Choice*, edited by Paul Engle and Joseph Langland. New York: Dell, 1962, p. 259.
"No Man's Goody." *Blue Grass*, no. 1 (1962), 19. [Brief allegory on wisdom.]
"To Name the Wrong." *Nation*, 194 (Feb. 24, 1962), 176–78. [Biographical/critical essay on Agostinho Neto, Angolan poet. Reprinted in *Black Orpheus* (Ibadan, Nigeria), 15 (Aug. 1964), 34–37 and *Introduction to African Writing*, edited by Ulli Beier. Evanston: Northwestern University Press and London: Longman, 1967, pp. 132–35, and London: Longman, 1979, pp. 142–45.]
"The Terrible Meek." *Nation*, 194 (June 16, 1962), 533–36. [Essay on the demonstration, arrest, and trial of elderly Quaker antinuclear demonstrators.]
* "Act of Conscience." *Nation*, 195 (Dec. 29, 1962), 463–80. [Essay on the antinuclear protest voyage of the *Everyman* and subsequent demonstrations and trial.]
"Introduction." *The Song of Roland*. In *Medieval Epics*. New York: Modern Library, 1963, pp. 87–95. [Historical/critical essay.]

* "Return to the Mountains." *Evergreen Review*, 7 (Oct.–Nov. 1963), 91–106. [Story. Reprinted in *The Poet's Story*, edited by Howard Moss. New York: Simon and Schuster, 1973. Also reprinted in *Evergreen Review Reader 1957–1967*, edited by Barney Rosset. New York: Grove Press, 1968.]

* "A New Right Arm." *Kulchur*, 3 (Autumn 1963), 3–16. [Reprinted, with a new prefatory note, Oshkosh: Road Runner Press, 1970. Satirical essay: a modest proposal for dealing with atomic age mutants.]

* "The Museum." *Atlantic Monthly*, 213 (May 1964), 68–73. [Story.]

* "The Church of Sounds." *Atlantic Monthly*, 214 (Dec. 1964), 85–87. [Story.]

"On the Bestial Floor." *Nation*, 200 (Mar. 22, 1965), 313–14. [Review of C. P. Idyll, *The Abyss*; Colin Bertram, *In Search of Mermaids*; George B. Schaller, *The Year of the Gorilla*; Ruth Harrison, *Animal Machines*.]

"Death of the Gorilla." *Nation*, 200 (June 28, 1965), 685. [Letter about the plight of the gorilla.]

* "Notes for a Preface." *The Distinctive Voice*, edited by William F. Martz. Glenview, Ill.: Scott, Foresman and Co., 1966, pp. 268–72. [Comments on poetry.]

"A Poet in Exile." *New York Review of Books*, 6 (Mar. 17, 1966), 16–18. [Review of Edwin Muir, *Collected Poems*.]

* "Sidelights." *Contemporary Authors*, edited by James M. Ethridge and Barbara Kopala. Detroit: Gale Research Co., 1966, vols. 15–16, pp. 299–300. [Reprinted in *200 Contemporary Authors: Bio-bibliographies of Selected Leading Writers of Today with Critical and Personal Sidelights*, edited by Barbara Harte and Carolyn Riley. Detroit: Gale Research Co., 1969, pp. 187–88, and, with updated bibliography, in *Contemporary Authors*, first revision, edited by Claire Kinsman. Detroit: Gale Research Co., 1975, vols. 13–16, pp. 553–54.] [Comments on his life and work.]

"Foreword." *Selected Translations 1948–1968*. New York: Atheneum, 1968, pp. vii–ix. [Comments on translation, influence of Pound.]

"Into English." *New York Times Book Review*, Mar. 17, 1968, p. 6. [Review of George Seferis, *Collected Poems*; *Selected Poems of Gunnar Ekelof*; *Chinese Moonlight*.]

"Foreword." *Transparence of the World*. New York: Atheneum, 1969, pp. v–viii. [Brief comments on Jean Follain. Parts reprinted as "Poems by Jean Follain." *Atlantic Monthly*, 224 (Feb. 1969), 77.]

* "The Academy"; * "Campbell"; * "The Flyover." *Quarterly Review of Literature*, 16 (1969), 390–422. [Stories.]

"Preface"; "Introduction"; "A Note on the Translation." *Products of the Perfected Civilization: Selected Writings of Chamfort*. New York: Macmillan, 1969, pp. 14–103. [Biographical/critical essay on Chamfort.]

* "On Open Form." *Naked Poetry*, edited by Stephen Berg and Robert Mezey. Indianapolis: Bobbs-Merrill Co., 1969, pp. 270–72. [Comments on poetic form.]

* "On Being Loyal." *New York Review of Books*, 15 (Nov. 19, 1970), 17.

[Statements on his refusal to sign a loyalty oath. Reprinted in *Newsletter on Intellectual Freedom*, 20 (Mar. 1971), 37–38 and in *Index on Censorship*, 1, no. 1 (1972), 71–74.]

* "On Being Awarded the Pulitzer Prize." *New York Review of Books*, 16 (June 3, 1971), 41. [Statement giving his prize money to draft resistance and to painter Alan Blanchard. W. H. Auden's rebuke of Merwin's statement, and Merwin's reply to Auden, are printed under the title "Saying No." *New York Review of Books*, 16 (July 1, 1971), 41.]

"Sebastien Roch Nicolas Chamfort"; "François Villon." *Atlantic Brief Lives: A Biographical Companion to the Arts*, edited by Louis Kronenberger. Boston: Little, Brown, 1971, pp. 145–47, 841–43. [Brief biographical essays.]

* "The Hawk and the Mules." *New Yorker*, 47 (Nov. 13, 1971), 52–53. [Story.]

"A Sight of the Bright Life." *New York Review of Books*, 18 (Apr. 20, 1972), 16–19. [Review of Munro S. Edmonson, trans. *The Book of Council: The Popol Vuh of the Quiche Maya of Guatemala*.]

* "Foreword." *Asian Figures*. New York: Atheneum, 1973, pp. i–iii. [Comments on aphorisms, proverbs, succinct poetic forms.]

* "Aspects of a Mountain." *Shenandoah*, 26 (Spring 1975), 10–89. [Autobiographical story.]

"Notes on a Way." In *Loka 2: A Journal from Naropa Institute*, edited by Rick Fields. Garden City, N.Y.: Doubleday, 1976, pp. 141–45. [Transcribed from a recording of an informal talk.]

"Foreword." To Robert Aitken. *A Zen Wave: Basho's Haiku and Zen*. New York: Weatherhill, 1978, pp. 11–15.

"The Snow." *New Yorker*, 54 (Apr. 24, 1978), 35. [Story.]

* "Air." *New Yorker*, 54 (Sept. 18, 1978), 152–53. [Story.]

* "Foreword." *Selected Translations 1968–1978*. New York: Atheneum, 1979, pp. vii–xiv. [Comments on problems and paradoxes of translating poetry.]

"Letter from William S. Merwin to Investigative Poetry Group." In *The Party: A Chronological Perspective on a Confrontation at a Buddhist Seminary*, edited by Ed Sanders. Woodstock, N.Y.: Poetry, Crime, and Culture Press, n.d. [c. 1980], pp. 79–89. [Portions of Merwin's letter were printed in the shorter version of "The Party" published in the Mar. 1979 issue of *Boulder Monthly*; Merwin's letter is dated July 20, 1977.]

"From a Letter." *For Rexroth*, ed. Geoffrey Gardner. New York: The Ark, 1980, p. 60. [Comments on Kenneth Rexroth.]

"A House Abroad." *New Yorker*, 57 (Mar. 23, 1981), 34–41. [Becomes part of "Hotel" in *Unframed Originals*, but with changes.]

"Anna." *New Yorker*, 57 (Aug. 3, 1981), 31–37. [Becomes part of "La Pia" and "Hotel" in *Unframed Originals*, but with changes.]

"Preface." *Robert the Devil*. Iowa City: Windhover Press, 1981, p. 5. [Comments on his translation.]

"Impact of Chinese Poetry on American Poets." *Ironwood*, 9, no. 1 (1981),

18. [Comments on Chinese poetry that has been translated into English.]

* "Affable Irregular." *Grand Street*, 1 (Winter 1982), 151–64. [Personal essay on R. P. Blackmur and on Merwin's days at Princeton.]

"Invisible Father," *New York Times Book Review*, Feb. 27, 1983, pp. 10–11, 29. [Review of Paul Auster, *The Invention of Solitude*.]

"Foie Gras." *New Yorker*, 60 (Nov. 19, 1984), 46–85. [Story.]

"On the Road with the Greek Gods." *New York Times Book Review*, Dec. 30, 1984, pp. 12–13. [Review of Friedrich Hölderlin, *Hymns and Fragments*, translated by Richard Sieburth.]

"Aloha, Malathion: Hawaii Wakes Up to Pesticides." *Nation*, 240 (Mar. 2, 1985), 235–37.

"Foreword." *From the Spanish Morning*. New York: Atheneum, 1985, pp. v–xvi.

"Foreword." *Four French Plays*. New York: Atheneum, 1985, pp. v–xii.

"Molokai Problems." *Honolulu Star-Bulletin*, May 18, 1985, A-7. [Letter to the editor about conflicts of interest in those urging further development on the island of Molokai.]

"W. S. Merwin on Ezra Pound." *Iowa Review*, 15 (Spring/Summer 1985), 70–73. [Comments from various sources, edited by Ed Folsom.]

TRANSLATIONS

Robert the Devil. Produced BBC Third Programme, 1954; Iowa City: Windhover Press, 1981. [310 copies printed. Wood engravings by Roxanne Sexauer. Anonymous fourteenth-century French play. Reprinted in *Four French Plays*.]

Vega, Lope de. *Punishment without Vengeance*. Produced BBC, 1954. [Microfilm, Columbia University.]

Vega, Lope de. *The Dog in the Manger*. Produced BBC, 1954.

The Poem of the Cid. New York: Las Americas, 1959, and London: Dent, 1959. [Reprinted New York: New American Library, 1962 (Mentor Edition), and 1975 (Meridian Edition). Reprinted in *Medieval Epics*. New York: Modern Library, 1963, pp. 443–590.]

The Satires of Persius. Bloomington: Indiana University Press, 1961. [Reprinted Port Washington, N.Y.: Kennikat Press, 1973, and London: Anvil Press, 1981.]

Some Spanish Ballads. London: Abelard-Schuman, 1961. [Reprinted as *Spanish Ballads*. Garden City, N.Y.: Doubleday Anchor, 1961. Reprinted in *From the Spanish Morning*.]

Lesage, Alain-René. *Turcaret*. In *The Classic Theatre*, edited by Eric Bentley. Garden City, N.Y.: Doubleday Anchor, 1961, vol. 4, pp. 187–274. [Reprinted in *Four French Plays*.]

Marivaux, Pierre de. *The False Confession*. In *The Classic Theatre*, edited by Eric Bentley. Garden City, N.Y.: Doubleday Anchor, 1961, vol. 4, pp. 275–351. [Produced New York, 1963. Reprinted in *Four French Plays*.]

The Life of Lazarillo de Tormes. Garden City, N.Y.: Doubleday Anchor,

1962. [Reprinted Gloucester, Mass.: Peter Smith, 1970, and in *From the Spanish Morning.*]

The Song of Roland. In *Medieval Epics.* New York: Modern Library, 1963, pp. 97–203. [Reprinted as a separate volume, New York: Vintage, 1970.]

Lorca, Federico García. *Yerma.* Produced Lincoln Center, New York, 1966.

Selected Translations 1948–1968. New York: Atheneum, 1968.

Follain, Jean. *Transparence of the World.* New York: Atheneum, 1969.

Chamfort, Sebastien. *Products of the Perfected Civilization: Selected Writings.* New York: Macmillan, 1969. [Reprinted San Francisco: North Point, 1984].

Neruda, Pablo. *Twenty Love Poems and a Song of Despair.* London: Cape, 1969, and New York: Grossman, 1969. [The first printing included a number of errors because Merwin was not given the opportunity to check proofs.] [Reprinted New York: Penguin, 1976. Seven of the twenty love poems are reprinted in Pablo Neruda, *Selected Poems: A Bilingual Edition,* edited by Nathaniel Tarn. London: Cape, 1969, and New York: Delacorte, 1972, pp. 15–38.]

Porchia, Antonio. *Voices.* Chicago: Follett, 1969. [Reprinted Consigny, France: Embers Handpress, 1978. Illustrated by Patrick Burke. 226 copies printed.]

Chinese Figures: Second Series. Mount Horeb, Wis.: Perishable Press, 1971. [120 copies printed. Reprinted, except for "The children who steal needles / grow up"; "Even if it's shaped like a god / mud / can't cross the river"; and "Gold can't buy back / the darkness / of the hair" in *Asian Figures;* "Heaven can't / be tied" is revised, in *Asian Figures,* to read "Can't keep Heaven / on a rope."]

Japanese Figures. Santa Barbara: Unicorn Press, 1971. [375 copies printed. Reprinted, except for "Writes well / with any pen," in *Asian Figures.*]

Asian Figures. New York: Atheneum, 1973.

Mandelstam, Osip. *Selected Poems.* London: Oxford University Press, 1973, and New York: Atheneum, 1974. [Translated with Clarence Brown.]

Juarroz, Robert. *Vertical Poems* [Cover reads *Vertical Poetry*]. Santa Cruz: Kayak, 1977. [Drawings by Susana Wald.]

Sanskrit Love Poetry. New York: Columbia University Press, 1977. [Reprinted as *The Peacock's Egg.* San Francisco: North Point, 1981. Translated with J. Moussaieff Masson.]

Euripedes. *Iphigenia at Aulis.* New York: Oxford University Press, 1978. [Translated with George E. Dimock, Jr.]

Selected Translations 1968–1978. New York: Atheneum, 1979.

Four French Plays. [*Robert the Devil;* Alain-René Lesage, *The Rival of His Master;* Alain-René Lesage, *Turcaret;* Pierre de Marivaux, *The False Confessions.*] New York: Atheneum, 1985.

From the Spanish Morning. [*Spanish Ballads;* Lope de Rueda, *Eufemia; The Life of Lazarillo de Tormes.*] New York: Atheneum, 1985.

[Translation projects in progress include Robert Juarroz, *Vertical Poetry* [expanded edition]; Rumi, *66 Poems* [with Talat Sait Halman]; Poems of

Aihei Dogen, Zenji [with Kazuaki Tanahashi]; *Denkoroku* [with Kazuaki Tanahashi].]

UNCOLLECTED TRANSLATIONS

Richard I of England. "Chanson." *Hudson Review,* 1 (Winter 1949), 523–24. [French.]

DuBellay, Joachim. "Les Amours XIII." *Hudson Review,* 1 (Winter 1949), 524–25.

Peitau, Guillem Comte de. "Vers" ("That the fevered breath attain relief"). *Hudson Review,* 3 (Autumn 1950), 432–34.

Bornelh, Giraut de. "Alba" ("Glorious Lord, fountain of clarity"). *Hudson Review,* 3 (Autumn 1950), 434–36.

Vaqueiras, Raimbaut de. "Planh" ("High waves that shift and gather from the sea"). *Hudson Review,* 3 (Autumn 1950), 437.

Anonymous. "The Old Woman of Beare"; "The Complaint of Eve." *Hudson Review,* 4 (Winter 1952), 540–44. [Ancient Irish from the English of Kuno Meyer.]

Meogo, Pero. Untitled ("He goes, my lover"). *Hudson Review,* 5 (Spring 1952), 66.

Miranda, Francisco de Sa de. Untitled ("At the voice of the enchanter"). *Hudson Review,* 5 (Spring 1952), 66.

Guilhade, Joan de. Untitled ("Friends, I cannot deny"). *Hudson Review,* 5 (Spring 1952), 67.

Torneol, Nuno Fernandes. "Alba" ("Waken, my love, who sleeps in the cold morning"). *Hudson Review,* 5 (Spring 1952), 69–71.

Anonymous. "El Prisionero." *Western Review,* 17 (Autumn 1952), 54. [Spanish.]

Jiménez, Juan Ramón. "Before the Virgin Shadow"; "The Newly Arrived"; "The Street Car in the Field"; "Air and Water in Darkness"; "Wait for Me in the Still Water"; "Invisible Reality"; "The Small Hours"; "The Truth and Grunewald"; "Sun"; "Street"; "Song of Vigil"; "Sunrise in August"; "Day after Day"; "The Green Bird"; "The Poem"; "Outside"; "Open Entirely"; "Great Moon"; "To the Sonnet with My Soul"; " To Winter in Summer"; "New Voice"; "To a Friend"; "Clouds"; "To My Soul"; "The Yellow Wave"; "This Nothing"; "In October"; "Dream"; "Solitude." *Poetry,* 82 (July 1953), 187–208.

Guillén, Jorge. "Passage to Dawn"; "The Nymphs"; "Time unto Time, or The Garden." *Hudson Review,* 7 (Summer 1954), 210–21.

Lorca, Federico García. "Night-Song of the Sailors of Andalusia." *The Listener,* 52 (Sept. 30, 1954), 527.

Peitau, Guillem Comte de. "Canso" ("With the sweetness of the new season"). *Hudson Review,* 8 (Summer 1955), 209.

Montaudon, Le Monge de. "Plazer" ("Game I enjoy, and gaiety"). *Hudson Review,* 8 (Summer 1955), 211.

Lorca, Federico García. "The Interrupted Concert," pp. 13–15; "Arrow,"

pp. 23–25; "Balcony," p. 25; "Early Morning," p. 27; "Half Moon," p. 29;
"The Street of the Mutes," pp. 45–47; "The Little Mad Boy," pp. 51–53;
"Farewell," p. 53; "Useless Song," p. 59; "Desire of a Statue," pp. 61–63;
"Song of the Barren Orange Tree," p. 63; "Gacela of Unforeseen Love,"
p. 157; "Gacela of the Terrible Presence," p. 159; "Gacela of Desperate
Love," pp. 159–61; "Casida of the Reclining Woman," p. 175; "Casida of
the Golden Girl," pp. 175–77. *The Selected Poems of Federico García
Lorca*, edited by Francisco García Lorca and Donald M. Allen. New
York: New Directions, 1955. [Also contains two poems published in *Se-
lected Translations 1948–1968.*]

Char, René. "Lightning Victory," pp. 265–67; "Vermillon," pp. 267–69;
"The Room in Space," p. 269; "Mourning at Nevons," pp. 271–75. René
Char, *Hypnos Waking*, edited by Jackson Mathews. New York: Random
House, 1956. ["Lightning Victory" and "Room in Space" also appear in
The Random House Book of Twentieth-Century French Poetry, edited
by Paul Auster. New York: Random House, 1982, pp. 401, 403.]

Vega, Lope de. Untitled ("Dawns hung with flowers"); "Harvest Song"; "On
the Triumph of Judith." *Hudson Review*, 9 (Winter 1956–57), 512–13.
[Also contains one poem printed in *Selected Translations 1948–1968.*]

Anonymous. "Plaint for the Death of Guillen Peraza." *Nation*, 186 (May 10,
1958), 420. [Medieval Spanish.]

Anonymous. "Is úar geimred; at-racht gáeth." *Nation*, 187 (Dec. 27, 1958),
501. [From the Finn cycle, based on Gerard Murphy's translation from
the Gaelic.]

Anonymous. "In the Shade of My Hair." *Nation*, 190 (May 21, 1960), 454.
[Spanish.]

Deibe, Hernan. "After the Conquest: Pampas Indian Song." *Nation*, 191
(July 23, 1960), 55.

Vega, Lope de. "Strange Shepherd, Set My Bellwether Free . . . ," pp. 115–16;
"At Dawn the Virgin Is Born . . . ," pp. 118–19; "Ice and Fires Contend
with My Child . . . ," pp. 119–20; "Where Are You Going, Maiden . . . ?"
pp. 120–21. *An Anthology of Spanish Poetry from Garcilaso to García
Lorca in English Translation*, edited by Angel Flores. Garden City, N.Y.:
Doubleday, 1961.

Neto, Agostinho. "African Poem." *Nation*, 194 (Feb. 24, 1962), 177.

Kegels, Anne-Marie. "Night," *Chelsea*, no. 11 (Mar. 1962), 115. [Also, on
p. 114, is "Nocturnal Heart," which appears in *Selected Translations
1948–1968*, but in a quite different translation.]

Anonymous. "My Mother," p. 48. *The Sea and the Honeycomb*, edited by
Robert Bly. Madison, Minn.: Sixties Press, 1966. [Spanish.]

Neto, Agostinho. "My Desire," p. 145. *Introduction to African Literature*,
edited by Ulli Beier. London: Longman Group Ltd., 1967.

Parra, Nicanor. "Puzzle," p. 19; "Landscape," p. 21; "Travel Notes," p. 23;
"The Pilgrim," p. 25; "The Vices of the Modern World," pp. 41–45;
"The Tablets," pp. 47–49. Nicanor Parra, *Poems and Antipoems*, edited
by Miller Williams. New York: New Directions Press, 1967. [Also in-

cludes four translations that appear in *Selected Translations 1948– 1968.*]

Anonymous. "Myrddyn." *Latitudes,* 2 (Spring 1968), 27. [Welsh.]

Essenin, Sergei. "Translations from Sergei Essenin." *Hudson Review,* 21 (Spring 1968), 94–96. [With Olga Carlisle.]

Porchia, Antonio. "Voces." *Harper's Bazaar,* 101 (July 1968), 47, 50–51, 104–5. [Reprinted in *Voices* but often with significant revisions.]

Tyutchev, Feydor. "Cicero," p. 35. *Poets on Street Corners: Portraits of Fifteen Russian Poets,* edited by Olga Carlisle. New York: Random House, 1968.

Brodsky, Joseph. "We are no harder of hearing," p. 400; "Memories," pp. 415– 17. *Poets on Street Corners: Portraits of Fifteen Russian Poets,* edited by Olga Carlisle. New York: Random House, 1968. [Also contains four other Brodsky poems published in *Selected Translations 1948–1968.*]

Neruda, Pablo. "Weak with the Dawn," p. 45; "Absence of Joaquín," p. 51; "Nocturnal Collection," pp. 53–57; "Serenade," p. 59; "The Night of the Soldier," pp. 69–71; "Nocturnal Statutes," p. 73; "Burial in the East," p. 75; "Poet (Sonata)," pp. 127–29; "Being Born in the Woods," pp. 135–37; "Battle of the Jarama River," pp. 159–61; "Ode to the Yellow Bird," pp. 301–7; "Ode to Laziness," pp. 309–11; "Ode to a Watch at Night," pp. 313–17; "Ode to the Clothes," pp. 333–35; "Ode to Cesar Vallejo," pp. 337–43. Pablo Neruda, *Selected Poems: A Bilingual Edition,* edited by Nathaniel Tarn. London: Cape, 1969, and New York: Delacorte, 1972. [Also reprints seven of the *Twenty Love Poems,* and six translations that appear in *Selected Translations 1948–1968.*]

Ghalib. "Ghazal" ("Few, only a few, are revealed in the flowers"). *Quarterly Review of Literature,* 16 (1969), 151. [With Aijaz Ahmad. Ghazal XV in *Ghazals of Ghalib,* but a completely different translation.]

Salinas, Pedro. "Put Her Far Away from Me, Mirror." *English Record,* 19 (Feb. 1969), 21. [Appeared in a significantly revised version as "Set Her Far from Me, Mirror" in *Roots and Wings: Poetry from Spain 1900– 1975,* edited by Hardie St. Martin. New York: Harper and Row, 1976, p. 109.]

Quevedo, Francisco de. "Portrait of Lisi which he bore in a circlet." *Tri-Quarterly,* no. 16 (Fall 1969), 49.

Anonymous. "Postlude: Song of Cajamarca." *Nation,* 209 (Oct. 27, 1969), 446. [Quechua.]

Follain, Jean. "Age." *Chelsea,* no. 27 (Dec. 1969), 131.

Aridjis, Homero. "Sometimes We Touch a Body," p. 25; "It's Your Name and It's Also October," p. 27; "Before the Kingdom," p. 29. *New Poetry of Mexico,* edited by Mark Strand. New York: E. P. Dutton, 1970.

Oliva, Oscar. "While Drinking a Cup of Coffee," p. 39. *New Poetry of Mexico,* edited by Mark Strand. New York: E. P. Dutton, 1970.

Shelley, Jaime Augusto. "The Birds," p. 45; "The Ring," p. 47. *New Poetry of Mexico,* edited by Mark Strand. New York: E. P. Dutton, 1970.

Mondragón, Sergio. "Guru," p. 51. *New Poetry of Mexico*, edited by Mark Strand. New York: E. P. Dutton, 1970.

Oca, Marco Antonio Montes de. "The Light in Its Stand," p. 61; "The Garden Which the Gods Frequented," p. 63. *New Poetry of Mexico*, edited by Mark Strand. New York: E. P. Dutton, 1970.

Sabines, Jamie. "I Don't Know for Certain . . . ," p. 71; "Tarumba," p. 73. *New Poetry of Mexico*, edited by Mark Strand. New York: E. P. Dutton, 1970.

Arreola, Juan José. "The Toad," p. 99; "Metamorphosis," p. 103. *New Poetry of Mexico*, edited by Mark Strand. New York: E. P. Dutton, 1970. [Also contains four other Arreola translations published in *Selected Translations 1968–1978*.]

Tablada, José Juan. "Dry Leaves," p. 207; "Panorama," p. 211; "Flying Fish," p. 213. *New Poetry of Mexico*, edited by Mark Strand. New York: E. P. Dutton, 1970.

Terrés, Jaime García. "Ipanema." *Extensions*, no. 5/6 (1970), 19. [Also printed in *New Poetry of Mexico*, edited by Mark Strand. New York: E. P. Dutton, 1970, p. 91.]

Anonymous. "The Substituted Poem of Laureate Quynh," p. 76. *Poetry Brief*, edited by William Cole. New York: Macmillan, 1971. [Vietnamese. With Nguyen Ngoc Bich.]

Ghalib. "Ghazal I" ("There is only one beloved face"), p. 7; "Ghazal XIV" ("Wings are like dust, weightless"), p. 71; "Ghazal XV" ("Here and there in a rose or a tulip,"), p. 76; "Ghazal XVII" ("If you were frail of heart"), p. 85; "Ghazal XIX" ("Where I'm going is farther at every step"), p. 91; "Ghazal XXI" ("Dewdrop on poppy petal"), p. 102; "Ghazal XXIII" ("Alright it's not love it's madness"), p. 110; "Ghazal XXVI" ("It is a long time since my love stayed with me here"), p. 124; "Ghazal XXX" ("Pine and cypress"), p. 138; "Ghazal XXXI" ("Flame is not so wonderful nor has the lightning"), p. 143; "Ghazal XXXIII" ("Everybody looking but it makes no difference"), p. 150; "Ghazal XXXV" ("If he fell in love with her that was only human"), p. 160; "Ghazal XXXVI" ("To me this world is a children's playground"), p. 163; "Ghazal XXXVII" ("There are a thousand desires like this"), p. 170. *Ghazals of Ghalib*, edited by Aijaz Ahmad. New York: Columbia University Press, 1971. [Also contains four Ghazals (V, XII, XV ["Almost none"], XXV) that appear in *Selected Translations 1968–1978*. Ghazal XXI also appears in *Selected Translations 1968–1978*, but in a completely different translation.]

Anonymous. "Prayer" ("You / from whom the universe came"); "Herder's Song" ("I wish for a llama"); Untitled ("Joy in your mouth"); Untitled ("My mother brought me to life"). *Hudson Review*, 24 (Spring 1971), 17–21. [Quechua. With others published in *Selected Translations 1968–1978*.]

Anonymous. Untitled ("Now you're ripe for me"). *Madrona*, 1 (Summer 1971), 21. [Malgache. From *Les Hain-Tenys*, by Jean Paulhan.]

Anonymous. "Burmese Pieces." *Antaeus*, no. 4 (Winter 1971), 18–21. [Burmese.]

Borges, Jorge Luis. "Unknown Street," p. 3; "Empty Drawing Room," p. 9; "Remorse for Any Death," p. 15; "Inscription for Any Tomb," p. 17; "Sunset over Villa Ortúzar," p. 45; "Ars Poetica," p. 143; "Someone," p. 185; "Ode Written in 1966," pp. 205–7. Jorge Luis Borges. *Selected Poems 1923–1967*, edited by Thomas Di Giovanni. New York: Delacorte Press, 1972. [Also includes two translations published in *Selected Translations 1948–1968* and three published in *Selected Translations 1968–1978*. "Someone" originally appeared in *Tri-Quarterly*, 13–14 (Fall 1968/Winter 1969), 364.]

Mendes, Murilo. "Map," pp. 49–53; "Horses," p. 55. *An Anthology of Twentieth-Century Brazilian Poetry*, edited by Elizabeth Bishop and Emanuel Brasil. Middletown, Conn.: Wesleyan University Press, 1972.

Melo Neto, João Cabral de. "Daily Space," p. 115; "Poem," p. 119. *An Anthology of Twentieth-Century Brazilian Poetry*, edited by Elizabeth Bishop and Emanuel Brasil. Middletown, Conn.: Wesleyan University Press, 1972. [Also contains three other Melo Neto translations published in *Selected Translations 1968–1978*.]

Parra, Nicanor. "This Has to Be a Cemetery," p. 257. *Doors and Mirrors: Fiction and Poetry from Spanish America 1920–1970*, edited by Hortense Carpentier and Janet Brof. New York: Grossman, 1972. [Also contains three other Parra translations published in *Selected Translations 1948–1968* and *Selected Translations 1968–1978*.]

Mutis, Alvaro. "Every Poem," pp. 267–69; "The Death of Matias Aldecoa," pp. 269–71. *Doors and Mirrors: Fiction and Poetry from Spanish America 1920–1970*, edited by Hortense Carpentier and Janet Brof. New York: Grossman, 1972.

Sabines, Jaime. From *The Signal* ("On Hope," "On Night," "On Illusion," "On Death," "On Myth"), pp. 327–29. *Doors and Mirrors: Fiction and Poetry from Spanish America 1920–1970*, edited by Hortense Carpentier and Janet Brof. New York: Grossman, 1972. [Also contains three other Sabines translations published in *Selected Translations 1968–1978*.]

Palomares, Ramón. "Night," p. 383. *Doors and Mirrors: Fiction and Poetry from Spanish America 1920–1970*, edited by Hortense Carpentier and Janet Brof. New York: Grossman, 1972.

Khiem, Nguyen Binh. "Conclusion," p. 65. *Toward Winter: Poems for the Last Decade*, edited by Robert Bonazzi. New York: New Rivers Press, 1972. [Also in *A Thousand Years of Vietnamese Poetry*, edited by Nguyen Ngoc Bich. New York: Alfred A. Knopf, 1975, p. 85.]

Anonymous. "Why Souls Are Lost Now." *New York Review of Books*, 18 (Apr. 20, 1972), 18. [Tzotzil.]

Automedon. "The Impotent Lover," p. 228; "The Gymnastics Teacher," p. 229. *The Greek Anthology and Other Ancient Greek Epigrams*, edited by Peter Jay. New York: Oxford University Press, 1973. [Also contains a translation of Automedon published in *Selected Translations 1968–1978*.]

Antiphilos. "A Torrent Cuts Off the Poet's Path," p. 246; "On Diogenes the

Cynic," p. 248. *The Greek Anthology and Other Ancient Greek Epigrams*, edited by Peter Jay. New York: Oxford University Press, 1973. [Also contains three other translations of Antiphilos published in *Selected Translations 1968–1978.*]

Julianus. "I kept singing this, and I will call it out from the grave," p. 312; "Drink was the end of you, Anacreon," p. 312; "Though you rule the dead, under the earth, who never smile," p. 312; "Anastasia, the Graces blossom and you were their flower," p. 313; "An Unguarded House," p. 313. *The Greek Anthology and Other Ancient Greek Epigrams*, edited by Peter Jay. New York: Oxford University Press, 1973.

Aridjis, Homero. "Blue Spaces," parts 1–6. *Nation*, 216 (Mar. 12, 1973), 346. [With Betty Ferber.]

Juarroz, Roberto. Three untitled poems ("The last light always welds itself to the hand"; "Sometimes death grazes our hair"; "Without meaning to I break off with my fingers"). *Nation*, 217 (Oct. 8, 1973), 348.

Aridjis, Homero. "From 'Blue Spaces,'" parts 7–11 [with Betty Ferber]; "The Word." *Nation*, 217 (Dec. 17, 1973), 662.

Juarroz, Roberto. Three untitled poems ("We will all die"; "I don't want to get God mixed up with God"; "A net of looking"). *Field*, no. 10 (Spring 1974), 6–8.

Khuyen, Nguyen. "Giving Up Drinking." *Antaeus*, no. 15 (Autumn 1974), 104. [With Nguyen Ngoc Bich. Also in *A Thousand Years of Vietnamese Poetry*, edited by Nguyen Ngoc Bich. New York: Alfred A. Knopf, 1975, p. 150.]

Tan, Do. "Twenty Years." *Antaeus*, no. 15 (Autumn 1974), 105. [With Nguyen Ngoc Bich and Burton Raffel. Also in *A Thousand Years of Vietnamese Poetry*, edited by Nguyen Ngoc Bich. New York: Alfred A. Knopf, 1975, p. 205, though Merwin is not acknowledged there.]

Thai-Tong, Tran. "Two Persimmons." *Antaeus*, no. 15 (Autumn 1974), 101. [With Nguyen Ngoc Bich. Also in *A Thousand Years of Vietnamese Poetry*, edited by Nguyen Ngoc Bich. New York: Alfred A. Knopf, 1975, p. 59.]

Luu, Ngo Chan. "To a Chinese Ambassador Leaving for Home," p. 4. *A Thousand Years of Vietnamese Poetry*, edited by Nguyen Ngoc Bich. New York: Alfred A. Knopf, 1975. [With Nguyen Ngoc Bich.]

Hanh, Van. "The Body of Man." p. 5. *A Thousand Years of Vietnamese Poetry*, edited by Nguyen Ngoc Bich. New York: Alfred A. Knopf, 1975. [With Nguyen Ngoc Bich.]

Giac, Man. "Rebirth," p. 6. *A Thousand Years of Vietnamese Poetry*, edited by Nguyen Ngoc Bich. New York: Alfred A. Knopf, 1975. [With Nguyen Ngoc Bich.]

Khiem, Nguyen Binh. "To an Old Fisherman," p. 84. *A Thousand Years of Vietnamese Poetry*, edited by Nguyen Ngoc Bich. New York: Alfred A. Knopf, 1975. [With Nguyen Ngoc Bich.]

Khoan, Phung Khac. "On War," p.89. *A Thousand Years of Vietnamese Poetry*, edited by Nguyen Ngoc Bich. New York: Alfred A. Knopf, 1975. [With Nguyen Ngoc Bich.]

Xuong, Tran Te. "Women," p. 150. *A Thousand Years of Vietnamese Poetry*, edited by Nguyen Ngoc Bich. New York: Alfred A. Knopf, 1975. [With Nguyen Ngoc Bich.]

Juarroz, Roberto. Untitled ("Efficacy of the light"), *New Yorker*, 51 (Jan. 26, 1976), 38. [With others published in *Vertical Poetry*.]

Salinas, Pedro. "So Transparent Your Soul," p. 99; "The Trouble with the Light," p. 107; "Set Her Far from Me, Mirror," p. 109; "And If the Shadows Weren't," p. 115; "Do You Hear How They Beg for Realities?," p. 117. *Roots and Wings: Poetry from Spain 1900–1975*, edited by Hardie St. Martin. New York: Harper and Row, 1976. [Also contains two other Salinas translations published in *Selected Translations 1948–1968* and *Selected Translations 1968–1978*; "The Dead" in *Selected Translations 1948–1968* is revised significantly here as "Deaths."]

Aleixandre, Vicente. "Closed," pp. 181–83; "The Old Man and the Sun," p. 193. *Roots and Wings: Poetry from Spain 1900–1975*, edited by Hardie St. Martin. New York: Harper and Row, 1976.

Felipe, León. "Let the Poet Come," p. 95; "Now I Am Going," p. 95. *Roots and Wings: Poetry from Spain 1900–1975*, edited by Hardie St. Martin. New York: Harper and Row, 1976. [Also includes one poem, "I Am Going because the Ear of Wheat and the Dawn Are Not Mine," published in *Selected Translations 1948–1968*, but revised significantly here.]

Rumi. "Ghazal." *Nation*, 224 (Feb. 12, 1977), 190. [With Talat Sait Halman.]

Rumi. "What Is the Whirling Dance." *American Poetry Review*, 7 (Jan./Feb. 1978), 3. [With Talat Sait Halman.]

Rumi. Two untitled poems ("Come come you are the soul"; "Don't fall asleep tonight"). *Chicago Review*, 30 (Autumn 1978), 9–11. [With Talat Sait Halman.]

Éluard, Paul. "Liberty," pp. 211–17. *The Random House Book of Twentieth-Century French Poetry*. New York: Random House, 1982.

Drama

Rumpelstiltskin. Produced BBC television, 1951. [Verse play for children.]

Pageant of Cain. Produced BBC Third Programme, 1952.

Huckleberry Finn. Produced BBC television, 1953. [Six-part children's play.]

Darkling Child. Produced London, England, Arts Theatre, 1956. [Written with Dido Milroy.]

Favor Island. Produced Cambridge, Massachusetts, Poet's Theatre, 1957, and BBC Third Programme, 1958. [Act 1 in *New World Writing 12* (New York: New American Library, 1957), pp. 122–54.]

The Gilded West. Produced Coventry, England, Belgrade Theatre, 1961.

(Typescripts of all these plays (except *Huckleberry Finn*) are part of the Merwin archive in the Rare Book Room, University Library, University of Illinois at Urbana-Champaign. The archive also includes drafts of a number of

Merwin's other plays, including "A Peacock at the Door," "Shadows of Horses," "The Wood of Women," and "Dr. Heidegger's Experiment.")

BROADSIDES

"When the War Is Over." N.p. [c. 1967]. [Printed in red, above a design of spilled blood. It may have been distributed at an antiwar demonstration or poetry reading.]

"A Letter from Gussie." Buffalo, N.Y.: Yorick Books, 1969. [Designed and illustrated by Serge Arnoux. Reprinted from *The Moving Target.*]

"The Approaches." Buffalo, N.Y.: Lockwood Memorial Library, State University of New York, 1969. Christmas broadside No. 2. [Reprinted in *The Carrier of Ladders.*]

"Two Poems" ["Other Travellers to the River" and "The Approaches"]. San Luis Obispo: Solo Press, 1971. [300 copies printed. Reprinted from *Lillabulero* and *New Directions Annual.* Reprinted in *The Carrier of Ladders.*]

"Japanese Figures," Santa Barbara: Unicorn Press, 1971; Unicorn Postcard Series 3 [Reprinted in *Asian Figures.*]

"Japanese Figures." Santa Barbara: Unicorn Press, 1971; Unicorn Broadside Series 2, no. 8. [Reprinted, except for "If the bird hadn't sung / it wouldn't have died," in *Asian Figures.*]

"For a Coming Extinction." Santa Cruz: Bookshop Santa Cruz, 1974–75. [Reprinted Pacific Grove, Calif.: Bookworks, 1976–77. Calligraphy by Elizabeth Tobisch. Design by Bill Prochnow. Reprinted from *The Lice.*]

"High Water." [San Francisco]: Black Stone Press, Square Zero Editions, 1978. [100 copies printed. Reprinted in *Opening the Hand.*]

"Tidal Lagoon." [San Francisco]: Black Stone Press, Square Zero Editions, 1978. [126 copies printed. Designed by Shelley Hoyt-Koch. Reprinted in *Opening the Hand.*]

"Sun and Rain." [San Francisco]: Black Stone Press, Square Zero Editions, 1979. [126 copies printed. Calligraphy by Yasutani Roshi. Reprinted in *Opening the Hand.*]

"Strawberries." West Branch, Iowa: Toothpaste Press, 1981. [90 copies printed. Reprinted in *Opening the Hand.*]

"To Dana for Her Birthday." N.p.: Meadow Press, Published by Intersection, 1981. [100 copies printed. Drawing by Andrew Rush. Reprinted in *Opening the Hand.*]

[Untitled. Three poems forthcoming in *Finding the Islands:* "Half the night sky deep cloud"; "Moonlight before dawn"; "Birds' feet."] West Branch, Iowa: Toothpaste Press, 1982. [700 copies printed as part of the Bookslinger exhibit at the 1982 A.B.A. Convention, Anaheim, Calif.]

"Berryman." In *Northern Lights.* Winston-Salem, N.C.: Palaemon Press Limited, 1983. [95 copies printed. A Portfolio of individual broadsides by fifteen different poets. "Berryman" is reprinted in *Opening the Hand.*]

"West Wall." [San Francisco]: Black Stone Press, Square Zero Editions, 1983. [100 copies printed.]

INTERVIEWS

"A Conversation with W. S. Merwin." *Audience*, 4, nos. 3–4 (1956), 4–6.
Ossman, David. "W. S. Merwin." In *The Sullen Art*. New York: Corinth Books, 1967, pp. 65–72.
Gerber, Philip L., and Robert J. Gemmett. "'Tireless Quest': A Conversation with W. S. Merwin." *English Record*, 19 (Feb. 1969), 9–18. [Edited version of a television interview conducted by Gregory Fitz Gerald and William Heyen.]
"An Interview with W. S. Merwin." *Road Apple Review*, 1 (Spring 1969), 35–37.
MacShane, Frank. "A Portrait of W. S. Merwin." *Shenandoah*, 21 (Winter 1970), 3–14.
Hall, Melissa Mia. "Poetry Dead? Not to W. S. Merwin." *Fort Worth Star-Telegram*, Dec. 12, 1982, pp. 7, 10.
Folsom, Ed, and Cary Nelson. "'Fact Has Two Faces': An Interview with W. S. Merwin." *Iowa Review*, 13 (Winter 1982), 30–66. [Parts reprinted in *American Poetry Observed: Poets on Their Work*, edited by Joe David Bellamy. Urbana: University of Illinois Press, 1984, pp. 168–80.] Revised and expanded in W. S. Merwin, *Regions of Memory: Uncollected Prose*, edited by Ed Folsom and Cary Nelson.
Pettit, Michael. "W. S. Merwin: An Interview." *Black Warrior Review*, 8 (Spring 1982), 7–20.
Myers, Jack, and Michael Simms. "Possibilities of the Unknown: Conversations with W. S. Merwin." *Southwest Review*, 68 (Spring 1983), 164–80.
Clifton, Michael. "W. S. Merwin: An Interview." *American Poetry Review*, 12 (July/Aug. 1983), 17–22.
Jackson, Richard. "Unnaming the Myths." In *Acts of Mind: Conversations with Contemporary Poets*. Tuscaloosa: University of Alabama Press, 1983, pp. 48–52.

MISCELLANEOUS

Merwin, W. S., ed. *West Wind: Supplement of American Poetry Edited by W. S. Merwin for the Poetry Book Society Christmas 1961*. London: John Roberts Press Limited, 1961. [Eleven-page pamphlet with "Shapes" (Michael Benedikt), "Flight" (Anne Sexton), "To find love I will first create it around you" (Jerome Rothenberg), "The Bay" (Robert Kelly), "The Body Snatcher" (Barbara Guest), "flowers of emergent occasions" (Armand Schwerner), "I Can Be Seen" (David Ignatow), "Tornado" (William Stafford), "In Fear of Harvests" and "The American Frontier" (James Wright), "The Sign Board" (Robert Creeley), and "The Redwoods" (Louis Simpson).]
Merwin, [Self-portrait]. In *Self-Portrait: Book People Picture Themselves*, edited by Burt Britton. New York: Random House, 1976, p. 85.

ARTICLES AND BOOKS ABOUT MERWIN

Albahari, David, and Raŝa Livada. "Nenapisano," Život, 55 (1979), 516–20. [Two poems translated and short biography.]

Altieri, Charles. "The Struggle with Absence." Enlarging the Temple. Lewisburg, [Pa.]: Bucknell University Press, 1979, pp. 193–220. [Reprinted in a revised version in W. S. Merwin: Essays on the Poetry.]

Anderson, Kenneth. "The Poetry of W. S. Merwin." Twentieth Century Literature, 16 (1970), 278–86.

Atlas, James. "Diminishing Returns: The Writings of W. S. Merwin." American Poetry since 1960: Some Critical Perspectives, edited by Robert B. Shaw. Chester Springs, Pa.: Dufour, 1974, pp. 69–81. Also Cheadle Hulme, Eng.: Carcanet Press, 1973.

Auden, W. H. "Foreword." In W. S. Merwin. A Mask for Janus. New Haven: Yale University Press, 1952, pp. vii–xi.

Benston, Alice. "Myth in the Poetry of W. S. Merwin." Poets in Progress, edited by Edward Hungerford. [Evanston, Ill.]: Northwestern University Press, 1962, pp. 179–204.

Bloom, Harold. "The New Transcendentalism: The Visionary Strain in Merwin, Ashbery, and Ammons." Chicago Review, 24 (Winter 1972), 25–43. [Reprinted in Figures of Capable Imagination. New York: Seabury Press, 1976, pp. 123–49.]

Bly, Robert. ["Crunk."] "The Work of W. S. Merwin." The Sixties, 4 (Fall 1960), 32–43.

Byers, Thomas B. "Believing Too Much in Words: W. S. Merwin and the Whitman Heritage." Missouri Review, 3 (Winter 1980), 75–89.

———. "The Peace in the Middle of the Floor: W. S. Merwin's Prose." Modern Language Quarterly, 44 (Mar. 1983), 65–79.

Carroll, Paul. "The Spirit with Long Ears and Paws." The Poem in Its Skin. Chicago: Big Table, 1968, pp. 139–52. [On "Lemuel's Blessing."]

Chamberlin, J. E. "Poetry Chronicle." Hudson Review, 26 (Summer 1973), 391–93.

Christhilf, Mark. "W. S. Merwin: The Poet as Creative Conservator." Modern Age, 23 (1979), 167–77.

———. W. S. Merwin the Mythmaker. Columbia: University of Missouri Press, 1986.

Clark, Tom. "When the Party's Over: An Interview with Allen Ginsberg." Boulder Monthly, Mar. 1979, 41–51.

———. The Master. Milwaukee: Pentagram Press, 1979. [Fictionalized account of the Naropa incident.]

———. The Great Naropa Poetry Wars. Santa Barbara: Cadmus Editions, 1980.

Contoski, Victor. "W. S. Merwin: Rational and Irrational Poetry." Literary Review, 22 (1978–79), 309–20.

Davis, Cheri. W. S. Merwin. Boston: Twayne, 1981.

Davis, Cheri Colby. "Merwin's Odysseus." Concerning Poetry, 8 (Spring 1975), 25–33.

———. "Time and Timelessness in the Poetry of W. S. Merwin." *Modern Poetry Studies*, 6 (Winter 1975), 224–36.

Davis, William V. "'Like the Beam of a Lightless Star': The Poetry of W. S. Merwin." *Poet and Critic*, 14 (1982), 45–56.

———. "'The Writing on the Void': W. S. Merwin's 'For the Anniversary of My Death.'" *Notes on Contemporary Literature*, 10, no. 4 (1980) 4–5.

Folsom, L. Edwin. "Approaches and Removals: W. S. Merwin's Encounter with Whitman's America." *Shenandoah*, 29 (Spring 1978), 57–73.

Frawley, William "Merwin's Unpunctuated Verse." *Notes on Contemporary Literature*, 7, no. 4 (1977), 2–3.

Frost, Lucy. "The Poetry of W. S. Merwin: An Introductory Note." *Meanjin*, 30 (1971), 294–96.

Gordon, Jan B. "The Dwelling of Disappearance: W. S. Merwin's *The Lice*." *Modern Poetry Studies*, 3 (1972), 119–38.

Gorman, Michael. "W. S. Merwin: Translator, Poet: Questions Raised by the W. S. Merwin Translation Papers." *Translation Review*, 9 (1982), 30–33.

Gross, Harvey. "The Writing on the Void: The Poetry of W. S. Merwin." *Iowa Review*, 1 (Summer 1970), 92–106.

Hoffman, Daniel. "Poetry: Schools of Dissidents," in *Harvard Guide to Contemporary American Writing*, edited by Daniel Hoffman. Boston: Harvard, 1979, pp. 538–45 and 559–60.

Howard, Richard. "W. S. Merwin." *Alone with America*. Enlarged edition. New York: Atheneum, 1980, pp. 412–49.

Hummer, T. R. "Roethke and Merwin: Two Voices and the Technique of Nonsense." *Western Humanities Review*, 33 (1979), 273–80.

Ingrasci, Hugh J. "Merwin's *The Miner's Pale Children*." *Explicator*, 37 (Spring 1979), 27–29.

Kyle, Carol. "A Riddle for the New Year: Affirmation in W. S. Merwin." *Modern Poetry Studies*, 4 (Winter 1973), 288–303.

Lazer, Hank. "For a Coming Extinction: A Reading of W. S. Merwin's *The Lice*." *ELH*, 49 (1982), 262–85.

Libby, Anthony. "W. S. Merwin and the Nothing That Is." *Contemporary Literature*, 16 (Winter 1975), 19–40. [Reprinted in a revised version in *Mythologies of Nothing*. Urbana: University of Illinois Press, 1984, pp. 185–209.]

Libby, Anthony. "Merwin's Planet: Alien Voices." *Criticism*, 24 (Winter 1982), 48–63.

Liberthson, Daniel. *The Quest for Being: Theodore Roethke, W. S. Merwin, and Ted Hughes*. New York: Gordon, 1977.

Link, Franz H. "W. S. Merwin: Metaphysiker des Schweigens." *Literaturwissenschaftliches Jahrbuch im Auftrage der Gorres-Gesellschaft*, 21 (1980), 303–20.

McFarland, Ronald E. "W. S. Merwin's 'Home for Thanksgiving.'" *Contemporary Poetry*, 2, no. 2 (1977), 38–44.

McPherson, Sandra. "Saying No." *Iowa Review*, 4 (1973), 84–88.

MacShane, Frank. "A Portrait of W. S. Merwin." *Shenandoah*, 21 (Winter 1970), 3–14.

Marin, Peter. "Spiritual Obedience: The Transcendental Game of Follow the Leader." *Harper's* (Feb. 1979), 43–58.

Messer, Richard. "W. S. Merwin's Use of Myth." *Publications of Arkansas Philological Association*, 1, no. 3 (1975), 41–48.

Mitgutsch, Waltraud. "Metaphorical Gaps and Negation in the Poetry of W. S. Merwin, Mark Strand, and Charles Simic." *On Poets and Poetry: Second Series*. Salzburg: Institut für Anglistik & Amerikanistik, University of Salzburg, 1980, pp. 3–30.

Nelson, Cary. "The Resources of Failure: W. S. Merwin's Deconstructive Career." *Boundary 2*, 5 (Winter 1977), 573–98. [Reprinted in a revised version in *Our Last First Poets* (Urbana: University of Illinois Press, 1981), pp. 179–215; revised again in *W. S. Merwin: Essays on the Poetry.*]

Peters, Robert. "The Great American Poetry Bake-Off: or, Why W. S. Merwin Wins All Those Prizes." *The Great American Poetry Bake-off*. Metuchen, N.J.: Scarecrow Press, 1979, pp. 258–68.

Ramsey, Jarold. "The Continuities of W. S. Merwin: 'What Has Escaped Us We Bring with Us.'" *Massachusetts Review*, 14 (1973), 569–90. [Reprinted in *W. S. Merwin: Essays on the Poetry.*]

Rexroth, Kenneth. "Poetry in the Sixties." *With Eye and Ear*. New York: Herder and Herder, 1970, pp. 69–77.

Rosenthal, M. L. "Exquisite Chaos: Thomas and Others." *The Modern Poets*. New York: Oxford University Press, 1960, pp. 261–64.

Sanderlin, Reed. "Merwin's 'The Drunk in the Furnace.'" *Contemporary Poetry*, 2, 1 (1975), 24–27.

Sanders, Ed, ed. "The Party: A Chronological Perspective on a Confrontation at a Buddhist Seminary," *Boulder Monthly*, Mar. 1979, pp. 25–39. [See also the letters to the editor printed together as "Feedback on Boulder Buddhism," in the July, 1979, issue of *Boulder Monthly*.]

———. ed. *The Party: A Chronological Perspective on a Confrontation at a Buddhist Seminary* (Woodstock, N.Y., n.d., c. 1980). [Substantially expanded from the *Boulder Monthly* version.]

Scholes, Robert. "Semiotics of the Poetic Text." *Semiotics and Interpretation*. New Haven: Yale University Press, 1982, pp. 37–56. [Reprinted in *W. S. Merwin: Essays on the Poetry.*]

Sherry, Vincent. "W. S. Merwin's *The Compass Flower*: The Angles of Convergence." *New Poetry*, 26, 1 (Apr. 1978), 44–54.

Stepanchev, Stephen. "W. S. Merwin." *American Poetry since 1945*. New York: Harper and Row, 1965, pp. 107–23.

Stiffler, Randall. "The Sea Poems of W. S. Merwin." *Modern Poetry Studies*, 11 (1983), 247–66.

———. "'The Annunciation' of W. S. Merwin." *Concerning Poetry*, 16 (Fall 1983), 55–63.

Swann, Brian. "The Poetry of W. S. Merwin: Carrier of Ladders." *Annali di Ca' Foscari*, 12 (1973), 135–47.

Taylor, L. Loring. "W. S. Merwin: Fereastřa în casa orbilor," *Steaua*, 25, no. 5 (1974), 45–47.

Trengen, Linda, and Gary Storhoff. "Order and Energy in Merwin's *The Drunk in the Furnace.*" *Concerning Poetry*, 13, no. 1 (1980), 47–52.

Veza, Laurette. "La Poésie de W. S. Merwin: Silence, notre premier langage." *Etudes Anglaises*, 29 (1976), 510–21.

Vogelsong, John. "Toward the Great Language: W. S. Merwin." *Modern Poetry Studies*, 3, no. 3 (1972), 97–118.

Watkins, Evan. "W. S. Merwin: A Critical Accompaniment." *Boundary 2*, 4 (1975), 187–99. [Reprinted in *The Critical Act: Criticism and Community*. New Haven: Yale University Press, 1978.]

Weinberger, Eliot. "Dharma Demagogy." *The Nation*, 230 (Apr. 19, 1980), 470–76. [Review of Ed Sanders, ed., *The Party* and Tom Clark, *The Great Naropa Poetry Wars*.]

Williamson, Alan. "Language against Itself." *Introspection and Contemporary Poetry*. Cambridge: Harvard University Press, 1984, pp. 87–92.

Woods, Robert [pseud. for Tom Clark]. " 'Buddha-gate': Scandal and Cover-up at Naropa Revealed." *Berkeley Barb*, no. 698 (Mar. 29-Apr. 11, 1979), 1, 4. [Letters of response from Allen Ginsberg and Jim Hartz appear in *Berkeley Barb*, no. 701 (May 10–23, 1979).]

HANDBOOKS, BIBLIOGRAPHIES, ETC.

Carruth, Hayden. "W. S. Merwin." *Contemporary Poets of the English Language*, edited by Rosalie Murphy. Chicago: St. James, 1970, pp. 747–49. [Reprinted in *Contemporary Poets*. 2d ed., edited by James Vinson. New York: St. Martins, 1975, pp. 1039–42.]

Christensen, Paul. "W. S. Merwin." *Twentieth-Century American Literature*. Great Writers Student Library, vol. 13, edited by James Vinson. New York: St. Martins, 1980, pp. 390–92.

Coffin, Arthur B. "W. S. Merwin." *Encyclopedia of World Literature in the Twentieth Century*, 2d ed., vol. 3, edited by Leonard S. Klein. New York: Frederick Ungar, 1983, pp. 270–71.

Davis, Cheri. "Selected Bibliography." *W. S. Merwin*. Boston: Twayne, 1981, pp. 171–75.

Gordon, Lois. "W. S. Merwin." *Contemporary Poets*. 3d ed., edited by James Vinson. New York: St. Martin's, 1980, pp. 1030–34.

Hartley, Eric. "W. S. Merwin." *American Poets since World War II*, edited by Donald J. Greiner. Detroit: Gale Research, 1980, vol. 2, pp. 65–74.

Jones, Peter. "W. S. Merwin." *A Reader's Guide to Fifty American Poets*. London: Heinemann, 1980, pp. 328–33.

Malkoff, Karl. "W. S. Merwin." *Crowell's Handbook of Contemporary American Poetry*. New York: Thomas Y. Crowell, 1973, pp. 208–17.

Roche, Thomas P., Jr. "Green with Poems." *Princeton University Library Chronicle*, 25 (1963), 89–104.

Seymour-Smith, Martin. "W. S. Merwin." *Who's Who in Twentieth Century Literature*. New York: Holt, Rinehart and Winston, 1976, p. 356.

Spacks, Barry. "W. S. Merwin." *Penguin Companion to Literature*. Vol. 3, *U.S.A.*, edited by Eric Mottram and Malcolm Bradbury. London: Penguin Books, 1971, p. 176.

Unsigned. "W. S. Merwin." *Contemporary Authors*, edited by Clare D. Kinsman. Detroit: Gale Research, 1975, 13–16:553–54. [See listing under "Sidelights" in the section on Merwin's uncollected prose for earlier versions.]

REVIEWS OF MERWIN'S WORKS

A MASK FOR JANUS (1952): John Holmes, "Of Time and Place and Versifiers," *New York Times Book Review* (Aug. 3, 1952), 6; Unsigned, "Individual Voices," *Times Literary Supplement* (Jan. 2, 1953), 6; Richard Wilbur, *Furioso* (Spring 1953), 57–61; Frederick Morgan, "Six Poets," *Hudson Review* (Spring 1953), 136–38; Harry Roskolenko, "A Variety of Poets," *Poetry* (Apr. 1953), 34–35; David Daiches, "Six Poets," *Yale Review* (Summer 1953), 630–31.

THE DANCING BEARS (1954): R. W. Flint, "Poets of the 50s," *Partisan Review* (Winter 1954), 679; Gerald D. McDonald, *Library Journal* (June 15, 1954), 1232; Unsigned, *U.S. Quarterly Book Review* (Sept. 1954), 343–44; Gerard Previn Meyer, "Nature's Various Vitality," *Saturday Review* (Oct. 9, 1954), 19; Louis L. Martz, "New Poetry: In the Pastoral Mode," *Yale Review* (Winter 1955), 309; William Meredith, "A Lot of Poems and a Bit of Theory," *Hudson Review* (Winter 1955), 596–97; W. D. Snodgrass, "Voice as Vision," *Western Review* (Spring 1955), 235–39; John Edward Hardy, "Of Promise, Achievement, and Vision," *Sewanee Review* (Spring 1955), 296–307.

DARKLING CHILD (1956): Unsigned, *London Times* (Jan. 28, 1956), 8.

GREEN WITH BEASTS (1956): G. S. Fraser, "Matter and Art," *New Statesman and Nation* (Oct. 13, 1956), 459; Philip Larkin, "Chosen and Recommended," *Manchester Guardian* (Oct. 16, 1956), 4; Unsigned, "Flying High," *Times Literary Supplement* (Oct. 26, 1956), 635; Robert Conquest, "Poems and Proses," *Spectator* (Nov. 23, 1956), 743; Gerald D. McDonald, *Library Journal* (Dec. 1, 1956), 2863; Unsigned, *Booklist* (Dec. 1, 1956), 170; John Logan, "Literary Noise and Poetic Art," *Commonweal* (Dec. 28, 1956), 340–41; David Ignatow, "Plain Statement of Poetic Loss," *Saturday Review* (Jan. 5, 1957), 32; Richard Eberhart, "Like a Broad River Flowing," *New York Times Book Review* (Jan. 13, 1957), 6; Melvin Maddocks, "Poems from New and Familiar Voices," *Christian Science Monitor* (Jan. 17, 1957), 7; Joseph Bennett, "Sawdust and Wine," *Hudson Review* (Spring 1957), 130–31; John Malcolm Brinnin, "Eleven Poets," *Yale Review* (Spring 1957), 454–55; Joseph Warren Beach, "A Fair Sampling," *Prairie Schooner* (Spring 1957), 171–81; John

Hollander, "Poetry Chronicle," *Partisan Review* (Spring 1957), 296–304; Roy Fuller, *London Magazine* (Mar. 1957), 71–79; Louise Bogan, *New Yorker* (Mar. 2, 1957), 114; M. L. Rosenthal, "The Sea of Hazard," *Nation* (Aug. 17, 1957), 74; Norman K. Dorn, "Amidst Smoky Jazz or 'Neath the Bough, the Poets Create," *San Francisco Chronicle* (Sept. 8, 1957), 29.

FAVOR ISLAND (1957): Unsigned, "'Favor Island' Is Season Finale at Poet's Theatre," *Boston Sunday Globe* (May 19, 1957), sec. a, p. 19; Elinor Hughes, "Poet's Theatre: 'Favor Island,'" *Boston Herald Traveler* (May 21, 1957), p. 33; Elinor Hughes, "Poet's Theatre Worth a Visit," *Boston Herald Traveler* (May 26, 1957), sec. i, p. 4.

THE POEM OF THE CID (1959): Allan R. Zoll, *New Mexico Quarterly* (Autumn 1961), 271–72; Robert Bly, "Rewriting vs. Translation," *Hudson Review* (Autumn 1962), 474–75; Barbara Gibbs, "Merwin as Translator," *Poetry* (Feb. 1963), 353–55.

THE DRUNK IN THE FURNACE (1960): Elizabeth Jennings, "Searching with Words," *New Statesman and Nation* (Oct. 15, 1960), 576; T. Francis Smith, *Library Journal* (Nov. 15, 1960), 4150–51; Dom Moraes, "Poems from Many Parts," *Time and Tide* (Nov. 19, 1960), 1413; John Holloway, *London Magazine* (Jan. 1961), 74–78; Robert D. Spector, "A Cloud of Quiet Terror," *Saturday Review* (Jan. 28, 1961), 30; Dudley Fitts, "A Varied Quintet," *New York Times Book Review* (Feb. 26, 1961), 12; James Dickey, "The Death and Keys of the Censor," *Sewanee Review* (Spring 1961), 327–29 [reprinted as "W. S. Merwin" in *Babel to Byzantium: Poets and Poetry Now* (New York: Farrar, Straus and Giroux, 1968), pp. 142–43]; James G. Southworth, *College English* (Spring 1961), 442; James Edward Tobin, "Narrative Skill and Portraiture," *Spirit* (Mar. 1961), 24–25; X. J. Kennedy, "Five Poets in Search of Six Lines," *Poetry* (May 1961), 122–23; Paul Later, "Poetry Demanding and Detached," *New Leader* (May 15, 1961), 23; Thom Gunn, "Outside Faction," *Yale Review* (Summer 1961), 588–89; John Holmes, "Poets All, Each Hewing to His Line," *New York Herald Tribune* (Aug. 27, 1961), 10; Louis Simpson, "Important and Unimportant Poems," *Hudson Review* (Autumn 1961), 464–65; Peter Davison, "Self-Revelation in the New Poetry," *Atlantic* (Nov. 1961), 174; Harry Fainlight, "Four Poets," *Encounter* (Nov. 1961), 73, 75; John Napier, "Poetry in the Vernacular and Otherwise," *Voices* (Sept.-Dec. 1961), 53–54; John Fandel, "A First and Fourth," *Prairie Schooner* (Fall 1962), 284.

SOME SPANISH BALLADS (1961): Paul Selver, "Sundry Translations," *Poetry Review* (Jan.-Mar. 1961), 171; J. M. Cohen, "Romances," *Time and Tide* (May 11, 1961), 787; Ray Smith, *Library Journal* (June 15, 1961), 2321; Unsigned, "From the Spanish," *Times Literary Supplement* (June 16, 1961), 374; Robert D. Spector, "Muse of Many Voices," *Saturday Review* (July 22, 1961), 16; Frank Goodwyn, *Inter-American Review of Bibliography*, 12 (1962), 163; Arthur L. Campa, *Midwest Folklore* (Spring 1962), 59; John Frederick Nims, "Young Stoic in Gray Flannels," *New*

York Times Book Review (Nov. 4, 1962), 38; Boyd Carter, "The 'Romance' of Spain," Prairie Schooner (Winter 1962/63), 366–67; Barbara Gibbs, "Merwin as Translator," Poetry (Feb. 1963), 353–55.

THE SATIRES OF PERSIUS (1961): Robert Bly, "Rewriting vs. Translation," Hudson Review (Autumn 1962), 474–75; John Frederick Nims, "Young Stoic in Gray Flannels," New York Times Book Review (Nov. 4, 1962), 38; Barbara Gibbs, "Merwin as Translator," Poetry (Feb. 1963), 353–55; C. H. Sisson, "Translating the Stoic Sage," Times Literary Supplement (June 5, 1981), 643.

THE LIFE OF LAZARILLO DE TORMES (1962): John R. Browne, Hispania (May 1963), 438–39.

THE MOVING TARGET (1963): James Dickey, "The Many Ways of Speaking in Verse," New York Times Book Review (Dec. 22, 1963), 4; Joseph Bennett, "The Moving Finger Writes," Hudson Review (Winter 1963–64), 624–25; Edward Dorn; "Some Questions of Precision," Poetry, 101 (1964), 184–85; Stephen Stepanchev, Shenandoah (Summer 1964), 69–77; Unsigned, Virginia Quarterly Review (Winter 1964), 24–25; Phillip Booth, "Poetry: A Contrast in Strategies," Christian Science Monitor (Jan. 9, 1964), 7; Richard K. Burns, Library Journal (Jan. 15, 1964), 268; Robert D. Spector, "The Poet's Other Voices, Other Rooms," Saturday Review (Feb. 1, 1964), 37; G. S. Fraser, "Three Poets," New York Review of Books (Feb. 20, 1964), 12–13; David Galler, "Versions of Accident," Kenyon Review (Summer 1964), 581–83; Ralph J. Mills, Jr., "Some New Poetry," Modern Age (Fall 1964), 436; R. K. Meiners, "The Necessary and Permanent Revolution," Southern Review (Autumn 1965), 931–37; Unsigned, "International Anonymous," Times Literary Supplement (Sept. 14, 1967), 820; Julian Symons, "Ragged Edges," New Statesman (Sept. 15, 1967), 328; Ian Hamilton, "Dead Ends and Soft Centres," Observer (Nov. 12, 1967), 28; Michael Thorpe, English Studies (June 1968), 279.

THE LICE (1967, 1969): William Dickey, Hudson Review (Winter 1967–68), 695–96; Thomas E. Luddy, Library Journal (Jan. 1, 1968), 87; Unsigned, Booklist (Jan. 1, 1968), 527; Peter Davison, "New Poetry: The Generation of the Twenties," Atlantic (Feb. 1968), 141–42; Lisel Mueller, "Five Poets," Shenandoah (Spring 1968), 68–69; Miller Williams, "Transaction with the Muse," Saturday Review (Mar. 9, 1968), 32–33; Denis Donoghue, "Object Solitary and Terrible," New York Review of Books (June 6, 1968), 22–23; Laurence Lieberman, "Recent Poetry in Review: Risks and Faiths," Yale Review (Summer 1968), 597–601 [reprinted in Unassigned Frequencies (Urbana: University of Illinois Press, 1977), pp. 257–60]; Lawrence Raab, American Scholar (Summer 1968), 538; Samuel French Morse, "Twelve Poets," Virginia Quarterly Review (Summer 1968), 510–11; Louis Simpson, Harper's (Aug. 1968), 76; Stanley Cooperman, "The Experience of Having Poemed," Prairie Schooner (Fall 1968), 269–71; Hayden Carruth, Poetry (Sept. 1968), 421–22; Robert Haas, "Death Camps of the Free World," Nation (Sept. 16, 1968),

253–54; Louise Bogan, *New Yorker* (Dec. 28, 1968), 63; Vern Rutsala, "The End of the Owls: W. S. Merwin, *The Lice*," *Far Point*, 2 (1969), 40–44; Unsigned, "Promiscuous Despair," *Times Literary Supplement* (May 29, 1969), 585; Derek Stanford, "Inner Landscapes," *Books and Bookmen* (Aug. 1969), 22; Brian Jones, "Black Feathers," *London Magazine* (Oct. 1969), 98; Fred Moramarco, "A Gathering of Poets," *Western Humanities Review* (Spring 1970), 206; R. K. Meiners, "The Way Out: The Poetry of Delmore Schwartz and Others," *Southern Review* (Winter 1971), 320–24; Harold Bloom, "Harold Bloom on Poetry," *New Republic* (Nov. 26, 1977), 25.

SELECTED TRANSLATIONS 1948–1968 (1968): Philip Levine, "Comment," *Poetry*, 115 (1969), 187–89; Ray Smith, *Library Journal* (Mar. 15, 1969), 1150; Robert D. Spector, "Lyrics, Heroic and Otherwise," *Saturday Review* (Mar. 15, 1969), 35; William J. Smith, *New York Times Book Review* (Nov. 16, 1969), 26, 28; Roger Mitchell, *Modern Language Journal* (Mar. 1970), 216.

PRODUCTS OF THE PERFECTED CIVILIZATION (1969): Unsigned, *Kirkus Reviews* (June 15, 1969), 664; Melvin Maddocks, "When Wit Is Serious," *Christian Science Monitor* (Sept. 11, 1969), 10; Judith Adelson, *Library Journal* (Sept. 15, 1969), 3056; Unsigned, *New Yorker* (Oct. 25, 1969), 191–92.

ANIMAE (1969): Jon M. Warner, *Library Journal* (Feb. 1, 1970), 502; Hayden Carruth, "End of the Sixties," *Hudson Review* (Spring 1970), 192.

TRANSPARENCE OF THE WORLD (1969): Stephen Berg, "Transparencies," *Poetry* (July 1970), 262–64; Vernon Young, "October Thoughts," *Hudson Review* (Winter 1970–71), 746.

THE CARRIER OF LADDERS (1970): Peter Cooley, "Transfiguring the World," *North American Review* (Winter 1970), 72–74; John W. Charles, "The New Austere Poetry of Merwin," *Library Journal* (Sept. 15, 1970), 2926; Helen Vendler, "Desolation Shading into Terror," *New York Times Book Review* (Oct. 18, 1970), 28, 30 [reprinted in *Part of Nature, Part of Us* (Cambridge: Harvard University Press, 1980), pp. 233–36]; Robert Scholes, *Saturday Review* (Oct. 31, 1970), 30–31; Michele Murray, "In New Volumes, the Poem Is Its Own Reward," *National Observer* (Nov. 30, 1970), 24; Vernon Young, "October Thoughts," *Hudson Review* (Winter 1970–71), 744–45; Richard Howard, "A Poetry of Darkness," *Nation* (Dec. 14, 1970), 634–38; David H. Zucker, "Shadow and Light," *Modern Poetry Studies*, 2 (1971), 182–86; Unsigned, *Virginia Quarterly Review* (Winter 1971), 18; John Vernon, *Western Humanities Review* (Spring 1971), 187–89; Sister Mary Anthony Weinig, *Best Sellers* (Mar. 1, 1971), 518–19; Denis Donoghue, "Waiting for the End," *New York Review of Books* (May 6, 1971), 27–31; G. S. Fraser, "The Magicians," *Partisan Review* (Winter 1971–72), 475–76; H. T. Kirby-Smith, Jr., "Miss Bishop and Others," *Sewanee Review* (Summer 1972), 490–93.

THE MINER'S PALE CHILDREN (1970): Gail Godwin, "Healing Fragments," *North American Review* (Winter 1970), 69–71; Unsigned,

Kirkus Reviews (Aug. 1, 1970), 824; Unsigned, *Publisher's Weekly* (Aug. 10, 1970), 50; J. D. O'Hara, "Which Is the Sweeter Song, the Iceberg's or the Whale's?" *Book World* (Sept. 20, 1970), 5; Phoebe Adams, *Atlantic* (Oct. 1970), 150; Unsigned, *Yale Review* (Oct. 1970), 34–36; Helen Vendler, "Desolation Shading into Terror," *New York Times Book Review* (Oct. 18, 1970), 28, 30 [reprinted in *Part of Nature, Part of Us* (Cambridge: Harvard University Press, 1980), pp. 233–36]; [See also letters by J. W. Ramsey and Helen Vendler, *New York Times Book Review* (Nov. 15, 1970), 58.] Robert Scholes, *Saturday Review* (Oct. 31, 1970), 30—31; John W. Charles, *Library Journal* (Nov. 15, 1970), 3926; Unsigned, *Saturday Review* (Nov. 28, 1970), 32; Unsigned, *Booklist* (Dec. 15, 1970), 328; Carolyn F. Ruffin, "How to Unchop a Tree," *Christian Science Monitor*, Dec. 23, 1970, 9; Vernon Young, "October Thoughts," *Hudson Review* (Winter 1970–71), 744–45; John Vernon, *Western Humanities Review* (Spring 1971), 187–89; Sister Mary Anthony Weinig, *Best Sellers* (Mar. 1, 1971), 518–19; G. S. Fraser, "The Magicians," *Partisan Review* (Winter 1971–72), 475–76; Unsigned, *Prairie Schooner* (Winter 1971–72), 370; Jay L. Halio, "First and Last Things," *Southern Review* (Spring 1973), 463.

WRITINGS TO AN UNFINISHED ACCOMPANIMENT (1973): Unsigned, *Kirkus Reviews* (Jan. 1, 1973), 45; Carey Horowitz, *Library Journal* (Jan. 1, 1973), 89; Unsigned, *Publisher's Weekly* (Jan. 29, 1973), 261; Brian Swann, *Library Journal* (Mar. 1, 1973), 748; Laurence Lieberman, "New Poetry: The Church of Ash," *Yale Review* (Summer 1973), 602–13 [reprinted in *Unassigned Frequencies* (Urbana: University of Illinois Press, 1977), pp. 122–30]; J. E. Chamberlin, "Poetry Chronicle," *Hudson Review* (Summer 1973), 391–93; Unsigned, *Virginia Quarterly Review* (Summer 1973), 110; Harvey Shapiro, "The Journey through a Poem," *New York Times* (June 22, 1973), 33; James Finn Cotter, *America* (July 21, 1973), 46–48; Michele Murray, "The Year's Poetry: Exactitude, Joy, Love, and More," *National Observer* (Aug. 18, 1973), 25; Richard Howard, "Names, Emblems, Tongues," *North American Review* (Fall 1973), 68; Stephen Spender, "Can Poetry Be Reviewed?" *New York Review of Books* (Sept. 20, 1973), 8–14; John Bayley, "How to Be Intimate without Being Personal," *Parnassus*, 2 (Fall/Winter 1973), 115–21; David Zuker, "In Search of Simplicities," *Modern Poetry Studies*, 5 (1974), 87–91; Paul Ramsey, *Sewanee Review* (Spring 1974), 397–98; Douglas Blazek, "Falling into Triteness," *Poetry* (June 1974), 176–78; Donald Newlove, *Village Voice* (July 4, 1974), 20; G. S. Fraser, "Free and Uneasy," *Partisan Review* (Spring 1978), 156.

ASIAN FIGURES (1973): Carey Horowitz, *Library Journal* (Jan. 1, 1973), 89; Linda Pastan, *Library Journal* (Apr. 15, 1973), 1290; Unsigned, "Feeling Big," *Times Literary Supplement* (June 8, 1973), 646; Harvey Shapiro, "The Journey through a Poem," *New York Times* (June 22, 1973), 33; James Finn Cotter, *America* (July 21, 1973), 46–48; Unsigned, *Choice* (Nov. 1973), 1394; David Zuker, "In Search of Simplicities," *Modern*

Poetry Studies, 5 (1974), 87–91; Gerrit Henry, *Poetry* (Aug. 1974), 297; Edward Engelberg, "Discovering America and Asia: The Poems of Wright and Merwin," *Southern Review* (Spring 1975), 442–43.

SELECTED POEMS OF OSIP MANDELSTAM (1973, 1974): Donald Davie, *New Statesman* (Dec. 7, 1973), 863; Madeline G. Levine, *Library Journal* (Dec. 15, 1973), 3640; Simon Karlinsky, "An Emerging Reputation Comparable to Pushkin's," *New York Times Book Review* (Jan. 20, 1974), 1, 10, 12, 14, 16; Victor Howes, "Testament of Courage," *Christian Science Monitor* (Jan. 23, 1974), F5; Susan Jacoby, "Power of the Word," *Saturday Review World* (Jan. 26, 1974), 42; Charles Newman, "A People Does Not Choose Its Poets," *Harper's* (Feb. 1974), 83–84; Benjamin DeMott, "The Capital of Russia," *Atlantic* (Feb. 1974), 86–87; Joseph Brodsky, "Beyond Consolation," *New York Review of Books* (Feb. 7, 1974), 14–16; Unsigned, *Virginia Quarterly Review* (Spring 1974), 58; John Heidenry, "Mandelstam—Searching for Signals," *Commonweal* (Apr. 12, 1974), 138–40; Unsigned, *Choice* (June 1974), 608; Michael Mesic, "Three of Them," *Poetry* (July 1974), 234–37.

THE FIRST FOUR BOOKS OF POEMS (1975): Terence Winch, "A Master Poet's Early Art—and Artifice," *Washington Post Book World* (Aug. 31, 1975), 3; Edmund Fuller, "Rich Evocations of Holy Themes," *Wall Street Journal* (Sept. 15, 1975), 10; Harold Bloom, "Harold Bloom on Poetry," *New Republic* (Nov. 29, 1975), 26; Lindley H. Clark, Jr., "Looking Over the Year's Books," *Wall Street Journal* (Dec. 5, 1975), 16; Turner Cassity, "Dresden Milkmaids: The Pitfalls of Tradition," *Parnassus* (Fall/Winter 1976), 295–304; Calvin Bedient, "Horace and Modernism," *Sewanee Review* (Spring 1977), 366–67; Vernon Young, "Same Sea, Same Dangers: W. S. Merwin," *American Poetry Review* (Jan./Feb. 1978), 4–5.

THE COMPASS FLOWER (1977): Unsigned, *Publisher's Weekly* (Dec. 27, 1976), 59; G. E. Murray, *Georgia Review* (Winter 1977), 962–71; Unsigned, *Kirkus Reviews* (Jan. 15, 1977), 84; H. W. Dillard, *Hollins Critic* (Feb. 1977), 15; Unsigned, *North American Review* (Spring 1977), 15; R. W. Flint, "Exiles from Olympus," *Parnassus* (Spring/Summer 1977), 97–102; C. W. Truesdale, *Library Journal* (Mar. 1, 1977), 612; Paul Gray, "A Quartet of Poets Singing Solo," *Time* (Mar. 21, 1977), 91; Connie Fletcher, *Booklist* (Apr. 15, 1977), 1236; David Bromwich, "Verse Chronicle," *Hudson Review* (Summer 1977), 282–83; Unsigned, *Choice* (June 1977), 534–35; Hayden Carruth, *New York Times Book Review* (June 19, 1977), 15F; Terrence Winch, *Washington Post Book World,* July 17, 1977, K4; Andrew Waterman, "The Illusions of Immediacy," *Times Literary Supplement* (July 29, 1977), 836; Linda W. Wagner, "The Most Contemporary of Poetics," *Ontario Review* (Fall-Winter 1977–78), 88–90; Harold Bloom, "Harold Bloom on Poetry," *New Republic* (Nov. 26, 1977), 25; Susan Wood, "Bards of America," *Washington Post Book World* (Dec. 11, 1977), E6; Victor Contoski, "The Mysterious Journey," *Moons and Lion Tailes,* 2 (1978), 96–99; L. L. Lee,

Western American Literature (Winter 1978), 321–23; Vernon Young, "Same Sea, Same Dangers: W. S. Merwin," *American Poetry Review* (Jan./Feb. 1978), 4–5; William Marling, "Indiscriminately Prolific Poet," *Southwest Review* (Spring 1978), 198–202; J. D. McClatchy, "Grace and Rude Will," *Poetry* (Aug. 1978), 288–90; Richard Jackson, "Worlds Created, Worlds Received," *Michigan Quarterly Review* (Fall 1978), 551–53; Vincent B. Sherry, Jr., "W. S. Merwin," *Contemporary Literature* (Winter 1980), 159–60; Timothy Steele, "Recent Verse of W. S. Merwin," *Southern Review* (Apr. 1980), 483–91.

HOUSES AND TRAVELLERS (1977): Unsigned, *Publisher's Weekly* (May 30, 1977), 36; Unsigned, *Kirkus Reviews* (June 1, 1977), 594–95; Rosaly DeMaios Roffman, *Library Journal* (July 1977), 1525–26; Unsigned, *Booklist* (July 1, 1977), 1621; Phoebe-Lou Adams, *Atlantic* (Oct. 1977), 107; Linda Pastan, *New Republic* (Oct. 22, 1977), 35–36; Victor Contoski, "The Mysterious Journey," *Moons and Lion Tailes*, 2 (1978), 96–99; Unsigned, *Choice* (Jan. 1978), 1497; Robert Bly, "Mixed Parable," *New York Times Book Review* (Feb. 5, 1978), 14–15; William Marling, "Indiscriminately Prolific Poet," *Southwest Review* (Spring 1978), 198–202; Richard Tobias, *World Literature Today* (Spring 1978), 287; Charles Molesworth, *Georgia Review* (Fall 1978), 683–87; Martin Kirby, "A Writer under the Influence," *Carleton Miscellany* (Spring 1979), 232–33; William Marling, *Arizona Quarterly* (Autumn 1979), 277–81.

SANSKRIT LOVE POETRY (1977): Unsigned, *Virginia Quarterly Review* (Autumn 1978), 146; Samuel Hazo, "The Experience of the Idea," *Hudson Review* (Autumn 1978), 546; Unsigned, *Choice* (Sept. 1978), 882; Carlo Coppola, *World Literature Today* (Winter 1979), 183–84; Unsigned, *Babel* (Summer 1979), 179; Jay Peter, "Ravishing and Rendering," *Poetry Review* (July 1979), 65–66; Richard A. Williams, *Journal of Asian Studies* (Aug. 1979), 790–92; Ludwik Sternbach, *Journal of the American Oriental Society* (July-Oct. 1980), 315–19; Edwin Gerow, *Journal of the American Oriental Society* (July-Oct. 1982), 546–47; M. K. Stocking, *Beloit Poetry Journal* (Winter 1983–84), 37–39.

FEATHERS FROM THE HILL (1978): Timothy Steele, "Recent Verse of W. S. Merwin," *Southern Review* (Apr. 1980), 483–91.

IPHIGENIA AT AULIS (1978): Bernard Knox, "A Four Handkerchief Tragedy," *New York Review of Books* (Feb. 9, 1978), 15–19; Tom T. Tashiro, *Library Journal* (Apr. 1, 1978), 753.

SELECTED TRANSLATIONS 1968–1978 (1979): Edward Butscher, *Booklist* (July 1, 1979), 1566; Marilyn Gaddis Rose, *Library Journal* (Aug. 1979), 1570; D. M. Thomas, *Times Literary Supplement* (Jan. 18, 1980), 66; Richard Tobias, *World Literature Today* (Summer 1980), 494.

UNFRAMED ORIGINALS (1982): Unsigned, *Kirkus Reviews* (Apr. 15, 1982), 538; Unsigned, *Publisher's Weekly* (May 14, 1982), 208; Joyce Carol Oates, *New York Times Book Review* (Aug. 1, 1982), 7; Reid Beddow, *Washington Post Book World* (Aug. 15, 1982), 8–9; George Core,

"Procrustes' Bed," *Sewanee Review* (Fall 1982), 108–9; Joseph Parisi, *Booklist* (Sept. 1, 1982), 22; Phoebe Pettingell, "Lives by the Poets," *New Leader* (Oct. 18, 1982), 16–17; Sandra Prewitt Edelman, "A Patch of Vacancy," *Southwest Review* (Winter 1983), 92–93; Edmund Fuller, "Autobiographies of a Satirist in Line and a Gifted Poet," *Wall Street Journal* (Jan. 3, 1983), 22; James Finn Cotter, "Poets Then and Now," *America* (Jan. 29, 1983), 75–76; Mark Irwin, *World Literature Today* (Spring 1983), 294; Waltraud Mitgutsch, *Western Humanities Review* (Spring 1983), 91–93; David St. John, "Raised Voices in the Choir: A Review of 1982 Poetry Selections," *Antioch Review* (Spring 1983), 232; Unsigned, *Virginia Quarterly Review* (Spring 1983), 62; Unsigned, *Publisher's Weekly* (Aug. 12, 1983), 64; M. K. Stocking, *Beloit Poetry Journal* (Winter 1983–84), 37–39; Unsigned, *New York Times Book Review* (Jan. 15, 1984), 34.

FINDING THE ISLANDS (1982): Unsigned, *Kirkus Reviews* (Sept. 15, 1982), 1099–1100; Sally A. Lodge, *Publisher's Weekly* (Oct. 8, 1982), 61; Gary Brown, *Library Journal* (Oct. 15, 1982), 1991; Joseph Parisi, *Booklist* (Oct. 15, 1982), 289; Kenneth Funsten, *Los Angeles Times Book Review* (Jan. 23, 1983), 3; Unsigned, *Virginia Quarterly Review* (Spring 1983), 62; M. K. Stocking, *Beloit Poetry Journal* (Winter 1983–84), 37–39; John Martone, *World Literature Today* (Winter 1984), 105.

OPENING THE HAND (1983): Unsigned, *Publisher's Weekly* (May 6, 1983), 97; Inge Judd, *Library Journal* (June 15, 1983), 1261; Joseph Parisi, *Booklist* (June 15, 1983), 1321; John Lucas, "A Mouthful of Pebbles," *New Statesman* (Aug. 5, 1983), 23; Holly Prado, *Los Angeles Times Book Review* (Aug. 21, 1983), 9; Michael Garcia-Simms, "Time and the Maker," *Southwest Review* (Autumn 1983), 403–5; John J. Murray, *Best Sellers* (Sept. 1983), 224–25; David Bromwich, "Remembered Gestures," *New York Times Book Review* (Oct. 9, 1983), 12–13; Karl Keller, "Nominees, 1983 Poetry Prize," *Los Angeles Times Book Review* (Oct. 30, 1983), 12–13; M. K. Stocking, *Beloit Poetry Journal* (Winter 1983–84), 37–39; Unsigned, *Virginia Quarterly Review* (Spring 1984), 60; David St. John, "Raised Voices in the Choir: A Review of 1983 Poetry Selections," *Antioch Review* (Summer 1984), 364–66.

DISSERTATIONS CONCERNING W. S. MERWIN

W. S. Merwin Only

Breslow, Stephen P. "W. S. Merwin: An American Existentialist." Columbia University, 1978.

Chapman, Wayne Alvin. "Strategies for Silence: W. S. Merwin's Disembodied Voice." University of Utah, 1978.

Christhilf, Mark MacNeal. "W. S. Merwin: An Appreciation." University of Maryland, 1979.

Kerman, Judith Berna. "Merwin's Journey: The Poems of W. S. Merwin as a Hero-Journey." State University of New York at Buffalo, 1977.

Lazer, Henry Alan. "For a Dissolving Music: The Poetry of W. S. Merwin." University of Virginia, 1976.

Murphey, Allene Arnholter. "Tokens of What There Is No Word For: Problems of Expression in W. S. Merwin." University of Pennsylvania, 1981.

Quinn, Theodore Kinget. "W. S. Merwin: A Study in Poetry and Film." University of Iowa, 1972.

Slowik, Mary Helen. "The Loss That Has Not Left This Place: The Problem of Form in the Poetry of W. S. Merwin." University of Iowa, 1975.

Swift, Keith. "The Poetry of W. S. Merwin: A Study of Theme and Style." University of Alberta, Canada, 1980.

Thompson, Ruth Fosness. "The Quest for Harmony: A Thematic Analysis of the Poetry W. S. Merwin." University of Minnesota, 1977.

Wilson, Carol Young. "'What You See Vanishing': Landscapes of Self in the Poetry and Prose of W. S. Merwin." Georgia State University, 1984.

W. S. MERWIN AND OTHERS

Buechler, Scott Howard. "Tracking over Empty Ground: Primitivism in the Poetry of Galway Kinnell and W. S. Merwin." University of Utah, 1979.

Byers, Thomas Beall. "What I Cannot Say: Self, Word, and World in Walt Whitman, Wallace Stevens, and W. S. Merwin." University of Iowa, 1979.

Clifton, Michael Edward. "The Intuitive Project in Bly and Merwin." Indiana University, 1984.

Davis, Cheri Colby. "Radical Innocence: A Thematic Study of the Relationship between the Translator and the Translated in the Poetry of W. S. Merwin and Jean Follain." University of Southern California, 1973.

Elliott, David Lindsey. "The Deep Image: Radical Subjectivity in the Poetry of Robert Bly, James Wright, Galway Kinnell, James Dickey, and W. S. Merwin." Syracuse University, 1978.

Hoeppner, Edward Haworth. "Icon and Hyperbola: Strategies for Verse in the Poetry of W. S. Merwin and John Ashbery." University of Iowa, 1984.

Levine, Ellen Sue. "From Water to Land: The Poetry of Sylvia Plath, James Wright, and W. S. Merwin." University of Washington, 1974.

Liberthson, Daniel. "The Quest for Being: Theodore Roethke, W. S. Merwin, and Ted Hughes." State University of New York at Buffalo, 1976.

McCorkle, James Donald Bruland. "Gaze, Memory, and Discourse: Self-Reflexivity in Recent American Poetry (Bishop, Ashbery, Merwin, Wright)." University of Iowa, 1984.

Seyffert, Henriette. "Three Contemporary Translator Poets: W. S. Merwin, W. Barnstone, and J. Wright." Indiana University, 1970.

Stiffler, Harold Randall. "The Good Darkness: Affirmation in the Poems of Robert Bly, W. S. Merwin, and James Wright." University of Illinois at Urbana-Champaign, 1981.

Notes on Contributors

CHARLES ALTIERI teaches English at the University of Washington and is the author of *Enlarging the Temple: Ontological Themes in American Poetry of the 1960's, Act and Quality: A Theory of Literary Meaning and Humanistic Interpretation*, and *Self and Sensibility in Contemporary American Poetry*.

EDWARD BRUNNER works in Iowa City and is the author of *Splendid Failure: Hart Crane and the Making of* The Bridge.

THOMAS B. BYERS teaches English at the University of Louisville and is the author of numerous essays on English and American literature.

ED FOLSOM teaches English at the University of Iowa, where he also edits the *Walt Whitman Quarterly Review* and coedits the *Iowa Review*. He is coeditor of *Walt Whitman: The Measure of His Song*. He has published numerous essays on American literature and is presently completing *Talking Back to Walt Whitman*.

MICHAEL GREER is a Ph.D. candidate at the University of Illinois.

WALTER KALAIDJIAN teaches English at Mercer University. He has published several essays on contemporary American poetry and is presently completing *Postmodern Poetics: The Social Text of Contemporary American Poetry*.

CHARLES MOLESWORTH teaches English at Queens College. He is the author of *The Fierce Embrace: A Study of Contemporary American Poetry, Words to That Effect* (poetry), *Donald Barthelme's Fiction: The Ironist Saved from Drowning*, and *Gary Snyder*.

CARY NELSON teaches English and criticism and interpretive theory at the University of Illinois. He is the author of *The Incarnate Word: Literature as Verbal Space* and *Our Last First Poets: Vision and History in Contemporary American Poetry*, the editor of *Theory in the Classroom*, and the coeditor of *Marxism and the Interpretation of Culture*, forthcoming. He is presently completing *Reading Criticism: The Literary Status of Critical Discourse.*

MARJORIE PERLOFF teaches English at Stanford University. She is the author of *Rhyme and Meaning in the Poetry of Yeats, The Poetic Art of Robert Lowell, Frank O'Hara: Poet among Painters, The Poetics of Indeterminacy: Rimbaud to Cage,* and *The Dance of the Intellect: Studies in the Poetry of the Pound Tradition.*

JAROLD RAMSEY teaches English at the University of Rochester. He is the author of *Love in an Earthquake* (poems) and editor of *Coyote Was Going There: Indian Literature of the Oregon Country.*

WILLIAM H. RUECKERT teaches English at the State University College of New York at Geneseo. He is the author of *Kenneth Burke and the Drama of Human Relations* and the editor of *Critical Responses to Kenneth Burke.* He is presently completing a book on William Faulkner and a book on contemporary poetry and critical theory.

ROBERT SCHOLES teaches English at Brown University. He is the coauthor of *The Nature of Narrative* and the author of *The Fabulators, Structuralism in Literature, Fabulation and Metafiction, Semiotics and Interpretation,* and *Textual Power: Literary Theory and the Teaching of English.*

General Index

Index to the Works of W. S. Merwin